# BANK
# VALUATION
# &
# VALUE-BASED MANAGEMENT

*Deposit and Loan Pricing, Performance Evaluation, and Risk Management*

# JEAN DERMINE

New York   Chicago   San Francisco   Lisbon   London
Madrid   Mexico City   Milan   New Delhi
San Juan   Seoul   Singapore   Sydney   Toronto

To Isabelle,
Nicolas, Martin, Suzanne,
Alexandre, Augustin, and Juliette

2 3 4 5 6 7 8 9 0 DOC/DOC    1 0

ISBN:   978–0–07–162499–2
MHID:      0–07–162499–6

This publication is designed to provide accurate and authoritative information in regard to the subject matter covered. It is sold with the understanding that the publisher is not engaged in rendering legal, accounting, or other professional service. If legal advice or other expert assistance is required, the services of a competent professional person should be sought.

—*From a Declaration of Principles Jointly Adopted by a Committee of the American Bar Association and a Committee of Publishers and Associations*

McGraw-Hill books are available at special quantity discounts to use as premiums and sales promotions, or for use in corporate training programs. To contact a representative please e-mail us at bulksales@mcgraw-hill.com.

This book is printed on acid-free paper.

# CONTENTS

Chapter 26

Supplemental chapters and solutions to the exercises are available online at http://www.mhprofessional.com/bankvaluation.

## BANK VALUATION AND VALUE-BASED MANAGEMENT

This book is the result of 25 years of research and development for a course on bank management at INSEAD. Unlike banking textbooks that emphasize institutional arrangements in the banking world, the primary purpose of this book is to propose a sound valuation model for banks. Surprisingly, very few publications on the subject are available. Anchored in the fields of economics and finance, this book provides not only useful tools for valuing banks, but also an integrated value-based management framework for discussing managerial issues such as fund transfer pricing, risk-adjusted performance evaluation, deposit pricing, capital management, loan pricing and provisioning, securitization, and the measurement of interest-rate risk. To create value in banking, it is necessary to first understand the drivers of value. A sound and explicit bank valuation model is, as shown in this book, a very powerful tool for evaluating decisions that enhance shareholder value. In short, the book provides rigorous foundations for discussing asset and liability management, the control of value creation and risks in banks.

Moreover, the book addresses two specific issues that are of increasing relevance for banks around the world: portfolio credit risk and liquidity risk. A large literature on the measurement of credit risk for a portfolio of assets or for CDO (collateralized debt obligations) tranches is rapidly emerging. Two chapters (22 and 25) provide an integrated summary of the statistical methodologies used to measure aggregate credit risk, helping to identify some key pending issues in the measurement of portfolio credit risk. The book discusses liquidity risk with implications for advanced fund transfer pricing. An integral part of many banking services, liquidity risk has recently resurfaced in many countries. References to the U.S. subprime crisis help to illustrate these issues.

While the discussion is rigorous, I have maintained a pedagogical approach. Concepts are often introduced with numerical examples. The idea is to build an intuitive understanding first. This is then followed by rigorous mathematical formulas.

Exercises are provided at the end of most chapters, with complete solutions available on the McGraw-Hill Web site at www.mhprofessional.com/bankvaluation. Throughout the book, examples from the international banking world help to illustrate the relevance of the theory.

Also available at the Web site are two additional chapters covering special topics: Chapter 27, "Islamic Banking, Interest-Free Banking"; and Chapter 28, "Prudential Regulations, Safety Nets, and Corporate Structure of International Banks (Branches vs. Subsidiaries)."

I acknowledge the patience and comments of the many MBA participants and bankers who have tested the concepts and exercises, and I would like to thank the Stern School of Business at New York University, where I spent a sabbatical year in 2006–2007, for its hospitality. My colleague Denis Gromb volunteered helpful comments on the bank valuation chapters. Finally, I acknowledge the creative environment at INSEAD, the international business school, where every day the rigor of academic research meets a constant effort for relevant and crystal-clear classroom delivery.

At the time this manuscript is being sent to the publisher, the U.S. subprime crisis is unfolding, with spillover effects being felt around the world. There is no need anymore to draw attention to the importance of sound bank management skills.

Jean Dermine
Fontainebleau, October 2008

# CHAPTER 1

# Discounting, Present Value, and the Yield Curve

Before embarking on a discussion of bank valuation and value-based management, it is necessary to review some fundamental tools used in financial economics. These include discounting, analysis of the yield curve, and statistics. Readers who are familiar with these tools can go directly to Chapter 4.

The first tool that is needed for valuation is discounting or present value. To make the presentation easier and allow readers to develop an intuitive understanding of this tool, this chapter starts with a simple numerical example. This is followed by general formulas. The chapter discusses

1. The present value of a single risk-free cash flow
2. The present value of a series of risk-free cash flows
3. The risk-free interest-rate yield curve
4. Some useful mathematical shortcuts: perpetuity, annuity, and constant-growth perpetuity

## PRESENT VALUE OF A SINGLE RISK-FREE CASH FLOW

### Numerical Example

Consider a cash flow[1] of 30 that is paid at the end of Year 3 and a current risk-free interest rate of 5 percent. Because the amount of this cash flow is known with certainty, it is called a risk-free cash flow. Cash flows from government bonds denominated in the local currency are often considered risk-free because, in principle, the government's ability to raise taxes or to print money allows it to meet its obligations.[2] The discount rate that is used to value the cash flow will be the interest rate, or return, currently available on a risk-free government bond.

|            | Year 1 | Year 2 | Year 3 |
|------------|--------|--------|--------|
| Cash flows | —      | —      | +30    |

The present value of the cash flow of 30 received at the end of Year 3 is the cash flow of 30 divided by a discount factor:

$$\text{Present value} = \frac{30}{(1.05) \times (1.05) \times (1.05)} = \frac{30}{1.05^3} = 25.92$$

The present value of the cash flow of 30 received at the end of Year 3 is 25.92. The present value figure is just the result of a mathematical calculation. What does it represent? A useful interpretation is that the present value is the *cash equivalent*, or the maximum amount that someone would be willing to pay today to receive the right to a cash flow of 30 at the end of Year 3, given an investment return of 5 percent.

Indeed, with a cash flow of 25.92 available today, an investor can either buy a new bond that yields 5 percent return over three years or buy the right to this cash flow of 30. If he buys a new bond, this is what he will receive in three years' time:

$$\text{Future cash flow} = 25.92 \times (1.05 \times 1.05 \times 1.05)$$
$$= 25.92 \times 1.05^3 = 30$$

Therefore, the present value of a cash flow can be said to represent the *fair value* of an asset. In an efficient market, it also represents the market price. Indeed, if the price were lower than 25.92, the asset would be a bargain, as the return would be above 5 percent, and everybody would rush to obtain this high return. If the price were above 25.92, nobody would buy the asset, since investors would receive a larger cash flow if they invested in a different bond yielding 5 percent. Arbitrage ensures that the market price will be very close to the present value calculation.

### Mathematics

Denoting the cash flow received at end of Year $t$ as $CF_t$ and the discount rate as $R$,

$$\text{Present value} = \frac{CF_t}{(1 + R)^t}$$

The present value of a single cash flow represents the maximum amount of cash that someone would be willing to pay in order to receive the right to that cash flow, given an investment return R. In an efficient market, the present value is equal to the market price of the asset.

## PRESENT VALUE OF A SERIES OF RISK-FREE CASH FLOWS

The first example discussed a single cash flow paid in Year 3. Next, the present value of a series of cash flows is covered.

### Numerical Example

Consider a series of risk-free cash flows paid at the end of each of the next three years[3] and a risk-free rate of 5 percent. Remember, this is the interest rate, or return, that is currently available on an alternative investment with similar risk.

|            | Year 1 | Year 2 | Year 3 |
|------------|--------|--------|--------|
| Cash flows | + 25   | + 40   | + 30   |

The present value of a series of cash flows is simply the sum of the present values of the individual cash flows; that is,

$$\text{Present value} = \frac{25}{1.05} + \frac{40}{1.05^2} + \frac{30}{1.05^3}$$
$$= 23.81 + 36.28 + 25.92$$
$$= 86.01$$

Again, the interpretation of the present value figure is that someone would be willing to pay a maximum of 86.01 to have the right to the cash flows to be received at the end of each of the next three years. Indeed, an investor could break the total investment of 86.01 into three smaller investments of 23.81, 36.38, and 25.92. She would invest the first amount in a one-year investment returning 25, the second amount in a two-year investment returning 40, and the third amount in a three-year investment returning 30.

$$23.81 \times (1.05) \quad = 25$$
$$36.28 \, x \times (1.05)^2 = 40$$
$$25.92 \, x \times (1.05)^3 = 30$$

Buying these three bonds for a total amount of 86.01 and buying the right to the series of cash flows provide the same cash flows in Years 1, 2, and 3. The present value of the series of cash flows, 86.01, is the *cash equivalent* or the *fair value* of the asset.

## Mathematics

Denoting a series of cash flows received at the end of the year as $CF_t$, where $t = 1, 2, \ldots, T$, and the discount rate as $R$, the present value of the series of cash flows is equal to

$$\text{Present value} = \frac{CF_1}{1 + R} + \frac{CF_2}{(1 + R)^2} + \cdots + \frac{CF_T}{(1 + R)^T}$$

The present value of a series of cash flows represents the maximum amount that someone would be willing to pay to receive the right to that series of cash flows, given an investment return $R$.

A series of cash flows over Years 1, 2, 3, . . . can be perceived as a portfolio containing a series of single cash flows with maturity 1, 2, 3, . . . Each separate single cash flow is discounted at the investment return $R$.

### RISK-FREE INTEREST-RATE YIELD CURVE

In the previous discussion on the present value of a series of risk-free cash flows, each cash flow was discounted at an identical discount rate of 5 percent. So far, the analysis has proceeded as if there were a single risk-free interest rate $R$. In reality, however, the interest rate often varies depending on the maturity of the asset. Consider the case where the rate for cash flows with a one-year maturity is 4.5 percent, that for cash flows with a two-year maturity is 5 percent, and that for cash flows with a three-year maturity is 5.5 percent.

|  | **Year 1** | **Year 2** | **Year 3** |
|---|---|---|---|
| Cash flows | + 25 | +40 | + 30 |
| Discount rate | 4.5% | 5% | 5.5% |

Figure 1.1 shows the relationship between interest rates and maturity. This curve is known as the *term structure of interest rates* or the *yield curve*.

Since the present value is a cash equivalent, each individual cash flow must be discounted at the appropriate interest rate, and the cash flow arriving in a particular year should be discounted at the interest rate for the corresponding maturity.

$$\begin{aligned}
\text{Present value} &= \frac{25}{1.045} + \frac{40}{1.05^2} + \frac{30}{1.055^3} \\
&= 23.92 + 36.28 + 25.55 \\
&= 85.75
\end{aligned}$$

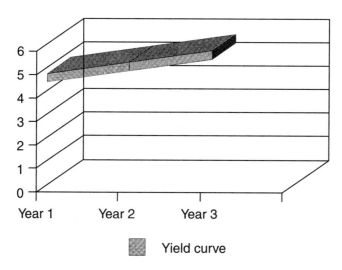

Figure 1.1 Yield curve.

## Mathematics

Denoting a series of cash flows received at the end of the year as $\mathrm{CF}_t$, where $t = 1, 2, \ldots, T$, and the return on an investment in Year $t$ as $R_t$, the present value of the series of cash flows is equal to

$$\text{Present value} = \frac{\mathrm{CF}_1}{1 + R_1} + \frac{\mathrm{CF}_2}{(1 + R_2)^2} + \cdots + \frac{\mathrm{CF}_T}{(1 + R_T)^T}$$

The present value of a series of cash flows represents the maximum amount that someone would be willing to pay to receive the right to that series of cash flows, given investment returns $R_t$.

## USEFUL SHORTCUTS: PERPETUITY, ANNUITY, AND CONSTANT-GROWTH PERPETUITY

So far, the discussion has considered a series of different cash flows with each cash flow being discounted separately. The first special case is when cash flows are *perpetual*. This means that an identical cash flow is received year after year, forever. A famous case of perpetuity was the *consols*, perpetual bonds issued by the United Kingdom that were especially common during the nineteenth and early twentieth centuries. As it was assumed that Britain would live forever, the king or queen could issue a perpetual bond. More surprisingly, some private banks have also issued perpetual bonds, or a promise to pay an interest coupon forever. Needless to say, these bonds cannot be considered risk-free. A second special case is an *annuity*, a series of constant cash flows that lasts for a finite period. A third special case considers perpetual cash flows *growing at a constant annual rate*, up to infinity. Simplified valuation formulas apply in these three cases.

### Perpetuity: A Perpetual Series of Constant Cash Flows

Consider a discount rate of 5 percent and a cash flow of 6, paid at the end of every year forever.

|            | Year 1 | Year 2 | Year 3 | ... |
|------------|--------|--------|--------|-----|
| Cash flows | 6      | 6      | 6      | 6   |

$$\text{Present value} = \frac{6}{1.05} + \frac{6}{1.05^2} + \cdots = \frac{6}{0.05} = 120$$

The present value of a constant perpetual cash flow is simply the cash flow divided by the discount rate.

### Mathematics

The value of a perpetual cash flow CF discounted at the interest rate $R$ is equal to

$$\text{Present value} = \frac{CF}{1+R} + \frac{CF}{(1+R)^2} + \cdots = \frac{CF}{R}$$

### Annuity: A Series of Constant Cash Flows over a Finite Period

Consider a discount rate of 5 percent and a cash flow of 6, paid at the end of every year for five years.

|            | Year 1 | Year 2 | Year 3 | Year 4 | Year 5 |
|------------|--------|--------|--------|--------|--------|
| Cash flows | 6      | 6      | 6      | 6      | 6      |

$$\text{Present value} = \frac{6}{1.05} + \frac{6}{1.05^2} + \frac{6}{1.05^3} + \frac{6}{1.05^4} + \frac{6}{1.05^5} = 25.98$$

A shortcut to calculate the present value of an annuity is to multiply the constant cash flow (6) by an annuity discount factor (ADF). The ADF for five years can easily be calculated using the formula for a perpetuity. Indeed, an annuity that lasts five years is equivalent to a perpetuity reduced by a perpetuity that starts in Year 6.

$$\begin{array}{cccccccc} \underline{0} & \underline{1} & \underline{2} & \underline{3} & \underline{4} & \underline{5} & \underline{6} & \underline{7} & \underline{8}\ldots \\ \text{CF} & \text{CF} & \text{CF} & \text{CF} & \text{CF} & \text{CF} & \text{CF} & \text{CF}\ldots \end{array}$$

The annuity discount factor is the difference between the discount factor for a perpetuity and the present value of the discount factor for a perpetuity that starts in Year 6 (discounted from the end of Year 5, the timing of the last cash flow on the annuity).

$$\text{Annuity discount factor for five years} = \text{ADF} = \frac{1}{0.05} - \left( \frac{1}{0.05} \times \frac{1}{1.05^5} \right)$$

$$= 4.3295$$

$$\text{Present value} = 6 \times \text{ADF (5 years, 5\%)} = 6 \times 4.3295 = 25.98$$

## Mathematics

The value of a constant cash flow CF discounted at an interest rate $R$ over a specific number of years $n$ is equal to

$$\text{Value} = \frac{\text{CF}}{1 + R} + \frac{\text{CF}}{(1 + R)^2} + \cdots + \frac{\text{CF}}{(1 + R)^n} = \text{CF} \times \left( \frac{1}{R} - \frac{1}{R \times (1 + R)^n} \right)$$

### Constant-Growth Perpetuity: A Series of Cash Flows in Perpetuity, Growing at a Constant Speed

The value of a cash flow growing at a constant rate forever is also given by a simple formula. Consider a cash flow of 6 paid at the end of Year 1, growing at a constant annual rate of 3 percent in perpetuity.

|  | **Year 1** | **Year 2** | **Year 3** | . . . |
|---|---|---|---|---|
| Cash flows | 6 | $+ 6 \times 1.03$ | $+ 6 \times 1.03^2$ | . . . |

$$\text{Present value} = \frac{6}{1.05} + \frac{6 \times 1.03}{1.05^2} + \frac{6 \times (1.03) \times (1.03)}{1.05^3} + \cdots$$

$$= \frac{6}{0.05 - 0.03} = 300$$

The present value is simply the cash flow for the first year divided by the discount rate reduced by the annual rate of growth. This formula is valid as long as the constant rate of growth $g$ is lower than the discount rate $R$.[4]

## Mathematics

The value of a perpetual series of cash flows growing at a constant annual rate $g$ ($g < R$), where CF1 is given, $\mathrm{CF}_2 = \mathrm{CF}_1 \times (1 + g)$, $\mathrm{CF}_3 = \mathrm{CF}_2 \times (1 + g)$, and so on, discounted at a rate $R$ is equal to

$$\text{Present value} = \frac{\mathrm{CF}_1}{1 + R} + \frac{\mathrm{CF}_1 \times (1 + g)}{(1 + R)^2} + \frac{\mathrm{CF}_1 \times (1 + g)^2}{(1 + R)^3} \cdots$$

$$= \frac{\mathrm{CF}_1}{R - g} \qquad g < R$$

Given the simplicity of the present value formulas for perpetuity and constant-growth perpetuity, they will be used repeatedly to introduce the bank valuation formula.

## CONCLUSION

This chapter has introduced the tools of present value and the yield curve. These tools will be used in many other chapters, such as those on bank valuation and loan pricing.

## APPENDIX: SEMIANNUAL, MONTHLY, AND CONTINUOUS DISCOUNTING

The period of reference used for discounting in this discussion, one year, is arbitrary. Cash flows can arrive every six months, every month, or even at shorter intervals. The framework discussed in Chapter 1 can be applied directly in such cases by replacing the time interval of one year with the actual period of reference: six months, one month, or some other period.

### Semiannual Compounding

For instance, the cash flows of a bond with a one-year maturity that pays a semiannual coupon of 5 every six months are as follows, with the time period now being six months:

| Period (Half a Year) | 1 (0.5 Year) | 2 (1 Year) |
| --- | --- | --- |
| Cash flow | 5 | 105 |

To discount, it is simply necessary to know the interest rate that applies over a six-month period. Here, it is important to be aware of a bank convention used in most countries with regard to interest-rate quotation: a quoted rate, say 12 percent, is generally an annual rate, even if payments are made more often. If the quoted annual rate of 12 percent refers to an interest rate that is compounded twice a year, it means that the interest rate applied for a six-month period is

$$\text{Six-month rate} = \frac{12\%}{2} = 6\%$$

Let us be clear: this is a market convention that is used in most countries.[5] Before signing a financial contract, the investor should verify the method used to calculate the interest rate applied in discounting.

The value of the one-year bond with a semiannual coupon is

$$\text{Present value} = \frac{5}{1.06^1} + \frac{105}{1.06^2} = 98.17$$

The relevant time period is six months. Thus, the interest rate that applies over a period of six months is used as the discount rate. The discounting is done over the relevant number of periods.

## Mathematics

The discount factor for an annual rate $R$, compounded twice a year, with $n$ denoting the number of years, is

$$\text{Semiannual discount factor (DF)} = \frac{1}{\left(1 + \dfrac{R}{2}\right)^{(2 \times n)}}$$

Thus, moving from annual discounting to six-month discounting is easy: the length of a period is changed from one year to six months, and the interest rate prevailing over a six-month period is used as the discount rate.

*Caution:* As quoted interest rates are usually annual rates, it is necessary to compute the six-month rate that applies over a six-month period.

## Monthly Compounding

Similarly, in the case of monthly compounding, the one-year period is replaced by a time interval of one month, and a one-month rate is used for discounting. Again, following the market convention used in most countries, a quoted annual rate $R$ compounded once a month means that the discount rate over one month is

$$\text{Monthly compounded rate} = \frac{\text{quoted annual rate } R}{12}$$

And the monthly discount factor, with $n$ denoting the number of years, is

$$\text{Monthly discount factor (DF)} = \frac{1}{\left(1 + \dfrac{R}{12}\right)^{(12 \times n)}}$$

## Continuous Compounding

Instead of compounding every month, it is possible to divide the year into a very large number of intervals $m$. It can be shown that as the time interval becomes extremely small ($m$ goes to infinity), the discount factor, with $R$ denoting the annual quoted rate compounded continuously and $n$ denoting the number of years, becomes

$$\text{Continuous discount factor (DF)} = \lim_{m \to \infty} \frac{1}{\left(1 + \dfrac{R}{m}\right)^{m \times n}}$$

$$= e^{-R \times n} = (2.71828)^{-R \times n}$$

This formula for continuous compounding is used in option pricing.

*Example:* We are going to compare the discount factors for annual discounting, semiannual discounting, monthly discounting, and continuous compounding. The quoted annual rate is 12 percent, and the one-year discount factor ($n = 1$) is calculated for each.

1. Compounding once a year:

$$\text{Annual discount factor} = \frac{1}{(1 + R)^1} = \frac{1}{1.12} = 0.893$$

2. Compounding twice a year:

$$\text{Semiannual discount factor} = \frac{1}{\left(1 + \dfrac{R}{2}\right)^{2 \times n}} = \frac{1}{\left(1 + \dfrac{0.12}{2}\right)^{2 \times 1}} = 0.89$$

### 3. Compounding once a month:

$$\text{Monthly discount factor} = \frac{1}{\left(1+\dfrac{R}{12}\right)^{12\times n}} = \frac{1}{\left(1+\dfrac{0.12}{12}\right)^{12\times 1}} = 0.8875$$

### 4. Continuous compounding:

$$\text{Continuous discount factor } DF = e^{-R\times n}$$

$$= (2.71828)^{-R\times n} = (2.71828)^{-0.12\times 1} = 0.8869$$

Not surprisingly, it can be seen that, for an identical quoted annual rate of 12 percent, the discount factor decreases as we increase the number of discounting periods, from 0.893 for annual discounting to 0.8869 for continuous discounting. This is to be expected, as with a larger number of discounting periods, instead of paying an interest rate of 12 percent once, at the end of the year, payments have to be made at a number of times during the year.

In many countries, consumer protection laws are forcing banks to disclose information on the *effective rate* that is really applied annually on a loan, taking into account the number of compounding periods. For instance, in the case of a quoted annual rate of 12 percent compounded monthly, the *effective rate* is calculated as follows:

$$\text{Effective rate} = \left(1+\frac{12\%}{12}\right)^{12} - 1 = (1.01)^{12} - 1 = 1.1268 - 1$$

$$= 0.1268 = 12.68\%$$

It is also possible to compute the *instantaneous interest rate r* that is equivalent to an interest rate $R$ compounded once a year:

$$e^r = 1 + R$$

$$\Rightarrow \ln(e^r) = r = \ln(1 + R)$$

For instance, if $R$ = 12 percent, $r = \ln(1.12) = 0.113329$
$r$ = 11.3329%

It is possible to verify that $e^{0.113329} = 1.12$.

As stated earlier, the instantaneous interest rate and continuous compounding are used in option pricing. In some countries, this formula is also applied to the calculation of installments on credit card loans.

## EXERCISES FOR CHAPTER 1

1. Compute the present value of a cash flow of 100 paid at the end of Year 3. The discount rate is 5 percent.
2. Compute the present value of a series of cash flows. A first cash flow of 100 is paid at the end of Year 1, and a second cash flow of 200 is paid at the end of Year 2. The discount rate is 6 percent.
3. Compute the present value of a series of cash flows. A first cash flow of 100 is paid at the end of Year 1, and a second cash flow of 200 is paid at the end of Year 2. The one-year discount rate is 6 percent, and the two-year discount rate is 7 percent.
4. Compute the present value of a cash flow of 100 paid at the end of Year 1. The annual quoted rate is 12 percent, and monthly discounting is applied.
5. You need to borrow $1 million to buy a house. A bank advertises a rate of 10 percent, with *constant* monthly payments at the end of each month (and monthly discounting). Compute the *monthly* payment on a 10-year loan.
6. A bond with two years to maturity (principal = €1 million) is yielding a fixed annual coupon of 5 percent. The current yield to maturity on a two-year bond is 7.8 percent. You want to buy back the 5 percent bond from the bondholders (ignore transaction costs). This will be financed by the issue of a perpetual bond at par (the issue price = the principal). The current yield to maturity on a perpetual bond is 9 percent.
7. Calculate the annual (€) interest expense on the new perpetual bond.

### Notes

1. A cash flow is an amount of money received in (disbursed from) a bank account or paid in bank notes or coins.
2. Although domestic-currency bonds are considered risk-free, there have been some cases of default. A famous one is Russia's default on its short-term domestic-currency Treasury bills, the GKOs, in 1998. Bonds issued by European governments in the euro zone present an interesting case, as the common European Central Bank could abstain from helping a national domestic government that is in financial distress.

3. The assumption about the timing of the cash flows, that they are paid at the end of the year, is made for simplicity. In the appendix to this chapter, we discuss the discounting of cash flows over a six-month period (semiannual discounting), a monthly period (monthly discounting), and continuously (continuous discounting).

5. An alternative that is used more rarely is

$$\text{Semiannual rate} = \sqrt{1.12} - 1 = 1.0583 - 1 = 5.83\%$$

# Coupon Bond Rate, Zero Coupon Bond Rate, Forward Rates, and the Shape of the Yield Curve

Chapter 1 showed that risk-free interest rates often vary depending on their maturity. The relationship between risk-free rates and maturity is called the *yield curve* or the *term structure of interest rates*. However, for bonds with an identical maturity, there is an additional distinction, discussed in this chapter, between the rates on zero coupon bonds and those on coupon bonds. A second topic discussed in this chapter is the very useful information on expected future interest rates, or *forward rates*, provided by the yield curve. This is a key piece of information to take into account in managing the maturity profile of a bond portfolio. Finally, the chapter covers different shapes of yield curves: a *flat* yield curve, an *upward-sloping* yield curve, an *inverted* or *downward-sloping* yield curve, and a *humped* yield curve.

## RATES ON COUPON BONDS AND ZERO COUPON BONDS

There are two types of bonds that have to be distinguished. *Coupon bonds* have interest payments, or *coupons*, at regular intervals (every year or every six months) and repay the principal at maturity. *Zero coupon bonds*, as the name indicates, have no coupon payments over the life of the bond and make a single *bullet* payment at maturity.

When referring to the investment return on a three-year bond, $R_3$, it is necessary to ask whether it is the return on a fixed coupon bond or the return on a zero coupon bond.

Consider two bonds. Bond C pays a fixed coupon of 5 percent at the end of each year and a principal payment of $100 at maturity. Bond Z, a zero coupon bond, pays a single cash flow of $119.1 at maturity. Both bonds are currently priced at $100.

| | Price | Year 1 | Year 2 | Year 3 | Yield |
|---|---|---|---|---|---|
| Bond C | $100 | $5 | $5 | $105 | 5.00% |
| Bond Z | $100 | 0 | 0 | $119.1 | 6.00% |

The bond yield is by definition the discount rate that makes the present value of the cash flows equal to the price.[1] For instance:

$$\text{Price}_{\text{Bond C}} = 100 = \frac{5}{1.05} + \frac{5}{1.05^2} + \frac{105}{1.05^3}$$

$$\text{Price}_{\text{Bond Z}} = 100 = \frac{0}{1.06} + \frac{0}{1.06^2} + \frac{119.1}{1.06^3}$$

In these examples, the two three-year bonds have the same price, $100, but a different yield: 5.00 percent for the coupon bond, Bond C, and 6.00 percent for the zero coupon bond, Bond Z. In such a case, what is the relevant interest rate to use to discount a three-year cash flow?

The answer is: the return on a zero coupon bond.

Indeed, remember the interpretation of present value in Chapter 1. Discounting is the search for a fair value such that someone would be indifferent between receiving a cash flow three years from now or a cash flow today that can be invested for three years at the specified rate. The yield of 6.00 percent on the zero coupon bond represents the effective return available on a three-year investment. By investing $100 in a risk-free asset today, the person is certain to receive $119.1 in three years' time, ensuring an annual return of 6.00 percent over three years. The yield of 5.00 percent on the coupon bond does not necessarily represent the effective return on a three-year investment because it does not tell us anything about the rate at which the coupons can be reinvested when they are paid at the end of Year 1 and at the end of Year 2.[2] With zero coupon bonds, there is no problem with reinvestment of coupons, so a zero coupon rate represents the effective rate that is currently available. It should be used for discounting. The appendix to this chapter shows how to derive zero coupon rates from information on the interest rates of coupon bonds.

When the return on a zero coupon bond $R_t$ is available, it should be used to discount cash flows with the specific maturity $t$.

The present value of a series of cash flows represents the amount of money someone would be willing to pay to obtain the right to this series of cash flows. The cash flows should be discounted at the investment return available for specific maturities. Whenever possible, they should be discounted at the effective return on a zero coupon bond.

## GOING LONG OR SHORT TERM: WATCH THE FORWARD RATES

A key decision for a bond portfolio manager is to decide whether he wants to invest in short-term or long-term risk-free bonds.[3] Information on *forward rates* will be a great help in making that decision.

Consider a situation where there is a zero coupon return of 4.5 percent for a bond with one year to maturity and a zero coupon yield of 5 percent for a bond with two years to maturity.

| Price | Year 1 | Year 2 | Yield |
|-------|--------|--------|-------|
| $100  | $104.50 |        | 4.5%  |
| $100  | 0      | $110.25 | 5%    |

Imagine that you need money two years from now. Two investment strategies are available. You can purchase a one-year investment and reinvest (*roll over*) the funds for an additional year at the end of the first year. Alternatively, you can make a two-year investment directly.

The forward rate, $f_{2,1}$, is *by definition* the one-year rate available in Year 1 that would make a two-year investment equivalent to a one-year investment with rollover.[4]

One-year strategy with rollover = two-year strategy,
$$100 \times (1.045) \times (1 + f_{2,1}) = 100 \times (1.05)^2 = 1.1025$$

Therefore,
Forward rate $f_{2,1} = 5.5\%$

The *forward* rate is thus a *breakeven* future rate, a rate to be observed in the future that makes two investment strategies equivalent. It is often called the market implied future rate or the market expectation about future rates. Here's why.

The forward rate provides very useful information for making a choice between long-term and short-term investments. If your own expectation about the rate to be observed next year is equal to the forward rate, you are indifferent between the two investment strategies, as they will provide identical returns two years down the road.[5] If your expectation about the rate that is likely to prevail next year is higher than the forward rate, you should buy the short-term investment, as reinvesting the principal at the higher rate than you expect will give you an overall better return over two years. In contrast, if your expectation for next year's rate is lower than the forward rate, you should buy the long-term bond.

For example:

Your expectation = 5.52% > forward rate = 5.5%
Revenue from one-year bond strategy = 100 × (1.045) × (1.0552)
= 110.27 > 110.25 = revenue from two-year bond strategy

Therefore, you should buy the one-year bond.

Your expectation = 5.48% < forward rate = 5.5%
Revenue from one-year bond strategy = 100 × (1.045) × (1.0548)
= 110.23 < 110.25 = revenue from two-year bond strategy

Therefore, you should buy the two-year bond.

A choice between investing in short-term and long-term bonds must be guided by a comparison between your own expectation about future rates and the forward rates.

Expectation > forward rate: buy short-term bond
Expectation < forward rate: buy long-term bond

If all market participants start to play this game, the market will reach an equilibrium at which the supply of one-year bonds and two-year bonds is equal to the quantity of each being demanded by investors. The market is happy, as its expectations are equal to the forward rate. This is why it is often said that forward rates represent the market expectations for future interest rates.

## A Common Fallacy

It is frequently said that an investor should buy a long-term bond if she expects the long-term rate to go down and a short-term bond if she expects the long-term rate to go up. This is not correct advice most of the time. It is true that if the interest rate goes down, the value of long-term bonds will increase, but the total return, or the coupon plus the capital gain, should be compared to that of investing in a one-year bond. If the market has anticipated the rate's going down, short- and long-term rates will already have adjusted to ensure market equilibrium. The only proper way to make a decision is to compare your own expectation with the forward rate, which is, by definition, the breakeven rate. If your expectation differs from the forward rate, there is a profit opportunity. But do not forget that thousands of experts in banks, insurance companies, and investment funds are searching for these profit opportunities. As a result, these situations are likely to be rare.

## Mathematics

Given $R_t$ and $R_{t+1}$, the returns on zero coupon bonds with $t$ and $t + 1$ years to maturity, the one-year forward rate at time $t$, $f_{t,1}$, is defined as the rate such that

$$(1 + R_{t+1})^{t+1} = (1 + R_t)^t \times (1 + f_{t,1})$$

## FORWARD RATES AND MATURITY RISK PREMIUM

If the market demands an extra risk premium for holding a long-term asset, the forward rate will represent the market expectations plus the risk premium. For example, the return on a two-year asset will exceed the return on a one-year asset with reinvestment at the expected interest rate in Year 2:

$$(1 + R_2)^2 > (1 + R_1) \times (1 + \text{expected rate})$$
$$(1 + R_2)^2 = (1 + R_1) \times (1 + \text{expected rate} + \text{market risk premium})$$
$$= (1 + R_1) \times (1 + \text{forward rate})$$

Therefore,

Forward rate = expected rate + maturity risk premium

The maturity risk premium can have two sources: the fact that there is some probability that the two-year asset might have to be sold at the end of Year 1 at a price different from the expected price, or, in a case in which the two-year asset is funded with short-term one-year funding, the fact that the short-term rate in Year 2 might be different from the expected rate.[6]

## FORWARD RATES AND YIELD CURVE SHAPES

The forward rates determine the slope of the yield curve. Frequently observed shapes for zero coupon bond yield curves are the upward-sloping yield curve, the downward-sloping or inverted yield curve, the flat yield curve, and the humped yield curve (see Figures 2.1 to 2.4).

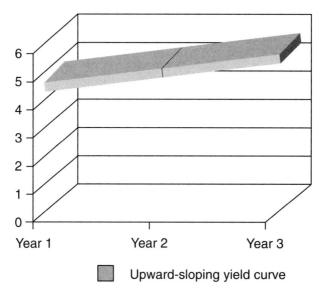

Upward-sloping yield curve

**Figure 2.1** The upward-sloping yield curve is the one most frequently observed in financial markets. It implies that forward rates are higher than the current short-term rate.

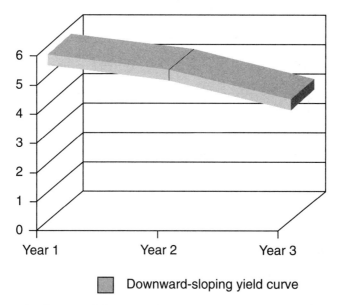

Downward-sloping yield curve

**Figure 2.2** The downward-sloping yield curve has received a lot of attention, as it is a good indicator of a recession in the United States. An inverted yield curve implies that the forward rates are lower than the current short-term rate. One interpretation is that interest rates will go down in the future because of an anticipated recession (Estrella and Trubin, 2006).

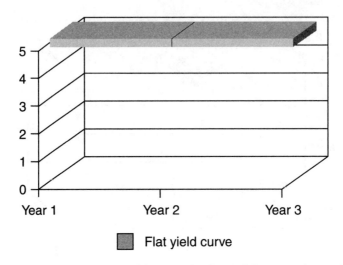

**Figure 2.3** In the case of a flat yield curve, the forward rates are identical to the current short-term rate.

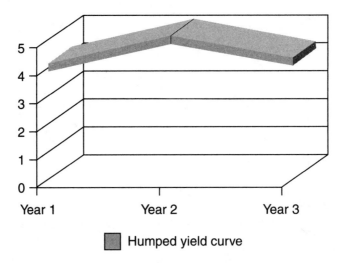

**Figure 2.4** A humped yield curve is rising in the early years and downward-sloping for longer-term maturities.

## CONCLUSION

This chapter has distinguished coupon bonds from zero coupon bonds. The latter provide more accurate information on bond returns, as there is no need for the reinvestment of coupons. It also introduced forward rates.

By definition, these are breakeven future rates that make short-term and long-term investments in bonds equivalent. Forward rates provide useful information on market expectations for future interest rates. Finally, the chapter introduced various shapes of yield curves: upward-sloping, flat, downward-sloping, and humped.

## APPENDIX: ESTIMATING THE ZERO COUPON RATE FROM COUPON BOND RATES—THE BOOTSTRAPPING METHOD

In many countries, zero coupon bonds are not available, and investors have access only to coupon bonds. Still, it is possible to derive the implicit term structure of interest rates for zero coupon bonds.

Take, for example, the following three coupon bonds:

| Price | Year 1 | Year 2 | Year 3 |
|-------|--------|--------|--------|
| $100 | $105 | | |
| $100 | $6 | $106 | |
| $100 | $7 | $7 | $107 |

To estimate the interest rates on zero coupon bonds, it is necessary to work recursively (*bootstrapping*). First, use the one-year maturity bond to calculate the one-year zero coupon rate $R_1$:

$$100 = \frac{105}{1 + R_1}$$

Therefore,

$$R_1 = 5\%$$

Then use the price of the two-year bond to calculate what is implicitly the two-year zero coupon rate, discounting the first cash flow at the calculated one-year zero coupon rate:

$$100 = \frac{6}{1.05} + \frac{106}{(1 + R_2)^2}$$

Therefore,

$$R_2 = 5.98\%$$

Finally, use the previous estimates of the one-year and two-year zero coupon rates to estimate the three-year zero coupon bond rate:

$$100 = \frac{7}{1.05} + \frac{107}{(1.0598)^2} + \frac{107}{(1 + R_3)^3}$$

Therefore,

$$R_3 = 7.1\%$$

The bootstrapping method allows investors to recover the zero coupon interest rates that are implicit in the prices of coupon bonds.

## EXERCISES FOR CHAPTER 2

1. You have the following information on current (spot) interest rates on zero coupon bonds with one, two, and three years to maturity:

   $R_1$: 7 percent
   $R_2$: 8 percent
   $R_3$: 9 percent

   What are the implicit *forward* rates for a one-year-maturity bond maturing two and three years from now?

2. Repeat Exercise 1 for the following yield curve:

   $R_1$: 7 percent
   $R_2$: 6 percent
   $R_3$: 5 percent

3. The current yield curve is as follows: the spot rate for zero coupon bonds with two years to maturity is 5 percent, while the spot rate for zero coupon bonds with one year to maturity is 6 percent.

   a. Compute the forward rate.

   b. If your own expectation is that, next year, the one-year-to-maturity zero coupon rate will be 3 percent, which would you prefer to buy today, the bond with two years to maturity or the bond with one year to maturity? Why?

### Notes

1. The bond yield is identical to the internal rate of return (IRR) on the bond.
2. It can be shown that the yield on a coupon bond represents the return on the investment if the coupons can be reinvested at a rate that is identical to the yield.

3. Risky bonds and credit risk are discussed in Chapter 15.
4. In the forward rate $f_{2,1}$, the first digit, 2, indicates the timing of the forward rate, while the second digit refers to the maturity of the forward rate, which is usually one year.
5. In this reasoning, we ignore the value at risk related to movements in interest rates. Indeed, an increase in the interest rate would lead to a reduced bond price. Interest-rate risk and price sensitivity to changes in interest rates are discussed in Chapters 18, 19, and 20.
6. Maturity premium, liquidity risk, and value creation are discussed in Chapter 21.

CHAPTER 3

# Statistics: A Review

This chapter reviews some of the fundamental elements of statistics that will be used in the chapters related to the measurement of trading and credit risk. Readers who are familiar with elementary statistics can turn directly to Chapter 4. This chapter discusses

1. The case of a single random variable, with its expected value and standard deviation
2. The case of two random variables with a joint probability distribution, marginal probabilities, covariance, and correlation
3. The Gaussian or normal probability distribution
4. The lognormal distribution

## RANDOM VARIABLES: DISCRETE AND CONTINUOUS

An example of a random variable is the interest rate on a government bond with five years to maturity to be observed in the future—for instance, in a week. It is random because the interest rate can take several values, low or high, with a probability attached to each value. Other examples include the foreign exchange rate between the U.S. dollar and the euro and the price of a share or a commodity, such as gold, silver, or oil.

A random variable can be either discrete or continuous. It is *discrete* if it can take only a finite number of values, for instance, $R_1, R_2, \ldots R_n$. A random variable is *continuous* if it can take any value over an interval $[a, b]$.

### Probability Distribution of a Random Variable

The probability distribution of a random variable gives the different values that the random variable can take and the probability attached to each value. An example of a discrete random variable follows. To make the example easier, assume that the euro interest rate in one year's time can have three possible values, each with its own probability:

| Euro Interest Rate | Probability |
|---|---|
| 3% | 0.3 (30%) |
| 4% | 0.4 (40%) |
| 5% | 0.3 (30%) |

For a visual representation of a probability distribution, imagine that you have a bag containing 100 balls. There are 30 balls with a value of 3 written on each ball, 40 balls with a value of 4, and 30 balls with a value of 5. You shake the bag and pick one ball with your eyes closed. What is the probability of picking a ball with 3 written on it? Answer: 30 percent, or 30 out of 100.

### Expected Value and Standard Deviation of a Random Variable

Several statistics, called *moments*, are used to describe the probability distribution of a random variable. Two of them are the mean or expected value, $E(R)$, and the standard deviation, $\sigma$.

### Mean or Expected Value of a Random Variable

Imagine that you have a random variable with a probability distribution and that you conduct an experiment. From the bag of 100 balls, you draw one ball, note the value written on the ball, and then put the ball back in the bag. You repeat this experiment many times (for example, a thousand times). The expected value gives you the average value of the random variable.

Mathematically, the expected value is defined as, $\pi_i$ denoting the probability attached to the specific values $R_i$:

$$\text{Expected value} = E(R) = R_1 \times \pi_1 + R_2 \times \pi_2 + \cdots + R_n \times \pi_n$$

$$= \sum_{i=1}^{n} R_i \times \pi_i$$

In the euro interest-rate example, the expected value is equal to

$$\text{Expected value} = E(R) = (3\% \times 0.3) + (4\% \times 0.4) + (5\% \times 0.3) = 4\%$$

### Standard Deviation of a Random Variable

In the experiment in which you drew a ball from the bag many times, returning the ball to the bag after each draw, the expected value was the average value of the draws. Some balls will have a higher value, while others will have a lower value. The standard deviation, $\sigma$, gives a measure of the average deviation from the average value. A random variable is said to have a large standard deviation or large volatility if some values deviate from the average by a large amount. Other random variables with less variation are said to display a low volatility or small standard deviation.

The computation of the standard deviation proceeds in two steps. In the first step, you compute the variance, which is the square of the standard deviation ($\sigma^2$).

$$\text{Variance } (R) = \sigma^2 = \pi_1 [R_1 - E(R)]^2 + \pi_2 [R_2 - E(R)]^2$$
$$+ \cdots + \pi_n [R_n - E(R)]^2$$
$$= \sum_{i=1}^{n} \pi_i [R_i - E(R)]^2$$

In the second step, you compute the standard deviation $\sigma$, the average value by which a random variable deviates from the average, by simply taking the square root of the variance[1]:

$$\text{Standard deviation} = \sigma = \sqrt{\text{variance}} = \sqrt{\sigma^2}$$

In the euro interest-rate example,

$$\text{Variance } (R) = \sigma^2 = 0.3 \times (0.03 - 0.04)^2 + 0.4 \times (0.04 - 0.04)^2$$
$$+ 0.3 \times (0.05 - 0.04)^2$$
$$= 0.00006$$

## TWO RANDOM VARIABLES AND JOINT PROBABILITY DISTRIBUTIONS

Consider the interest rates in both euro and U.S. dollars. Each interest rate is a random variable. The joint probability distribution indicates the probability of observing a particular pair of values for each of the two random variables. Table 3.1 describes the probability distribution for the two interest rates.

The top horizontal line gives the potential values for the euro interest rate, which are identical to those in the single random variable example, ranging from 3 percent to 5 percent. The first column gives the potential values for the dollar interest rate, which range from 3 percent to 7 percent. The numbers inside the table give the *joint probabilities*, that is, the probability of observing a pair of values, a specific value for the

**T A B L E   3.1**

Joint Probability Distribution for Euro and U.S. Dollar Interest Rates

| $R_\varepsilon$ <br> $R_\$$ | 3% | 4% | 5% | Marginal Probability of $R_\$$ |
|---|---|---|---|---|
| 3% | 0.15 | 0.03 | 0.02 | 0.2 |
| 5% | 0.1 | 0.22 | 0.18 | 0.5 |
| 7% | 0.05 | 0.15 | 0.1 | 0.3 |
| marginal probability of $R_\varepsilon$ | 0.3 | 0.4 | 0.3 | |

euro interest rate and a specific value for the dollar interest rate, at the same time. For example, the probability of observing a euro interest rate of 4 percent and a dollar interest rate of 7 percent is 0.15 (15 percent). The *joint probability distribution* gives us the potential values for the two random interest rates along with the probabilities of observing specific pairs of interest rates.

The last column and the bottom line of the matrix give the *marginal probability distribution* for the dollar interest rate and the euro interest rate. The marginal probability distribution for the dollar interest rate gives the probability of observing a specific dollar interest rate, regardless of the value of the euro interest rate. For example, the marginal probability of observing a dollar interest rate of 7 percent, no matter what the value of the euro interest rate may be, is 0.3. The marginal probability of the dollar interest rate is obtained by taking the sum of the joint probabilities over the horizontal line. For example,

Marginal probability $R_\$ = 7\% = 0.05 + 0.15 + 0.1 = 0.3$

Similarly, the marginal probability distribution for the euro interest rate is given in the bottom horizontal line. The marginal probability of the euro interest rate is obtained by taking the sum of the joint probabilities over the column. For example,

Marginal probability $R_\varepsilon = 5\% = 0.02 + 0.18 + 0.1 = 0.3$

The marginal probability distribution for the euro interest rate is identical to the probabilities given for the case with a single random euro interest rate. The marginal probability distribution allows the computation of the expected value and standard deviation, using formulas identical to those given earlier. It can be verified that

> Expected euro interest rate: 4%; standard deviation of euro interest rate: 0.77%
>
> Expected dollar interest rate: 5.2%; standard deviation of dollar interest rate: 1.4%

## Covariance and Correlation

When there are two random variables, it is often useful to know whether these two variables are related to each other. Do interest rates tend to go up and down together, or do they move independently of each other? Two measures in statistics, *covariance* and *correlation*, measure the degree of co-movement of two random variables. The covariance is a weighted sum of cross products. The weight is the joint probability, and each term of the cross products is the deviation from the mean:

$$
\begin{aligned}
\text{Covariance} &= \pi_{R\euro=3\%, R\$=3\%} \times [3\% - E(R\euro)] \times [3\% - E(R\$)] \\
&+ \pi_{R\euro=4\%, R\$=3\%} \times [4\% - E(R\euro)] \times [3\% - E(R\$)] \cdots \\
&+ \pi_{R\euro=5\%, R\$=7\%} \times [5\% - E(R\euro)] \times [7\% - E(R\$)] \\
&= 0.15 \times (3\% - 4\%) \times (3\% - 5.2\%) \\
&+ 0.03 \times (4\% - 4\%) \times (3\% - 5.2\%) \cdots \\
&+ 0.1 \times (5\% - 4\%) \times (7\% - 5.2\%) = 0.000036
\end{aligned}
$$

As it is not easy to give an economic interpretation of a covariance, the measure is transformed into a *correlation*, a standardized measure with a range of values from $-1$ to $+1$. A correlation of $+1$ indicates perfect positive correlation, with two random variables going up and down in parallel. A correlation of $-1$ indicates a perfect negative correlation, with the two random variables moving in opposite directions: when one interest rate goes up, the other one goes down. A correlation close to zero indicates that the two variables are largely independent of each other.

The definition of the correlation and the correlation for the euro and dollar interest-rate example are

$$
\text{Correlation} = \frac{\text{covariance}}{\sigma_{R\euro}\, \sigma_{R\$}} = \frac{0.000036}{0.0077 \times 0.014} = 0.33
$$

In this example, the positive correlation of 0.33 indicates that the euro and dollar interest rates tend to go up and down together.

## CONTINUOUS RANDOM VARIABLES AND
## THE NORMAL DISTRIBUTION

All the previous examples involved *discrete* random variables. The variables could take only a finite number of values. As indicated previously, a continuous random variable can take any value over some interval. A well-known continuous probability distribution is the Gaussian probability distribution, also called the normal distribution or the bell-shaped curve. The random variable can vary from $-\infty$ to $+\infty$.

The probability distribution of the continuous random variable $R$, shown in Figure 3.1, is given by the probability density function (pdf), denoted as $f(R)$:

$$f(R) = \frac{1}{\sqrt{2\pi}\,\sigma} e^{\frac{[r-E(R)]^2}{\sigma^2}} \qquad -\infty < R < +\infty$$

Often, the variable of interest $R$ is transformed into a *standard random variable z*, which is the original random variable $R$ transformed into a number of standard deviations from the mean,

$$z = \frac{R - E(R)}{\sigma}$$

The expected value of the standard random variable is equal to 0, and its standard deviation is equal to 1.

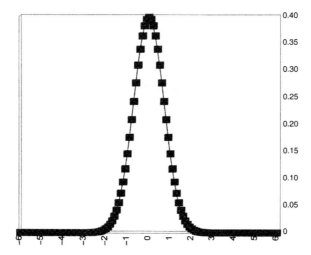

**Figure 3.1** Standard normal distribution.

The probability density function for the standard normal random variable $z$ is equal to

$$f(z) = \frac{1}{\sqrt{2\pi}} e^{-z^2} \qquad -\infty < z < +\infty$$

Finally, there is the cumulative probability distribution. By definition, it measures the probability that the random variable $R$ is below a certain value, let us say $c$. It is the area to the left of the value $c$ on the probability density function curve.

$F_R(c)$ = cumulative probability distribution = probability of $R < c$

The cumulative normal distribution for a standard random variable is given in Figure 3.2.

Some values for a cumulative standard normal distribution are

$F_R(+\infty)$ = probability $(R < +\infty)$ = 100%
$F_R(0)$ = probability $(R < 0)$ = 50%
$F_R(1)$ = probability $(R < 1 \times \sigma)$ = 84%
$F_R(1.96)$ = probability $(R < 1.96 \times \sigma)$ = 97.5%
$F_R(2.33)$ = probability $(R < 2.33 \times \sigma)$ = 99%
$F_R(-\infty)$ = probability $(R < -\infty)$ = 0

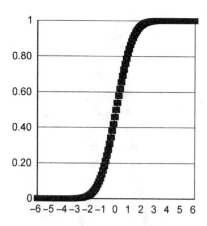

**Figure 3.2** Cumulative standard normal distribution.

## LOGNORMAL DISTRIBUTION

The lognormal distribution is the probability distribution of a random variable whose logarithm is normally distributed. If $P = e^R$, with $R$ a normally distributed random variable, then $\ln(P) = R$, and $P$ is said to have a lognormal distribution. The lognormal distribution is often used to describe the probability distribution of stock prices. The normally distributed variable $R$ is the instantaneous rate of return on the shares, and the stock price is given by $P = e^R$.

Using the lognormal distribution ensures that the lowest possible value for the share price is zero, which is compatible with the limited liability of shareholders. The probability density function for $P$ is

$$f(P) = \frac{1}{P\sigma\sqrt{2\pi}} e^{\frac{[\ln(P) - \mu]^2}{2\sigma^2}} \qquad P > 0$$

This distribution has two parameters, $\sigma$ and $\mu$, which are the mean and standard deviation of the variable's logarithm, $\ln(P) = R$.

## CONCLUSION

This chapter has introduced both discrete and continuous random variables. The joint probability distribution is described by various parameters, such as expected value, standard deviation, and correlation. Two frequently used continuous probability distributions are the normal and lognormal distributions.

## EXERCISE FOR CHAPTER 3

The following table describes the probability distribution for two interest rates, $R$ and $R_\$$.

|        | R    |      |      |
|--------|------|------|------|
| $R_\$$ | 4%   | 5%   | 6%   |
| 3%     | 0.1  | 0.03 | 0.07 |
| 5%     | 0.1  | 0.22 | 0.18 |
| 7%     | 0.5  | 0.15 | 0.1  |

1. Calculate:

    a. The marginal probabilities of each interest rate
    b. The expected value and the standard deviation of each interest rate
    c. The covariance and correlation between the two interest rates

2. With the help of a PC spreadsheet, calculate the probability that a standard normally distributed variable belongs to the interval [0, 2.33]. *Hint:* First draw the relevant area under the normal probability density function. Then use the PC spreadsheet to compute the probability.

## Note

1. The intuitive reason for the two-step procedure for computing the standard deviation is as follows: a measure of volatility that gives equal weight to negative and positive deviations from the mean is needed. In computing the variance, squaring each deviation eliminates the negative signs.

# CHAPTER 4

# The Economics of Banking, and a Bank's Balance Sheet and Income Statement

Before embarking on a bank valuation model, it is useful to review the main economic services provided by banks and present a representative balance sheet and income statement for a bank. Understanding these will greatly facilitate modeling.

## THE ECONOMICS OF BANKING: FIVE MAIN FUNCTIONS

Through financial markets, economic units with surplus funds, such as some households and firms (and, more rarely, governments), can finance economic units with a shortage of funds, such as other firms, other households, or governments. On the financial markets, savers can buy bonds or shares issued by units that are running a deficit. This is referred to as *direct finance*. An alternative, *indirect finance*, is to create an intermediary between the units with a surplus and those with a deficit. A bank is such a financial intermediary. Other financial intermediaries include insurance companies, pension funds, and investment funds such as mutual funds and hedge funds.

A bank is a firm whose assets are mostly made up of financial claims issued by borrowers, such as households, corporate firms, governments, and other financial intermediaries, and whose liabilities are sold to units with a capital surplus in various forms, such as demand deposits, savings deposits, term deposits, subordinated debt (loan capital), and equity shares.

Besides acting as a financial intermediary between economic units with a surplus and those with a deficit, banks engage in various insurance-related activities, such as buying or selling credit derivatives. With these instruments, the bank insures one party against the risk that another party,

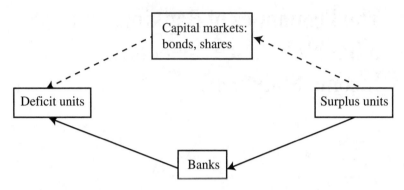

**Figure 4.1** Financial markets: direct finance (---) and indirect finance (—).

such as a corporation or a government, will default on its obligations. Other insurance-type claims include financial derivatives, such as forwards, options, and swaps, the payoffs of which are related to movements in interest rates, exchange rates, or equity or commodity prices.[1] With the exception of the transaction cost and the cash premium received or paid, these activities do not create an asset or a liability on the balance sheet. They are *off-balance sheet* activities.

Although the services provided by banks are interrelated, it is convenient to distinguish five categories of increasing complexity: underwriting and placement, portfolio management, payment (transmission) services, monitoring and information-related services, and risk sharing.

### Underwriting and Placement

The first service provided by banks is bringing together savers and borrowers. The underwriting and placement of securities—bonds or shares— is a function that helps borrowers (corporate firms or public institutions) to meet economic units with a surplus; the bank structures or customizes the type of securities issued so that they meet the risk/return requirements of both borrowers and lenders. In this function, the underwriter is involved not only in designing the securities, but also in the valuation of assets and the pricing of the securities to ensure that the terms of the issue are competitive. Increasingly, rating agencies are playing a crucial role by providing an independent evaluation of the risks incurred on these claims.

As investors may wish to transform these claims into cash or other securities in the future, the securities need to be able to be exchanged. Broker/dealers and market makers provide exchange services to ensure the existence of secondary trading and liquidity. In a pure underwriting and placement situation, it is assumed that the return and risk of the securities can be properly defined, so that there is no major problem of asymmetrical information (agency problem) between lenders and borrowers. In this case, monitoring is not an issue. A pure case is the financing of public debt in countries where the sovereign risk is minimal. When banks perform an underwriting and placement service, the end investors hold the claims on deficit units directly.

## Portfolio Management

Investors can acquire a diversified portfolio of securities issued by deficit spending units at low cost. The pure vehicle for doing this is the mutual fund or unit trust (called SICAV in France and Luxembourg), which supplies a diversified portfolio to the holders of its shares. The income derived from the financial assets is paid to the holders of the shares, less a fee paid to the fund manager.[2] The reason for the existence of these funds is twofold. The first is to reduce the transaction cost incurred in purchasing many securities. The second is that investors may wish to delegate the assessment of companies' economic prospects and the management of the fund to specialists.

## Payment Services

A third function performed by financial intermediaries is the management of the payment system, i.e., facilitating and keeping track of transfers of wealth among individuals. This is the bookkeeping activity of banks, carried out by debiting and crediting individual accounts. Although the payment system is limited by regulation to a specific type of deposits (demand deposits), it could achieve the same result by debiting or crediting any type of liquid assets. The so-called cash management or sweep account, which automatically transfers money from mutual funds into demand deposits, is a perfect illustration of the possibility of extending the payment system to other assets.

## Monitoring and Information-Related Services

Private information held by borrowers leads to contracting problems, because assessing the solvency of a borrower or monitoring his actions after a loan has been made is costly (Stiglitz and Weiss, 1981). Sometimes it is useful to package these claims in a portfolio, and banks perform a useful function by reducing the costs of screening and monitoring borrowers. The delegation of screening and monitoring to banks has been shown to be an efficient mechanism.[3] This fourth service is linked to the first one, underwriting and placement. It is considered a separate service here because it applies in those cases where significant information asymmetries make it difficult to issue financial claims that can be traded on securities markets. While the second service, portfolio management, refers to the management of liquid assets, this fourth function refers to the management of the credit portfolio, which is often the largest part of a bank's balance sheet.

### Risk-Sharing Service

An increasingly important function of banks is to make the market more complete, i.e., to provide some form of insurance against several sources of risk. First, banks not only supply diversified assets, but they also organize the efficient distribution of risky income earned on the asset pool. The debt holders receive a fixed payment, and the shareholders receive the residual income. Other insurance services include interest-rate insurance (floating-rate lending with various ceilings on interest rates called *caps* or *floors*), inflation insurance with real contracts, and liquidity insurance, an option allowing a deposit holder or the holder of a line of credit to withdraw funds quickly at face value (Diamond and Dybvig, 1983; Rajan, 1998). Allen and Santomero (1998, 2001) have emphasized the growing importance of risk management services provided by banks.

This section explained the generic economic functions of banks. The Second Banking Directive[4] of the European Commission lists the specific activities that can be authorized by regulators in the European Union:

- Deposit taking and other forms of borrowing
- Lending
- Financial leasing
- Money transmission services
- Issuing and administering means of payments (credit cards, traveler's checks, and bankers' drafts)
- Guarantees and commitments
- Trading for the bank's own account or the accounts of customers in
  - Money market instruments
  - Foreign exchange
  - Financial futures and options

      ◦ Exchange- and interest-rate instruments
      ◦ Securities
- Participation in share issues and the provision of services related to such issues
- Money brokering
- Portfolio management and advice
- Safekeeping of securities
- Credit reference services
- Safe custody service

This complete list describes the activities of a *universal bank*. In some countries, such as the United States and Japan, the list of permissible activities has in the past been greatly reduced (Saunders and Walter, 1994). But there has recently been a regulatory convergence toward the universal banking model. For instance, the Financial Modernization Act (Gramm-Leach-Bliley) of 1999 in the United States repealed the Glass-Steagall Act, which separated commercial banking from securities underwriting. The banking systems of most countries in Latin America and Central and Eastern Europe were deregulated with the adoption of the universal banking model. The 2008 U.S. credit crisis[5] created a cataclysm in the specialized investment banking industry. Two players, Bear Stearns and Merrill Lynch, were bought by banks (JPMorgan and Bank of America); Lehman Brothers Holdings filed for bankruptcy; and the remaining two, Morgan Stanley and Goldman Sachs, changed their status from investment banks to bank holding companies.

## A BANK'S BALANCE SHEET AND INCOME STATEMENT

Before discussing modeling, it is useful to present the balance sheet and income statement of a representative bank. The consolidated balance sheet shown in Table 4.1 is that of the Royal Bank of Canada for the year ended October 31, 2007.

The consolidated income statement of the Royal Bank of Canada for the year ended October 31, 2007, is shown in Table 4.2.

With respect to the five functions of banks discussed earlier, it can be seen that noninterest revenues, originating from insurance, trading of securities, management of the payment system, and fund management, exceed net interest income; the figures are Can$14,930 million and Can$7,352 million, respectively. Over the years, banks have diversified their sources of revenue, and the share coming from fee-based services has increased.

**TABLE 4.1**

Consolidated Balance Sheet, Royal Bank of Canada, 2007

| Assets (Can $ million) | | Liabilities and Shareholders' Equity (Can $ million) | |
|---|---|---|---|
| Cash and due from banks | 4,226 | Deposits | |
| Interest-bearing deposits with other banks | 11,881 | Personal | 116,557 |
| | | Business and government | 219,886 |
| | | Bank | 28,762 |
| | | | 365,205 |
| Securities | | Other | |
| Trading | 148,246 | Acceptances | 11,786 |
| Available-for-sale | 30,009 | Obligations related to securities sold short | 44,689 |
| Investments | — | Obligations related to assets sold under repurchase agreements | 37,033 |
| | | Derivatives | 72,010 |
| | | Insurance claims and policy benefit liabilities | 7,283 |
| | | Liabilities of operations held for sale | — |
| | | Other liabilities | 28,483 |
| | | | 201,284 |
| Assets purchased under repurchase agreements | 64,313 | Subordinated debentures | 6,235 |
| | | Trust capital securities | 1,400 |
| | | Preferred shares liabilities | 300 |
| Loans | | Noncontrolling interest in subsidiaries | 1,483 |
| Retail | 69,462 | | |
| Wholesale | 69,967 | | |
| | 239,429 | | |
| Allowance for loan losses | (1,493) | | |
| | 237,936 | | |
| Other | | Shareholders' equity | |
| Customers' liability under acceptances | 11,786 | Preferred shares | 2,050 |
| Derivatives | 66,585 | Common shares | 7,300 |
| Premises and equipment, net | 2,131 | Contributed surplus | 235 |
| Goodwill | 4,752 | Treasury shares: preferred | (6) |

(Continued)

**TABLE 4.1**

*(Continued)*

| Assets (Can $ million) | | Liabilities and Shareholders' Equity (Can $ million) | |
|---|---|---|---|
| Other intangibles | 628 | Treasury shares: common | (101) |
| Assets of operations held for sale | — | Retained earnings | 18,167 |
| Other assets | 17,853 | Accumulated other comprehensive income (loss) | (3,206) |
| | 103,735 | | 24,439 |
| **Total assets** | 600,346 | **Total liabilities and shareholders' equity** | 600,346 |

Source: Royal Bank of Canada, Annual Report, 2007.

**TABLE 4.2**

Consolidated Income Statement, Royal Bank of Canada, 2007

| | |
|---|---|
| **Interest income** (Can$ million) | |
| Loans | 14,724 |
| Securities | 7,665 |
| Assets purchased under reverse repurchase agreements | 3,450 |
| Deposits with banks | 538 |
| | 26,377 |
| **Interest expense** | |
| Deposits | 13,770 |
| Other liabilities | 4,737 |
| Subordinated debentures | 338 |
| | 18,845 |
| **Net interest income** | 7,532 |
| **Non-interest income** | |
| Insurance premiums, investment and fee income | 3,152 |
| Trading revenues | 2,261 |
| Investment management and custodial fees | 1,579 |
| Mutual funds revenues | 1,473 |
| Securities brokerage commissions | 1,353 |

(Continued)

**TABLE 4.2**

*(Continued)*

| | |
|---|---:|
| Service charges | 1,303 |
| Underwriting and other advisory fees | 1,217 |
| Foreign exchange revenue, other than trading | 533 |
| Card service revenue | 491 |
| Credit fees | 293 |
| Securitization revenues | 261 |
| Net gain (loss) on sale of available-for-sale securities | 63 |
| Net gain on sale of investment securities | — |
| Other | <u>951</u> |
| **Noninterest income** | 14,930 |
| **Total revenue** | 22,462 |
| **Provisions for credit losses** | 791 |
| **Insurance policyholders benefits, claims and acquisition expense** | 2,173 |
| **Noninterest expenses** | |
| Human resources | 7,890 |
| Equipment | 1,009 |
| Occupancy | 839 |
| Communications | 723 |
| Professional fees | 530 |
| Outsourced item processing | 308 |
| Amortization of other intangibles | 96 |
| Other | <u>1,108</u> |
| | 12,473 |
| **Business realignment charges** | — |
| **Income from continuing operations before income taxes** | 7,025 |
| Income taxes | 1,392 |
| **Net income before noncontrolling interest** | 5,633 |
| Noncontrolling interest in net income of subsidiaries | 141 |
| **Net income from continuing operations** | 5,492 |
| **Net loss from discontinued operations** | — |
| **Net income** | 5,492 |
| Preferred dividends | (88) |
| Net gain on redemption of preferred dividends | — |
| **Net income available to common shareholders** | 5,404 |

Source: Royal Bank of Canada, Annual Report, 2007.

**TABLE 4.3**

A Bank's Simplified Balance Sheet

| Assets | Liabilities and Shareholders' Equity |
|---|---|
| Reserves with central banks | |
| Retail loans | Retail deposits |
| | Demand deposits |
| | Savings deposits |
| | Term deposits |
| Corporate loans | Corporate deposits |
| | Demand deposits |
| | Term deposits |
| Interbank loans | Interbank deposits |
| Government bonds | Subordinated debt |
| Fixed assets | Equity |

To model the bank, we will very much simplify the balance sheet and income statement. The balance sheet of a bank used for modeling purposes is shown in Table 4.3.

Banks collect deposits from the retail and corporate markets. Some of these can be withdrawn on demand (demand deposits used for the payment system). Others, such as savings deposits, can be transferred into other deposit accounts on demand. The maturities of these first two types of deposits are said to be *undefined*, as deposits can stay in the bank for only a few days or for several years. The undefined maturity creates a specific problem of pricing these deposits and measuring their interest-rate and liquidity risks. These issues will be addressed in Chapters 18 to 21. Other deposits, the term deposits, have a fixed contractual maturity. Finally, the pricing could be a fixed rate or a floating or adjustable rate linked to a short-term benchmark rate, such as the interest rate on government Treasury bills or the interbank rate.

In addition to raising money from the public, banks borrow from one another on the interbank market with interbank deposits. Finally, two sources of long-term funds are subordinated bonds and equity. Subordinated debt plays a special role in banks, as, with some eligibility limits, it qualifies as part of regulatory capital, along with equity.[6]

On the asset side, banks must hold some reserves at the central bank, reserves that pay a low (often zero) interest rate. As discussed earlier, a main function of banks is to lend money to individuals and corporations. Excess funds can be lent to other banks (interbank loans) or used to purchase government bonds. Finally, a small proportion of funds is used to purchase fixed assets, such as buildings and computers.

In addition to balance sheet items, banks are involved in a large number of off-balance sheet activities, such as derivatives (forward rate agreements, options, or swaps), loan commitments, and loan guarantees. These are called off-balance sheet or contingent claims because, except for incurring a small transaction cost or a premium, they have no impact on the balance sheet at origination. They will create a cash flow (positive or negative) when some contingency occurs.

The simplified income statement used for modeling purposes is shown in Table 4.4.

Interest income is earned on loans and bonds, while fee and trading income is generated from providing various services[7] or through trading. Interest expense includes the cost of deposits and subordinated debt. A very specific and difficult issue in banking concerns the creation of loan provisions to take into account the loss of value of loans. As loans usually are not traded on capital markets, there is no information readily available on what the fair value of a loan is. Moreover, if the borrower gets into difficulties and enters bankruptcy proceedings, it may take several years to know the exact amount of loan losses. As a consequence, a method must be devised to set the *fair* level of provisions for credit risk. This is discussed in Chapters 14 and 15.

**T A B L E   4.4**

A Bank's Simplified Income Statement

Interest income
       − Interest expense
= *Net interest income*
       + Fee/trading income
= *Gross revenue*[8]
       − Loan provisions
       − Operating (noninterest) expense
= *Earnings before taxes*
       − Taxes
= *Earnings after taxes*

## CONCLUSION

This chapter has reviewed the five main services provided by banks: underwriting, portfolio management, payment services, credit screening and monitoring, and risk sharing. In a *universal banking* system, such as those in most countries, banks are authorized by regulators to provide all these services. The balance sheet and income statement of a representative bank were introduced. Although a balance sheet can be quite complex, it is useful to simplify it by relating assets and liabilities to four market segments: retail, corporate, interbank, and capital markets (bonds or shares).

## EXERCISES FOR CHAPTER 4

  1. List the five main economic services provided by universal banks.
  2. Define gross revenue (also called gross income).

### Notes

1. Financial and credit derivatives are discussed in Chapters 24 and 25.
2. See Black (1970), Fama (1980), and Dermine, Neven, and Thisse (1991) for a portfolio view of financial firms.
3. See Diamond (1984) and Fama (1985).
4. Directive 89/646/EEC.
5. The 2008 U.S. credit crisis is discussed in Chapters 15, 16, and 21.
6. Regulatory capital is discussed in Chapters 12 and 13.
7. Fee-based activities are discussed in Chapter 8.
8. Gross revenue is also called gross income.

# PART ONE

# Bank Valuation

# CHAPTER 5

# The Valuation of Banks, Part 1

## MARKET MULTIPLES, DISCOUNTING FUTURE DIVIDENDS, PRESENT VALUE OF FUTURE ECONOMIC PROFITS, AND THE FUNDAMENTAL VALUATION MODEL (NO CORPORATE TAXES, NO RISK)

To create value in banking, it is first necessary to understand the drivers of value. As shown in this and the following chapters, a sound and explicit bank valuation model is a very powerful tool for evaluating decisions and enhancing shareholder value. These decisions include deposit and loan pricing, risk-adjusted performance evaluation, and capital management. While many books discuss the valuation of nonfinancial companies, very little has been written on bank valuation. In a bestselling book on the valuation of business firms written by consultants (Koller et al., 2005), there is one chapter on bank valuation toward the end. It states: "Valuing banks is conceptually difficult." The purpose of this chapter and the next is to present a clear framework that will help to identify the various sources of value for a bank.

There are at least four approaches to valuing banks:

1. The applications of market multiples, such as the price/earnings (P/E) ratio or the market/book value (MBV) ratio
2. The discounted value of future dividends
3. The discounted value of future economic profits
4. A "fundamental" valuation model

All of these approaches will be presented, but the emphasis will be on the fourth one, the fundamental valuation model. We call it *fundamental* because not only does it present a transparent framework for valuing banks, but it also helps greatly in discussing managerial issues such as fund transfer pricing, risk-adjusted performance evaluation, capital management, loan and deposit pricing, loan-loss provisioning, and the measurement of interest-rate risk on the banking book. These managerial issues are discussed in later chapters.

## MARKET MULTIPLES

The market multiple approach is the simplest way to value a bank. It certainly does not require hiring expensive consultants or investment bankers.

### P/E Multiple

A very common multiple used by bank analysts is the price/earnings (P/E) ratio. Determining this multiple requires three steps.

### Step 1: Evaluate the Market P/E for Comparable Banks

The first step is to search for comparables (the *comps*), similar banks that are listed on a stock market, and to compute the ratio of the stock price to the earnings per share for each. This is the P/E ratio. The share price used is the most recent trading price. The earnings per share can be either the last published earnings per share figure (*historical P/E*) or an average of the future earnings per share forecasted by analysts (*forward P/E*). The average P/E of the comparable banks is then computed. In the OECD countries, the P/E ratio for the banking sector was around 11 in early 2007. It went down by 50 percent during the U.S. subprime credit crisis.[1]

### Step 2: Forecast the Bank's Earnings per Share (EPS)

The second step entails forecasting the bank's earnings per share. This could be an extrapolation based on last year's realized earnings, or it could be based on available information about the bank's likely earnings in the future.

### Step 3: Valuation of the Shares

In the third step, it is assumed that the stock market will value the earnings of the bank in the same way it is valuing the earnings of other banks:

$$\text{Value of shares}_{\text{bank}} = \text{P/E}_{\text{comparables}} \times \text{forecasted EPS}_{\text{bank}}$$

Although this approach is frequently used to value companies in many industries, a specific problem arises in valuing banks. As banks sometimes take large provisions for credit losses, they can report a very low income during a particular year. As the market understands that the very low earnings are temporary and that earnings will return to normal in the following years, the P/E ratio goes up substantially because the price is divided by exceptionally low earnings. In other words, the timing of a one-time provision for credit losses can create large volatility in the P/E ratio of a bank. As a consequence, more stable market multiples are needed.

## MBV Multiple

In banking, the market/book value (MBV) ratio, the ratio of the market value of shares to the book value of equity, is a much more stable figure. For this reason, it is the author's preferred market multiple for valuing banks. Calculating it requires two steps.

### Step 1: Evaluate the MBV Ratio for Comparable Banks

The first step is to search for comparables, similar banks that are listed on a stock market, and then to compute the ratio of the market value of the shares to the accounting book value of equity for each. This is the market/book value ratio. The share price refers to the last trading price. The accounting value of equity is the shareholders' equity reported in the financial accounts. The average MBV ratio for the comparables is then computed. In the OECD countries, the average MBV ratio for the banking sector was close to 2 before the 2007 U.S. subprime crisis. Table 5.1 gives the MBV and P/E ratios of banks in a few countries, just eight months into the U.S. subprime credit crisis.

Banks in *emerging* or *new* markets, such as Brazil and Russia, show MBVs of above 3, an indicator of large expected growth in the future. The P/E ratios observed in April 2008 display the unwelcome volatility mentioned earlier. For example, the very large P/Es of 31.7 for Merrill Lynch and 42.3 for Citigroup were caused mainly by very low earnings resulting from heavy provisions for loan losses.

### Step 2: Determine the Price of Equity

In the second step, it is assumed that the stock market will value the equity of the bank the same way it is valuing the equity of other banks:

$$\text{Value of equity}_{bank} = \text{MBV}_{comparables} \times \text{book value of equity}_{bank}$$

**T A B L E   5.1**

Market/Book Value Ratio and Price/Earnings Ratio, April 29, 2008

| Bank | MBV (P/E) |
|---|---|
| *United Kingdom* | |
| Barclays | 1.32 (6.9) |
| Lloyds-TSB | 2.06 (8.5) |
| Royal Bank of Scotland | 0.66 (6.7) |
| Standard Chartered Bank | 2.42 (15.1) |
| *United States* | |
| Merrill Lynch | 1.87 (31.7) |
| Citigroup | 1.25 (42.3) |
| Goldman Sachs | 1.84 (11.5) |
| *Germany and Switzerland* | |
| Deutsche Bank | 1.04 (8.92) |
| Crédit Suisse | 1.33 (10.28) |
| UBS | 1.99 (—) |
| *Brazil and Russia* | |
| Banco Itau | 3.63 (12.2) |
| Rosbank | 5.58 (10.6) |

Source: Thomson ONE Banker Analytics.

Two widely used market multiples have been presented, the P/E ratio and the MBV ratio. The mathematical relationship between these two multiples is shown in Appendix A to this chapter: the market/book value ratio is the product of the P/E ratio and the return on equity.

The market multiple approach is used a great deal by bank analysts. Opponents of this approach recommend focusing not on accounting figures, such as earnings or the book value of equity, but on the reality of the future cash flows to be generated by the bank. A second problem with the market multiple approach is that it requires believing implicitly that the stock market values the shares of banks correctly. This may often be true in efficient markets. Still, it is useful to understand which economic or business assumptions justify the current valuation figures. With that information, the analyst can exercise judgment and decide whether or not he is comfortable with that set of assumptions. A cash flow–based approach is discussed next. It must be emphasized, however, that the market multiple approach should not be dismissed, as it provides a useful benchmark, the current valuation by the stock market. Strong arguments are needed to deviate substantially from the current market valuation.

## DISCOUNTING FUTURE DIVIDENDS

The second approach recognizes that the owners of shares, the shareholders, are likely to receive dividends in the future. In this approach, the dividend stream expected from this equity investment is forecasted and discounted. In practice, this method begins with a detailed forecast of future annual profits and a forecast of the part of earnings that needs to be retained to grow the equity (the amount needed to finance the growth of the bank) to arrive at a forecast of future expected dividends. A detailed dividend forecast can be made for up to five years, after which dividends are simply assumed to grow in perpetuity at a constant annual rate $g$. Table 5.2 gives an example.

Table 5.2 provides a dividend forecast for the next four years, assuming constant perpetual growth thereafter. The dividend payout ratio, the fraction of profit paid as a dividend, is 50 percent in the first three years and, because of limited growth opportunities, 75 percent thereafter. With a constant return on equity (ROE) of 15 percent (in Year 1, $15,000/$100,000), dividends grow by 7.5 percent in the first three years[2] and then, after the increase in the dividend payout ratio in Year 4, by 3.75 percent forever.

Based on the financial mathematics discussed in Chapter 1, the first three dividends are discounted as a series of different cash flows, and it can be seen that there is a constant-growth perpetuity starting in Year 4, with a first cash flow of $13,975.8 in Year 4 growing by 3.75 percent thereafter.

Unlike the risk-free cash flows of Chapter 1, dividends are risky, so it is no surprise that shareholders will use a higher rate to discount these

**T A B L E   5.2**

Dividend Forecast, an Example

|  | Year 1 | Year 2 | Year 3 | Year 4 | Year 5 ... |
|---|---|---|---|---|---|
| Earnings | 15,000 | 16,125 | 17,334.38 | 18,634.5 | 19,333.3 |
| Dividends paid at end of year | 7,500 | 8,062.5 | 8,667.2 | 13,975.8 | 14,499.9 |
| Retained earnings | 7,500 | 8,062.5 | 8,667.2 | 4,658.6 | 4,833.3 |
| Equity at start of year | 100,000 | 107,500 | 115,562.5 | 124,229.7 | 128,888 |

cash flows. The higher discount rate is justified by the risk aversion of investors, who need to be compensated for taking some risk. The risk-adjusted discount rate used to value shares, $R_s$, is the risk-free rate plus a risk premium. In banking, a risk premium of around 5 percent is regularly used to value bank shares.[3]

$$\text{Value} = \frac{D_1}{1+R_s} + \frac{D_2}{(1+R_s)^2} + \frac{D_3}{(1+R_s)^3} + \frac{\dfrac{D_4}{R_s - g}}{(1+R_s)^3}$$

$$= \frac{7,500}{1.1} + \frac{8,062.5}{(1.1)^2} + \frac{8,667.2}{(1.1)^3} + \frac{\dfrac{13,975.8}{0.1 - 0.0.375}(= 223,610)}{(1.1)^3}$$

$$= 188,000$$

The first three terms give the discounted value of dividends over the first three years. The last term in the numerator, the value of the future stream of dividends with constant growth in perpetuity ($223,610), estimated at the end of Year 3, is referred to as the *terminal value*. In this calculation, a series of yearly dividends is discounted over a certain period, and then a terminal value that captures the value of dividends beyond that initial period is added.

A question that is frequently raised is, what is a reasonable perpetual growth rate for dividends, and is the estimated terminal value "reasonable"? The growth rate is often related to the nominal growth of GNP in a country, that is, real growth plus inflation. Indeed, the growth of a banking system often parallels the growth in GNP. An ad hoc sanity check for whether the terminal value estimate is reasonable is to divide the terminal value estimated at the beginning of Year 4 ($223,610) by the book value of equity at that time ($124,230). This gives an implicit MBV ratio (1.8 in the numerical example), and the analyst can check whether or not this is a reasonable figure.

## PRESENT VALUE OF FUTURE ECONOMIC PROFITS

As discussed previously, the market value of shares is equal to the present value of future dividends, discounted at the appropriate rate of return on shares ($R_s$):

$$\text{Market value of shares} = \frac{D_1}{1+R_s} + \frac{D_2}{(1+R_s)^2} + \cdots$$

An alternative approach that is fully consistent with the present value of dividends is to relate the share price to the so-called economic profit (EP) of the bank, that is, the value created by the bank on top of the expected rate of return on shareholders' equity:

$$\text{Economic profit (EP)} = \text{profit} - (\text{equity} \times \text{cost of equity})$$
$$= \text{profit} - (\text{equity} \times R_s)$$

Economic profit is an intuitive concept.[4] It recognizes that shareholders can invest in bank shares with an expected return $R_s$. Value is created during a year when the profit exceeds this return.

It can be shown (see Appendix B to this chapter) that the market value of equity today is equal to the current equity, $E_0$, plus the present value of future economic profits:

$$\text{Market value of equity}_0 = \text{equity}_0 + \sum_{t=1}(\text{profit}_t - \text{cost of equity}_t)$$
$$= \text{equity}_0 + \sum_{t=1}(\text{ROE}_t \times \text{equity}_t - \text{equity}_t \times R_s)$$

A special case is that in which equity, dividends, and economic profit are growing in perpetuity at a constant rate $g$ (with $g < R_s$).[5] Applying the financial mathematics discussed in Chapter 1 for the case of a constant-growth perpetuity gives

$$\text{Market value}_0 = E_0 + \frac{(\text{ROE} - R_s) \times E_1}{R_s - g}$$

For this special case of perpetual growth, the formula provides insights into the MBV ratio:

$$\frac{MV_0}{E_0} = \frac{\text{ROE} - R_s}{R_s - g} + 1$$

It can be seen that the MBV ratio is driven by the ROE and growth in earnings.

For example, with a cost of equity $R_s$ of 10 percent, an ROE of 15 percent, and a growth rate of 5 percent, the result is

$$\frac{MV}{E} = \frac{15\% - 10\%}{10\% - 5\%} + 1 = 2$$

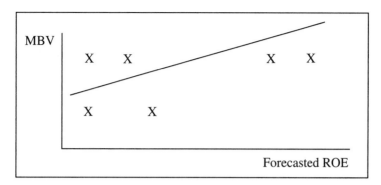

**Figure 5.1** The MBV-ROE valuation graph.

Consistent with this analysis, bank analysts use a simple tool to iden-tify undervalued or overvalued banks (see Figure 5.1).

Each entry (indicated by X) represents a bank at a specific point in time, with its forecasted ROE and its current MBV. The diagonal line is rep-resentative of the current stock market relationship between MBV and fore-casted ROE. A point above the line indicates that the bank is overvalued relative to the market (based on this, a sell recommendation would follow). Conversely, a point below the line indicates undervaluation and suggests a buy recommendation. Although any investor could draw such a chart, the value created by good analysts is in forecasting future ROE correctly.

Three approaches to bank valuation have been discussed so far: the use of market multiples, such as the P/E or MBV ratio; the present value of future expected dividends; and the sum of equity plus the present value of future economic profits. These three approaches are not specific to banking, but can be applied to the valuation of any company. The next step is to build on these approaches and introduce the *fundamental* bank valuation model.

## FUNDAMENTAL VALUATION MODEL (NO TAXES, NO RISK)

The fundamental valuation model is important for two reasons. First, it provides a transparent framework for analyzing the sources of value of banks. Second, it provides a tool for discussing, in an integrated manner, several bank managerial decisions, such as fund transfer pricing, risk-adjusted performance evaluation, capital management, loan pricing and loan-loss provisioning, and the measurement of interest-rate risk on the banking book.

For ease of presentation, this discussion ignores taxes and risk. These will be introduced in the next chapter.

The fundamental valuation formula breaks the bank into two major parts: on-balance sheet business, such as deposit taking and lending, and off-balance sheet business, such as trading activities, advisory work, and asset management. In terms of the income statement and gross revenue discussed in Chapter 4, the on-balance sheet business generates net interest income, while the off-balance sheet business generates fee income and trading profit. The fundamental bank valuation formula applies to the value of on-balance sheet business. This is the object of this section. The valuation of off-balance sheet banking business[6] is presented in Chapter 8.

To introduce the fundamental bank valuation formula, this section starts with a simple example that encompasses most of the theory behind this approach. More general formulas will follow.

### Valuing a Bank: An Example (No Taxes, No Risk)

Consider a bank that is funded with deposits of $95 and equity of $5. The funds are invested in fixed-rate government bonds with one year to maturity. They were purchased at a time when the fixed coupon rate was 6 percent. Today, similar bonds yield a 9 percent return. Deposits with short-term maturity yield 7 percent, the current rate available on new short-term deposits. The bonds are recorded at their historical book value of $100. A question might be, why would depositors accept a return of 7 percent when the current bond rate is 9 percent? Lack of competition among banks, ignorance on the part of some depositors, or convenience can explain why some depositors will invest in 7 percent deposits.

To keep the example simple, assume that this bank is going to live for two years with the same deposit base of $95. There is no risk, so the risk premium is 0 percent, and dividends will be discounted at the current risk-free bond rate of 9 percent At the end of two years, the bank will be closed and a liquidating dividend will be paid to shareholders. Finally, for the moment, ignore operating (noninterest) expenses. Here is the balance sheet:

| Assets (6 percent): 100 | Deposits (7 percent): 95 |
|---|---|
| (risk-free bonds) | Equity:                   5 |

Assets are risk-free government bonds with a maturity of one year and a coupon of 6 percent.

Short-term deposits yield 7 percent.

The current (risk-free) interest rate on assets is 9 percent.

The current interest rate on deposits is 7 percent.

The bank will be closed in two years.

The annual profit of this bank over the next two years can be forecasted:

$$\text{Profit}_{\text{Year 1}} = (6\% \times 100 - 7\% \times 95) = -0.65$$
$$\text{Profit}_{\text{Year 2}} = (9\% \times 100 - 7\% \times 95 - 9\% \times 0.65) = 2.29$$

In Year 1, the bank is losing money ($-\$0.65$), and it takes out a small loan on the market, $0.65, to finance that loss,[7] paying the current market rate of 9 percent. In Year 2, the *old* 6 percent coupon bond matures, and the proceeds are reinvested at the current bond rate of 9 percent.

Looking at this simple example, it can be argued that there are three methods of valuing this bank's equity.

### Valuation Method 1: The Book Value of Equity

This is the easiest method. The book value of equity is the difference between the accounting value of the assets and that of the debt, $100 − $95 = $5. The argument against this method is that the result is not very meaningful because it does not take into account the fair value of the assets, risk-free bonds that yield only 6 percent at a time when the current market rate is 9 percent.

### Valuation Method 2: The Liquidation Value

The liquidation value is the difference between the current value of the assets and that of the deposits.

$$\text{Value of assets} = \frac{106}{1.09} = 97.25$$

The value of short-term deposits yielding the current rate of 7 percent will be equal to the book value, $95.

$$\text{Value of deposits} = \frac{95 \times 1.07}{1.07} = 95$$

$$\text{Liquidation value} = \text{value of assets} - \text{value of deposits}$$
$$= \$97.25 - \$95 = \$2.25$$

The *liquidation* value represents the value that would accrue to shareholders if the bank were closed and liquidated immediately.

Ignoring transaction costs, the bonds can be sold at $97.25. After repayment of the short-term debt of $95, the shareholders receive a liquidating dividend of $2.25.

## Valuation Method 3: Present Value of Future Dividends

The third method of valuation is to compute the present value of the dividends paid to shareholders over the two-year life of the bank. Since, in this example, the bank is losing money in the first year, no dividend is paid in Year 1. A liquidating dividend is paid in Year 2. It includes the profit for the year ($2.29) plus the principal of the asset ($100), minus the repayment of the debts, deposits ($95), plus the small additional amount of debt raised to finance the loss during the first year ($0.65).

$$\text{MV of equity} = \text{PV of dividends}$$
$$= \frac{0}{1.09} + \frac{2.29 + 100 - 95 - 0.65}{1.09^2} = 5.59$$

The accounting book value of $5 can be ignored because the assets were not marked to market, so the result is two relevant concepts of the value of equity:

1. The liquidation value
2. The present value of future dividends

The *liquidation* value, as discussed earlier, represents the value that would accrue to shareholders if the bank were liquidated immediately. Ignoring transaction costs, the bonds can be sold at $97.25. After reimbursement of the short-term debt of $95, shareholders receive a liquidating dividend of $2.25.

The present value of future dividends represents a different concept. This is the value of the equity of a company as a *going concern*, that is, the value of the equity of a bank that is going to live for two years. In this example, the going-concern value of $5.59 exceeds the liquidation value of $2.25. This raises an interesting question as to what is driving the wedge (the difference) between the liquidation value and the going-concern value. In this example, the single key assumption that explains the wedge is that the bank is assumed to finance itself at a low interest rate of 7 percent when the market rate is 9 percent. The low-cost deposits are, intuitively, the source of value creation. This can be shown mathematically. It can be proved (see Appendix C to this chapter) that the present value of future dividends can be written as the sum of two terms: the liquidation value (the value if the bank were closed today) and an additional component, the franchise value, that is the present value of the future profits on low-cost deposits:

MV of equity = PV of dividends

$$= \frac{0}{1.09} + \frac{2.29 + 100 - 95 - 0.65}{1.09^2} = 5.59$$

$$\text{MV of equity} = \left[ \frac{106}{1.09} - \frac{95 \times 1.07}{1.07} \right]$$

$$+ \left[ \frac{(9\% - 7\%) \times 95}{1.09} + \frac{(9\% - 7\%) \times 95}{1.09^2} \right]$$

MV of equity = liquidation value + franchise value

$$= 2.25 + 3.34 = 5.59$$

Note that it is not possible to move directly from the first approach (the present value of dividends) to the second one (liquidation value + franchise value). As stated earlier, the mathematical proof is given in Appendix C.

There are two comments to make with respect to the second approach. In determining the liquidation value, assets and deposits have to be evaluated at their *own* current rate. That is, bonds are discounted at the current rate prevailing on the bond market, 9 percent, while deposits are discounted at the rate prevailing on new deposits, 7 percent. This is consistent with *fair valuation* accounting rules, which require evaluation of assets and liabilities at their own current rates.[8] The value of \$95 for deposits represents the amount of money that depositors should be willing to receive in the event of liquidation, because they can invest their money in another bank at an identical deposit rate of 7 percent.

Second, it can be observed that the franchise value[9] over two years is the margin between the *current* market rate of 9 percent and the rate paid on deposits of 7 percent. The franchise value represents the value created by the bank as a going concern. For two years, it is able to raise deposits at a cost below the market rate of 9 percent. Notice that in Year 1, the margin is computed based on the current market rate of 9 percent even though the government bond on the balance sheet is yielding only 6 percent. The reason is that the low interest rate of 6 percent has already been taken into account in determining the liquidation value of the bonds.

This example is simple, even simplistic. However, the basic concepts it illustrates are at the heart of this valuation methodology. It proposes evaluating the equity of banks in two steps. First, focusing on the current balance sheet of the bank, it is necessary to move from accounting book value figures to current liquidation values. Second, the franchise value will be assessed with a forecast of future volumes of deposits and margins.

This approach also helps in understanding some policy debates of recent decades. In the 1980s in the United States, long-term bond rates went up to 14 percent, precipitating a fall in the fair value of fixed-rate mortgages. On a liquidation value basis, the equity of many American savings and loan associations (S&Ls) was clearly negative. But they were kept open by regulators in the hope that the future franchise value would more than compensate for the negative liquidation value. Bad luck: the franchise value did not fully materialize, as increased competition and financial innovations, such as money market funds, substantially reduced the margins on deposits and the franchise value. This led to heavy losses and a government-sponsored bailout at a cost of $300 billion. In the S&L case, instead of talking of a *going-concern value*, it would be possible to talk of a *gone-concern value!*

The simple numerical example given in this section was useful for providing a basic understanding of the fundamental valuation model. Next, the actual fundamental valuation model is introduced. As already mentioned, two steps are needed. The first step is valuation in a risk-free and no-tax world. This is followed in the next chapter by the introduction of taxes and risk.

### Valuing a Bank (No Taxes, No Risk)

This section generalizes the previous simple example. The representative balance sheet of the bank is given here (symbols in parentheses are returns):

| Loans $L$ $(l)$ | Deposits $D$ $(d)$ |
|---|---|
| Bonds $B$ $(b)$ | Equity $E$ $(b^*)$ |
| Fixed assets | |

There are three types of bank assets: loans, bonds, and fixed assets. Funding comes from two sources: deposits and equity. Loans, bonds, and deposits are recorded at their historical book value. That is, a loan of $1 million granted two years ago is booked at $1 million. In practice, there will be several categories of loans and several types of deposits.

Some will be recorded at historical book value. Others could be marked to market. The model can accommodate all of this. However, in introducing the valuation model, it is simplified to allow concentration on the essentials.

At this point, it is necessary to distinguish between the *contractual, historical* interest rates on the assets and deposits and the *current* interest rates that would be applicable to new assets or deposits of identical maturity. For instance, for bonds, $b$ is the historical return on a bond purchased a few years ago. The rate $b^*$ denotes the current return on a new bond with a maturity identical to that remaining for the bond that is currently held. With reference to the previous example, the historical return was 6 percent, while the current return on a new bond with a one-year maturity was 9 percent.

So, the *historical, contractual* returns on loans, bonds, and deposits are denoted as $l$, $b$, and $d$.

The *current* returns are denoted as $l^*$, $b^*$, and $d^*$. Notice that in some cases (for instance, for short-term deposits or short-term loans), the historical return could be identical to the current return.

In the absence of risk, the discount rate at which shares are valued, the investment return available to shareholders, will be the current risk-free bond rate $b^*$. There can be many reasons why there are different interest rates for assets and liabilities. The longer maturity of assets may command a risk premium, and, given that deposits can be withdrawn at short notice, the posted deposit rate does not include the extra cost of refinancing in the event of deposit withdrawals. However, this does not explain the differential in the model. The assumption has been that the return and the cost, $l^*$ and $d^*$, are net of the price for risk, and it has been postulated that it is imperfect competition, imperfect information, or regulation in some markets that creates the interest-rate differentials. Barriers to entry or regulation (such as regulations on interest rates paid on demand deposits) prevent the creation of perfect substitutes that would erase the interest-rate differentials. The relevance of imperfect competition can be questioned in a period of global deregulation, but it would seem that market concentration resulting from bank mergers or asymmetrical information can create imperfections in at least some markets. In any case, the model is quite general, as perfect competition will appear as a special case.

The market value of equity is equal to the present value of future dividends:

Market value of equity = present value of future dividends

It can be shown (the proof is in Appendix C on page 71) that the market value of equity can be decomposed into two terms: the liquidation value and a franchise value:

$$\text{Market value of equity} = \text{liquidation value} + \text{franchise value}$$
$$= \text{current value of assets} - \text{current value of deposits} + \text{franchise value}$$

$$\text{MV of equity}_0 = L_0^* + B_0^* - D_0^*$$

$$+ \frac{(b_1^* - d_1^*) \times D_1^*}{1 + b_1^*} + \frac{(b_2^* - d_2^*) \times D_2^*}{(1 + b_1^*) \times (1 + b_2^*)} + \cdots$$

$$+ \frac{(l_1^* - b_1^*) \times L_1^*}{1 + b_1^*} + \frac{(l_2^* - b_2^*) \times L_2^*}{(1 + b_1^*) \times (1 + b_2^*)} + \cdots$$

$$- \frac{\text{operating expenses}_1}{1 + b_1^*} - \frac{\text{operating expenses}_2}{(1 + b_1^*) \times (1 + b_2^*)} - \cdots$$

where

$D_1^*$ = value of deposits in Year 1, discounted at the current deposit rate $d_1^*$

$L_1^*$ = value of loans in Year 1, discounted at the current loan rate $l_1^*$

$B_1^*$ = value of bonds in Year 1, discounted at the current bond rate $b_1^*$

The value of equity is the sum of the four parts. Each part represents something specific, and it is necessary to look at each part individually.

## Liquidation Value
The first term is the liquidation value.

$$\text{Liquidation value} = L_0^* + B_0^* - D_0^*$$

As in the example, the liquidation value is the current value of the assets net of the current value of debt, with each item being discounted at its current rate. This requires some interpretation. When a loan is discounted at its current loan rate, what does the present value represent? Remember the discussion of present value as "cash equivalent" in Chapter 1. The present value represents the amount of money that a borrower would be willing to pay back to the bank immediately, in the event of liquidation, if that borrower were able to take out a new loan at the current rate $l^*$. A similar reasoning applies to deposits. The present value is the amount of money a depositor would be willing to receive today from the bank if she could invest the money at a new rate $d^*$. These current values are identical to the *fair* value of financial instruments reported by U.S. banks in their annual report [as required by Statement of Financial Accounting Standards (SFAS) 107]. The liquidation value represents the amount of money available to shareholders in the event of liquidation and closure of the bank. Notice that the fixed assets do not appear in this liquidation value concept. This will be explained later.

## Franchise Value of Deposits

The second term is the franchise value of deposits.

$$\text{Franchise value of deposits} = \frac{(b_1^* - d_1^*) \times D_1^*}{1 + b_1^*} + \frac{(b_2^* - d_2^*) \times D_2^*}{(1 + b_1^*) \times (1 + b_2^*)} + \cdots$$

The franchise value of deposits represents the present value of the profits made from collecting deposits in the future. As discussed in Chapter 2, discounting for each year is done at the appropriate maturity rate.[10] Notice that for each year, the margin refers to the difference between the deposit rate paid in that year and the rate available on the bond market in that year. Notice also that, for each year, the calculation takes into account the current value of the book of deposits available in that year. These deposits can include both deposits from the past and new deposits collected during that year. For example, the deposits in Year 1, $D_1^*$, would include the initial deposits, $D_0^*$, plus possible new deposits collected during the first year. Estimating the franchise value of deposits therefore requires an estimate of the growth of deposits over time, and of the margin likely to be earned on these deposits. The expression for the franchise value of deposits is identical to that in the example discussed earlier. In that example, there was a constant deposit base of $95 over two years, a rate on deposits of 7 percent, and a rate on bonds of 9 percent. Often, banks collect fees for managing deposit accounts. This additional source of cash flow could be added to the interest margin. The third and fourth terms were not present in the previous simple example.

## Franchise Value of Loans

The third term is the franchise value of loans.

$$\text{Franchise value of loans} = \frac{(l_1^* - b_1^*) \times L_1^*}{1 + b_1^*} + \frac{(l_2^* - b_2^*) \times L_2^*}{(1 + b_1^*) \times (1 + b_2^*)} + \cdots$$

The franchise value of loans is the present value of future profits on loans, again evaluated in terms of the current bond rate. This term did not exist in the simple example because the bank was not lending money; it was only holding government bonds. Again, an estimate of the franchise value of loans requires a forecast of growth in the loan portfolio and of margins made on loans.

### Present Value of Operating (Noninterest) Expenses

Finally, the last term affects the market value of the bank's equity negatively. This is the present value of operating (noninterest) expenses, such as the remuneration of employees.

$$\text{Value of operating (noninterest) expenses}$$
$$= -\frac{\text{operating expenses}_1}{1 + b_1^\circ} - \frac{\text{operating expenses}_2}{(1 + b_1^\circ) \times (1 + b_2^\circ)} - \cdots$$

Again, this fourth and last term was not present in the simple example because operating expenses were ignored. Since the franchise value of deposits and loans included interest margins before operating expenses, the discounted value of cash operating expenses must be deducted. This would include, when relevant, the cash outflows related to capital expenditures, such as investment in technological infrastructure, needed to sustain the growth of the bank.

To complete the discussion of the fundamental valuation formula requires three additional observations related to the value of fixed assets, to the absence of a franchise value for holdings of bonds, and to the value created by fee-based income.

### Fixed Assets

Fixed assets, such as headquarters buildings in prime locations, do not show up in the fundamental valuation formula. The reason is that the bank is being valued as a going concern. If it does not sell its fixed assets, no cash flow is realized, and so these assets do not affect the valuation formula. However, some people have argued correctly that fixed assets would be sold in the event of a liquidation, generating a cash flow in that situation. Therefore, it would be possible to include the value of fixed assets to get a liquidation value and then take it back from the franchise value to recognize that the fixed assets would be needed to run the bank as a going concern. The fundamental valuation formula in that case would be

$$\text{MV of equity}_0 = L_0^* + B_0^* - D_0^* + FA_0^*$$

$$+ \frac{(b_1^* - d_1^*) \times D_1^*}{1 + b_1^*} + \frac{(b_2^* - d_2^*) \times D_2^*}{(1 + b_1^*) \times (1 + b_2^*)} + \cdots$$

$$+ \frac{(l_1^* - b_1^*) \times L_1^*}{1 + b_1^*} + \frac{(l_2^* - b_2^*) \times L_2^*}{(1 + b_1^*) \times (1 + b_2^*)} + \cdots$$

$$- \frac{\text{operating expenses}_1}{1 + b_1^*} - \frac{\text{operating expenses}_2}{(1 + b_1^*) \times (1 + b_2^*)} - \cdots$$

$$- FA_0^*$$

In the following discussion, fixed assets will be ignored, on the assumption that they will not be sold.[11]

## No Franchise Value for Holdings of Bonds
Both in the numerical example and in the formula, there is no franchise value for government bonds. The reason is that the bank does not create value through holding bonds, since its shareholders can buy bonds themselves.

## Value Derived from Fee-Based Income
The model has focused exclusively on valuing on-balance sheet businesses, such as loans and deposits. No value has been attached to off-balance sheet activities, such as asset management, corporate advisory services on mergers and acquisitions and initial public offerings, or trading. Of course, these off-balance sheet activities are additional sources of value. However, as methods of valuing these are directly inspired by standard corporate valuation approaches, and they will be discussed, as indicated earlier, in a separate chapter, Chapter 8. The treatment of the valuation of fee-based activities in a subsequent chapter does not imply that these activities do not create much value. It is just that balance sheet banking and off-balance sheet banking require different valuation methodologies.

### The Fundamental Valuation Model: An Example
To get some insights into the valuation formula, it is helpful to consider the example of a loan funded exclusively with equity. Of course, in real life, loans will also be funded with debt. But this extreme example helps in understanding the valuation model. Consider a one-year loan of $100 funded with equity. In a year's time, the loan portfolio will grow to $150.

$$\overline{\text{Loan} = 100\ (20\%)\ \Big|\ \text{Equity} = 100}$$

The contractual interest rate on the loan $l$ is 20 percent, equal to the current rate $l^*$ on a new loan.

Operating expenses are 4 percent, and the current rate on government bonds is 9 percent. To simplify the example, the bank will be closed after two years.

The market value of the equity is the present value of future dividends:

MV of equity = present value of future dividends

$$= \left[\frac{(20\% - 4\%) \times 100}{1.09}\right] - \frac{50}{1.09} + \left[\frac{(20\% - 4\%) \times 150 + 150}{1.09^2}\right]$$

$$= 115.26$$

The first term is the present value of the dividend paid to shareholders in Year 1. It has two parts: the profit on the loan, (20 percent − 4 percent) × 100, reduced by the retained earnings[12] needed to grow the loan portfolio, $50 = $150 − $100.

The second term represents the present value of the dividend paid in Year 2. That includes two terms: the profit in Year 2 and a liquidating dividend when the bank is closed at the end of Year 2.

An alternative is to apply the fundamental valuation formula:

MV of equity = liquidation value + franchise value

$$= \left(\frac{20 + 100}{1.2}\right) + \left[\begin{array}{c}\dfrac{(20\% - 9\% - 4\%) \times 100}{1.09} \\ + \dfrac{(20\% - 9\% - 4\%) \times 150}{1.09^2}\end{array}\right]$$

$$= 100 + (6.42 + 8.84) = 115.26$$

The liquidation value is the discounted value of cash flows on the current loan portfolio, discounted at the current rate on new loans. In this case, the liquidation value, $100, is identical to the book value because the current rate $l^*$ is the same as the historical rate $l$. The franchise value over two years is the difference between the current return on the loan and the current opportunity bond rate, net of operating expenses.

Notice that in the second formulation, the fundamental valuation formula, the analysis focuses exclusively on two things: the liquidation value of current assets and the franchise value. There is no need to calculate retained earnings, as this term is implicitly taken into account.

The absence of a retained earnings calculation often surprises analysts who are used to dividend forecasts (profit net of retained earnings). They ask: are you really sure that the fundamental valuation formula is taking the necessary retained earnings into account?

The answer is yes, and this can be proven fairly intuitively. Retained earnings create an immediate negative cash flow (dividends are reduced or shareholders need to invest fresh equity to finance the growth), followed by a positive cash flow when the money invested in new loans is paid back:

$$
\begin{aligned}
\text{Net present value of retained earnings} &= \frac{-50}{1.09} + \frac{50 \times (1 + 20\%)}{1.09^2} = \frac{-50}{1.09} \\
&\quad + \frac{50 \times (1.09)}{1.09^2} + \frac{50 \times (20\% - 9\%)}{1.09^2} \\
&= \frac{50 \times (20\% - 9\%)}{1.09^2}
\end{aligned}
$$

This illustrates that the present value of cash flows linked to retained earnings is identical to the franchise value of $50 on the new loan, which is included in the fundamental formula. If retained earnings were simply invested at the bond rate, their present value would be zero. The value is coming entirely from the extra return generated by the retained earnings. So, a benefit of the fundamental valuation formula is that it does not require computing retained earnings explicitly.

The fundamental valuation formula framework allows the sources of value—liquidation value of the current balance sheet, franchise value of deposits, franchise value of loans, and operating expenses—to be disentangled.

The liquidation value is the value of the current balance sheet $(L_0^* + B_0^* - D_0^*)$, while the going-concern value requires a second term, the value of the franchise, i.e., the bank's ability to earn rents in the future. Rents can be created by lending, but also by collecting low-cost deposits.[13] The solvency of banks must be evaluated as the greater of the *liquidation* and *going-concern* values. This was already noted by Nobel Prize-winner Paul Samuelson many years ago (1945, p. 24): "It should not be necessary to argue before economists that the banking system is a going concern and should be treated as such."

In anticipation of the discussion of interest-rate risk in Chapter 19, it can be seen that the market value of the equity of a bank will be affected not only by changes in the liquidation value of its assets and liabilities, but also by the impact of the interest rate on the franchise value.

## CONCLUSION

This chapter provides an introduction to bank valuation. Three approaches that are not specific to banks have been covered: market multiples, present value of future dividends, and current equity plus present value of future economic profits. The fundamental bank valuation model has also been introduced. To simplify the discussion, taxes and risk were ignored in this chapter. They are introduced in the next chapter. The fundamental valuation formula approach shows that the present value of future dividends is equal to the liquidation value of the bank if it were closed immediately, plus a franchise value that represents the value created by the bank as a going concern. The franchise value represents the present value of future profits on loans and deposits. As will be shown in coming chapters, the fundamental valuation model is useful not only for valuing banks, but also for discussing value-enhancing decisions such as the choice of a fund transfer price, deposit and loan pricing, and the measurement of interest-rate risk.

## APPENDIX A: RELATIONSHIP BETWEEN THE P/E RATIO AND THE MARKET/BOOK VALUE RATIO

Bankers sometimes wonder whether the P/E ratio or the market/book value ratio is a better indicator of value creation. Should investors be impressed by a P/E of 14 (above the average of 11 for the banking industry observed before the subprime crisis) or an MBV of 2.5 (above the average of 2 for the banking sector in OECD countries)?

As is shown here, the mathematical relationship between the P/E and the MBV helps in understanding why the MBV is a better indicator of value creation.

Let

$n$ = number of shares
$P$ = price per share
EPS = earnings per share
BVS = book value per share = equity/$n$

$$\frac{\text{Market value of equity}}{\text{Book value of equity}} = \frac{P \times n}{BVS \times n} = \frac{P \times EPS}{BVS \times EPS} = \frac{P}{EPS} \times \frac{EPS}{BVS}$$
$$= P/E \text{ ratio} \times ROE$$

The MBV ratio is the product of the P/E ratio and the return on equity (ROE). The P/E ratio is an indicator of the expected future growth of earnings and of the degree of risk, but it does not say anything about the current level of earnings, high or low. The MBV ratio incorporates not only the P/E, but also the current level of ROE. Intuitively, a high P/E that applies to low earnings is not an indicator of value creation. Therefore, the MBV is a better indicator of value creation. Still, it is not a perfect indicator, as it is a relative index that does not say anything about either the size of a firm or the amount of equity invested in it. Clearly, a large MBV for a very small firm with a low equity base will not indicate much value creation. Therefore, the best indicator of value creation, which takes the size of the bank into account, is

$$\text{Market value added (MVA)} = \text{market value of shares} -$$
$$\text{equity invested by shareholders}$$

## APPENDIX B: VALUE OF EQUITY AS DISCOUNTED VALUE OF FUTURE ECONOMIC PROFITS

Consider first the case of equity generating a constant ROE every year in perpetuity, with the full profit being paid out as a dividend. Thus, there is no retained earnings and zero growth:

$$
\begin{aligned}
\text{Value of equity} &= \frac{\text{dividend}}{1+R_s} + \frac{\text{dividend}}{(1+R_s)^2} + \frac{\text{dividend}}{(1+R_s)^3} + \cdots \\
&= \frac{E \times \text{ROE}}{1+R_s} + \frac{E \times \text{ROE}}{(1+R_s)^2} + \frac{E \times \text{ROE}}{(1+R_s)^3} + \cdots \\
&= \frac{E \times R_s + E \times (\text{ROE} - R_s)}{1+R_s} + \frac{E \times R_s + E \times (\text{ROE} - R_s)}{(1+R_s)^2} + \cdots \\
&= \frac{E \times R_s}{R_s} + \frac{(\text{ROE} - R_s) \times E}{1+R_s} + \frac{(\text{ROE} - R_s) \times E}{(1+R_s)^2} + \cdots \\
&= \text{equity}_0 + \sum (\text{ROE} - R_s) \times E
\end{aligned}
$$

The value of equity is equal to the current equity plus the present value of future economic profits.

Next, assume that at the end of Year 1 the firm has retained earnings ($RE_1$) that are reinvested forever at a constant ROE. Compute the present value of a negative cash flow followed by positive additional dividends:

Value of retained earnings$_1$

$$= \frac{-\text{RE}_1}{1+R_s} + \frac{\text{ROE}\times\text{RE}_1}{(1+R_s)^2} + \frac{\text{ROE}\times\text{RE}_1}{(1+R_s)^3} + \cdots$$

$$= \frac{-\text{RE}_1}{1+R_s} + \frac{R_s\times\text{RE}_1 + (\text{ROE}-R_s)\times\text{RE}_1}{(1+R_s)^2} + \frac{R_s\times\text{RE}_1 + (\text{ROE}-R_s)\times\text{RE}_1}{(1+R_s)^3} + \cdots$$

$$= \frac{-\text{RE}_1}{1+R_s} + \frac{\dfrac{R_s\times\text{RE}_1}{R_s}}{1+R_s} + \frac{(\text{ROE}-R_s)\times\text{RE}_1}{(1+R_s)^2} + \frac{(\text{ROE}-R_s)\times\text{RE}_1}{(1+R_s)^3} + \cdots$$

$$= \frac{(\text{ROE}-R_s)\times\text{RE}_1}{(1+R_s)^2} + \frac{(\text{ROE}-R_s)\times\text{RE}_1}{(1+R_s)^3} + \frac{(\text{ROE}-R_s)\times\text{RE}_1}{(1+R_s)^4} + \cdots$$

The value of retained earnings is equal to the present value of the future economic profits on these retained earnings. This calculation could be repeated for retained earnings in Year 2, Year 3, and so on. Adding the value of retained earnings to the zero-growth valuation yields

$$\text{Value of equity} = \frac{\text{dividend}_1}{1+R_s} + \frac{\text{dividend}_2}{(1+R_s)^2} + \frac{\text{dividend}_3}{(1+R_s)^3} + \cdots$$

$$= \text{equity}_0 + \sum_{t=1}(\text{ROE}-R_s)\times E_i$$

The value of equity is the current equity plus the present value of future economic profits.

If a constant rate of growth for equity $g$ (with $g < R_s$) is assumed, this simplifies to

$$\text{Value of equity} = \text{equity}_0 + \frac{(\text{ROE}-R_s)\times\text{equity}}{R_s - g}$$

Denoting the dividend payout ratio (dividend/profit) by $p$,[14] the growth of equity $g$ is equal to

$$g = \frac{\text{retained earnings}}{\text{equity}} = \frac{(1-p)\times\text{profit}}{\text{equity}}$$

$$= \frac{(1-p)\times\text{ROE}\times\text{equity}}{\text{equity}} = (1-p)\times\text{ROE}$$

With a constant ROE and $p$ implying a constant perpetual growth $g$ (with $g < R_s$) for equity, profit, and dividends, the value of equity is equal to

$$\text{Value of equity} = \text{equity}_0 + \frac{(\text{ROE} - R_s) \times \text{equity}}{R_s - (1-p) \times \text{ROE}}$$

## APPENDIX C: PROOF OF FUNDAMENTAL VALUATION FORMULA

This appendix shows that the value of a two-period asset $A$ with a historical return $a$, a current (one-period) return $a^*$, and a discount rate of $b^*$ is equal to

$$MV = \frac{aA}{1+b^*} + \frac{(1+a)\,A}{(1+b^*)^2}$$

$$= A_1^° + \left[ \frac{(a^* - b^*) \times A_1^°}{1+b^*} + \frac{(a^* - b^*) \times A_2^°}{(1+b^*)^2} \right]$$

where

$$A_1^° = \frac{aA}{1+a^*} + \frac{(1+a)\,A}{(1+a^*)^2}$$

$$A_2^° = \frac{(1+a)\,A}{1+a^*}$$

The analysis can be repeated for loans, bonds, and deposits to obtain the valuation formula.

Proof:

$$MV = \frac{aA}{1+b^*} + \frac{(1+a)\,A}{(1+b^*)^2} = \left[ \frac{aA}{1+a^*} + \left( \frac{aA}{1+b^*} - \frac{aA}{1+a^*} \right) \right]$$

$$+ \left\{ \frac{(1+a)\,A}{(1+a^*)^2} + \left[ \frac{(1+a)\,A}{(1+b^*)^2} - \frac{(1+a)\,A}{(1+a^*)^2} \right] \right\}$$

$$= \left[ \frac{aA}{1+a^*} + \frac{(1+aA)}{(1+a^*)^2} \right] + \left\{ \begin{array}{l} \dfrac{aA\,(a^* - b^*)}{(1+a^*)(1+b^*)} + \\[2mm] \dfrac{(1+a^*)(a^* - b^*)[(1+a^*) + (1+b^*)]}{(1+a^*)^2\,(1+b^*)^2} \end{array} \right\}$$

$$= A_1^° + \frac{(a^* - b^*)\left[ \dfrac{aA}{1+a^*} + \dfrac{(1+a)\,A}{(1+a^*)^2} \right]}{1+b^*} + \frac{(a^* - b^*)\dfrac{(1+a)\,A}{1+a^*}}{(1+b^*)^2}$$

$$= A_1^° + \left[ \frac{(a^* - b^*) \times A_1^°}{1+b^*} + \frac{(a^* - b^*) \times A_2^°}{(1+b^*)^2} \right]$$

## EXERCISES FOR CHAPTER 5

1. Bank Alpha is a fast-growing company. As of January 1, 2009, it has not yet paid a single dividend, and it has announced that it will not pay any for the next two years. Given that the earnings per share (EPS) for December 2008 was 10, that the ROE is 15 percent, that the expected return on shares with similar risk is 10 percent, and that the company is expected to pay 60 percent of profit as a dividend in three years' time (December 2011) and in the future, compute the value of the shares on January 1, 2009, assuming that all parameters (EPS and dividend excepted) will be constant forever.

2. In an article titled "Risk and Reward on Wall Street," an analyst wrote several years ago:

    The top 30 U.S. banks are currently trading at 75% of book value. This implies that retained earnings of $100 millions are being marked down to $75 millions by the market; this in turn implies that the market's opinion of the banking industry's future ability to earn profit is bleak (poor).

    In the context of the bank fundamental valuation framework, is this statement true or false? Justify your answer.

3. The volume of demand deposits during Year 1 is $100. It is expected to grow to $105 in Year 2. The interest rate paid on deposits is 0 percent. The level of operating expenses is 3 percent, the tax rate is 0 percent, and the shareholders' rate of return is 10 percent.

    The volumes of deposits are as follows:

    | Year 1 | + | Year 2 |
    |--------|---|--------|
    | 100    |   | 105    |

    Taking a two-year horizon (i.e., the bank will be closed at the end of Year 2), compute the value of this deposit liability (that is, the present value of net cash outflows) from the shareholders' perspective.

    Decompose this value into a liquidation value, a franchise value, and the present value of operating expenses.

4. A bank is investing exclusively in perpetual risk-free bonds (principal of $100, fixed annual coupon 9 percent). The asset is funded with perpetual deposits ($95) and equity ($5). The current risk-free rate on the bond market is 7 percent, and the

bank pays interest of 6 percent on deposits. Operating expenses are ignored. The current rate on new deposits is also 6 percent. The corporate tax rate is 0 percent.

| Risk-free bonds: 100 | Deposits: | 95 |
|---|---|---|
| | Equity: | 5 |

**a.** Compute the value of the equity of this perpetual bank (assuming a zero equity risk premium).

**b.** Break the value of equity into a liquidation value and a franchise value.

## Notes

1. The U.S. subprime credit crisis is discussed in Chapters 15, 16, and 21.
2. In the case of a constant ROE, it can be shown that the rate of growth of dividends is equal to $(1 - \text{dividend payout ratio}) \times \text{ROE}$. Growth is equal to $(1 - 50\%) \times 15\% = 7.5\%$ for the first three years, and $(1 - 75\%) \times 15\% = 3.75\%$ thereafter in perpetuity. See the proof at the end of Appendix B of this chapter.
3. Remember that the discount rate represents the return available to investors. Instead of buying the bank's shares, investors could buy shares in other banks with similar risk. Historical studies show that buying bank shares earns an investor, on average, an extra return of 5 percent over the risk-free government bond rate. This historical extra return is called the *realized risk premium*. It is consistent with theoretical asset pricing models, such as the capital asset pricing model (CAPM).
4. Economic profit (EP) is discussed in greater detail in Chapter 9, which covers performance metrics for value centers.
5. As discussed at the end of Appendix B of this chapter, in the case of a constant ROE and a constant dividend payout ratio $p$, the annual growth rate for dividends, $g$, is equal to $(1 - p) \times \text{ROE}$.
6. As will be discussed in Chapter 8, off-balance sheet banking business will most often include some on-balance sheet assets and liabilities, such as fixed assets (offices, computers, and other such things) or financial assets (interbank assets or bonds that are part of a trading portfolio, for example).
7. Alternative ways to finance the loss of $0.65 are to sell part of the bonds or to increase the volume of low-cost deposits. The market-borrowing approach was chosen here for ease of exposition.

8. U.S. Statement of Financial Accounting Standards (SFAS) 107, "Disclosures about Fair Value of Financial Instruments."

9. The word *franchise* arises from the fact that banks have received from central banks a bank license, the authorization to collect deposits (and/or grant loans), giving them access to a banking *franchise*.

10. With reference to Chapter 2, discounting at the spot (current) zero coupon rate is equivalent to discounting, year by year, at the one-year forward rate [for example, in Year 2, $(1 + b_1^*) \times (1 + b_2^*)$].

11. It would also be possible to discuss a *sale and leaseback* agreement, with an initial cash inflow linked to the sale of the asset, followed by the flow of after-tax rental expenses. Another case is the sale of an expensive building in the center of a city, followed by the building of a new headquarters outside the city (as was done by the Spanish Banco Santander in Madrid). As a sale could take place in the future, it might be necessary to attach some probability to the sale of fixed assets and its associated cash flows, clearly not an easy exercise.

12. In this example, the profit of $16 is not large enough to cover the growth of equity of $50. Shareholders have to provide additional equity of $34 ($50 − $16).

13. This is a major difference from nonfinancial firms, such as industrial or service firms. These firms create value on assets when the net present value of investment is positive (as is the case for banks with loans), but they do not create value through the funding of assets because it is assumed that they must pay the market rate on their debt.

14. The *plowback ratio* is defined as $(1 - p)$, the complement of the dividend payout ratio.

CHAPTER 6

---

# The Valuation of Banks, Part 2

## THE FUNDAMENTAL VALUATION MODEL
## (WITH CORPORATE TAXES AND RISK)

The previous chapter introduced four methods for the valuation of banks: market multiples, present value of dividends, present value of economic profits, and a "fundamental" bank valuation model for valuing on-balance sheet banking business. The last approach decomposes the value of a bank into four components:

1. The liquidation value of the current balance sheet
2. The franchise value of deposits
3. The franchise value of loans
4. The present value of operating expenses

The step-by-step presentation in the previous chapter ignored corporate taxes and risk. This chapter provides the complete framework, with taxes and risk included. A numerical example to build understanding will be followed by formal bank valuation formulas.

## VALUING A LOAN: AN EXAMPLE

Consider a loan of $100 that is funded exclusively with equity. Again, this extreme example is chosen only to facilitate the introduction of corporate taxes and risk.

$$\text{Loan} = 100\ (8\%) \mid \text{Equity} = 100$$

This risky loan yields expected interest revenue $l$ (net of expected loan losses) of 8 percent. To simplify the example, assume that this is a perpetual loan, paying an expected revenue $l$ of 8 percent every year. The loan is funded exclusively with equity. The expected return on a new loan $l^*$ is 11 percent. The differential between the expected contractual return,

$l$ = 8 percent, and the return on a new loan, $l^*$ = 11 percent, could be caused by an increase in fixed interest rates in the country. The corporate tax rate $t$ is 40 percent. Finally, since these are risky cash flows, they are discounted at a risk-adjusted rate $b^{**}$ of 10 percent, which is the risk-free rate $b^*$ plus a risk premium. A discussion on estimating the relevant risk premium will appear later in the chapter.

So, three different interest rates must be considered:

1. The expected return on the loan on the balance sheet: $l$ = 8 percent
2. The expected current return on a new loan: $l^*$ = 11 percent
3. A shareholder risk-adjusted discount rate: $b^{**}$ = 10 percent

The value of the equity of the bank is the present value of the perpetual dividends, the profit after corporate tax that is paid to shareholders every year in perpetuity.

$$\text{Market value of equity} = \text{present value of dividends}$$

$$= \frac{(1-40\%)\times 8}{1.1} + = \frac{(1-40\%)\times 8}{1.1^2} + \cdots = \frac{(1-40\%)\times 8}{0.1}$$

$$= 48$$

As discussed in Chapter 1, the value of a perpetual cash flow is the annual cash flow divided by the discount rate.

In the spirit of the fundamental valuation formula, the value of equity can be written in a different manner:[1]

$$\text{Market value} = \frac{\text{annual dividend}}{\text{discount rate}} = \frac{(1-40\%)\times 8}{0.1} = 48$$

$$= \frac{(1-40\%)\times 8}{(1-40\%)\times 0.11} + \frac{(1-40\%)\times(11\%-10\%)\times 72.7}{0.1}$$

$$- \frac{40\%\times 0.1\times 72.7}{0.1}$$

$$= 72.7 + 4.4 - 29.1 = 48$$

The market value of equity is the sum of three terms. As in the model with no tax, the first steps are to find the current liquidation value of the loan ($72.7) and the franchise value of loans ($4.4). Now, a third term, the last one ($-29.1$), has been added. Here are some comments on each of these three terms.

## After-Tax Liquidation Value

The after-tax liquidation value is $72.7. In this case, the *after-tax* expected cash flows on the loans must be discounted by an *after-tax* current return on new loans. In the special case of a perpetuity, the tax factors $(1 - t)$ in the numerator and the denominator would cancel out, but they would not do so in the case of assets with finite maturities.

## After-Tax Franchise Value

The after-tax franchise value is $4.4. It will not be a surprise that the franchise value must be calculated after tax. The after-tax margin is now the difference between the current expected return on the loan and the shareholders' risk-adjusted return, the cost of equity (to be discussed later).

## Tax Penalty

The third term, a negative figure $(-\$29.1)$, represents a tax penalty. In the numerator is the tax rate $t$ multiplied by a return on the loan (10 percent $\times$ $72.7). Corporate finance specialists should be familiar with this term. Since Modigliani and Miller (1958), it has been well known that debt creates value because the cost of debt, the interest expense, is tax-deductible. Corporate debt allows a company to reduce its before-tax earnings and corporate tax payments. Our case is just the reverse of the Modigliani-Miller interest expense tax shield. The bank does not have debt; instead, since it is holding a financial asset, it has to pay corporate tax on the interest income earned on the asset.[2] So what is an interest tax shield in the case of debt becomes a corporate tax penalty in the case of a financial asset. This third term is referred to as the *corporate tax penalty*.

Notice that in this example, the tax penalty is very large. This is because the loan is funded exclusively with equity. There is no interest tax shield on equity. It is no surprise, as is discussed in Chapters 12 and 13, that bankers have lobbied very hard to be allowed to finance loans with a maximum amount of debt, with tax-deductible interest expense, and with a minimum amount of equity.

Before generalizing this example with the introduction of holdings of bonds and funding with deposits, it is first necessary to discuss the risk-adjusted cost of equity, the discount rate needed to value dividends.

## RISK-ADJUSTED DISCOUNT RATE FOR VALUING LOANS

The framework has ignored the element of risk and the difficulty of choosing a *risk-adjusted* discount rate for valuing assets and liabilities. Standard corporate finance theory suggests discounting dividends at the cost of equity, the expected return on the stock market. In this case, the rate is calculated as the expected return on bank shares, which can be estimated with a standard capital asset pricing model (CAPM), a dividend discount model, or a multifactor model (Brealey, Meyers, and Allen, 2006; Lajéri and Dermine, 1999). The CAPM shows that the risk premium on shares is the product of two terms: the beta of the shares and the market premium.

Risk premium = beta of shares × market premium

The market premium is the difference between the expected return on the overall stock market and that on government bonds. International research[3] has evaluated the market premium as being close to 5 percent. The beta of a stock indicates the degree of covariation between that specific stock and the overall stock market. A beta of 1 indicates that the returns on that stock are highly correlated with those on the stock market. A beta of zero indicates no correlation at all.[4]

As an illustration, the betas of the shares of several European and American banks are reported in Table 6.1.

The betas in Table 6.1 are computed on bank stocks and represent the overall risk of the bank, the risk of the net cash flows, which have two components: cash flows from multiple assets and cash flows on liabilities. They can be used to calculate the overall risk premium for a bank. Whenever the risk of specific assets is different from the average corporate risk, the standard corporate finance textbook recommends finding listed shares of firms with risk similar to that of the one analyzed, the *comparables*. For instance, in the case of a conglomerate firm with businesses in

**TABLE 6.1**

### Betas of Banks' Shares

| | | | |
|---|---|---|---|
| BNP-Paribas | 1.08 | JPMorgan Chase | 1.11 |
| UBS | 1.37 | Citigroup | 1.31 |
| Santander | 1.22 | Bank of America | 0.87 |
| ING Group | 1.36 | Goldman Sachs | 1.43 |

Source: *Thomson Analytics*, September 2008.

both the chemical sector and other sectors, the textbook recommends using the expected return on the shares of chemical companies to estimate the cost of equity for projects in the chemical sector. It recommends searching for specialized, sisterlike, comparable companies listed on a stock exchange whenever there is a need for a risk-specific discount rate.

In principle, since a bank has assets with many different types of risk, from very safe to very risky, making a similar recommendation could be tempting. Specialized banks, such as monoline credit card providers (e.g., Capital One), global custodians (e.g., State Street or Bank of New York), private banks (Vontobel in Switzerland), or investment banks (Goldman Sachs or Merrill Lynch), can help in estimating a specific risk premium for some activities of a universal bank. However, the standard corporate finance recommendation is very unlikely to work for bank lending, because specialized banks that lend to just one business sector are unlikely to be found in the stock market. Banks diversify their credit risk by lending to companies in many different industries. It is for this reason, the absence of specialized bank lenders listed on the stock market, that banks often use a single average cost of equity, the expected return on the bank's own shares, to evaluate different activities (Zaik et al., 1996). This section proposes a methodology for valuing bank lending that takes specific risk-adjusted discount rates into account.

The argument here is that, rather than searching in the stock market for listed banks specializing in lending to a single business sector to determine the beta of their shares and the relevant equity risk premium, an alternative is to use the *expected return on corporate bonds with risk similar to that of loans* as an opportunity cost for the bank's shareholders. Indeed, shareholders can find an alternative similar-risk investment by buying a corporate bond with risk similar to that of the loan. For example, a very safe loan can be compared to an AAA-rated bond. So, unlike the corporate finance literature, which advocates the use of information on risk premiums from the equity markets, this chapter advocates the use of information on risk premiums available on the corporate bond, asset-backed securities, and credit derivative markets.

Although data on the expected return on corporate bonds are currently not as widely available as data on the expected return on shares, with the growth of the corporate bond, asset-backed securities, and credit derivative markets, more information on the expected return on corporate bonds can be expected to become available. Studies by Kaplan and Stein (1990) for the junk bond markets and Delianedis and Santa-Clara (1999) for the graded bond markets provide the realized excess premiums, or the difference between the realized returns on corporate bonds of different

**TABLE 6.2**

Excess Return on Corporate Bonds (Realized Return on Corporate Bonds Minus
Return on U.S. Government Bonds) and Equities

| | |
|---|---|
| AAA | 27 bp |
| AA | 48 bp |
| A | 69 bp |
| BBB | 83 bp |
| Junk | 200 bp |
| Equity | 500 bp |

Source: Kaplan and Stein (1990) and Delianedis and Santa-Clara (1999).

grades and the return on federal risk-free bonds with a matched maturity,
that are reported in Table 6.2.

This table shows a reasonable range from a low 27-bp risk premium
for holding AAA bonds to 200 bp for holding higher-risk junk bonds.[5] For
reference, the risk premium for the overall stock market is around 500 bp.

Kozhemiakin (2007) reports the realized excess premium for investing in corporate bonds relative to risk-free Treasury bills (Table 6.3). As
expected, he obtains higher risk premiums, as long-term risk-free bonds
already include a maturity risk premium.

The excess return on AAA bonds must include a long-term maturity
premium that is unrelated to credit risk. So, it would appear that studies

**TABLE 6.3**

Historical Realized Excess Returns (1985–2005)

| Rating | Annualized Realized Excess Returns |
|---|---|
| AAA | 1.4% |
| A | 1.7% |
| BBB | 1.8% |
| BB | 3.3% |
| B | 2% |

Source: Kozhemiakin (2007).

that compute the realized excess return on matched-maturity bonds provide better information on the credit risk premium.

More recent evidence on risk premiums on corporate credit risk compares the risk-neutral probability of default[6] observed in credit default swaps to the actual probability of default coming out of Moody's KMV (Amato, 2005; Berndt et al., 2005). These studies observe, on average, a risk premium of 35 bp for a portfolio of 125 entities with credit ratings ranging from A to BBB; however, the risk premium exhibits large variation over time.

It can be seen that the margin in the loan franchise is the difference between the return on the loan ($l^*$) and the return on a similar-risk asset ($b^{**}$). This seems intuitive. A loan will create a positive franchise when the expected return on that loan exceeds the expected return on a similar-risk corporate bond[7] that the bank can buy as an alternative investment.[8]

## RISK PREMIUM ON EQUITY SHARES VS. RISK PREMIUM ON CORPORATE BONDS: A CLARIFICATION

At this stage, the reader might be confused between two types of risk premium in the banking sector: a 5 percent risk premium on the bank's shares and a much lower risk premium on the corporate bond market that is used to value bank loans (0.25 to 2 percent). A clarification is needed. The risk premium on the bank's shares is the risk premium for *leveraged* cash flows, the cash flows from the bank's assets net of the cost of debt funding. As leverage, or funding with debt, increases risk, the risk premium on the bank's shares includes both a risk premium for the riskiness of the asset and a risk premium for leverage. The lower risk premium on corporate bonds was used to value a loan funded exclusively with equity, with no debt and no leverage. In this case, as there is no debt and no leverage, the resulting risk premium is much lower. In corporate finance, this is referred to as an *unlevered* (zero-debt) cost of capital. This approach to bank valuation involves separating the net leveraged cash flows of a bank (cash flow from assets net of debt funding expense) into a sum of unlevered cash flows. This will allow the choice of a specific risk premium for particular assets, such as the use of the expected return on corporate bonds to evaluate loan portfolios with risk similar to that of the bonds.

The next step is to look at the example of the value of equity invested in a loan.

## VALUING EQUITY INVESTED IN A LOAN

Consider the equity of a bank invested in loans. This discussion focuses on one asset for expository convenience and further assumes that the loan is perpetual. The single-asset approach is generalized next.

This discussion uses the following terms:

$L$ = loan (perpetuity)

$l$ = expected return on loan on balance sheet

$t$ = corporate tax rate

$l^*$ = expected current return on new loan

$b^{**}$ = shareholders' risk-adjusted rate of return

The balance sheet for this position is as follows:

Loan $L$ $(l)$ $\mid$ Equity $(b^{**})$

As discussed earlier in this chapter, rather than searching for banks that specialize in lending to a single business sector in order to determine the beta of their shares and the relevant risk premium, an alternative is to use the *expected return on corporate bonds with similar risk* as an opportunity cost for the banks' shareholders. To value a loan to a particular business sector with a specific credit grade, the analyst can use information from the corporate bond, asset-backed securities, and credit derivative markets.

It is now possible to value the equity of this bank. It is the present value of the (perpetual) flows of dividends discounted at the shareholders' rate of return:

$$\text{MV of equity} = \text{PV of dividends} = \frac{(1-t)\times l \times L}{b^{**}}$$

This can be shown to be equal to[9]

$$\text{Market value of equity} = \frac{(1-t)\times l \times L}{(1-t)l^*} + \frac{(1-t)(l^* - b^{**})L^*}{b^{**}} - \frac{t\,b^{**}L^*}{b^{**}}$$

$$= L^* + \frac{(1-t)(l^* - b^{**})L^*}{b^{**}} - \frac{t\,b^{**}L^*}{b^{**}}$$

The value of the equity is the sum of three terms: the value of the after-tax cash flows from the loan discounted at the loan after-tax current rate, the after-tax value of the franchise, and the Modigliani-Miller tax penalty. The valuation formula highlights that the relevant rate used to calculate the franchise value of loans should be the expected rate on a corporate bond with risk similar to that of the loan ($b^{**}$).

If the same approach is repeated for bonds and deposits, the valuation formula for the equity of a bank can be obtained. That is, the net cash flows earned by the bank are broken into several components: net cash flows from loans, net cash flows from bonds, and net cash flows on debt. Each is evaluated separately. This will be done later in this chapter.

At this stage of the discussion of the bank fundamental valuation formula, and before the complete formula for valuing a bank is introduced, it is useful to clarify the issue of the impact of *personal tax* on valuation, an issue that is not discussed much in valuation practice.

## Corporate and Personal Taxes

Until now, this discussion has considered only *corporate* taxes, that is, taxes paid by the bank on its before-tax profit. But individual shareholders also pay *personal* taxes when they receive dividends. As personal taxes are often ignored in valuation, it is implicitly assumed either that the personal tax rate on dividends is zero or that it does not have any impact on the value of equity. Let us clarify the often neglected impact of personal taxes on valuation.

In many corporate finance textbooks, there is hardly any discussion of the impact of personal taxes. The argument is that investment funds, which do not pay personal taxes, drive share prices. But what if you are an investor who pays personal taxes? In fact, it is fairly simple to introduce personal taxes into this framework. Valuation was the calculation of a fair value, a cash equivalent such that investors would be indifferent between buying the asset at a price equal to the present value of future cash flows and buying another similar asset. To take personal taxes into consideration, simply compute the net cash flows after personal taxes and use the discount rate equal to the return after personal taxes. Indeed, if the buyer chose an alternative investment, he would also have to pay personal taxes on income earned on that alternative investment. In the case of the perpetual loan, with $t_p$ and $t$ denoting the personal tax rate and the corporate tax rate, respectively,

$$\text{MV of equity} = \text{PV of dividends} = \frac{(1-t_p)\times\text{dividend}}{b^{**}\times(1-t_p)}$$

$$= \frac{(1-t_p)\times[(1-t)\times l\times L]}{b^{**}\times(1-t_p)} = \frac{l\times(1-t)\times L}{b^{**}}$$

Since the personal tax factor affects both the numerator and the denominator, it cancels out. So, in this case, personal taxes are neutral (not to your wallet, but to valuation). This is a paradox: personal taxes reduce the cash flows received, but not the value. The reason is that value is driven not only by cash flows after personal tax, but also by the return on an alternative investment, which is also taxed at the personal level.

Whenever taxes are not neutral, analysts need to care about the specific tax status of shareholders and should compute the cash flows after personal taxes for the numerator and the investment rate after personal taxes for the denominator. The following discussion ignores the personal tax rate, assuming that personal taxes are value-neutral.

So far, this discussion has been concerned with the valuation of a bank's equity invested exclusively in loans. This approach can now be generalized to obtain the bank valuation formula.

## VALUATION OF A BANK'S EQUITY: THE COMPLETE MODEL (WITH CORPORATE TAX AND RISK)

The previous discussion dealt with the case of equity that was invested exclusively in loans. In general, the equity of a bank is a (long) position in loans and bonds, and a (short) position in debt (using the principle of value additivity of Modigliani and Miller, 1958). The same framework can be applied to each component to obtain the value of the equity of the bank. So consider the balance sheet of the bank:

| Loans ($l$) | Deposits ($d$) |
|---|---|
| Bonds ($b$) | Equity |
| Fixed assets | |

The contractual rates on these assets and deposits are $l$, $b$, and $d$, respectively, while the current expected returns are $l^*$, $b^*$, and $d^*$.

The market value of the equity of the bank is the risk-adjusted value of future dividends, discounted at the overall risk-adjusted cost of equity. The alternative is to use this framework to obtain a fundamental valuation formula. The idea is that the dividend flow can be decomposed into the cash flows linked to loans, cash flows linked to bonds, and cash flows linked to debt. Equity is then a portfolio of long positions in assets and short positions in debt. Applying the decomposition framework discussed earlier to loans, bonds, and deposits and adding up the results produces

Market value of equity$_0$

$$= [L_0^* + B_0^* - D_0^*]$$

$$+ \frac{(1-t) \times (b_1^* - d_1^{**}) \times D_1^*}{1 + b_1^{**}} + \frac{(1-t) \times (b_2^* - d_2^{**}) \times D_2^*}{(1 + b_1^{**}) \times (1 + b_2^{**})} + \cdots$$

$$+ \frac{(1-t) \times (l_1^* - b_1^{**}) \times L_1^*}{1 + b_1^{**}} + \frac{(1-t) \times (l_2^* - b_2^{**}) \times L_2^*}{(1 + b_1^{**}) \times (1 + b_2^{**})} + \cdots$$

$$+ \frac{(1-t) \times \text{operating expenses}_1}{1 + b_1^{**}} - \frac{(1-t) \times \text{operating expenses}_2}{(1 + b_1^{**}) \times (1 + b_2^{**})} - \cdots$$

$$- \frac{t \times b_1^{**} \times (L_1^* + B_1^* - D_1^*)}{1 + b_1^{**}} - \frac{t \times b_2^{**} \times (L_2^* \times B_2^* - D_2^*)}{(1 + b_1^{**}) \times (1 + b_2^{**})} - \cdots$$

The valuation formula includes five terms.

### Liquidation Value

The first term is the current value, with each asset and debt being the value of the after-tax expected cash flows discounted at the after-tax current expected rate on new assets or debts $[(1 - t) \times l^*, (1 - t) \times b^*,$ and $(1 - t) \times d^*]$.

### Franchise Value of Deposits

This is the after-tax franchise value of deposits, evaluated relative to a risk-adjusted rate. For simplicity, the formula uses one single risk-adjusted rate, $b^{**}$, but, in theory, there should be a specific rate for each asset and liability.[10]

### Franchise Value of Loans

The after-tax franchise value of loans is evaluated relative to the return on similar-risk corporate bonds.

### Present Value of Operating Expenses

As the volatility of operating expenses is similar to that of deposits, these expenses can be discounted at the risk-adjusted rate applied to deposits.

### Modigliani-Miller Tax Penalty

The last term captures the tax effect. Note that there will be a tax penalty on assets and a tax shield on the debt. As banks are usually net holders of financial assets, the net tax effect is likely to be negative.[11]

As stated previously, with this framework, it is not necessary to calculate the retained earnings needed to finance the growth of the bank. They are implicitly taken into account in the calculation of the franchise value.

## NUMERICAL EXAMPLE OF THE FUNDAMENTAL VALUATION FORMULA

To provide some understanding of the fundamental bank valuation formula, it is applied here to a simple exercise.

Balance Sheet (beginning of Year 1)

| Bond ($b$ = 10%) = 100 | Deposits ($d^*$ = 9%) = 90 |
|---|---|
|  | Equity = 10 |

A three-year fixed-coupon bond ($b$ = 10 percent) is funded with short-term deposits of $90 (deposit rate $d$ = 9 percent, constant for three years). The current three-year bond rate is 12 percent, and the corporate tax rate $t$ is 40 percent. The bank is to be closed in three years. There are no loans.

Forecasts deposits, equity (funded out of retained earnings), and bonds for the next three years are

|  | Year 1 | Year 2 | Year 3 |
|---|---|---|---|
| Deposits | 90 | 92 | 94 |
| Equity | 10 | 11 | 12 |
| Bonds | 100 | 103 | 106 |

All the data, estimated at the start of each year, are known with certainty. The risk premium used to value shares is thus zero.

Assuming that the additional funding is invested in new bonds, the annual dividends are forecasted and the market value of equity (discounting at the risk-free rate of 12 percent) is calculated.

Profit before tax in Year 1:

$$10\% \times 100 - 9\% \times 90 = 1.9$$

Profit after tax in Year 1:

$$1.9 \times (1 - 0.4) = 1.14$$

Dividend in Year 1:

Profit after tax − retained earnings = 1.14 − 1 = 0.14

Profit before tax in Year 2:

$$10\% \times 100 + 12\% \times 3 - 9\% \times 92 = 2.08$$

Profit after tax in Year 2:

$$2.08 \times (1 - 0.4) = 1.248$$

Dividend in Year 2:

Profit after tax − retained earnings = 1.248 − 1 = 0.248

Profit before tax in Year 3:

$$10\% \times 100 + 12\% \times 6 - 9\% \times 94 = 2.26$$

Profit after tax in Year 3:

$$2.26 \times (1 - 0.4) = 1.356$$

The dividend in Year 3 (13.356) includes the reimbursement of ending equity (12) and the profit after tax (1.356).

|                   | Year 1 | Year 2 | Year 3 |
|-------------------|--------|--------|--------|
| Profit before tax | 1.9    | 2.08   | 2.26   |
| Profit after tax  | 1.14   | 1.248  | 1.356  |
| Dividend          | 0.14   | 0.248  | 13.356 |

MV of equity = PV (future dividends)

$$= \frac{0.14}{1.12} + \frac{0.248}{1.12^2} + \frac{13.356}{1.12^3} = 9.829$$

The value of equity can be decomposed into three terms: liquidation value, franchise value, and tax penalty. This means that the value of the existing bonds over the next three years must be calculated. It will differ from par value, since the coupon of 10 percent differs from the current bond rate of 12 percent.

|                                      | Year 1 | Year 2 | Year 3 |
|--------------------------------------|--------|--------|--------|
| Value of initial bonds$_{\text{after tax}}$ | 96.862 | 97.836 | 98.881 |

Careful: the value of bonds is the present value of the after-tax cash flows discounted at the after-tax discount rate.

$$\text{Value of bonds}_{\text{Year 1}} = \frac{10\times(1-0.4)}{1+12\%\times(1-0.4)} + \frac{10\times(1-0.4)}{[1+12\%\times(1-0.4)]^2}$$

$$+ \frac{100+10\times(1-0.4)}{[1+12\%\times(1-0.4)]^3} = 96.862$$

$$\text{Value of bonds}_{\text{Year 2}} = \frac{10\times(1-0.4)}{1+12\%\times(1-0.4)} + \frac{100+10\times(1-0.4)}{[1+12\%\times(1-0.4)]^2} = 97.836$$

$$\text{Value of bonds}_{\text{Year 3}} = \frac{10\times(1-0.4)+100}{1+12\%\times(1-0.4)} = 98.881$$

MV of equity

$$= 96.862 - 90$$

$$+ \frac{(1-40\%)\times(12\%-9\%)\times 90}{1.12}$$

$$+ \frac{(1-40\%)\times(12\%-9\%)\times 92}{1.12^2}$$

$$+ \frac{(1-40\%)\times(12\%-9\%)\times 94}{1.12^3}$$

$$- \frac{40\%\times12\%\times(96.862-90)}{1.12}$$

$$- \frac{40\%\times12\%\times(100.836-92)}{1.12^2}$$

$$- \frac{40\%\times12\%\times(104.881-94)}{1.12^3} = 6.862 + 3.9709 - 1.00395$$

$$= 9.829$$

The application of the fundamental valuation formula can be seen to lead to a market value of equity ($9.829) that is identical to the present value of future dividends. Some technical comments on the calculation of the terms of the valuation formula follow. For the tax penalty in Year 2, the bond asset includes the *old* bonds at market value (97.836) + the new bond (3) = 100.836. In Year 3, it includes the *old* bond at market value (98.881) + the new bonds (6) = 104.881.

As can be seen from this numerical example, a correct calculation of the liquidation value of assets and debt[12] in each year is needed to obtain a perfect equivalence between the value of equity calculated as the present value of future dividends and the value obtained with the fundamental bank valuation formula. In real-life valuation applications, this could appear to be a very demanding task. However, do not be misled by the mathematics. As is discussed in Chapter 7, key issues in bank valuation concern the assumptions about the magnitude of the franchise value, the growth of future businesses, the likely margins on loans and deposits, and the growth in operating expenses. In practical applications, the validity of these assumptions will matter much more than the choice of a risk premium or the precise calculation of the liquidation values.

## CONCLUSION

This chapter has completed the presentation of the fundamental bank valuation model by adding corporate taxes and risk. The value of equity is broken down into four major components: a liquidation value, a franchise value of deposits and loans, a present value of operating expenses, and a tax penalty. The tax penalty incorporates the tax benefit from debt finance and the tax penalty on financial assets. The argument here is that the corporate bond and credit derivative markets provide useful information for estimating credit risk–specific risk premiums. Some of the main economic and strategic determinants of the market value of banks are discussed in Chapter 7, followed by the valuation of off-balance sheet businesses in Chapter 8.

Appendixes B and C to this chapter include technical comments on the estimation of the liquidation value and on the valuation methods for the "new age" Internet banks. Appendix D in this chapter deals explicitly with the value resulting from the limited liability of banks' shareholders, the so-called put option value. The funding of illiquid loans, liquidity risk, and value creation by banks are discussed explicitly in Chapter 21.

## APPENDIX A: BANK VALUATION, THE CORPORATE TAX CASE

The after-tax value of a one-year asset $A$ issued at par with historical return $a$, current (one-period) return $a^*$, and discount rate $b^*$ is equal to

$$\frac{[1+a(1-t)]\,A}{1+b^*} = \frac{[1+a(1-t)]\,A}{1+a^*(1-t)} + \frac{[1+a(1-t)]\,A}{1+b^*} - \frac{[1+a(1-t)]\,A}{1+a^*(1-t)}$$

$$= A^* + \frac{[1+a^*(1-t)][1+a(1-t)]\,A - (1+b^*)[1+a(1-t)]\,A}{(1+b^*)\times[1+a^*(1-t)]}$$

$$= A^* + \frac{\{[1+a^*(1-t)]-(1+b^*)\times[1+a(1-t)]\,A\}}{(1+b^*)[1+a^*(1-t)]}$$

$$= A^* + \frac{[a^*(1-t)-b^*+b^*t-b^*t]\times A^*}{1+b^*}$$

$$= A^* + \frac{(1-t)(a^* - b^*)A^*}{1+b^*} - \frac{tb^*A^*}{1+b^*}$$

A proof for a two-year asset is available in Dermine (2007).

## APPENDIX B: TWO FURTHER COMMENTS ON ESTIMATION OF THE LIQUIDATION VALUE

To complete the presentation of the fundamental bank valuation framework, two further comments on the computation of the liquidation value are needed.

### From Accounting Book Value to Current Values

In valuation applications, the accounting book values of assets and liabilities are available. The formula demands an estimate of their current values. There are two economic reasons why current liquidation values can differ from accounting book values.

The first reason is the existence of fixed-interest-rate instruments in a period when market rates change. If interest rates go up (down), the current value of fixed-rate instruments goes down (up).

The second reason is credit risk and the need to adjust the value of loans by a satisfactory level of loan-loss provisions. The issue of loan-loss provisions for performing and nonperforming loans is discussed in Chapters 14 and 15.

### Valuing Before Tax vs. Valuing After Tax

It should be emphasized that the liquidation value demands the valuation of after-tax cash flows at an after-tax discount rate. In general, this is not equivalent to discounting before-tax cash flows at a before-tax discount rate. A simple example will illustrate.

Consider a three-year bond with a coupon of 8 percent, a tax rate of 40 percent, and a current market rate of 15 percent. The value is first computed on a before-tax basis. Next, the valuation after tax is computed.

Before tax:

| 0 | 1 | 2 | 3 |
|---|---|---|---|
| | 8 | 8 | 108 |
| Value = 84.01742 | 88.62004 | 93.91304 | |

$$\text{Value}_0 = 84.01742 = \frac{8}{1.15^1} + \frac{8}{1.15^2} + \frac{108}{1.15^3}$$

$$\text{Value}_1 = 88.62004 = \frac{8}{1.15^1} + \frac{108}{1.15^2}$$

$$\text{Value}_2 = 93.91304 = \frac{108}{1.15^1}$$

After tax:

| 0 | 1 | 2 | 3 |
|---|---|---|---|
| | $8 \times (1 - 0.4) = 4.8$ | 4.8 | 104.8 |

$$\text{Value}_0 = 89.36856 = \frac{4.8}{[1+15\%\times(1-0.4)]^1} + \frac{4.8}{[1+15\%\times(1-0.4)]^2}$$
$$+ \frac{104.8}{[1+15\%\times(1-0.4)]^3}$$

In this example, the value computed on an after-tax basis, $89.37, is higher than the value computed on a before-tax basis, $84.02. What is the extra source of value creation? It is related to the taxation regime. Taxes were computed only on interest income, with no tax on annual capital gains. Buying or holding a bond at a discount creates additional value if it allows you to avoid taxes on capital gains. It can be shown that the difference in value before tax and after tax is precisely the present value of the taxes on annual capital gains:

$$\text{Value}_{\text{after tax}} = \text{value}_{\text{before tax}} + \text{present value of taxes on capital gains}$$

$$89.36856 = 84.01742 + \frac{0.4\times(88.62004 - 84.01742)}{1+15\%\times(1-0.4)}$$
$$+ \frac{0.4\times(93.91304 - 88.62004)}{[1+15\%\times(1-0.4)]^2}$$
$$+ \frac{0.4 \times (100 - 93.91304)}{[1+15\%\times(1-0.4)]^3}$$

The before-tax and after-tax values would be identical only if taxes were also applied on unrealized capital gains (Samuelson tax invariance theorem, 1964).

The practical message of this discussion is that, in the presence of unrealized capital gains or losses, it is advisable to calculate the liquidation values of assets and deposits as the present value of after-tax cash flows discounted at an after-tax discount rate.[13]

## APPENDIX C: VALUING INTERNET BANKS

At the time of the Internet boom in the late 1990s, a question arose as how to value Internet banks. There were two specific issues related to the valuation of Internet banks: first, they were growing very fast, starting from a very low base, and second, these new banks were losing money in the early years, as their scale had to increase to cover the cost of fixed investment. Since they were losing money, these banks were not paying dividends. Four types of valuation methods can be applied to Internet banks.

### E-premium

A former MBA student turned consultant told the author that investment banks were adding an *e-premium* to standard valuation multiples, such as market/book value. This did not help the author very much, but raised his interest concerning what this e-premium could be.

### Value per Customer

This approach forecasts the number of potential clients and multiplies this number by a "value per client." Again, this is interesting, but it raises the question of what the value per client might be.

### Fundamental Valuation Formula

The fundamental valuation formula can be used to value Internet banks. The franchise value net of operating expenses is likely to be negative in the early years, but it could become positive if the bank can attract new clients and cross-sell several banking services. Certainly it will not be easy to forecast the success of an Internet bank, but this is inherent in the new technology world.

### Real-Option Approach

In simple terms, the real-option approach relies on Monte Carlo techniques to simulate many potential paths, or scenarios, for the future of the bank. Each path includes assumptions about growth, cross-selling, and margins. For each path, the present value of cash flows is computed. One advantage of the real-option approach is that it highlights the significant bankruptcy risk of new ventures (Dermine, 2000).

## APPENDIX D: VALUE OF THE LIMITED LIABILITY OF SHAREHOLDERS—THE PUT OPTION VALUE

In the bank valuation model discussed in this chapter, it was implicitly assumed that either the risk of bank default was extremely small (negligible) or shareholders had full liability, meaning that if the bank were in default, the shareholders would stand ready to finance the losses out of their own pocket. Indeed, when the expected revenue on loans ($l^*$) was computed, the case of bank default and limited liability, where the shareholders would not face the entire losses on loans, was not considered. In the banking world, limited liability is most often the case. There are a very few exceptions, such as some private banks in Switzerland, where shareholders face full liability. This appendix provides an example[14] to derive and clarify the value resulting from the limited liability of shareholders. This value is often referred to as the *put option value*.

Consider a bank that is going to live for one year. The asset of $110 is financed by deposits ($100) and equity ($10). At the end of the year, the asset can take a value of $131 with probability of 50 percent or $100 with probability of 50 percent. The expected value of the asset is $115.5 (= 50% × $131 + 50% × $100). The depositors have been promised a return of 5 percent on the deposits. The risk-free rate is 5 percent, and, for simplicity of exposition, there is no risk premium. This is a risk-neutral world. The contractual return of 5 percent promised to depositors could appear low, as the bank could default if the asset generates a revenue of only $100. There could be two reasons for this: either uninformed depositors do not realize that there is a risk of default, or depositors are fully insured by a deposit insurance system.

Asset: 110 — 131 (50%) / 100 (50%)      Deposits: 100 (105)      Equity: 10

The case of full liability will be considered first. After that, the case of limited liability will be considered.

### Full-Liability Case

In this case, bank shareholders must be ready to fund losses.

Market value of equity = value of asset − value of debt

$$= \frac{50\% \times 131 + 50\% \times 100}{1.05} - \frac{50\% \times 105 + 50\% \times 105}{1.05}$$

$$= 110 - 100 = 10$$

In this full-liability case, the value of equity is equal to $10, the liquidation value, as there is no franchise value of the asset or of the deposit. Competition is perfect. Next, consider the market value of equity when shareholders can default on their obligations.

### Limited-Liability Case

Market value of equity = value of asset − value of debt

$$= \frac{50\% \times 131 + 50\% \times 0}{1.05} - \frac{50\% \times 105 + 50\% \times 0}{1.05}$$

$$= 12.38$$

In the limited-liability case, shareholders default (receive and pay nothing) when the asset of $100 cannot cover the contractual liability of $105. In the default case, the depositors take control of the bank's assets ($100). As can be seen, the option to default increases the market value of equity, since shareholders do not have to finance losses. This can be made explicit:

Market value of equity

= value of asset$_{\text{full liability}}$ − value of debt$_{\text{full liability}}$ + option to default

$$= \frac{50\% \times 131 + 50\% \times 100}{1.05} - \frac{50\% \times 105 + 50\% \times 105}{1.05} + \frac{50\% \times 105 - 50\% \times 100}{1.05}$$

$$= 110 - 100 + 2.38 = 12.38$$

The last term ($2.38) represents the value derived from the option to default: the shareholders do not have to pay the depositors ($105), but they receive nothing from the asset ($100), which is given to the depositors. This default option value is referred to as the *put option value*, as it is equivalent to a right given to the shareholders to sell the asset of the bank to the depositors at a face value of $105 (the precise terms of a put option[15]).

To summarize, under limited liability of shareholders, the market value of equity is equal to the market value of equity under full liability plus the value of a put option. It can be assumed that the value of the put option is directly related to the bank's probability of default.

If the default option increases the market value of equity, the question of where that value is coming from arises. Indeed, in the world of finance, there is rarely a free lunch. In this case, it is the depositors who suffer from the put option. To see this, the market value of deposits can be computed.

$$\text{Value of deposits} = \frac{50\% \times 105 + 50\% \times 100}{1.05} = 97.62$$

If the bank is solvent (the asset = $131), the depositors get paid ($105). If there is a default (asset = $100), the depositors receive $100. In this case, the value of the deposits, $97.62, is less than $100. The depositors have not priced the risk of default correctly. This can be rewritten in a different manner.

$$\begin{aligned}
\text{Value of deposits} &= \frac{50\% \times 105 + 50\% \times 100}{1.05} \\
&= \frac{50\% \times 105 + 50\% \times 105}{1.05} - \frac{50\% \times 105 - 50\% \times 100}{1.05} \\
&= 100 - 2.38 = 97.62
\end{aligned}$$

The value of deposits is equal to the value under full liability minus the put option that has been given to bank shareholders. Depositors have given shareholders the right to default, that is, to sell the asset to them at a price equal to the contractual payment promised on deposits (the put option value). In many countries, deposit insurance systems have been created to protect depositors. In that case, the put option value is fully assumed by the deposit insurance agency, which, in case of bank default, takes control of the bank's assets ($100) and pays the depositors the promised amount ($105). The value of the deposit insurance can be calculated as follows:

$$\text{Value of deposit insurance liability} = \frac{50\% \times 0 + 50\% \times (105 - 100)}{1.05}$$
$$= 2.38$$

If the bank is solvent (asset = $131), the deposit insurance agency pays nothing. If the bank defaults (asset = $100), the agency pays the depositors ($105) and receives the bank asset ($100).

It must be observed that, in this example, the bank did not have to pay for the deposit insurance. To prevent the transfer of wealth from the public sector to the bank, the bank should be charged a fair deposit insurance premium.

The practical implication of this put option discussion for bank valuation is that, whenever the probability of bank default is significant, it should be taken into account in computing the expected dividend flows.

## EXERCISES FOR CHAPTER 6

1. Assume a fixed-rate loan of $100 with two years to maturity, with interest payments at the end of the year and principal repayment at maturity. The corporate tax rate is 40 percent, annual expected revenue (net of loan losses) $l$ is 10 percent, expected return on new loans $l^*$ is 12 percent [after tax = 12 % × (1 − 0.4) = 7.2 %], and shareholders' expected rate of return $b^{**}$ is 11 percent.
The after-tax expected cash flows from the loan are as follows:

| Year 1 | Year 2 |
|---|---|
| 10 × (1 − 0.4) | 100 + 10 × (1 − 0.4) |

Compute the value of this asset (that is, the present value of future after-tax cash flows) from the shareholders' perspective. Decompose this value into a liquidation value, a franchise value, and a corporate tax penalty.

2. The volume of demand deposits is expected to be $100 in Year 1. It is expected to be $105 in Year 2. The rate paid on deposits is 0 percent. The level of operating expenses is 3 percent, the tax rate is 40 percent, and the shareholders' expected rate of return is 10 percent.
The volumes of deposits are as follows:

| Year 1 | Year 2 |
|---|---|
| 100 | 105 |

Taking a two-year horizon (i.e., the bank is closed at end of Year 2), compute the value of this deposit liability (that is, the present value of net cash outflows) from the shareholders' perspective. Decompose this value into a liquidation value, a franchise value, the present value of operating expenses, and a corporate tax penalty.

3. A bank is investing exclusively in perpetual risk-free bonds (principal of $100, fixed annual coupon 9 percent). The asset is funded with perpetual deposits ($95) and equity ($5). The current risk-free rate on the bond market is 7 percent, and the bank pays interest of 6 percent on deposits. The current rate on new deposits is also 6 percent. The corporate tax rate is 30 percent (the personal tax rate on interest and dividend income is 0 percent).

Risk-free bonds: 100  Deposits: 95

Equity: 5

**a.** Compute the value of the equity of this perpetual bank (assuming a zero equity risk premium).

**b.** Break the value of the equity into a liquidation value, a franchise value, and a tax penalty

## Notes

1. See the proof in Appendix A of this chapter for a one-year-to-maturity asset.
2. Notice that the tax penalty is calculated as the shareholders' discount rate of 10 percent (not the loan rate of 11 percent) times the value of the loan. The reason is that the margin on the loan (11 percent − 10 percent) was already taxed in the calculation of the franchise value.
3. Dimson et al. (2006).
4. Note that with a beta of zero, the risk premium of a risky share would be zero. The assumption in the CAPM is that the risk of that share would disappear in a well-diversified portfolio of shares.
5. It must be emphasized that the risk premium on corporate bonds refers to the difference between the expected return on the bonds (net of expected losses) and the risk-free rate. As is discussed in Chapter 15, this is different from the full contractual bond spread, which should include both the expected loss and the risk premium.
6. Risk-neutral probabilities of default are discussed in Chapter 15.
7. As an alternative to the expected return on corporate bonds, an attempt could be made to estimate a beta using CAPM theory: $beta_1 = cov\,(R_i, R_M)/\sigma^2_M)$. In the absence of empirical evidence from bank shares, the covariance can be estimated by the correlation between the accounting income or cash flow of a specific business and the market return. The key difference with the approach given here is that the expected return on corporate bonds can be estimated directly from market data, while the alternative beta approach makes the strong implicit assumption that the CAPM holds in reality.
8. Credit risk has been emphasized in this chapter. A second source of risk that is relevant for part of the loan book is liquidity risk. This additional source of risk and its implication for value creation are discussed in Chapter 21.
9. See the proof in Appendix A of this chapter, for a one-year-to-maturity asset.

10. The risk-adjusted rate for deposits should be lower than the risk-adjusted rate for loans (assets). Depositors are protected by the equity of the shareholders, who will absorb part of the losses.
11. The bank valuation approach is similar to the adjusted present value (APV) approach used in corporate finance. In that approach, the asset is first evaluated as if it were fully funded with equity. The assets are valued using an unlevered cost of equity. The present value of the tax savings created by debt financing is then added. In the bank valuation approach, the loans are valued as if they were funded exclusively by equity, and the unlevered discount rate is the expected return on corporate bonds with similar risk. A term incorporating the impact of taxes is then added.
12. In this example, the liquidation value of short-term deposits was equal to the book value.
13. In Dermine (1987, 2007), it is shown, relying on a theorem of Samuelson (1994), that an alternative and equivalent method for bank valuation is to compute the liquidation value on a before-tax basis and add an additional term equal to the present value of tax savings on unrealized capital gains. Note that fair value accounting concepts, based on the value of before-tax cash flows, ignore the eventual benefits resulting from the nontaxation of unrealized capital gains.
14. Complete models are available in Merton (1977), Ronn and Verma (1986), Dermine and Lajéri (2001), and Chen et al. (2006).
15. Put options are reviewed in Chapter 24.

# Economic and Strategic
# Drivers of Bank Valuation

## DETERMINANTS OF FRANCHISE VALUE, ECONOMIES OF SCALE
## AND SCOPE, AND INFLATION AND BANK VALUATION

The previous chapters introduced the fundamental bank valuation formula.
It applies to the on-balance sheet business of banks. (The valuation of
fee-based activities is discussed in Chapter 8.) It has been shown that the
present value of dividends can be decomposed into a series of five terms:

1. The liquidation value
2. The franchise value of deposits
3. The franchise value of loans
4. The present value of operating expenses
5. A Modigliani-Miller tax penalty

Before moving on to the discussion in Chapter 8 on how to value
fee-based bank activities, this chapter identifies several economic and
strategic factors that can affect the franchise value. A discussion of scale
and scope economies follows, as they can affect operating expenses
and revenues. Finally, the specific impact of inflation on bank valuation
(the *inflation tax penalty*) is covered.

## ECONOMIC AND STRATEGIC FACTORS AFFECTING
## THE FRANCHISE VALUE

At least six factors are likely to have an impact on the magnitude of
the franchise value of deposits and loans: economic growth, the level of
nominal interest rates, competition, financial innovation, the stock
market, and taxes and regulation.

## Economic Growth

Around the world, the nominal growth of the balance sheets of banks is closely linked to the nominal growth of gross domestic product (GDP). Nominal growth includes real growth plus inflation. The change in the volumes of bank deposits and loans mirrors the growth of GDP. As a consequence, the starting point for estimating the growth in franchise value is a forecast of the nominal growth of GDP. It is then possible to make adjustments if there are reasons to believe that the growth of particular types of assets or deposits could deviate from that of GDP.

For example, banking systems that have recently been deregulated tend to grow faster than GDP, to catch up with the rest of the world. To illustrate this, Table 7.1 gives the ratio of banking assets to GDP for the 15 "old" members of the European Union and the same ratio for eight new members from Central and Eastern Europe that joined the European Union in 2004.

While the ratio of total banking assets to GDP for the 15 old members of the European Union in 2006 was 297 percent, that ratio was substantially smaller in many of the eight new member countries; for example, it was 70 percent in Poland. From 2003 to 2006, however, there was rapid growth in the banking systems of those countries; for example, the ratio rose from 85 percent to 118 percent in Slovenia.

**TABLE  7.1**

Size of National Banking Systems

| Countries | Banking Assets/GNP (%), 2006 (2003) | Population (millions) |
|---|---|---|
| EU 15 | 297 (281) | 383 |
| Czech Republic | 101 (98) | 10.2 |
| Estonia | 115 (79) | 1.4 |
| Hungary | 104 (72) | 10.1 |
| Latvia | 144 (66) | 2.3 |
| Lithuania | 71 (52) | 3.5 |
| Poland | 70 (56) | 38 |
| Slovakia | 95 (74) | 5.4 |
| Slovenia | 118 (85) | 2 |

Source: European Central Bank.

## Level of Nominal Interest Rates

Around the world, it has been observed that retail interest rates are noto-riously sticky or rigid. For instance, when market interest rates rise, banks not only delay the adjustment of retail deposit rates, but they often make only a partial adjustment. Similarly, when interest rates in a country go down, banks delay and only partly adjust interest rates on consumer loans or credit card loans downward. The stickiness of retail interest rates is explained by the lack of competition and the relatively low elasticity of volumes to changes in interest rates. An implication of rate stickiness is that the margin on deposits, defined in the franchise value as the differ-ence between the market rate and the deposit rate, is going to be larger when market interest rates increase and lower when interest rates decrease. The level of nominal market interest rates is therefore a major determinant of the franchise value of deposits.

In a similar but opposite manner, when market interest rates go down, the margin on loans, defined in the franchise value of loans as the difference between the return on loans and the market rate, increases, and vice versa in the case of interest rates going up. The impact of the level of interest rates on the franchise value of deposits and loans is summarized in Table 7.2.

## Competition

The number of banks, the intensity of competition, and the threat of new entrants into the banking sector will affect the pricing of deposits and loans and interest margins. Domestic mergers in recent years have increased market concentration in many countries, leading to a fear of market power. This has forced some regulators to intervene to prevent the creation of a dominant position. For instance, in the United Kingdom, the

**TABLE 7.2**

Impact of Nominal Interest Rate on the Retail Franchise Value

|  | High Nominal Rates | Low Nominal Rates |
| --- | --- | --- |
| Franchise value of deposits | High | Low |
| Franchise value of loans | Low | High |

Competition Commission (2002) has recommended that the large banks not be allowed to buy additional local banks.

It should be emphasized, however, that it is not only the number of banks that has an impact on margins. It is also the threat of the entry of new players, which is related to the ease of entry. Markets that are *contestable* will display lower margins. Barriers to entry can be of a regulatory nature, but they often are related to the imperfect information available to customers, which substantially increases the perceived or effective cost of switching from one bank to another. Another factor that can affect margins is the existence of state-owned banks or mutually owned banks. Since the governance of these banks is different from that of other banks, they can have an incentive to increase market share at the expense of interest margins. For example, in Germany, the low retail interest margins were caused by aggressive pricing by the Landesbanks, owned by the regional Länder.

## Financial Innovation

Financial innovation refers to new investment vehicles that compete with traditional banking products. This is a particular type of competition. Two examples are *money market funds* and *commercial paper.*

For many years, banks were shielded from competition in the short-term deposit and short-term loan markets. By regulation, the only short-term investments available were bank deposits, and short-term borrowing was available only from banks. Central banks justified these regulations by their wish to control the economy. By forcing economic actors to use banking products, central banks could control the economy by controlling the size of the banking system. But the opening of international capital flows substantially increased competition among banking centers. To favor their own banking system and lure customers from other countries, central banks deregulated markets and allowed financial firms to offer money market funds and both financial and nonfinancial firms to issue commercial paper.

A money market fund is an investment fund that invests in short-term bonds, such as government Treasury bills. It pays its investors the return on the fund less a management fee. The introduction of money market funds has had a significant impact on the volume of short-term bank deposits in several countries, affecting the franchise value of deposits. Notice that the banks have not lost everything, as they manage many of these mutual funds. When they do, they still earn a management fee, although it is often substantially lower than the original interest margin on deposits.

Similarly, the introduction of commercial paper, short-term bonds issued by nonfinancial firms, has brought in a competitor to short-term bank loans.

## The Stock Market: Bullish or Bearish

In many countries, it has been observed that at the time of a stock market boom, investors chase good returns and shift part of their savings away from banks into the stock market. In contrast, at the time of a downturn in the market, money often comes back into safe bank deposits. The franchise value of deposits is thus affected by the state, bullish or bearish, of the stock market.

## Taxes and Regulation

In some countries, specific types of deposits are tax-free. In this case, banks can be tempted to pay a lower rate on these tax-attractive deposits. This usually increases the bank margin on deposits. A particular type of regulation is the reserve requirement on bank deposits. In most countries, banks have to hold a small part of their deposits, the reserve requirement, at the central bank. As no interest or a low rate of interest is paid on these reserves, this requirement reduces the profitability of bank deposits.[1]

The six strategic factors just discussed—economic growth, level of nominal interest rates, competition, financial innovation, the stock market, and taxes and regulation—will have a very significant impact on the franchise value of loans and deposits. Sound judgment concerning the evolution of these factors over time will be needed to estimate the franchise value of deposits and loans.

Another factor that is of great importance in bank valuation is the existence, or lack of it, of economies of scale and scope. This is discussed in the next section.

## ECONOMIES OF SCALE AND SCOPE IN BANKING

The market value of banks will be affected by the growth of revenue and by the control of operating (noninterest) expenses. An issue that has received a very large amount of attention around the world is the existence, or lack of it, of economies of scale and scope. Economies of scale refer to the fact that size can provide a bank with a source of competitive advantage. Economies of scope refer to the fact that the joint offering of several products can also be a source of competitive advantage.

Eleven potential sources of economies of scale and scope can be identified.[2] In principle, they should be related to their impact on shareholders' wealth. However, agency conflicts between shareholders and managers could also lead to situations in which they are related to the managers' self-interest.

The eleven sources of economies of scale and scope are

1. Cost-based economies of scale
2. Brand-based economies of scale
3. Revenue-based economies of scale
4. Safety net–based (too-big-to-fail) economies of scale
5. Cost-based economies of scope
6. Revenue-based economies of scope
7. Financial diversification–based economies of scope
8. X-efficiency
9. Market power
10. Defense-based economies of scale
11. "Quiet life"–based economies of scale

Each of these sources is discussed here.

### Cost-Based Economies of Scale

Cost efficiency is achieved by lowering the average cost per unit of output through expanding a single line of business.

The wide consensus is that only very small banks have the potential to achieve economies of scale and that the average cost curve for larger firms quickly becomes more or less flat. The relationship between the average cost per unit and bank size can be represented by an L-shaped curve, as shown in Figure 7.1.

As the L-shaped curve indicates, the important question is how to identify the minimum scale that will allow a bank to operate at an optimal

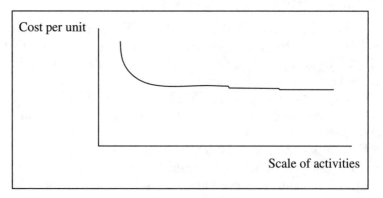

Figure 7.1 Economies of scale in banking.

efficiency level. In the United States, the scale-efficient point has ranged from $500 million of assets in the late 1980s to $25 billion of assets[3] in 2000.[4] This substantial increase in optimal size is explained by progress in information technology and by deregulation of interstate banking, both of which allow new forms of organization with larger size. In Europe, estimates report the existence of economies of scale up to an asset size of 25 billion euros. Vander Vennet (2002) estimates the optimal size to be in the range of 10 to 100 billion euros. Almost all of these studies conclude that there are no significant cost-based economies of scale to be gained from M&As involving very large banks.

Two words of caution should be expressed concerning the academic studies reporting the absence of economies of scale for large banks. The first one is that the minimum efficient scale seems to be increasing very rapidly over time. In only 15 years, it has increased from $0.5 billion to $25 billion. A size that is optimal today might be too small tomorrow. The second is that most studies, because of the lack of product data, have analyzed broad categories of banking products, such as deposits, loans, and securities holdings. It may well be that for very specific activities, such as global custody in securities markets, payment, or credit card processing, there are substantial economies of scale.

## Brand-Based Economies of Scale

Large size will allow brand recognition to be obtained at a lower cost. This is special type of cost-based economy of scale that is related to marketing costs per unit of product sold. The strategic importance of brand is often recognized as a potential source of competitive advantage for the future, when consumers of financial services will shop on the Internet and face a wide choice of products. To the best of the author's knowledge, there has been no published study on the linkage between size, brand recognition, and interest margins.

## Revenue-Based Economies of Scale

Size and a large capital base will allow a firm to underwrite large loans and securities issues, thus having a positive impact on the supply of underwriting services. In the context of the euro and integrated capital markets, size has become one source of competitive advantage in capital markets. There is anecdotal evidence that a large capital base helps in the capital markets. For instance, since its acquisition of National Westminster Bank, the Royal Bank of Scotland group has been much more active in international syndicated loan activities. Similarly, the Scandinavian bank Nordea, created through the merger of four Scandinavian banks, has developed the size necessary to compete in Nordic capital markets.

### Safety Net–Based Economies of Scale

When a bank becomes very large, it is more likely to be qualified as "too big to fail" by the public authorities.[5] Being too big to fail means that the indirect costs to the economy resulting from the default of a large bank would be so significant that the public authorities decide that they will bail out the bank in the event of financial distress. This implicit guarantee provides a competitive advantage in terms of both a lower funding cost for a given level of capital and risk and the acceptance of larger positions by counterparties. The rating agency Moody's recognizes the possibility of public bailouts and provides two ratings of banks: the bank financial strength ratings (BFSR), based solely on the bank's intrinsic safety and soundness on a legal stand-alone basis, and the ordinary long-term deposit ratings, which factor in credit support from owners, industry groups, and/or official institutions.

### Cost-Based Economies of Scope

Cost efficiencies can be achieved by offering a broad range of products or services to a customer base, for instance, both banking and insurance products. These could originate from the large fixed costs incurred in gathering an information database or acquiring computer equipment that can be used to provide a large set of services.

U.S. and European studies have measured efficiencies of scope by comparing the total cost of a firm with what the cost of that firm would be if it were broken into a set of firms offering a smaller set of products. There is overwhelming evidence pointing to the lack of economies of scope.

### Revenue-Based Economies of Scope

This source involves the hope of cross-selling new products to an existing customer base. It relies on investors' assumed preference for one-stop shopping. The case of banking and insurance products is often quoted. Here, it is interesting to observe that there is a wide divergence of views. In several continental European countries, such as the Netherlands, France, Belgium, and Italy, banks have been very successful in offering insurance products, especially life insurance. In other countries, such as the United States and the United Kingdom, banking remains separate from insurance. A famous case is Citigroup, which first merged an insurance group,

Travelers, with a bank, only to decide, in the end, to spin off the insurance component. This observed difference across countries is most likely explained by history. In countries where customers have been used to buying banking and insurance products from different vendors, such as the Anglo-Saxon countries, there is not much value in one-stop shopping. In other countries, however, customers value one-stop shopping.

### Financial Diversification–Based Economies of Scope

Standard portfolio theory holds that a portfolio of imperfectly correlated risks will reduce the overall volatility of profit. According to Pilloff and Santomero (1998), lower volatility may raise shareholder wealth in several ways.[6] First, the expected value of bankruptcy costs may be reduced. A large proportion of bankruptcy costs are incurred as a result of the loss of franchise value caused by a default. Second, if the firm faces a convex tax schedule, then the expected taxes paid may fall. Third, earnings from lines of business where customers value bank stability (such as long-term customer relationships) may be increased. Finally, levels of certain risky activities that are barely profitable could be increased because the necessary amount of capital would be reduced. The argument is that a business exhibiting a low correlation with an existing portfolio of business will have a low marginal risk, thus permitting a lower capital requirement and a lower threshold of acceptable earnings. Financial diversification can be obtained through offering a range of products, servicing different customer groups, or spreading credit risk across industries or regions. The assumption here is that firm-based diversification is more efficient than diversification purchased on the market, such as credit derivatives and loan sales.

Several studies have reported the potential benefits of diversification of loan portfolios (Boyd and Runkle, 1993; Dermine, 2003) or diversification across activities such as banking and insurance (Santomero and Chung, 1992; Boyd, Graham, and Hewitt, 1993). Simulation results indicating the benefits of diversification must be viewed with caution, however, as they make the implicit assumption that the combined firm can be managed as efficiently as the separate firms.

### X-Efficiency

X-efficiency refers to the fact that, given its current volume of output, a firm is not operating with maximum cost efficiency, i.e., it has too high a cost structure. This can be shown on the L-shaped curve in Figure 7.2. Instead of all banks being located on the curve, some banks of an identical size may be operating above the fitted average curve.

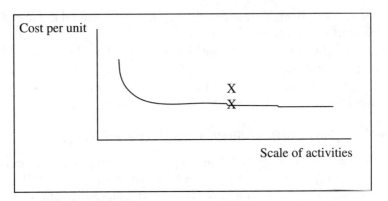

**Figure 7.2** X-efficiency in banking.

This source of efficiency is often cited as the prime motivation for a domestic merger, as two banks that merge can coordinate the reduction in the size of a too large branch network more easily. In a survey of 130 studies in 21 countries, Berger and Humphrey (1997) showed that inefficiency, i.e., operating with too high cost relative to the best bank, was on the order of 20 to 30 percent, and that operating efficiency was a much more relevant issue than economies of scale.

### Market Power

Horizontal mergers, which reduce the number of firms operating in an individual market, may lead to less competition and higher margins. Mergers across industries may allow higher profit as a result of *tying* strategies that allow the firm to package a bundle of goods. Finally, larger size creates *monopsony* power, as it reinforces the bargaining power of the bank with its suppliers, such as information technology firms.

The first nine motives were discussed from the perspective of increasing the value of shareholders' wealth.[7] However, agency conflicts between management and shareholders could lead managers to attempt to increase their own expected utility. Two such arguments are as follows: mergers to avoid being taken over, and attempts to increase the managers' own benefits.

### Defense-Based Economies of Scale

Achieving a certain size (capital clout) can act as a defensive measure against takeover. Thus, to protect their functions and related perks, senior managers might wish to increase the size of the company to reduce the threat of a takeover. It must be observed that, since globalization has made large pools of money accessible, activist hedge funds have been able to challenge even very large banks. In 2007, Christopher Hohn, managing partner at the hedge fund Children's Investment Fund (TCI),[8] challenged the strategy of the Dutch bank ABN-AMRO. This led to the hostile takeover of ABN-AMRO by a consortium of three European banks: Fortis, Royal Bank of Scotland, and Santander.

### The Expense Preference, "Quiet Life," and "Hubris" Hypotheses

The argument is that higher profit driven by economies of scale or market power can be captured by management in the form of higher salaries, perks, or reduction of risk (the "quiet life" hypothesis). A special case is the *hubris* hypothesis, according to which management arrogance (hubris) leads it to overstate the gain from a merger, with the result that it ends up overpaying for the target firm (Roll, 1986).

Table 7.3 summarizes the empirical evidence on the existence of scale and scope economies. Keep in mind that the last two items are related to the well-being of management, at the expense of shareholders.

Sources of scale and scope economies are numerous. They must be evaluated properly to arrive at a sound bank valuation model.

**TABLE 7.3**

Economies of Scale and Scope: A Summary Assessment

| Sources of Economies of Scale and Scope | Significance |
|---|---|
| Cost-based economies of scale | Low |
| Brand-based economies of scale | ? |
| Revenue-based economies of scale | Large in capital markets activities |
| Safety net–based economies of scale | Large |
| Cost-based economies of scope | Low |
| Revenue-based economies of scope | ? |
| Financial diversification–based economies of scope | Large |
| X-efficiency | Large |
| Market power in noncontestable markets | Large |
| Defense-based economies of scale | ? |
| The "quiet life" and "hubris" hypotheses | Large |

The next section discusses a driver of bank valuation that has not received wide attention: the impact of inflation on the market value of a bank's equity. The fundamental valuation model will help in identifying an inflation tax.

## INFLATION AND BANK VALUATION

Inflation can affect the market value of equity through various channels. It will affect the nominal growth of bank deposits and loans. The monetary policy of the central bank is likely to raise nominal interest rates. Interest margins on retail deposits and loans are likely to be affected by the overall level of nominal market rates. But there is an additional significant impact that is often overlooked: the impact of inflation on taxation. It is this last effect that needs to be clarified.

An example will help to identify the inflation tax channel. Consider the following balance sheet for a bank:

| Bonds: 100 ($b^* = 3\%$) | Deposits: 95 ($d^* = 2\%$) |
|---|---|
| Equity: 5 | |

Bonds of \$100 carry the current bond rate ($b^*$) of 3 percent, and the deposits of \$95 pay the current rate ($d^*$) of 2 percent. The corporate tax rate is 40 percent. To focus attention on the essentials, this discussion ignores loans and operating expenses.

At first, there is no inflation, and the asset and deposits are constant forever. The market value of equity is the present value of a perpetual dividend:

$$\text{Market value of equity}$$

$$= \frac{\text{Perpetual dividend}}{\text{Risk-free rate}}$$

$$= \frac{(3\% \times 100 - 2\% \times 95) \times (1 - 0.4)}{0.03} = 22$$

$$= \text{liquidation value} + \text{franchise value} - \text{tax penalty}$$

$$= (100 - 95) + \frac{(3\% - 2\%) \times (1 - 0.4) \times 95}{3\%} - \frac{40\% \times 3\% \times (100 - 95)}{3\%}$$

$$= 5 + 19 - 2 = 22$$

The market value of equity is equal to \$22. It is either the discounted value of future dividends or the sum of three terms: the liquidation value (\$5) plus the after-tax franchise value of deposits (\$19) minus the tax penalty (−\$2).

In this example, assume an inflation rate of 10 percent, and also assume that the volumes of bonds, deposits, and equity increase by exactly 10 percent every year. Growth in equity will be funded by retained earnings. Also assume that the nominal interest rates on both bonds and deposits increase by exactly the inflation factor, 10 percent, so as to keep the initial real interest rates on bonds and deposits constant:[9]

Bond rate factor: $(1.03) \times (1.1) = 1.133$
Bond rate $= 13.3\%$

Deposit rate factor: $(1.02) \times (1.1) = 1.122$
Deposit rate $= 12.2\%$

The next step is to forecast dividends, that is, the after-tax profit net of retained earnings:

$$\text{Dividend}_{\text{Year 1}} = (13.3\% \times 100 - 12.2\% \times 95) \times (1 - 0.4)$$
$$- 10\% \times 5 = 0.526$$

$$\text{Dividend}_{\text{Year 2}} = (13.3\% \times 100 \times 1.1 - 12.2\% \times 95 \times 1.1) \times (1 - 0.4\%)$$
$$- 10\% \times 5 \times 1.1 = 0.5786$$

$$\text{Dividend}_{\text{Year 3}} = (13.3\% \times 100 \times 1.1^2 - 12.2\% \times 95 \times 1.1^2) \times (1 - 0.4\%)$$
$$- 10\% \times 5 \times 1.1^2 = 0.63646$$

. . .

It can be seen that the annual dividend is growing each year by 10 percent, the rate of inflation. It is then possible to compute the value of shares as the present value of a constant-growth perpetuity:

$$
\begin{aligned}
\text{Market value of equity} &= \frac{\text{after-tax profit in Year 1} - \text{retained earnings in Year 1}}{\text{bond rate} - \text{growth rate}} \\
&= \frac{(13.3\% \times 100 - 12.2\% \times 95) \times (1 - 40\%) - 10\% \times 5}{13.3\% - 10\%} \\
&= \frac{0.526 - 0.5}{13.3\% - 10\%} = 15.93939
\end{aligned}
$$

Thus, under a scenario of apparently neutral inflation, where bonds, deposits, equity, and interest rates increase by the same inflation rate of 10 percent, the market value of equity has fallen from $22 to $15.93939, a significant relative fall of 28 percent. To identify the source of the inflation penalty, it is helpful to recompute the value of equity as the sum of three terms: liquidation value plus franchise value of deposits minus tax penalty.

Market value of equity

= liquidation value + deposit franchise − tax penalty

$$= (100 - 5) + \frac{(13.3\% - 12.2\%) \times (1 - 0.4) \times 95}{13.3\% - 10\%} - \frac{40\% \times 13.3\% \times (100 - 95)}{13.3\% - 10\%}$$

$$= 5 + 19 - 8.6061 = 15.93939$$

Compared with the case with no inflation, there is no change in the liquidation value ($5) and no change in the franchise value of deposits ($19), but a significant increase in the tax penalty ($8.6061 vs. $2).

The increase in the tax penalty can be explained by focusing on the impact of inflation on the contribution to the dividend of the income earned on equity funding in the first year:

- Without inflation, the equity of $5 invested in bonds contributes to the dividend:

$$\text{After-tax profit on equity of } \$5 = \text{dividend}$$
$$= (5 \times 3\%) \times (1 - 0.4) = 0.09$$

- With inflation, the equity of $5 invested in bonds contributes to profit, but the need for retained earnings to grow equity wipes out the entire dividend contribution.

$$\text{Dividend} = \text{after-tax profit} - \text{retained earnings}$$
$$= (5 \times 13.3\%) \times (1 - 0.4) - (5 \times 10\%)$$
$$= 0.399 - 0.5 = -0.101$$

Equity funds were a positive contributor to the dividend in the zero-inflation case. They contribute negatively under a 10 percent inflation scenario. This at first surprising result is due to an anomaly in the corporate tax system. Each year, the inflation of 10 percent reduces the real value of equity, 10 percent × 5 = 0.5 in the first year. To account for this loss of purchasing power, taxable income should be reduced by an inflation cost: 13.3 percent × 5 − 10 percent × 5. However, the tax authorities in most countries do not recognize this loss caused by inflation and tax the full interest income of 13.3 percent × 5 at the tax rate of 40 percent. This effect is known as the inflation tax.[10]

It is possible to verify that the difference in market value with and without inflation, $6.06061, is precisely equal to the present value of the inflation tax, growing forever at a constant rate of 10 percent:[11]

$$MV_{without\ inflation} - MV_{with\ inflation} = 22 - 15.93939 = 6.06061$$

$$= \frac{inflation\ tax}{13.3\% - 10\%} = \frac{40\% \times 10\% \times 5}{13.3\% - 10\%}$$

The practical implication of this discussion is that inflation is most likely to have an impact on the value of the equity of a bank. It will run through higher nominal growth for deposits and loans, a higher discount rate, most likely an impact on interest margins on the retail market, and an inflation tax. Therefore, careful attention has to be given to valuing the bank under several reasonable inflation scenarios. Once these scenarios are identified, the valuation methods discussed in the previous chapters — discounted value of future dividends and the fundamental valuation formula — will yield the correct value of equity, incorporating the impact of inflation correctly.

In the presence of uncertain inflation, analysts sometimes prefer to work as if inflation were 0 percent (that is, work in real terms), value the bank, and then assume that inflation is neutral, with no impact on the value of the bank. This approach is likely to be misleading because it ignores the several channels by which inflation can affect value. It is highly recommended that the analyst work in nominal terms, explicitly incorporating the inflation forecast into the analysis.

## CONCLUSION

The objective of this chapter was to call attention to the fact that a sound evaluation of banks requires identifying the strategic drivers of franchise value, the sources of economies of scale and scope, and the potential impact of inflation.

## EXERCISES FOR CHAPTER 7

1. What is the difference between economies of scale and economies of scope?
2. List and explain four different sources of economies of scale in banking.
3. List and explain three sources of economies of scope in banking.

4. Consider the following balance sheet for a bank:

Bonds: 100 ($b^* = 2\%$) Deposits: 92 ($d^* = 1\%$)
Equity: 8

Bonds of $100 carry the current bond rate ($b^*$) of 2 percent, and the deposits of $92 pay the current rate ($d^*$) of 1 percent. The corporate tax rate is 40 percent. Loans and operating expenses are ignored. There is no inflation, and the asset and deposits are constant forever.

Compute the market value of equity in the zero-inflation case. Next, decompose the value of equity into three terms (equity, franchise value, and tax penalty).

Now assume an inflation rate of 10 percent, and assume that the volumes of bonds, deposits, and equity increase by exactly 10 percent every year. Growth in equity will be funded by retained earnings. Also assume that the nominal interest rates on bonds and deposits exactly increase by the inflation factor 10 percent, so as to keep the initial real interest rates on bonds and deposits constant:

Bond rate factor:

$(1.02) \times (1.1) = 1.122$
   Bond rate $= 12.2\%$

Deposit rate factor:

$(1.01) \times (1.1) = 1.111$
   Deposit rate $= 11.1$ percent

Compute the annual dividends that can be paid over the next three years.

Compute the market value of equity in this 10 percent inflation case. Decompose the value of equity into three terms (equity, franchise value, and tax penalty). What explains the difference between the market value of equity in the 0 percent and 10 percent inflation cases?

## Notes

1. An exception is the European Central Bank, which pays a market rate on reserves.
2. This is discussed in Dermine (2003) in the context of mergers and acquisitions in European banking markets.

3. The scale of activities is often measured by total assets or number of accounts.
4. U.S. studies on the existence of cost-based economies of scale with multiple products have traditionally used a translog function (Berger and Mester, 1997). This has the advantage of allowing different economies of scale or scope at different levels of output.
5. Some central banks refer to these entities as LCFI, large and complex financial institutions.
6. The benefits of diversification and stability of income are discussed at greater length in Chapter 23.
7. It can be seen that in some cases, the increase in the wealth of shareholders does not correspond to a social optimum. Exploiting the benefits of a public safety net or market power can create economic inefficiencies at a national level. These issues must be dealt with by antitrust authorities and by the bank regulators.
8. Along with his wife, Jamie, Mr. Hohn has set up a foundation that, among other activities, finances the production of AIDS drugs for children.
9. As discussed previously, deposit rates might not increase as much as the market bond rate in reality. This example ignores the likely positive impact of inflation and interest rate on the deposit franchise value in order to identify whether or not inflation has a specific impact in an apparently neutral setting in which everything—volumes and interest rates—rises with inflation.
10. Some countries, such as Brazil or Israel, at a time of hyperinflation, have adjusted taxes to eliminate this costly inflation tax. Instead of taxing the full revenue of 13.3 percent × 5, they were taxing the revenue net of an inflation loss: 13.3 percent × 5 − 10 percent × 5 = 3.3 percent × 5. This inflation-adjusted tax would eliminate the tax penalty. Most countries with milder inflation have not bothered to adjust the tax system.
11. A formal model of the banking firm with inflation and retained earnings is available in Dermine (1985b, 1987).

# CHAPTER 8

# Valuation of Fee-Based Activities

The fundamental bank valuation formula is concerned with on-balance sheet activities, such as lending, deposit taking, and investing in bonds. As discussed in Chapter 4, banks also engage in off-balance sheet activities, such as asset management, private banking, corporate advisory services, brokerage, and proprietary trading. A characteristic of many of these activities is that they generate fees and are mostly conducted off-balance sheet. That is, few assets and liabilities related to these activities show up on the bank's balance sheet.

These activities should be valued separately from the on-balance sheet activities. For the latter, this book has introduced a specific method that relies on the fundamental valuation formula. For the off-balance sheet fee-based activities, the use of standard corporate finance valuation tools is recommended. Since many textbooks have been written on valuation and many readers are likely to be familiar with these techniques, this chapter summarizes, in a systematic manner, the key steps that need to be taken. Fee-based activities are described first. Next, the valuation methodology is proposed. A numerical example follows.

## FEE-BASED ACTIVITIES

Five lines of off-balance sheet business are discussed here: asset management, private banking, corporate advisory services, brokerage/dealership, and proprietary trading. The objective is to understand, from a valuation perspective, the types of cash flows generated by these activities and the eventual risks associated with them.

### Asset Management

As mentioned in Chapter 4, bonds and shares issued by deficit units, such as corporations or governments, are not always held directly by savers. Quite often, savers prefer to invest in investment funds, such as mutual funds or SICAVs. These are, in essence, corporate structures, funded by shares, that invest in financial assets, such as bonds or stocks. The investors delegate the management of the portfolio to the investment fund.

In many countries, banks are involved in asset management. They earn a management fee, typically a percentage of the assets under management,[1] and sometimes commissions on trades of the securities held by the fund.[2] The risk arising from the volatility of the returns on the fund is borne by the investors, not by the bank.[3] The risk for the bank arises from three elements. First, since the management fee is a fixed percentage of the asset base, it is directly affected by changes in the asset base driven by asset withdrawals or the return on the funds. Second, there have been cases where a bank has compensated clients for investment losses, not because it had a legal obligation to do so, but rather because it had a commercial obligation related to the desire to keep the person who was compensated as a client of the bank.[4] A third type of risk is legal risk, the risk that the fund managers do not carry out their fiduciary duty to act in the best interest of investors.[5] If that should happen, the sponsor of the fund, the bank, can be sued and face severe financial penalties.

## Private Banking

Wealthy investors receive advice from banks on managing their financial assets, managing their taxes, or arranging for the disposition of their estate. The minimum level of assets required to qualify for private banking services varies across banks, but is generally between $500,000 and $5,000,000. Again, banks earn a management fee, a percentage of assets under management. The risk is linked to changes in assets under management and to possible breaches of fiduciary duty.

## Corporate Advisory Services

Banks advise corporations on a different set of issues. They sell risk management services to help corporations evaluate and manage their exposure to changes in foreign exchange rates or interest rates. They advise corporations on the choice of financial structure, that is, the types of securities the corporations issue. They also help firms to issue these securities and place them with investors. A special case is the issuing of shares that are going to be listed on a stock exchange for the first time (an initial public offering, or IPO). Finally, banks are active in advising on mergers and acquisitions. Banks earn fees for advising corporations or facilitating the issuance of securities. When the bank underwrites a security issue, the risks can be of either a legal or a financial nature, that is, the bank promises to buy the securities if they cannot be placed with the public at a given price. Moreover, there is often a credit risk when the bank provides a short-term *bridge* loan to accelerate a transaction, before a security issue can take place.

## Brokerage/Dealership

The term *primary markets* refers to the exchange of shares or bonds at the time of issue. Later, when investors want to sell their investments, they can sell shares or bonds on the *secondary markets*. To facilitate the matching of buyers and sellers on the secondary markets, banks conduct brokerage and dealership activities. (A broker brings a buyer and a seller together; a dealer holds securities in its asset portfolio.) Again, banks earn commissions on trades. Over the years, competition has brought down these commissions as a result of progress in information technology and Internet-based trading.

## Proprietary Trading

Finally, banks can invest their own funds in shares, bonds, currencies, or commodities. In this case, the bank acts as an investor, bearing the entire risk and receiving the entire return from the investment. When financial derivatives are used, as is often the case, this activity will appear off-balance sheet. However, a straight investment in shares would be an on-balance sheet investment.

## VALUATION OF FEE-BASED ACTIVITIES

As mentioned in the introduction to this chapter, the valuation of off-balance sheet activities should be carried out using the standard corporate finance techniques discussed in most finance textbooks.[6] Two approaches are used to value the equity of companies. The first one, the flow to shareholders approach, is the present value of future dividends received by shareholders. This entails a forecast of future profits, retained earnings, and dividends. The second approach, which is more commonly used, is the asset-value-based approach (also called the enterprise-value approach). It involves four steps:

- *Step 1*: Assignment of assets linked to the fee-based activity, financial structure, and weighted average cost of capital (WACC)
- *Step 2*: Computation of free cash flows on assets

- *Step* 3: Valuation of assets
- *Step* 4: Valuation of equity

Each step is reviewed separately.

### Step 1: Assignment of Assets, Financial Structure, and Weighted Average Cost of Capital (WACC) to the Fee-Based Activity

Even if fee-based activities are often referred to as off-balance sheet activities, there will always be some assets associated with them on the balance sheet, even if a very small amount. For instance, an M&A department will need offices, desks, and computers. Once these assets have been identified, the critical issue of the financial structure arises: how much debt should be used in financing these assets, and how much equity? The issue of capital management will be discussed at greater length in Chapters 12, 13, 20, and 22. To keep the discussion at an intuitive level at this stage, assume that equity will be needed to cover risk, to absorb the potential losses resulting from these activities, and to meet regulatory capital requirements.

The balance sheet of a representative fee-based banking business will be as follows:[7]

| Accounts receivable | Accounts payable |
|---|---|
| Other assets | Net accruals |
| | Debt $(D, R_d)$ |
| | Equity $(E, R_s)$ |

Accounts receivable might arise if fees for services are not collected immediately. Accounts payable arise if the bank does not pay some suppliers of services directly. Net accruals refer to liabilities of a firm that are related to salaries or taxes to be paid. The debt used to finance these assets will pay a market rate on debt, $R_d$. This analysis does not include in debt the deposits, which could carry a below-market rate. These deposits are associated with the bank's on-balance sheet business, discussed previously, and are valued using the fundamental valuation formula. Additional off-balance sheet activities are financed on competitive debt markets, paying the market rate. The cost of equity, $R_s$, is the investment return available to shareholders on the stock market. It is the risk-free rate plus a risk premium.

Following the presentation by Hawawini and Viallet (2007), a balance sheet can be simplified as follows, with only two generic assets and two types of sources of funds:

| Working capital requirement (WCR) | Debt $(D, R_d)$ |
|---|---|
| Other assets | Equity $(E, R_s)$ |

where

$$\text{Working capital requirement} = \text{accounts receivable} - \text{accounts payable} - \text{net accruals}$$

The working capital requirement refers to the asset created by the operating and cash cycle of the firm, with a time lag between the supply of a service and its actual payment. The lag creates accounts receivable and accounts payable. As reviewed later, it has an important impact on the calculation of free cash flows.

A generic profit and loss account for fee-based activities is shown here. The format used is similar to that used for a standard corporate firm. This will facilitate the application of standard corporate finance tools.

Fee income

Trading income

− Operating (noninterest) expense

= Earnings before interest, taxes, depreciation, and amortization (EBITDA)

− Depreciation and amortization (DEP)

= Earnings before interest and taxes (EBIT)

− Taxes

= Earnings after tax (EAT)

Note that in accordance with standard accounting principles, fees are recognized at the time the firm provides a service, and expenses are recognized at the time a service is provided to the firm (*matching principle*). Whenever these services are not paid for immediately, they give rise to accounts receivable or accounts payable.

From the simplified balance sheet, it is possible to compute a company's average cost of funding, the weighted average cost of capital (WACC). This is simply the average cost of debt and equity weighted by the relative amounts of debt and equity funding in the financial structure.

$$\text{Weighted average cost of capital} = \left[ R_d \times (1-t) \times \frac{\text{debt}}{\text{debt} + \text{equity}} \right] + \left( R_s \times \frac{\text{equity}}{\text{debt} + \text{equity}} \right)$$

A question that often arises is whether to use the accounting book value of equity or the market value. From a logical point of view, since the value of equity being computed is the maximum price that should be paid for the equity of a business, given the return $R_s$ available to shareholders, the market value of equity should be used.[8]

### Step 2: Computation of Free Cash Flows Generated by the Assets

In the second step, it is necessary to forecast the free cash flows that will be generated by these assets.

The free cash flows are the cash flows available (free) to make payments to the suppliers of funds: debt holders (interest or principal) and shareholders (dividends or stock repurchase).

Students of corporate finance will remember the need to move from accounting flows (sales and cost) to a cash flow concept. For example, sales do not give rise to cash when they are not paid for immediately. In that case, sales create an increase in accounts receivable. To move from accounting flows to cash flows, it is necessary to take the increase in the working capital requirement away from the accounting flows.[9] There are two ways to calculate these free cash flows:

Free cash flow:

$$\text{Cash flow available (free) to meet funding obligations} = \text{EBIT} \times (1 - t) - \Delta\,\text{WCR} + \text{DEP} - \text{additional investment (CAPEX)}$$

where

$$
\begin{aligned}
\text{EBIT} &= \text{earnings before interest and taxes} \\
\text{DEP} &= \text{depreciation plus amortization} \\
\text{WCR} &= \text{working capital requirement} = \text{accounts receivable} - \\
&\quad\ \text{accounts payable} - \text{net accruals}
\end{aligned}
$$

As discussed earlier, a change in the working capital requirement, $\Delta\,\text{WCR}$ (an increase in accounts receivables, for example), is deducted to allow the move from an accounting concept (fee income or operating expenses) to a cash flow concept. This first approach starts with EBIT, an earnings concept calculated after depreciation. Since depreciation is not a direct cash flow (it is an indirect cash flow, as it affects taxes), it is added back. Capital expenditures (CAPEX) needed to sustain the operations of the firm will reduce the free cash flows. Therefore, they will be forecasted and deducted to compute the free cash flows.

Sometimes, the first approach is presented with different acronyms:

$$\text{Free cash flows} = \text{NOPLAT} + \text{DEP} - \Delta\,\text{WCR} - \text{CAPEX}$$

where

NOPLAT = net operating profit less adjusted taxes = EBIT × (1 − t)

The term *adjusted taxes* refers to the fact that tax calculations applied to EBIT have ignored the interest expense. The actual tax deductibility of interest is taken into account when the cost of debt after taxes in the weighted average cost of capital (WACC) is computed.

The second approach to calculating free cash flows starts with an earnings concept calculated before interest, taxes, depreciation, and amortization (EBITDA):

$$\begin{aligned} \text{Free cash flow} &= \text{cash flow available (free) to meet funding} \\ &\quad \text{obligations} \\ &= \text{EBITDA} \times (1 - t) - \Delta\,\text{WCR} + \\ &\quad (t \times \text{DEP}) - \text{CAPEX} \end{aligned}$$

In the second approach, the calculation of taxes is first applied to earnings calculated before depreciation and amortization (EBITDA). The result is then corrected by adding the tax savings (the tax shield) resulting from depreciation ($t \times$ DEP). As in the first method, changes in working capital requirements ($\Delta$+WCR) and capital expenditures (CAPEX) have been taken into account.

### Step 3: Valuation of Assets

The value of the assets is the present value of the free cash flows, discounted at the weighted average cost of capital. Often, as was discussed in Chapter 5 for dividends, a detailed forecast of free cash flows for a few years will be provided, and the assumption will then be that, starting in Year $t + 1$, the free cash flows will grow at a constant rate $g$ to infinity.

$$\begin{aligned} \text{Value of assets} &= \frac{\text{free cash flow}_1}{(1 + \text{WACC})^1} + \frac{\text{free cash flow}_2}{(1 + \text{WACC})^2} + \cdots \\[2mm] &+ \frac{\text{free cash flow}_t + \dfrac{\text{free cash flow}_{t+1}}{\text{WACC} - g}}{(1 + \text{WACC})^t} \end{aligned}$$

The calculation of a terminal value will again raise the issue of its relevance. Dividing the market value of assets by the book value of assets in the year in which the terminal value is calculated will allow a discussion of whether or not this multiple is reasonable.[10]

## Step 4: Valuation of Equity

The value of the equity of a fee-based activity is simply the difference between the value of the assets and the debt:

Value of equity = value of assets − value of debt

These four steps are standard in corporate finance valuation. Next, a simple numerical example to illustrate the methodology is provided.


## VALUATION OF FEE-BASED ACTIVITIES: NUMERICAL EXAMPLE

Consider the following balance sheet for a trading desk:

| | |
|---|---|
| Securities:  200 | Debt:  150  $(R_d = 5\%)$ |
| Fixed assets: 10 | Equity: 60  (cost of equity = $R_s = 19\%$) |
| 210 | 210 |

Because of a volatility of profit of $30 (one standard deviation), the bank decides to operate the trading unit with equity[11] of $60.

The expected revenue, based on the results of the last five years, includes revenue from commissions and from trading profits.

| | |
|---|---|
| Revenue (interest, fees, trading revenue): | 42.5 |
| − Operating (noninterest) expenses: | −3 |
| − Depreciation: | −2 |
| = Earnings before interest and taxes (EBIT): | 37.5 |
| − Interest expenses (5% × 150): | −7.5 |
| = Earnings before taxes (EBT): | 30 |
| − Taxes (40 %): | −12 |
| = Earnings after taxes (EAT): | 18 |

To make the example easier, assume that this expected profit will be stable until infinity. That is, there is no growth, and the full profit can be paid each year as a dividend. To keep the operation going, annual capital expenditures are estimated to be equal to $2. There will be no change in the working capital requirement (WCR).


### Flows to Shareholders Approach

First, the equity of the bank will be valued as the present value of perpetual dividends paid to shareholders. This is the flow to shareholders approach.

$$\text{Value of equity} = \frac{\text{perpetual dividend}}{\text{cost of equity}} = \frac{18}{0.19} = 94.73684$$

In this case, the calculation is straightforward because there is no growth and therefore no need for retained earnings.

### Asset-Value-Based Approach

As discussed earlier, the asset-value-based approach first calculates the value of the assets and then deducts the debt to obtain the value of equity. With access to the balance sheet and funding structure, four additional steps are needed:

- Calculation of free cash flows
- Calculation of WACC
- Calculation of asset value
- Calculation of the value of equity

#### Free Cash Flows

$$
\begin{aligned}
\text{Annual free cash flows} &= (1 - t) \times \text{EBIT} - \Delta\,\text{WCR} + \text{DEP} \\
&\quad - \text{CAPEX} \\
&= (1 - 40\%) \times (37.5) - 0 + 2 - 2 \\
&= 22.5
\end{aligned}
$$

#### Weighted Average Cost of Capital

The free cash flows generated by the assets will be discounted at a weighted average cost of capital WACC. Based on the previous discussion, the weights should be the market value of debt and equity,[12] $150 and $94.73684:

$$
\begin{aligned}
\text{WACC} &= \left[5\% \times (1 - 0.4) \times \frac{150}{150 + 94.73684}\right] + \left(19\% \times \frac{94.73684}{150 + 94.73684}\right) \\
&= 9.1935\%
\end{aligned}
$$

#### Value of Assets

The value of the assets is the present value of free cash flows (in this example, a perpetual cash flow) discounted at the WACC:

$$\text{Value of assets} = \frac{\text{free cash flow}}{\text{WACC}} = \frac{22.5}{9.1935\%} = 244.7368$$

## Value of Equity

The value of the equity is obtained by deducting the value of debt from the value of the assets:

Value of equity = value of assets − debt = 244.7368 − 150 = 94.7368

It can be seen that the two methods, flows to shareholders and value of assets, lead to the same value of equity. In this simple exercise, the first method, flows to shareholders, was the quicker methodology. In practice, the second approach, value of assets, is used most of the time. One of the reasons is that with this method, there is no need to forecast retained earnings and dividends. The discount rate, the WACC, ensures that the company is funded each year with a mix of debt and equity identical to that assumed in the WACC.

As the fundamental valuation model used to value a bank differs from the standard free cash flow–WACC methodology, it helps to clarify the origins of the differences in valuation methodology.

## FUNDAMENTAL BANK VALUATION VS. STANDARD CORPORATE VALUATION: A COMPARISON

There are two key differences between the bank valuation model presented in previous chapters and the standard corporate finance approach.

First, while bank valuation took the discounted value of dividends as a starting point, the standard finance approach focuses, as a first step, on the valuation of assets, free cash flows, and the weighted average cost of capital. A main reason for a special model for banks is that, unlike nonfinancial firms, banks create value not only on the asset side, but also on the liability side by collecting low-cost deposits. As these volumes of low-cost deposits change over time, there is no simple concept of weighted average cost of capital in banking.

A second difference is that the standard corporate valuation model focuses on the free cash flows received up to infinity. In the fundamental bank valuation model, the focus is on dividends received up to infinity, but after a mathematical transformation, the focus of the fundamental valuation formula is on the current value of equity augmented by the franchise value of loans and deposits and the tax penalty. The franchise value incorporates the value created by collecting deposits and loans beyond the return on investment or funding available to shareholders on capital markets.

## CONCLUSION

This chapter on the valuation of fee-based activities closes the first part of the book, "Bank Valuation." In practice, the analyst breaks the bank into two components: the on-balance sheet activities (loans, deposits, and bonds), and the off-balance sheet fee-based activities. The fundamental valuation formula is applied to the on-balance sheet business. The free cash flow–WACC approach is used to value the fee-based activities. The value of the equity of the bank is the sum of the two components: the banking part and the fee-based part.

The second part of the book discusses value-based management. It builds on the foundations provided by the bank valuation model.

## APPENDIX: FROM OPERATING ACCOUNTING FLOWS TO CASH FLOWS

This appendix shows the mathematical relationship between operating accounting flows (sales of services and related expenditures) and cash flows. Note that capital expenditures, depreciation, and taxes have not been taken into account in this appendix. The focus is exclusively on sales of services and related expenditures.

### Cash Inflows Linked to Sales of Services

Start with the accounting flows related to accounts receivable (A/R):

$$A/R_t = A/R_{t-1} + \text{sales of services}_t - \text{payments}_t$$

Therefore,

$$\text{Cash inflows} = \text{payments}_t = \text{sales of services}_t - (A/R_t - A/R_{t-1})$$
$$= \text{sales of services}_t - \Delta A/R$$

Cash inflows are equal to the sales for the year reduced by any increase in the stock of accounts receivables.

### Cash Outflows Linked to Expenditures[13]

Start from the accounting relationships for accounts payable (A/P) and accruals:

$$A/P_t = A/P_{t-1} + \text{expenditures}_t - \text{payments}_{\text{expenditures } t}$$
$$\text{Accruals}_t = \text{accruals}_{t>t} + \text{salaries}_t - \text{payments}_t$$

Therefore,

$$\text{Cash outflows}_t = \text{payments}_{\text{expenditures } t} + \text{payments}_{\text{salaries } t}$$
$$= \text{expenditures}_t + \text{salaries}_t - (\text{A/P}_t - \text{A/P}_{t-1}) -$$
$$(\text{Acc}_t - \text{Acc}_{t-1})$$
$$= \text{expenditures}_t + \text{salaries}_t - \Delta\text{A/P} - \Delta\text{Acc}$$

Cash outflows are equal to expenditures and salaries reduced by an increase in accounts payable or accruals.

## Net Cash Flow from Operations

The net cash flow from operations is just the difference between cash inflows and cash outflows, discussed previously:

$$\text{Net cash flows from operations}_t = \text{cash inflows}_t - \text{cash outflows}_t$$
$$= \text{sales of services}_t - \text{expenditures}_t$$
$$- \text{salaries}_t - (\Delta \text{ A/R} - \Delta \text{ A/P} -$$
$$\Delta \text{ Acc})$$
$$= \text{sales}_t - \text{expenditures}_t -$$
$$\text{salaries}_t - (\Delta\text{WCR})$$

where

WCR = working capital requirement
= accounts receivable (A/R) − accounts payable (A/P) − net accruals

## EXERCISES FOR CHAPTER 8

1. List four types of fee-based activity in banking.
2. Value the equity of the following investment fund business unit. Management fees are collected as a percentage of assets under management.

   The following is the balance sheet for the investment fund business unit:

| Fixed assets: | 100 | Debt: | 70 ($R_d$ = 5%) |
|---|---|---|---|
| | | Equity: | <u>30</u> (cost of equity = $R_s$ = 15%) |
| | 100 | | 100 |

   As a result of operational risk,[14] the bank decides to operate the investment fund unit with equity of $30.

The expected revenue next year, based on the results of the last five years, includes management fees.

| | |
|---|---|
| Management fees: | 30.5 |
| − Operating (noninterest) expenses: | −6 |
| − Depreciation: | −10 |
| = Earnings before interest and taxes (EBIT): | 14.5 |
| − Interest expense (5% × 70): | −3.5 |
| = Earnings before taxes (EBT): | 11 |
| − Taxes (40%): | 4.4 |
| = Earnings after taxes (EAT): | 6.6 |

Annual capital expenditures are estimated to be equal to $10. It is assumed that the free cash flows will grow by 4 percent forever. Assuming that the working capital requirement is equal to zero, value the equity of the fund management unit using the four steps of the asset-value-based approach.

## Notes

1. Remuneration of hedge funds is reported to be around 2 percent of funds under management plus 20 percent of excess returns over a stated benchmark.
2. This can give rise to "churning," or buying and selling securities too often in order to earn commissions on trades.
3. There are exceptions; for example, the manager of the fund may promise a guaranteed return, or a floor on the minimum return.
4. In 2007, so-called structured investment vehicles (SIVs) (mutual funds invested in real estate mortgages) were sold to investors as a quasi risk-free asset. When the fear of loan losses started to rise, some banks were forced to bail out these funds to protect the investors. SIVs and securitization are discussed in greater detail in Chapter 16.
5. In Europe, a November 2007 EU directive, MIFID ("Markets in Financial Instruments Directive"), is forcing banks to inquire explicitly about the risk appetite of their clients. A bank can be sued if it sells risky assets that do not match the risk preferences of its clients.
6. See Brealey, Myers, and Allen (2006) or Hawawini and Viallet (2006).
7. This discussion has ignored inventories, which are likely to be small in a financial services firm.
8. There is sometimes a loop in this calculation. Given a specific level of debt in the balance sheet, the value of equity is needed to compute

the weight in the WACC, but the WACC is needed to compute the value of equity. This creates a loop that can be solved with iterations. This will be illustrated in the numerical example.

9. A proof is given in the appendix to this chapter.
10. An alternative is to assume that the cash return on investment (free cash flows divided by assets) will go down over time as a result of competitive market pressure.
11. Equity allocation to the trading desk is discussed in Chapter 20.
12. Note that the figure used is the value of equity calculated using the flows to shareholders approach, $94.73684. If this information were not available (as is the case in real life), several iterations would be needed. The calculation would start with the book value of equity, $60. A WACC, value of assets, and value of equity would then be calculated. The iteration would then start. This value of equity would be inserted into the WACC calculation to obtain a new WACC, value of assets, and value of equity. The iteration would continue until the value of equity converged to a unique value.
13. Purchases linked to inventories, which are likely to be small in a financial services firm, have been ignored.
14. Operational risk is the risk of loss resulting from inadequate or failed internal processes, people, and systems or from external events. Operational risk is discussed in Chapter 26.

# Value-Based Management

CHAPTER 9

# Value-Based Management in Banking: An Introduction

## PERFORMANCE METRICS FOR VALUE CENTERS

This chapter introduces corporate financial objectives for banks, both at the overall level of the bank and at the decentralized level of profit centers.[1] This will lead to a discussion of fund transfer pricing for deposits and loans in the next chapter.

Value-based management refers to the corporate objective of increasing the wealth of the shareholders of a corporation. An increase in the share price and a dividend payment both contribute to increases in wealth. While this type of management might be expected in a capitalist society, it is often seen as contrary to stakeholders-based management, where the corporate objective is to increase the welfare not only of shareholders, but also of employees, clients, and society.[2]

The shareholder value–based management paradigm can be defended on two grounds. First, it is not really negative for stakeholders. Indeed, a well-functioning company cannot ignore the welfare of its employees,[3] its clients, or society. Second, economists have shown that, in well-functioning competitive markets, the maximization of shareholder value will lead to an efficient allocation of labor and capital. Nobel Prize winner Milton Friedman (1970) put it in simple terms: freely accepted transactions between a company and its clients or between a company and its employees must increase the welfare of both parties. Adam Smith and economic science have recognized market imperfections, such as monopoly power, externalities (such as pollution resulting from production), and the existence of the public good (such as national defense and fair income distribution). These market imperfections give rise to the need for public interventions.

In summary, in a competitive economy with a well-functioning political system that acts to correct market imperfections, it can be concluded that the maximization of shareholder value enhances public welfare. As noted by Jensen (2001), this has the great advantage of focusing management's attention on one single corporate objective, instead of having to focus on the often conflicting interests of a large number of stakeholders. This book adopts the shareholder value–based approach and leaves it to the board of directors of a bank to decide whether circumstances justify a deviation from this rule. In any case, the maximization of shareholder value remains a useful benchmark against which to evaluate any decision.

This chapter discusses both the corporate financial objectives at the overall level of the bank and financial objectives for decentralized business units, the value centers. The last section of the chapter covers a difficult issue that is of great relevance: in evaluating the realized performance of a business unit, how can good management be distinguished from good luck?

## VALUE-BASED MANAGEMENT FOR THE OVERALL BANK

At the top of the bank, corporate financial objectives have to be set. To be consistent with value-based management, these objectives must lead to an increase in the value of equity, the wealth of shareholders.

Chapter 5 introduced four methods of valuing a bank. The third approach showed that the value of equity is equal to the current equity plus the present value of future economic profits, that is, the value created by the bank on top of the cost of equity, which is the return available to shareholders on the stock market ($R_s$):

$$\text{Economic profit (EP)} = \text{profit after tax} - (\text{equity} \times \text{cost of equity})$$
$$= \text{profit after tax} - (\text{equity} \times R_s)$$

$$\text{Market value of equity}_0 = \text{equity}_0 + \sum_{t=1}(\text{profit}_t - \text{cost of equity}_t)$$
$$= \text{equity}_0 + \sum_{t=1}(\text{ROE}_t \times \text{equity}_t - \text{equity}_t \times R_s)$$

As is apparent from this valuation formula, there are two drivers of value: return on equity (ROE) and growth of equity when the return on equity exceeds its opportunity cost.[4] Therefore, it is no surprise that banks' CEOs, in presentations to analysts, focus on return on equity and growth prospects. Indeed, retained earnings, the part of profit that is not paid out as dividends, create additional value if they can be reinvested in assets yielding a good return. In recent years, banks have been investing massively in emerging "new" markets—for example, Turkey, Latin America, Egypt, and China—in a search for *top-line* revenue growth.

As the return on equity is a key determinant of value, the next step is to break down ROE to identify its key contributors.

### ROE Breakdown

Consider a simple balance sheet of a bank with assets funded by deposits and equity. We define EOA as the average earnings on assets. It is the sum of interest income + noninterest income (such as fees) − provisions for credit risk, as a percentage of total assets. The average cost of debt (deposits and other liabilities), CD, is the ratio of interest expenses to total debt. The operating expenses ratio, OE, is the ratio of operating expenses to total assets. Finally, the average effective tax rate is denoted by $t$ (taxes as a percentage of earnings before tax):

| Assets A (EOA) | Deposits D (CD) |
|---|---|
|  | Equity E |

where

$$EOA = \text{earnings on assets (\%) (interest income}$$
$$+ \text{ fee/trading income} - \text{provisions)}$$
$$CD = \text{cost of debt (\%)}$$
$$OE = \text{operating expenses (\% of assets)}$$
$$t = \text{corporate tax rate (\%)}$$

A first breakdown commonly used by analysts is as follows:

$$\text{Return on equity} = \text{ROE} = \frac{\text{net income}}{\text{equity}}$$

$$= \frac{\text{net income}}{\text{assets}} \times \frac{\text{assets}}{\text{equity}}$$

$$= \text{ROA} \times \text{leverage}$$

The return on equity is the product of the after-tax return on assets (ROA) and a leverage factor. As leverage is often close to 15, a 1 percent after-tax ROA objective would lead, for example, to an ROE of 15 percent.

A more transparent decomposition is

$$\text{Return on equity} = (EOA - OE) \times (1 - t)$$
$$+ (EOA - CD - OE) \times \frac{D}{E} \times (1 - t)$$

It can be shown that the ROE is the sum of two terms.[5] The first term, usually small, includes the earnings on assets net of operating expenses, taken after taxes. The second term is the product of three terms: a margin $(EOA - CD)$[6] net of operating expenses, a leverage factor $(D/E)$, and a tax factor. The second term shows explicitly that leverage is good for the bank as long as the margin exceeds the operating expenses ratio.

Leaving the mathematics aside, there are five key factors that affect the ROE:

1. Earnings on assets
2. Margin $(EOA - CD)$
3. Operating expenses
4. Corporate tax rate
5. Leverage $(D/E)$

A more detailed breakdown of ROE with specific ratios for credit risk and cost-income is provided in Appendix B of this chapter.

Banks use additional measures of corporate performance to compare themselves with their peers in the banking sector:

- Price/earnings ratio (P/E)
- Market/book value ratio (MBV)
- Debt ratings
- Cost-income or cost efficiency ratio

The last one, the cost-income or cost efficiency ratio, is defined as

$$\text{Cost-income ratio} = \frac{\text{operating expenses}}{\text{gross revenue}}$$

$$= \frac{\text{operating expenses}}{\text{net interest margin} + \text{fee/trading income}}$$

Many banks have been able to bring this ratio below 50 percent. However, this ratio is an imperfect measure of cost control, as it includes both a cost and a revenue figure. Thus, it can be affected by both cost and revenue factors. For instance, in markets that are characterized by heavy competition and low margins, the cost-income ratio will be relatively higher than in markets with less competition and higher margins. For control of costs, a ratio that links operating expenses to business activity, such as the operating expense (OE) ratio, is preferable.[7]

Banking supervisors, who focus on the solvency of banks, use the CAMEL system to evaluate banks:

- Capital
- Asset quality
- Management quality
- Earnings
- Liquidity

Most bank CEOs will agree that the return on equity (ROE) is one of the most important measures of performance used by bank analysts. The second most important ratio looked at by bank analysts is the cost-income ratio, an indicator of the bank's ability to control operating expenses.[8]

While the objective of achieving a high ROE is sound, it is still not fully operational in a complex organization. To ensure that the various business units contribute to the ROE objective, performance metrics for individual business units have been designed.

## PERFORMANCE METRICS FOR VALUE-CENTER MANAGEMENT

A value center could be a business unit such as a retail branch, a corporate and investment banking department, a large corporate client to whom the bank is selling several products, or a single product line. In developing measures or metrics of performance,[9] banks have been very creative with acronyms:

- ROC: return on capital
- RAC: return on allocated capital
- RAR: risk-adjusted return
- RORAC: return on risk-adjusted capital
- RAROC: risk-adjusted return on capital
- RARAC: risk-adjusted return on allocated capital
- RORIWAC: return on risk-weighted assets
- RORWA: return on risk-weighted assets
- ROARC: return on allocated risk capital
- RARORAC: risk-adjusted return on risk-adjusted capital

The measure that has received the most attention is RAROC, developed by the U.S. investment bank Bankers Trust. The concept is simple.

At the overall level of the bank, there is a return on equity objective:

$$\text{Return on equity} = \frac{\text{Profit after tax}}{\text{equity}}$$

The net income after tax and the equity of the bank can be viewed as two pies, as shown in Figure 9.1.

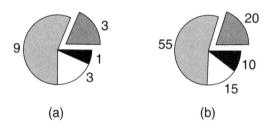

(a)                                        (b)

**Figure 9.1**  (a) Net income after tax and (b) equity of the bank.

Profit and equity are allocated to value centers. Essentially, this is an attempt to break up the bank, a complex organization, into a set of small firms, each with its own P&L and equity allocation. RAROC is the ROE calculated at the level of a value center:

$$\text{RAROC} = \frac{\text{allocated profit}}{\text{allocated equity}}$$

For instance, if a profit center has a net income allocation of $3 and an equity allocation of $20, its RAROC is

$$\text{RAROC} = \frac{\text{allocated profit}}{\text{allocated equity}} = \frac{3}{20} = 15\%$$

The RAROC figure will be satisfactory if it exceeds the cost of equity, the return available to shareholders on the stock market. Technical issues to be discussed later in the book concern the allocation of profit to the value centers, including such issues as the fund transfer price and provisions for credit risk, and the logic behind the allocation of equity. It does not take great skills in mathematics to understand that a business manager will prefer to receive a very low equity allocation.

RAROC is commonly used, and several banks include it in their annual reports. A Danish bank uses it as a way to compare the performance of different branches. However, this measure of performance suffers from a limitation: as it is a percentage figure, it does not take the size of operations into account. Intuitively, it can be recognized that even with a great RAROC, a small operation is unlikely to create much value for shareholders. To correct this weakness, a complementary measure of performance has been created: the economic profit, already introduced earlier at the level of the overall bank.

Economic profit for value center
= allocated after-tax profit − cost of allocated equity
= allocated after-tax profit − (allocated equity × cost of equity)

The economic profit measures the value created for shareholders on top of what the shareholders could achieve through buying shares on the market.[10] That is, it is the after-tax profit reduced by an opportunity cost of equity.

With a cost of equity of 10 percent, the economic profit of our profit center is

$$\text{Economic profit} = 3 - (20 \times 10\%) = 1$$

As pointed out earlier, the allocation of equity to a business unit will have a major impact on the economic profit, and therefore on strategy. The important issue of equity allocation will be dealt with in Chapters 12, 13, and 23. At this stage, it should just be said that it will be related to the riskiness of the activities and/or to bank regulations on capital.

The measurement of allocated profit after tax raises its own set of issues. Provisions for credit risk will be discussed in Chapters 14 and 15. In the next chapter, the issue of the fund transfer price used to evaluate the profitability of deposits and loans is covered. But before closing, one of the most challenging issues in the banking sector must be addressed: in evaluating the realized performance of a business unit, how can good management be distinguished from good luck, or bad management from bad luck?

## EVALUATION OF PERFORMANCE AND INCENTIVES: GOOD LUCK OR GOOD MANAGEMENT? BAD LUCK OR BAD MANAGEMENT?

This chapter has provided a methodology for evaluating realized performance (RAROC or economic profit). For example, consider the case in which a corporate business unit is granting a loan with a large contractual margin to a risky client. The economy begins an expansion and the loan is paid back, with a good profit margin for the bank. When the good performance of this business unit is observed, how can the analyst determine whether the good result was caused by good management (and therefore the manager deserves congratulations and possibly a bonus) or whether it was caused by good luck? Similarly, if a poor result is observed at the time of a recession, how can poor management be distinguished from bad luck?

Indeed, the banking business often involves taking risk, and it is therefore natural that a business should produce losses occasionally. The issue of performance evaluation in banking is not new, and it has been very much discussed in a specific sector: the fund management business. In that industry, a fund manager invests in a stock. If the stock market goes up and there is a profit, was the profit the result of superior management skills in picking the stock or was it the result of pure luck? This issue will always arise when a business unit invests in a risky venture that can produce either a good or a bad outcome. The issue is not only difficult, but of great importance. The goal is to avoid a performance evaluation system that leads to wrong actions, such as excessive or insufficient risk taking.

To address this issue of performance evaluation in banking, it is necessary to start with the fundamentals of value creation.

Assume that the bank invests its equity, $E$, and generates some value at the end of the year, $V$. It is necessary to make a distinction between the *origination date* (the time of the investment) and the *realization date* (the end of the year).

Equity $E$ is invested, producing an expected value $E(V)$ at the end of the year. This is a risky investment, with an end-of-year value given by the probability distribution shown in Figure 9.2.

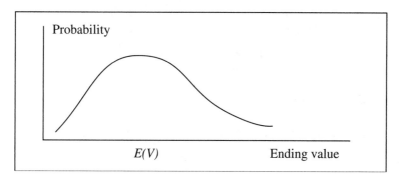

**Figure 9.2** Ending value of a risky investment.

Given a risk-adjusted opportunity return $R_s$ (the cost of equity, the expected risk-adjusted return on alternative investments), the value of the investment at the origination date is

$$\text{Value of equity}_0 = \frac{E(V)}{1 + R_s}$$

The value created by the investment is equal to

Value created = value of equity − equity invested

$$\frac{E(V)}{1 + R_s} - E = \frac{E(V) - (1 + R_s)E}{1 + R_s}$$

$$= \frac{[E(V) - E] - R_s \times E]}{1 + R_s} = \frac{E(\text{profit}) - R_s \times E}{1 + R_s}$$

$$= \frac{E(\text{economic profit})}{1 + R_s}$$

Note that the cost of equity, $R_s$, takes into account the risk of the project, including leverage (which would, as mandated by regulations, be zero for a mutual fund). This formula shows that a good decision is one that creates expected economic profit. In the jargon of the fund management industry,[11] it must create an *alpha* (that is, the expected return on investment must exceed the risk-adjusted opportunity cost of equity).

A year later, the value of the investment $V$ is realized. The result is a profit or a loss $(V - E)$. Suppose there is a profit. Should the company compliment the manager? Should he be paid a bonus? Was the good result caused by good luck or good management? Because of randomness, realized profit is likely to differ from the expected value: higher or lower. A practical question of great relevance is, how can the performance of the manager be evaluated *ex post* (after the revenue is realized)? Remember that the key issue is to reward good managers, and this requires separating luck from superior management skills.

Here are four ways to evaluate performance, with a discussion of the merits of each of them.

### Performance Evaluation Method 1: Realized Economic Profit (REP)

The first method of evaluating performance uses realized economic profit.

Realized economic profit (REP) = realized profit − (equity allocated × $R_s$)

An equity cost is charged for risk taking, but the main weakness of this approach is that the realized profit could be the result of either pure luck or good management skills. A second major weakness is that this measure of performance can sometimes create unintended incentives for excessive risk taking. If the manager's bonus is related to a positive outcome and is zero for a negative outcome, she could be tempted to take a large gamble, hoping for a large payoff. This is akin to a call option, whose value increases with volatility.[12]

### Performance Evaluation Method 2: Expected Economic Profit (at Origination Date) (EEP)

The second method of evaluating performance uses expected economic profit.

$$\text{Expected economic profit (EEP)} = \text{expected profit} - (\text{equity allocated} \times R_s)$$

This method, which focuses on expected profit and charges a cost for risk, allows firms to reward superior management skills. It also allows them to motivate/reward staff members rapidly, before the outcome of a long term-investment is fully realized.

The major drawback of this approach is that a tool is needed to evaluate the expected economic profit correctly (which entails charging a risk-adjusted cost for equity and calculating the expected profit properly, with a forecast not only of good outcomes, but also of bad outcomes with eventual effects on reputation). It is clear that determining the value of the expected economic profit at the origination date is not easy and that it is essential to send the right signal to those who are making transactions. Too often, staff members and dealers will have an incentive to present a rosy picture, so as to earn a performance fee easily.

### Performance Evaluation Method 3: Benchmarked Economic Profit (BEP)

The third method of evaluating performance uses benchmarked economic profit.

$$\text{Benchmarked economic profit (BEP)} = \text{realized profit} - \text{realized outcome on a risk-adjusted (benchmarked) alternative investment}$$

With this method, realized profit is compared to what would have been realized by investing in the risk-adjusted alternative investment (the risk-adjusted alternative investment has the same risk as the asset, but carries the expected return demanded by the market for this risk). The idea is that shareholders can buy risky investments as well.[13] This is a *relative* realized evaluation of performance, as it compares realized performance to that of a benchmark. This method is used frequently in the investment industry. How does the return on a specific investment fund compare to that on a benchmark, such as the overall stock market index?[14] An explanation beyond relative performance evaluation is as follows: if an economic variable (such as a recession) is driving both the realized return on the asset and the realized return on the alternative investment, then a superior realized return on the asset is indicative of a *superior* investment. The purpose of performance evaluation is to separate superior performance from good luck. With this method, a positive performance is not necessarily indicative of good management. The manager must also outperform the benchmark. And a negative performance is not always indicative of bad performance, if the manager still does better than the benchmark.[15]

Note that a relative evaluation can work only if a correct benchmark can be identified. The benchmark should have a probability distribution (including volatility) similar to that of the asset under review. Moreover, if the benchmarked economic profit (BEP) turns out to be positive, the realized profit could still be negative—for example, in the case of lending at the time of a recession. There should be two levels of evaluation: Ex ante (given the probability distribution of the outcomes), was it a good decision to take this type of risk and lend this amount to a specific sector? And given that the decision has been made, was the right asset chosen? The BEP answers the second question. The expected economic profit (EEP) would help to answer the first one.

### Performance Evaluation Method 4: Average Realized Economic Profit (AREP) over a Long Period

The fourth method of performance evaluation uses the average realized economic profit.

Average realized economic profit (AREP)
= average realized profit − average cost of equity

This approach seeks to eliminate the problem with the first approach: that a realized outcome can be the result of good or bad luck. When the average of realized economic profits is taken over a long period, the result will be a good measure of expected economic profit (with the good draws compensating for the bad draws). As the legendary investor Warren Buffett once said: "You only learn who has been swimming naked when the tide goes out." If you take risk, the potential loss will be seen only at the time of a shock. So, several years of data on performance are needed to assess average return and risk. Unlike the ex ante expected economic profit, this method does not require computation of the expected profit from the complete profit distribution (which is difficult to estimate), as the average realized economic profit will be observed over a long period. This method is used in part in the fund management industry, in which the average realized performance of a fund over both short and long periods is shown. Its major drawback is that several years of data are needed. If competition for talent in the market demands short-term bonuses, it may be difficult to implement. This raises incentives for banks to provide a stable environment for employees so that several years of data on performance can be collected.

This last approach is related to the so-called deferred account bonus schemes. Instead of paying a bonus based on the realized economic profit or the benchmarked economic profit that is 100 percent in cash, 25 percent is paid in cash, but 75 percent is invested in a fictitious "deferred bank account." Every year, the new bonus goes into that account (so that after several years, the bonus is really based on the average performance over several years). Again, this will work for long-term employees.

To the best of our knowledge, no empirical studies have demonstrated the benefits of delayed bonuses for risk taking. Interviews with bankers offer mixed reactions. Some believe that delayed bonuses would indeed be useful, while others think that they will not change aggressive risk behavior and, therefore, that an independent risk management system must be in place to limit risk taking.

## Summary

Banking (and business) often involves risky decisions. This implies that a realized outcome will be due partly to good (or bad) management skills and partly to good (or bad) luck. The noise provided by the random element means that it is necessary to be extremely careful in measuring performance. Two sound measures of performance are the expected economic profit and the average realized economic profit. The drawback with the first of these approaches is the difficulty of estimating the expected economic profit ex ante, while the drawback with the second approach is that it takes several years of data to compute an average economic profit.

If possible, the second approach should be implemented, but this also requires building an organization with long-term commitments by employees. This approach will work only if the system is accompanied by a loyalty program that allows employees to believe that they will be employed for a long time and that they should worry about average realized performance, not just short-term luck. Heads of business units within the bank that have longer horizons should be evaluated over a longer period or compensated with a deferred bonus scheme. Having to worry about the future of the bank, not just the short-term horizon, senior executives will have proper incentives to invest in strong risk management systems. Adequate risk management will then control the risk taken by short-term-minded junior managers.

Many commentators have attributed the 2007 subprime credit crisis[16] in the United States (involving more than $700 billion in credit losses) to wrong performance evaluation and bonus systems that are based on realized economic profit, leading to excessive risk taking. This issue of performance evaluation and risk-taking incentives in banking is not new, but shows up every time there is a crisis: "Those who do not learn from history are doomed to repeat it."[17] Senior management must be aware that the evaluation system and bonus schemes can sometimes induce some managers—in particular, those with a short time horizon—to take excessive risk. An adequate independent risk control system is needed to prevent a massive buildup of risk.

## CONCLUSION

This chapter has introduced measures of performance for the overall bank and for profit centers. For the overall bank, CEOs like to emphasize ROE, growth opportunities, and the cost-income ratio. At the level of profit centers, many banks rely on RAROC or economic profit. These last two measures involve the allocation of profit and equity to business units, issues that are discussed in the following chapters. A difficult issue in evaluating the performance of a business unit in a bank is how to separate good luck from good management and bad luck from bad management.

## APPENDIX A: PROOF OF ROE BREAKDOWN

$$ROE = EAT/E = [(EOA \times A - OE \times A - CD \times D) \times (1 - t)]/E$$
$$= \{[(EOA - OE) \times A - CD \times D] \times (1 - t)\}/E$$
$$= \{[(EOA - OE) \times (D + E) - CD \times D] \times (1 - t)\}/E$$
$$= (EOA - OE) \times (1 - t) + (EOA - CD - OE) \times D/E \times (1 - t)$$

## APPENDIX B: ALTERNATIVE ROE DECOMPOSITION

A more detailed presentation of ROE is given in this appendix.
Define:

Gross income = interest income + fees − interest expense

$\quad$ CIR $\quad$ = cost-income ratio = operating expenses/gross income

$\quad$ EOA $\quad$ = earnings on assets = interest income + fees as a percentage of assets

$\quad$ CD $\quad$ = interest expenses divided by total debt

$\quad$ PRO $\quad$ = provisions divided by assets [or more completely, (provisions/loans) × (loans/assets)]

Then,

$$ROE = [EOA \times (1 - CIR) - PRO] \times (1 - t) + [(EOA - CD) \times (1 - CIR) - PRO] \times (D/E) \times (1 - t)$$

Proof:

$$ROE = (\text{gross income} - \text{operating expenses} - \text{provisions}) \times (1 - t)/E$$
$$= (EOA \times A - CD \times D - CIR \times \text{gross income} - PRO \times A) \times (1 - t)/E$$
$$= \{EOA \times (D + E) - CD \times D - CIR \times [EOA \times (D + E) - CD \times D] - PRO \times (D + E)\} \times (1 - t)/E$$
$$ROE = [EOA \times (1 - CIR) - PRO] \times (1 - t) + [(EOA - CD) \times (1 - CIR) - PRO] \times (1 - t) \times D/E$$

## APPENDIX C: ROE VS. EPS

Executives are sometimes confused about the relationship between two corporate objectives, earnings per share (EPS) and return on equity (ROE). The mathematical relationship between these two variables is as follows:

Let:

$\quad$ EPS = earnings per share

$\quad$ # = number of shares outstanding

$\quad$ BVS = book value per share (equity/#)

$$EPS = \frac{\text{earnings after tax}}{\#}$$

$$= \frac{\text{earnings after tax} \times BVS}{\# \times BVS} = \frac{\text{earnings after tax} \times BVS}{\text{equity}} = ROE \times BVS$$

So, in many cases, a decision that increases ROE will also increase EPS. An exception is when a decision involves issuing equity, which can affect the average book value per share (dilution effect). But, as is discussed later, it should be emphasized that decisions should be evaluated on the basis of their effect on shareholder value, not just on EPS or ROE (which ignore risk and valuation effects).

## APPENDIX D: STANDARD PERFORMANCE RATIOS

A series of standard performance ratios is given here. They are measures of profitability, operating efficiency, credit risk, leverage, and liquidity.

### Profitability

$$ROE = \text{return on equity} = \frac{\text{net income}}{\text{equity}}$$

$$ROA = \text{return on assets} = \frac{\text{net income}}{\text{assets}}$$

$$RORWA = \text{return on risk-weighted assets} = \frac{\text{net income}}{\text{risk-weighted assets}}$$

Risk-weighted assets are defined in Chapters 12 and 13. As risky assets should yield higher income, RORWA is conceptually a superior measure to the standard ROA.

Often, the contribution of net interest margin and noninterest income needs to be known. Four additional ratios provide this information:

$$\frac{\text{Noninterest revenue}}{\text{Gross revenue}} = \frac{\text{noninterest revenue}}{\text{net interest income} + \text{noninterest revenue}}$$

$$\frac{\text{Net interest income}}{\text{Risk-weighted assets}};$$

$$\frac{\text{Noninterest revenue}}{\text{Risk-weighted asset}}$$

$$\frac{\text{Trading revenue}}{\text{Value at risk (VAR)}}$$

Value at risk (VAR), a measure of risk in the trading portfolio, is discussed in Chapter 20.

### Operating Efficiency

$$\text{Cost-income ratio (CIR) (also called efficiency ratio)} = \frac{\text{operating expenses}}{\text{gross revenue}}$$

with gross revenue = net interest income + noninterest revenue

$$\text{Operating expense ratio} = \frac{\text{operating expenses (noninterest expense)}}{\text{assets}}$$

### Credit Risk

$$\frac{\text{Annual credit risk provisions}}{\text{loans}};$$
$$\frac{\text{Nonperforming loans (NPL)}}{\text{loans}}$$
$$\frac{\text{Cumulative provisions (loan loss allowance)}}{\text{Nonperforming loans}}$$

### Leverage

$$\text{Leverage ratio} = \frac{\text{equity}}{\text{assets}}$$
$$\text{BIS ratio} = \frac{\text{BIS capital}}{\text{risk-weighted assets}}$$
$$\text{Tier 1 ratio} = \frac{\text{Tier 1 capital}}{\text{risk-weighted assets}};$$
$$\text{Tier 2 ratio} = \frac{\text{Tier 2 capital}}{\text{risk-weighted assets}}$$

BIS capital, Tier 1 capital, Tier 2 capital, and risk-weighted assets are defined in Chapters 12 and 13.

### Liquidity

$$\text{Loan-to-deposit ratio} = \frac{\text{loans}}{\text{deposits}}$$
$$\text{Contingency ratio} = \frac{\text{liquid assets}}{\text{short-term deposits}}$$

## EXERCISES FOR CHAPTER 9

1. The balance sheet and income statement of a bank are as follows:

### Balance Sheet (End of the Year, $ Millions)

| Assets 110 | Debt (including deposits) | 105 |
|---|---|---|
|  | Equity | 5 |
| Total 110 |  | Total 110 |

### Income Statement ($ Millions)

|   | Interest income | 8.2 |
|---|---|---|
| − | Interest expense | −5.25 |
| = | Net interest margin | 2.95 |
| + | Noninterest income | 0.8 |
| = | Gross revenue | 3.75 |
| − | Provision for bad debts | −1.3 |
| − | Operating expenses | −1.1 |
| = | Profit before tax | 1.35 |
| − | Taxes | −0.54 |
| = | Profit after tax | 0.81 |

Compute the return on equity (ROE), and show that it can be decomposed into a chain of ratios:

$$ROE = (EOA - OE) \times (1 - t) + (EOA - CD - OE) \times D/E \times (1 - t)$$

2. The allocated profit after tax of a corporate banking division is $4 million. Equity of $20 million has been allocated to this profit center. Compute the RAROC, the cost of equity, and the economic profit. The risk-free rate on government bonds is 10 percent, and the market demands a risk premium of 5 percent on bank shares.

## Notes

1. Corporate objectives are sometimes referred to as key performance indicators (KPIs).
2. The *Wall Street Journal* (January 4, 2007) has argued that some CEOs, such as Robert Nardelli, who was removed from Home

Depot, have failed to respond to a widening array of stakeholders' advocates: hedge funds, private-equity deal makers, legislators, regulators, attorneys general, nongovernmental organizations, and countless others who want a say in how public companies manage their affairs.

3. At a public forum in New York, Mrs. Dina Dublon, at the time CFO of JPMorgan Chase, reported management's enthusiasm about the bank's supporting a foundation helping children who were victims of war. Here is an example where (tax-efficient) concerns for society can increase the motivation of employees, promoting good management and shareholder value.

4. There is a third driver that is more difficult to change and is not discussed here: the cost of equity $R_s$. As the risk premium is set by shareholders, bankers have only an indirect way to affect it: lobby for an efficient and liquid stock market that increases investor participation and reduces the risk premium.

5. The proof is given in Appendix A of this chapter.

6. It is not exactly an interest margin, as the earnings on assets (EOA) includes the fee income and is net of credit risk provisions.

7. Economic-based measures of cost efficiency, such as data envelopment analysis (DEA), are superior measures of operational efficiency (Canhoto and Dermine, 2003).

8. A list of standard performance ratios is given in Appendix D of this chapter.

9. There has been a change in terminology over time. Profit centers are now called value centers, and measures of performance are called performance metrics or key performance indicators. Managers are called leaders. The author leaves it to linguists to explain the origin of the changes in terminology, but hypothesizes that new terminology is needed to catch the attention of a *zapping* society of executives. In a very different context, former U.S. Treasury Secretary James Baker III wrote in his 2007 report on the Iraq Study Group: "Our country deserves a debate that prizes substance over rhetoric." Similarly, in bank management, substance should prevail.

10. Economic profit is related to EVA, the economic value added concept used in the nonfinancial industry; EVA = $(1 - t) \times$ EBIT - (assets $\times$ WACC). As discussed in Chapter 8, banks focus on revenue from equity and cost of equity, while nonfinancial firms focus on revenue from assets and weighted average funding cost of assets.

11. Bodie, Kane, and Marcus (1996).

12. An introduction to options is provided in Chapter 24.

13. For a loan, a natural estimate of a risk premium is that available on corporate bonds. It is indicative, as the risk distribution announced by the loan manager could differ from that perceived by the overall market for corporate bonds.
14. In fund management evaluation, the return on a fund is compared to an alternative benchmark investment (it is a 100 percent funded equity benchmark, as there is no issue of adjusting for leverage).
15. If the realized negative performance is less negative than the performance of the benchmark, the unit would still receive a positive evaluation. As the bank would have realized a negative return, it might seem strange or difficult for it to pay a bonus, and in fact it might not be paid. However, the evaluation of relative performance should be separated from the general issue of whether or not shareholders want to pay higher (lower) bonuses when the absolute performance of the bank is good (bad). There are two issues: the evaluation of individual performance and whether to share the bank's shareholders' gains or losses with the heads of business units. The individual bonuses could be linked to both the performance of the individual business unit and the overall performance of the bank.
16. The U.S. subprime credit crisis is discussed in Chapters 15, 16, 21, and 25.
17. In 1995, the investment bank Salomon Brothers, under pressure from its main shareholder, Warren Buffett, introduced multiyear deferred accounts for its directors in proprietary trading (*Financial Times*, November 7, 1994). The plan had to be abandoned because of competitive pressure from peers who were offering a cash bonus. In 2008, Josef Ackermann, chief executive of Deutsche Bank, was reported to be "eye[ing] a multi-year bonus system" (*Financial Times*, May 30, 2008).

CHAPTER 10

# Fund Transfer Pricing: Foundation and Advanced Approaches

This chapter discusses the fund transfer price (FTP) used to evaluate the profitability of deposits and loans. The issue is as follows. In evaluating the profitability of deposits, the cost—the interest paid on deposits and the operating expenses allocated to deposits, such as employee time and IT expenses—is known. However, the choice of a return on deposits is more problematic, because deposits are used to finance various types of assets: consumer loans, corporate loans, interbank assets, bonds, and fixed assets. A revenue—a fund transfer price—must be identified to evaluate the return on deposits. The problem for loans is symmetrical: the return on loans—that is, the interest income net of average bad debt expense—is known, but the funding cost is not. The reason is that banks use several sources of funds to finance assets: demand deposits, savings deposits, time deposits, corporate deposits, interbank deposits, and subordinated debt. Again, there is a need for a specific fund transfer price to evaluate the cost of funding loans.

A *foundation* approach that is used around the banking world is first presented. Next, the chapter argues that liquidity risk, the credit risk premium introduced in the fundamental bank valuation model, and the effective maturity of some products call for a more *advanced* fund transfer pricing system.

## FUND TRANSFER PRICING: FOUNDATION APPROACH

Two economists, Klein and Monti,[1] have proposed a simple model of banking that allows a clear discussion of fund transfer pricing. The asset side of the bank's balance sheet consists of reserves with the central bank ($R$), loans ($L$), and market-traded assets such as government bonds ($B$) and interbank loans. The liability side includes deposits ($D$) and equity ($E$).

The regulatory reserves, yielding no interest, are a fraction $r$ of deposits. The supply of government bonds (yielding a current interest rate $b)^2$ is perfectly elastic in competitive markets. That means that the interest rate is set on the very large world market and that the purchase or sale of bonds by one bank has no impact on the interest rate. The balance sheet is as follows:

| Assets | Liabilities and Shareholders' Equity |
| --- | --- |
| Reserves $(R)$ | Deposits $(D)$ |
| Loan $(L)$ | Equity $(E)$ |
| Bonds, interbank $(B)$ | |

The loan demand by borrowers, $L(.)$, is a decreasing function of the interest rate $l$, and the deposit supply, $D(.)$, is an increasing function of the interest rate $d$. All these assets and deposits have the same maturity, say one year, and at this stage all parameters are known with certainty. Operating expenses linked to deposits and loans are left out for simplicity.

The opportunity cost of equity in this certain world is the exogenous current government bond rate $b$. There is no risk premium. The bank chooses deposit and credit rates to maximize its end-of-year economic profit (EP), that is, the accounting profit reduced by an opportunity cost of equity:

$$\text{Max EP} = (l \times L + b \times B - d \times D) - b \times E$$

subject to

$$R + L + B = D + E$$

Substituting the balance sheet constraint into the objective function gives

$$\text{Max EP} = [(1 - b) \times L] + \{[b \times (1 - r) - d] \times D\}$$

The economic profit is the sum of two terms: income on loans net of an opportunity cost (the government bond rate $b$), and income on deposits invested in securities with a return reduced by the central bank's reserve requirement $(r \times D)$. For each dollar raised, only $(1 - r)$ of that dollar is available for investment. This simple relationship has given rise to the important *separation theorem* in banking, which suggests pricing loans and deposits independently, with reference to the market rate (the rate on government bonds or the interbank rate). The separation theorem can be represented as shown in Figure 10.1, with the reserve requirement being set at zero for the sake of exposition.

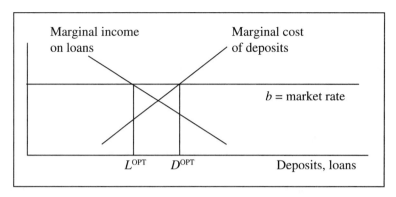

**Figure 10.1** The separation theorem.

The horizontal line represents the perfectly elastic market rate $b$. The two planted lines represent the marginal income on loans and the marginal cost of deposits. When a bank wishes to increase its loan portfolio, the income on an additional dollar of loans (the marginal or incremental income) is going down, either because the bank will need to lower the interest rate to attract the additional dollar of loans or because the bank is willing to accept loans of lower quality. Similarly, the cost of an additional dollar of deposits (the marginal or incremental cost of deposits) is going up, either because the bank needs to raise the deposit rate to attract the additional dollar of deposits or because the bank needs to open more expensive branches in remote areas.

Figure 10.1 illustrates that the optimal volume of deposits, $D^{OPT}$, is reached when the marginal cost of deposits is equal to the market rate $b$. You would not want to go beyond $D^{OPT}$ because the incremental cost would be higher than the cost of funds on money markets, $b$. Similarly, the optimal volume of loans, $L^{OPT}$, is reached when the marginal revenue from loans is equal to the marginal investment return, the market rate $b$. The separation between the lending and funding decisions can also be seen. The separation theorem says that both loans and deposits must be priced with reference to the market rate and that these decisions are independent of each other. The difference between the optimal volumes of deposits and loans is the net position in Treasury assets, bonds, or interbank loans. In Figure 10.1, this quantity is positive, with deposits exceeding the volume of loans. The bank is a net lender in the market. But it could be negative, with the bank being a net borrower.

An alternative, intuitive reason for the choice of the interbank rate as a transfer price is as follows. If a branch manager works very hard and succeeds in attracting more deposits, what is the impact of those new deposits on the balance sheet? In most countries, the impact will be on the interbank or bond position: it goes up when deposits are collected, and it goes down if deposits leave the bank. In such a case, the transfer price should be set to send the *right signal* to the manager. If the impact is on the interbank position, then the market rate, such as the interbank rate, should be used as the transfer price. Similar reasoning applies to increases or decreases in the loan portfolio. In countries with expanding economies, it can be seen that banks are reducing their holdings of bonds or interbank positions to fund the growth in the loan portfolio.

## MATCHED-MATURITY MARGINAL VALUE OF FUNDS (MMMVF)

In the model just discussed, the maturity of assets and deposits was identical at one year, and the fund transfer price was a one-year-maturity market rate. When the maturities of assets and debt vary, a question will arise as to which maturity should apply: a short-term market rate or a long-term market rate.

There is an organizational issue related to the choice of the maturity for the transfer price. If branch managers are best at marketing loans and deposits, they might not have the best expertise in managing a maturity mismatch. As a consequence, an asset and liability management (ALM) group is created to manage the maturity mismatch, and branch managers focus on increasing interest margins. How is this achieved?

Consider the following original balance sheet for a branch:

### Branch Original Balance Sheet

| | |
|---|---|
| Consumer loans (3 months):  100 | Term deposits (1 month):  100 |
| Consumer loans (12 months): 150 | Term deposits (6 months): 150 |
| Total: 250 | Total: 250 |

The three-month and twelve-month loans are funded with one-month and six-month deposits. There is a maturity mismatch and an interest-rate risk.[3] If short-term interest rates go up, the cost of the one-month deposits will increase before the return on assets can adjust. To focus the branch manager on interest margins and to protect him from interest-rate fluctuations, two other balance sheets are artificially constructed: a modified fully matched one for the branch and another for the ALM department. This is done as if the three-month consumer loans were funded with three-month interbank debt lent by the ALM department. Once the loan is granted, the margin is computed and is booked in the branch. The manager is protected from interest-rate fluctuation. The six-month term deposits collected by the branch are calculated as if the deposits were invested in a six-month inter-bank asset lent to the ALM department. Again, the margin for the branch is locked in. Repeating the same reasoning for the twelve-month loans and the one-month deposits, the end result is a fully matched balance sheet for the branch and a maturity mismatch that has been transferred to the ALM group. That group will be in charge of managing the mismatch, either on-balance sheet or with derivatives.[4] The fund transfer price applied to deposits and loans is called the matched-maturity marginal value of funds, the MMMVF. For an international bank, a matched-maturity and matched-currency marginal value of funds could be added.

### Branch Matched-Maturity Balance Sheet (Modified)

| | |
|---|---|
| Consumer loans (3 months): 100 | Interbank (3 months): 100 |
| Consumer loans (12 months): 150 | Interbank (12 months): 150 |
| Interbank (1 month): 220 | Term deposits (1 month): 220 |
| Interbank (6 months): 100 | Term deposits (6 months): 100 |

### ALM Balance Sheet

| | |
|---|---|
| Interbank (3 months): 100 | Interbank (1 month): 220 |
| Interbank (12 months): 150 | Interbank (6 months): 100 |

It can be seen that when the branch matched-maturity balance sheet and the ALM balance sheet are consolidated, the result is identical to the original balance sheet for the branch. The sum of the P&L of the matched-maturity branch and of the ALM department is thus equal to the actual profit of the branch.

The separation theorem allows the identification of the relevant interest rate for evaluating the profitability of loans and deposits. It permits the division of the bank into a set of profit centers. Indeed, the economic profit can be shown to be the sum of two terms: the profit on loans (net interest margin) and the profit on deposits (net interest margin adjusted eventually for reserves with the central bank). And once a maturity mismatch is introduced, a third entity emerges, the ALM group. It is therefore possible to break up the bank into different sources of economic profit or different value centers, with the transfer price needed to evaluate the profit on deposits or loans being identified as the market rate with the same maturity as the product. This rate is known as the MMMVF, the matched-maturity marginal value of funds. The expression "breaking up the bank" was used to refer to the fact that the deposit taking and lending activities could each be evaluated on its own.

## FUND TRANSFER PRICING: ADVANCED APPROACHES

The MMMVF fund transfer price is used widely in banking, and is implemented in the ALM information system of many banks. This can be referred to as the *foundation* approach to the choice of the fund transfer price. However, there are potential dangers with a naive or blind application of the MMMVF. Complex issues that must sometimes be taken into account include

1. Cases of liquidity constraints and/or the possible need for the joint maximization of profit on deposits and loans
2. The need for credit risk adjustment if the credit risk on the loans differs substantially from the average risk on the bank's assets
3. The difference between the *contractual* maturity of a product and its *effective* maturity

These three cases call for more advanced fund transfer pricing and are discussed here.

### Advanced FTP 1: The Case of Liquidity Constraints

The MMMVF allows the analyst to break up, or separate, the loan and deposit pricing decisions, with each one being made at the appropriate interbank market rate. However, there are cases when this simple separation breaks down. Two such cases are cases of joint cost or revenue functions in deposits and loans. A joint revenue function could exist if the volume of deposits received is linked to the volume of loans granted. For instance, the terms of a mortgage loan could impose the opening of a deposit account with the same bank. A joint cost function could be the result of joint operating expenses in delivering deposits and loans. When there is a joint cost or revenue function, the total profit on loans and deposits must be maximized jointly. A third case involves risk—the volatility of income related to loans or deposits. Total aggregated risk, discussed in Chapter 23, is most often a joint issue. Finally, a significant adjustment to fund transfer pricing is needed when the bank is facing liquidity constraints. This case is discussed next.

### The Case of Liquidity Constraints

Bank loans are notoriously illiquid; that is, they cannot be sold rapidly without a substantial loss of value. The reason is that, in the relationship with its client, the bank holds private information that is not known to other market participants. If the sale of a loan is proposed, the market will not know whether it is a safe loan or a risky loan (a so-called lemon). A *fire sale* of loans, or a sale of loans on short notice, will generate sharp capital losses. For this reason, banks want to avoid the sale of loans on short notice. Since, as discussed in Chapter 4, banks provide investors with useful short-term deposits that can be withdrawn upon demand, banks face a liquidity risk, or the risk of a deposit outflow. To avoid the risk of having to sell illiquid loans, banks hold a percentage of their short-term deposits as liquid assets, such as government bonds or assets that can be discounted at the central bank.[5]

For many years, banks were not particularly concerned with liquidity risk because, since their deposit base exceeded their loan portfolio, they were holding a large portfolio of liquid assets. With the rapid growth in their loan portfolios, however, the holding of excess liquid assets has been substantially reduced, and the arrival of the U.S. subprime crisis[6] in 2007 again drew attention to liquidity risk. For many banks, it called into question the adequacy of their current fund transfer pricing system.

Two cases that lead to a choice of specific fund transfer prices are discussed. In the first case, the funding of the bank is limited to clients' deposits. In the second case, funding is coming from both clients' deposits and an issue of long-term bonds.

### Liquidity Risk in the Case of Exclusive Funding with Clients' Deposits

In order to be able to finance an eventual outflow of short-term deposits, the bank invests part of the funds in short-term liquid assets. To make this operational, banks apply a liquidity ratio—for example, a 90 percent liquidity ratio:

Liquidity ratio: Illiquid loans $\leq 90\%$ of liquid short-term deposits

Deposits that are not invested in loans (a minimum of 10 percent in the example) are invested in contingency liquid market securities, such as risk-free government bonds. This ensures that the bank can fund a withdrawal of 10 percent of its deposits through a sale of liquid assets. As a consequence of liquidity risk and the liquidity ratio, a bank that is experiencing a large increase in loans can suddenly run up against the liquidity constraint. That is, it cannot increase its loan book further without raising additional deposits. ALM specialists refer to this case as moving from a situation of being *liability-driven* (deposits exceed loans) to a situation of being *asset-driven* (assets exceed funding and the liquidity constraint is binding).

This is a case in which the separation theorem breaks down, and pricing decisions for loans and deposits have to be considered jointly. This can be represented graphically in Figure 10.2 (ignoring the reserve requirement for the sake of simplicity). A mathematical derivation is given in Appendix A of this chapter.

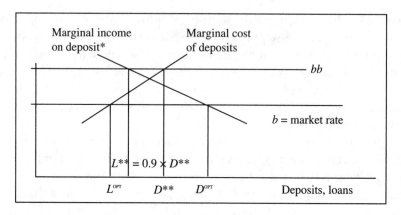

**Figure 10.2** Liquidity-constrained case.

*Marginal income on deposit is defined in Appendix A of this chapter. It is a weighted sum of the amount invested in contingency liquid bonds and the amount invested in loans.

$L^{OPT}$ and $D^{OPT}$ represent the optimal volumes of deposits and loans without the liquidity constraint. The loan volume ($L^{OPT}$) has to be reduced to $0.9 \times D^{OPT}$ because there are too few deposits ($D^{OPT}$) to meet the liquidity constraint. In this case, it is necessary to loosen the separation theorem. As, at $L = 0.9 \times D^{OPT}$, the marginal return on loans exceeds the marginal cost of deposits, there is an incentive to attract more deposits to finance profitable marginal loans. In this case of a bank facing a liquidity constraint, the optimal situation for the bank is when the marginal cost of one dollar of deposits is equal to the marginal return on this extra dollar of deposits (as discussed in Appendix A of this chapter, the marginal income from one dollar of deposits is a weighted sum of the amount invested in liquid bonds and the amount invested in additional loans). To get this result, the interbank rate can be artificially increased to $bb$ to attract a larger volume of deposits ($D^{**}$) and a reduced volume of loans ($L^{**} = 0.9 \times D^{**}$).

This will ensure the equality of the marginal cost of an extra unit of deposits and the marginal return, while meeting the liquidity ratio constraint. This is one of the ways banks can adjust the transfer price in a period of liquidity constraints. A higher fund transfer price is paid to those who collect deposits to entice them to collect more deposits. An alternative approach that banks use is to abandon the fund transfer price and allocated profit logic in setting quantitative deposit goals. That is, a bonus is paid if the branches succeed in raising the appropriate amount of deposits. A third approach is to estimate a single joint profit for the loan and deposit departments, explicitly recognizing the liquidity constraint and the impossibility of separating the deposit pricing decision from the loan pricing decision.

In the case discussed in this section, loans are funded exclusively with deposits. This would be the case in countries with poorly developed capital markets. In the second case, discussed in the next section, long-term bonds can be issued to fund the bank.

## Liquidity Risk in the Case of Funding with Clients' Deposits and the Issuance of Long-Term Bonds

In the previous example, funding was done entirely with customer deposits, and the loan portfolio was constrained to be equal to a maximum of 90 percent of the deposit base. In that case, the separation theorem breaks down. However, an alternative to funding the bank with stable retail deposits is to fund it with interbank deposits and an issue of long-term bonds. As there is a risk of a run and a deposit outflow, contingency liquid assets are funded with long-term funding (such as long-term bonds or covered bonds[7]). If there is a *reasonable* deposit outflow from retail or interbank deposits, it can be met through the sale of short-term liquid assets. A formal derivation follows.

If interbank and long-term funding are available, it might be optimal to reduce retail deposits when the marginal cost of those deposits exceeds the cost of an alternative funding mix (interbank + long-term funds). In this model, short-term deposits and interbank funding create the need for the bank to fund contingency liquid assets with long-term funding. If there is a deposit outflow, it can be met through the sale of liquid assets. The model in this case becomes

| Loans: $L$ $(l)$ | Deposits: $D$ $(d)$ |
|---|---|
| Bonds: $B$ $(b)$ | Interbank deposits: $I$ $(i)$ |
| | Long-term funding: $F$ $(f)$ |
| | Equity: $E$ $(b)$ |

The balance sheet constraint is

$$L + B = D + I + F + E$$

The contingency liquidity constraint is

$$B = (\beta \times D) + (\alpha \times I) \text{ and } B = F$$

The last constraint implies a revised balance sheet constraint:

$$L = D + I + E$$

It would be expected that the liquidity buffer ratio for deposits be smaller than the ratio for interbank deposits ($\beta < \alpha$ as interbank deposits, being more volatile, need a higher liquidity contingency) and that the cost of long term funds be larger than the return on liquid assets ($f > b$, as the liquidity premium raises the cost of longer-term funding).

$$
\begin{aligned}
\text{Economic profit} &= (l \times L + b \times B - d \times D - i \times I - f \times F) - b \times E \\
&= l \times L + b \times (\beta \times D + \alpha \times I) - d \times D \\
&\quad - i \times (L - D - E) - f \times (\beta \times D + \alpha \times I) - b \times E \\
&= l \times L + b \times (\beta \times D + \alpha \times L - \alpha \times D) - d \times D \\
&\quad - i \times (L - D) - f \times (\beta \times D + \alpha \times L - \alpha \times D) + (i - b) \times E \\
&= \{ L \times [l - I + \alpha \times (f - b)] \} \\
&\quad + \{ D \times [-d + i + (f - b) \times (\alpha - \beta)] \} + [(i - b) \times E]
\end{aligned}
$$

The result is that the separation theorem is restored. In this case, at the optimum, the marginal income on loans should equal the marginal funding cost given by the loan fund transfer price (L-FTP):

$$\text{Loan fund transfer price} = \text{L-FTP} = i + [\alpha \times (f - b)]$$

The marginal cost of funding the loan includes the interbank funding rate plus the net cost of long-term funding (the cost of long-term funds net of the return on the contingency liquid asset).

At the optimum, the marginal cost of deposits must be equal to the marginal return given by the deposit fund transfer price (D-FTP):

$$\text{Deposit fund transfer price} = \text{D-FTP} = i + [(f - b) \times (\alpha - \beta)]$$

The marginal return on deposits is equal to the interbank funding rate plus the net cost reduction resulting from a reduced contingency liquidity requirement (when $\beta < \alpha$). Notice that the transfer prices for loans and deposits are not identical anymore because the impact on the contingency liquidity requirement of an extra unit of loans and an extra unit of deposits is not identical. One extra dollar of loans demands one dollar of interbank funding plus a contingency liquid buffer. One extra dollar of deposits requires one dollar less of interbank deposits, with an impact on the contingency buffer that is a netted effect (a smaller buffer for stable retail deposits and a larger buffer for volatile interbank deposits). The buffer effect is zero when $\alpha = \beta$. The loan fund transfer price L-FTP is larger than the deposit fund transfer price D-FTP:

$$\text{L-FTP} = i + \alpha(f - b) > \text{D-FTP} = i + (f - b)(\alpha - \beta)$$

if $b < f$ and $\beta < \alpha$.

In the case of mix funding, with clients' deposits, interbank funding, and the issuing of long-term bonds, the separation theorem is restored, with the fund transfer price becoming a mix of interbank funding and the cost of the liquidity buffer, which includes the liquidity premium on long-term funding.

The discussion of liquidity risk and joint maximization has been presented in the context of the Klein-Monti microeconomic model. In practice, the problem is handled in the following way: The people granting loans and accepting deposits are given the market rates for different maturities. They then choose the best mix of loans and deposits so as to maximize profit. If there are no liquidity constraints, this is the end of the process. If the risk manager observes a liquidity risk that cannot be handled in a simple, cost-efficient manner, the issue is passed to the Asset and liability committee (ALCO) of the bank. This senior committee usually includes the chief executive officer (CEO); the chief financial officer (CFO); the chief risk officer (CRO); the heads of businesses, such as the heads of retail banking, treasury, and corporate banking; the head of accounting and control; and the chief economist. Jointly, the ALCO decides how to solve the liquidity problem: by reducing the loan portfolio, by raising more deposits, or by raising more expensive long-term funds. From an operational perspective, as discussed earlier, the targets for deposits and loans can be achieved either by adjusting the fund transfer price, by abandoning the transfer price logic and simply setting targets for volumes of loans and deposits, or by maximizing the profit on loans and deposits jointly.

Cases of liquidity constraints are to be found not only in emerging (transition) countries that are facing a large growth in their loan portfolios, but also in countries in which the deposit base of banks has been eroded by competing financial products, such as money market funds, mutual funds, or pension funds.

In summary, *joint maximization* of economic profit on loans and deposits will be the rule whenever an increase in loans (deposits) has an impact on the profit on deposits (loans). Joint maximization means that it is necessary to search for the appropriate combination of deposits and loans that creates the highest economic profit for the bank. In this case, it is necessary to abandon the simple interbank transfer price and the matched-maturity marginal value of funds (MMMVF), and decentralization into separate value centers disappears. But as was shown earlier, the availability of long-term funding can restore the separation theorem, albeit in a modified form.

### Advanced FTP 2: Credit-Risk-Adjusted MMMVF

When a matched-maturity market rate is being used as the transfer price, there could be an apparent paradox. An A-rated bank would never lend to a AAA-rated client because the return on the AAA-rated asset would probably be less than the bank's cost of funds, the A-rated matched-maturity market rate. According to this argument, holding a AAA-rated asset would lead to a loss. This is a paradox, as it would seem intuitively that banks should be able to hold safe assets. This paradox can be solved in two ways.

The first is to recognize that investing in a AAA-rated asset should reduce the average risk of the bank's asset portfolio and therefore reduce the average cost of funding the bank on the interbank market. The marginal cost of funding the AAA loan therefore has two parts: the funding cost of the loan and the reduction in the overall cost of the debt as a result of the risk reduction.[8] And, when the bank wants to keep its rating and its cost of funds constant, an investment in a safe asset should lead to a reduction of equity funding.

A complementary and alternative line of reasoning, which the author prefers, follows.

The logic of the matched-maturity interbank rate and the Klein-Monti separation theorem is very much a profit and loss account logic. You increase the loan portfolio and fund it on the interbank market. The margin is computed as the difference between the revenue from the loan and the cost of funds on the interbank market. An alternative and better logic would be to focus on *value creation*. The bank fundamental valuation formula indicates that the capital markets would discount a AAA-rated loan at the opportunity return available on AAA corporate bonds. It shows explicitly that the franchise value of loans is the difference between the return on the loan and a risk-adjusted return available on the corporate bond market.

As a reminder of the discussion in Chapter 6, the fundamental bank valuation formula shows that the franchise value of loans is calculated vis-à-vis a risk-adjusted rate ($b^{**}$).

Market value of equity$_0$

$$= [L_0^{\circ} + B_0^{\circ} - D_0^{\circ}]$$

$$+ \frac{(1-t)\times(b_1^{\circ} - d_1^{\circ\circ})\times D_1^{\circ}}{(1+b_1^{\circ\circ})} + \frac{(1-t)\times(b_2^{\circ} - d_2^{\circ\circ})\times D_2^{\circ}}{(1+b_1^{\circ\circ})\times(1+b_2^{\circ\circ})} + \cdots$$

$$+ \frac{(1-t)\times(l_1^{\circ} - b_1^{\circ\circ})\times L_1^{\circ}}{(1+b_1^{\circ\circ})} + \frac{(1-t)\times(l_2^{\circ} - b_2^{\circ\circ})\times L_2^{\circ}}{(1+b_1^{\circ\circ})\times(1+b_2^{\circ\circ})} + \cdots$$

$$- \frac{(1-t)\times \text{operating expenses}_1}{(1+b_1^{\circ\circ})} - \frac{(1-t)\times \text{operating expenses}_2}{(1+b_1^{\circ\circ})\times(1+b_2^{\circ\circ})} - \cdots$$

$$- \frac{t\times b_1^{\circ\circ}\times(L_1^{\circ} + B_1^{\circ} - D_1^{\circ})}{(1+b_1^{\circ\circ})} - \frac{t\times b_2^{\circ\circ}\times(L_2^{\circ} + B_2^{\circ} - D_2^{\circ})}{(1+b_1^{\circ\circ})\times(1+b_2^{\circ\circ})} - \cdots$$

Therefore, it is suggested that an *advanced* fund transfer pricing methodology be used to move from a P&L to a valuation perspective. To evaluate the profit on a new loan, its impact on the value of equity would be measured. A credit-risk-adjusted transfer price would be used to evaluate the franchise, that is, the return available on a AAA corporate bond, and the tax penalty originating from the funding structure of the loan would be added separately.

For example, consider a very safe (AAA-equivalent) loan of $100 yielding an expected return of 5.5 percent. The cost of the A-rated interbank debt of the bank is 5.6 percent. The expected return on AAA-rated corporate bonds is 5 percent, and the tax rate is 40 percent. The AAA-rated loan is funded with $2 of equity and $98 of interbank debt. The overall cost of equity is 10 percent.

If the overall cost of debt and the overall cost of equity are used, the *standard* economic profit would be measured as follows:

$$\begin{aligned}
\text{Standard economic profit} &= \text{profit} - \text{cost of equity} \\
&= (1 - 0.4) \times (5.5\% \times 100 - \\
&\quad 5.6\% \times 98) - (10\% \times 2) \\
&= -0.1928.
\end{aligned}$$

Since the economic profit is negative, the loan should not be accepted.

In this example, the standard economic profit would underestimate the value created by the safe loan because it would charge too high an average cost of interbank debt and equity. There are two flaws in this approach. The first and more significant one is that it fails to recognize that taking a AAA safe asset (partly funded with equity) reduces the overall risk of the bank's debt. The marginal cost of debt funding should be less than 5.2 percent.[9]

The second flaw is that the overall cost of equity of 10 percent does not recognize the specific risk of the loan. If a bank is not careful, it can lead itself into a vicious cycle, avoiding safe loans and funding risky loans that lead, later, to a further downgrade. The *advanced* economic profit approach allows a response to these two flaws.

$$
\begin{aligned}
\textit{Advanced} \text{ economic profit on loan} &= \text{franchise profit} - \text{tax penalty} \\
&= (1 - 0.4) \times (5.5\% - 5\%) \times 100 \\
&\quad - 0.4 \times 5\% \, (100 - 98) \\
&= 0.26
\end{aligned}
$$

The advanced approach[10] focuses directly on the impact of the new loan (with its specific risk) on the market value of equity. Since the economic profit is positive, the loan should be accepted.

The advanced economic profit formula can be rewritten as follows:

$$
\begin{aligned}
\textit{Advanced} \text{ economic profit on loan} &= (1 - 0.4) \times (5.5\% - 5\%) \times 100 \\
&\quad - 0.4 \times 5\% \, (100 - 98) \\
&= [(1 - 0.4) \times 5.5\% \times 100 - 5\% \times 100] \\
&\quad + (0.4 \times 5\% \times 98) \\
&= 0.26 \\
&= \text{unlevered economic profit} + \text{tax} \\
&\quad \text{shield on debt}
\end{aligned}
$$

The advanced economic profit is equal to the economic profit on an unlevered (100 percent equity financed) loan plus the tax benefit of the interest tax shield on debt.[11]

The advanced approach ignores the overall cost of debt and the overall cost of equity, but rather focuses on the marginal/incremental risk-adjusted specific opportunity rate.

As discussed in Chapter 6, the lack of empirical evidence on the risk premium on the corporate bond market explains why banks often use a single transfer price, the interbank rate. But as corporate bonds, asset-backed securities, and credit derivatives become increasingly an asset class, much more available information on the risk premium demanded in return for bearing credit risk can be expected to be available in the coming years.[12]

Note that in the case of the funding of a AAA-rated loan by an A-rated bank and in the case where the overall cost of bank debt is reduced because of lower risk, the reported net income of the bank could still be reduced. But this does not imply that the value of equity would fall if the funding of a AAA-rated loan reduces the overall riskiness of the bank and the risk-adjusted discount rate to value less risky dividends. It could be argued that financial markets are not that well informed, with the result that the risk premium will not adjust. In this case of *imperfect* capital markets that cannot recognize and price the correct risk, the bank would be advised to sell and securitize the safe asset to focus the attention of the market on the safety of the asset, justifying a lower discount rate.[13]

In summary, the advanced fund transfer pricing approach, which recognizes the specific credit risk of an asset, can be dealt with in two ways. The first is based on the bank valuation model and the franchise value, which recognizes the opportunity rate as being the expected return on corporate bonds with similar risk. A second approach, consistent with standard corporate finance and the weighted average cost of capital discussed in Chapter 8, is to assume that the loan is funded with both debt and equity. The risk-specific cost of debt and equity that applies to the loan must be used, and an adequate debt/equity mix for marginal funding must be chosen. The latter approach is not easy to implement in banking because, as discussed in the valuation model, it is not easy to identify a risk-adjusted rate for the equity used to finance a loan. Appendix B in this chapter shows the equivalence between using the expected rate on a corporate bond as a transfer price and using an interbank cost of debt with a specific risk-adjusted cost of equity.

### Advanced FTP 3: Effective Maturity vs. Contractual Maturity[14]

The previous discussion emphasized the use of a matched-maturity transfer price. However, for some products with undefined maturities, such as demand or savings deposits, the choice of a transfer price becomes problematic. Contractually, these deposits are short term because the depositor has the right to withdraw them on demand. In reality, they have a longer-term maturity, because many of these deposits are fairly stable. In countries with very low short-term rates and an upward-sloping curve, the choice of a relevant maturity for the fund transfer price is crucial. A low short-term rate would kill the profit on deposits, while a higher long-term rate would make them profitable.

In practice, banks analyze the historical behavior of deposit balances and divide the pool of deposits into short-term deposits (those that are likely to fluctuate in the short run) and permanent deposits (*core* deposits that are likely to stay in the bank permanently). A short-term market rate is used to reward the first pool, and a long-term rate is used to reward the second pool. This approach is useful, but a bit ad hoc. A multiperiod model of banking is needed to identify the correct transfer price.

There are two reasons justifying the need for a multiperiod model. First, consider the case where the supply of deposits is a lagged function of past deposit rates. This is likely to be the situation in the retail sector, in which customers, facing switching costs, will display some form of loyalty. This creates a lag in the deposit supply function. The volume of deposits tomorrow is related to what it is today. The second reason for dynamic consideration is that, for marketing reasons, it can be costly to adjust the deposit rate continuously. This is referred to as deposit-rate rigidity or "stickiness."[15] The choice of a deposit rate today will affect the volume of deposits both today and tomorrow. In both cases, it is necessary to model dynamic, multiperiod implications. A complete discussion of deposit pricing in a multiperiod setting is given in Chapter 11. In this chapter, the fund transfer price that will send a correct signal to branch managers, consistent with multiperiod optimization, is discussed.

Consider a two-period model, with $b_1$ being the bond rate in Year 1 and $b_2$ the forward rate in Year 2.

Year 1    Year 2
$b_1 = 3\%$   $b_2 = 5\%$

The intuition behind our fund transfer proposal is based on the fact that collecting one extra dollar of deposits in Year 1 will lead to $\alpha \times 1$ dollar of deposits in Year 2 (where $\alpha$, a *persistence* factor, represents the derivative, that is, the change of deposits in Year 2 resulting from one dollar of deposits collected in Year 1). In this example, the market rate is low in the first year, but higher in the second year. Attracting one dollar of deposits today could be profitable if the margin increases next year.

In a multiperiod setting, a correct evaluation of the profitability of a value center must take into account the profit over two years to incorporate the dynamic consideration. Intuitively, the proposal for the fund transfer price to be used to evaluate profit over two years will involve an average of the one-year rate and the two-year rate, weighted by the magnitude of the persistence factor $\alpha$. If the persistence factor is equal to 1 (that is, if one dollar of deposits today implies one dollar of deposits tomorrow), the fund transfer price to be used over a two-year period will be the two-year fixed-coupon bond rate.

A formal discussion follows. The lagged supply of deposit case is analyzed, i.e., $D_2 = D_2(d_2, d_1)$. In this case, the maximization of the present value of profit on deposits over two periods becomes

$$\text{Maximum present value of profits} = (b_1 - d_1) \times D(d_1) + \frac{(b_2 - d_2) \times D(d_1, d_2)}{1 + b_2}$$

The present value of the marginal profit over two years of collecting one extra dollar of deposits today is[16]

$$
\begin{aligned}
\text{Marginal profit} &= (b_1 - d_1) + \frac{(b_2 - d_2) \times \dfrac{\partial D_2}{\partial D_1}}{1 + b_2} \\[2em]
&= \left( b_1 + \frac{b_2 \times \dfrac{\partial D_2}{\partial D_1}}{1 + b_2} \right) - \left( d_1 + \frac{d_2 \times \dfrac{\partial D_2}{\partial D_1}}{1 + b_2} \right) \\[2em]
&= \left( b_1 + \frac{b_2 \times \alpha}{1 + b_2} \right) - \left( d_1 + \frac{d_2 \times \alpha}{1 + b_2} \right)
\end{aligned}
$$

with $\alpha = \text{persistence factor} = \dfrac{\partial D_2}{\partial D_1}$

The first term is the present value of the marginal revenue over two years on one dollar of deposits collected today, while the second term is the present value of the funding cost over two years. As the fund transfer price represents the marginal revenue on deposits, a two-period fund transfer price should be used in a multiperiod setting:

Fund transfer price FTP = marginal revenue over 2 years

$$= b_1 + \frac{b_2 \times \alpha}{1 + b_2} = b_1 + \frac{b_2}{1 + b_2} - \frac{(1 - \alpha)b_2}{1 + b_2}$$

$$= c + \frac{c}{1 + b_2} - \frac{(1 - \alpha)b_2}{1 + b_2}$$

where $(1 - \alpha)$ is a decay factor, the part of the original deposit that is lost, and $c$ is a fixed coupon on a two-year bond (see the proof in Appendix C of this chapter).

If the derivative $\partial D2 / \partial D1 \; 5 \; a \; 5 \; 1$, the result is

Fund transfer price = marginal revenue over 2 years

$$= b_1 + \frac{b_2 \times \alpha}{1 + b_2} = b_1 + \frac{b_2}{1 + b_2} = c + \frac{c}{1 + b_2}$$

with $c$ = fixed coupon on 2-year bond

So, the adjusted transfer price would take into account the marginal return over two periods, the return on a one-year investment rolled over for two years, which is identical to a fixed coupon, $c$, on a two-year bond. It can be seen that the use of a two-year coupon bond rate as a two-year transfer price is warranted in the case in which the dollar of deposits behaves like a fixed deposit with a fixed amount and a fixed deposit rate.

Chapter 11 presents optimal deposit pricing in a multiperiod environment. Anticipating that chapter, it should be made clear that single-period profit maximization will in many cases be suboptimal as compared to multiperiod optimization. So a correct evaluation of a value center that sends a signal compatible with multiperiod maximization is to evaluate performance over a two-period basis. As discussed in Chapter 11, it is only in special cases that single-period optimization will be optimal.

When a multiperiod setting applies, such as in the case of rigid deposit rates or a lagged supply of deposits resulting from customers' loyalty, it is necessary to ensure that the profit allocated to a value center over a short period does not lead to myopic maximization behavior that is incompatible with correct maximization over a multiperiod horizon.

In practice, measuring performance over a short horizon, say one year, is preferred. To entice the deposit manager to raise the appropriate amount of funds, the transfer price could again be manipulated (incorporating the benefit in future periods arising out of the *persistence* factor) to ensure that an adequate amount of funds is raised.

## CONCLUSION

Fund transfer pricing for loans and deposits has been developed to send the right signal to those in charge of collecting deposits and granting loans. In many countries, it has been based on the matched-maturity marginal value of funds (MMMVF), such as the interbank rate or bond rate. ALM software often includes the market rate as a transfer price for deposits and loans. This chapter has argued that the liquidity risk observed recently around the world, the need to incorporate a credit risk premium, and the need to take the effective maturity of deposits into account call for the use of an advanced fund transfer price system.

## APPENDIX A: LIQUIDITY CONSTRAINT AND JOINT PROFIT MAXIMIZATION

This appendix analyzes fund transfer pricing and optimization when the liquidity requirement is binding. A specific case is analyzed: that in which funding is limited to client deposits. A second case, with long-term funding available, is discussed in the chapter.

Mathematically, denoting the deposit supply and loan demand functions by $D(d)$ and $L(l)$, and the interest rates on deposits and loans by $d$ and $l$, the result is

$$\text{Net income} = l \times L + b \times B - d \times D$$

with constraints

$$L + B = D \text{ and } L < 0.9 \times D$$

When the liquidity constraint is binding $(L = 0.9\,D)$, the result is

$$\text{Net income} = l \times 0.9D + b \times 0.1D - d \times D$$

The first condition to optimize profit is equal to

$$\frac{\partial \text{ Net income}}{\partial D} = l \times 0.9 + 0.9 \times D \times \frac{\partial l}{\partial L} \times \frac{\partial L}{\partial D} + 0.1 \times b - d - D \times \frac{\partial d}{\partial D} = 0$$

$$= l \times 0.9 + L \frac{\partial l}{\partial L} \times 0.9 \times \frac{l}{l} + 0.1 \times b - dD \frac{\partial d}{\partial D} \times \frac{d}{d} = 0$$

$$\rightarrow 0.9 \times l \times (1 + \varepsilon_L^{-1}) + 0.1 \times b = d \times (1 + \varepsilon_D^{-1})$$

$$\rightarrow \text{marginal income} = \text{marginal cost}$$

with $\varepsilon_L$ = elasticity of loans and $\varepsilon_D$ = elasticity of deposits

It can be seen that, in the case of liquidity constraints, the separation is lost and that, at the optimum, the marginal cost of one dollar of deposits is equal to the marginal income on one dollar of deposits, a mix of investment in loans and in the liquid bond asset. A complete discussion of deposit pricing, marginal income, and price elasticity is available in Chapter 11.

## APPENDIX B: THE ADVANCED FUND TRANSFER PRICE: EQUIVALENCE BETWEEN USING THE RISK-ADJUSTED OPPORTUNITY RETURN ON THE CORPORATE BOND MARKET AND THE INTERBANK COST OF DEBT WITH A RISK-SPECIFIC COST OF EQUITY

In this chapter, it was recommended that the matched-maturity market rate (the interbank rate for short maturities and the swaps rates for long maturities) be used to evaluate the margin on deposits and loans. This is the widely used market practice, which focuses on the P&L account. However, in the fundamental bank valuation model, it was shown that the franchise value was calculated with respect to the risk-adjusted expected return on (similar-risk) corporate bonds, $b^{**}$. Can these two approaches, the P&L-based approach and the value-based approach, be reconciled?

For ease of presentation, $L$ refers to a perpetual loan. Here is the balance sheet:

| Loan $L$ $(l)$ | Interbank debt |
| | Equity $E$ (cost of equity $= R_s$) |

Book value = current value. The expected return on (similar-risk) corporate bonds is $b^{**}$.

### Foundation FTP Approach

$$\text{Market value of equity} = \frac{\text{dividend}}{R_S} = \frac{(1-t)\times(lL - iI)}{R_S}$$

$$\text{Value creation} = \text{MVE} = \frac{(1-t)\times(lL - iI) - R_S E}{R_S} \quad (1)$$

Perpetual profit = perpetual dividend = $(1 - t) \times (l \times L - i \times I)$

- To maximize value creation (market value of equity, MVE), you should maximize $(1 - t) \times (l \times L - i \times I) - R_s \times E$ = economic profit = EP.
- Use the interbank rate as a transfer price and $R_s$, the bond rate + an equity risk premium, as the cost of equity, which should be adjusted for the risk of the loan and leverage. This approach is equivalent to the use of the weighted average cost of capital (WACC), used extensively in corporate finance. As discussed in Chapter 6, it is not obvious how to estimate the equity risk premium specific to a particular loan.

### Advanced FTP Approach Consistent with the Fundamental Bank Valuation Model

The fundamental bank valuation model implies

$$\text{MV} = \text{liquidation value} + \text{franchise value} - \text{tax penalty}$$

$$\text{Market value of equity} = L - I + \frac{(1-t)(l - b^{**})L}{b^{**}} - \left[\frac{t\times b^{**} \times L}{b^{**}} + \frac{-t\times i\times I}{i}\right]$$

$$\text{MVE} = \frac{(1-t)\times(l - b^{**})\times L}{b^{**}} - \left[\frac{t\times b^{**}\times L}{b^{**}} + \frac{-t\times i\times I}{i}\right] \quad (2)$$

To maximize value creation (market value of equity, MVE), you should maximize

$$(1 - t) \times (1 \times L - i \times I) - R_s \times E = \text{economic profit (EP)}$$

The first term is the profit on the loan evaluated against the expected return on a similar-risk corporate bond. The second term is the Modigliani-Miller tax penalty (shield) for loans and debt. This can be expressed in an alternative form:

$$[(1 - t) \times (l \times L) - b^{**} \times L] + (t \times b^{**} \times I)]$$

This approach is equivalent to the APV (adjusted present value) approach in corporate finance, in which the assets are valued at the unlevered cost of capital (100 percent equity financed) and in which the value of a tax shield from the use of debt is calculated. Unlike the risk premium on equity needed for the foundation approach, it should be possible to find a risk premium for the expected return on (similar-risk) corporate bonds.[17]

## APPENDIX C: FORWARD-RATE ROLLOVER VS. COUPON ROLLOVER

This appendix shows that the present value of one-year forward rates over two years is equivalent to the present value of a fixed two-year coupon received over two years.

Given that $b_1$ is the one-year rate, $b_2$ is the forward rate to be observed next year, and $c$ is the coupon on a two-year fixed-rate bond, in equilibrium, investing in a one-year strategy with rollover yields the same return as investing in a two-year coupon bond:

$$(1 + b_1) \times (1 + b_2) = c \times (1 + b_2) + c + 1$$
$$1 + b_1 + b_2 + b_1 \times b_2 = c + c \times b_2 + c + 1$$
$$b_1 \times (1 + b_2) + b_2 = c \times (1 + b_2) + c$$
$$b_1 + b_2/1 + b_2 = c + c/1 + b_2$$

The present value of one-year forward rates over two years is equivalent to the present value of a fixed two-year coupon received over two years.

## EXERCISES FOR CHAPTER 10

1. The following is the balance sheet for a branch. Taking into account that the reserve requirement of the Central Bank is 10 percent (with no revenue paid on these reserves), calculate

the net interest margin on deposits, the net interest margin on loans, and the total net interest margin earned by that branch. The *foundation* approach should be used to evaluate the interest margins.

| Assets | Liabilities |
|---|---|
| Reserves (@10%): 30 | Deposits (one year, rate = 1.7%): 100 |
| Loans (three years, rate = 6%): 200 | Deposits (two years, rate = 2.15%): 200 |
| Loans (five years, rate = 8%): 300 | |

The interbank curve is as follows:

6-month-rate: 2%

1-year rate: 3%

2-year rate: 3.5%

3-year rate: 4%

4-year rate: 4.5%

5-year rate: 5%

2. On March 12, 2006, Capital One, the fourth-largest credit card issuer in the United States, bought North Fork, a New York bank, for $14.6 billion. It wanted North Fork for one main reason: to give Capital One a source of cheap and stable deposits. The bank justified the premium paid for the acquisition by the value of the synergy created between the credit card loans and the cheap and stable deposit base. Do you agree with this argument?

3. An A-rated bank has a cost of interbank funding of 5.6 percent and a cost of equity of 10 percent:

| Assets | Deposits |
|---|---|
| | Interbank (A-rated, 5.6%) |
| | Equity (cost of equity, 10%) |

It considers financing a AAA-type loan of $300, to be funded with $6 of equity and $294 of interbank debt. The expected return on this new asset is 5.5 percent. The corporate tax rate is 40 percent, and the expected opportunity return on AAA-rated bonds is 5 percent.

The bank's finance department recommends turning down the loan, as the economic profit (EP) on this new transaction is negative:

$$EP = \text{profit} - \text{cost of allocated equity}$$
$$= [(1-0.4) \times (5.5\% \times 300 - 5.6\% \times 294)] -$$
$$(10\% \times 6) = -0.579$$

What is your opinion? Should the bank finance the loan? Why or why not?

4. Consider a risky (BB-equivalent) loan of $100 yielding an expected return of 6.5 percent. The cost of the AA-rated interbank debt of the bank is 5.2 percent. The expected return on BB-rated corporate bonds is 5.7 percent, and the tax rate is 40 percent. The loan is funded with $8 of equity and $92 of interbank debt. The equity of $8 is chosen to keep the AA rating of the bank. The overall cost of equity is 10 percent. Using advanced fund transfer pricing, evaluate the economic profit on this loan.

## Notes

1. Klein (1971) and Monti (1972).
2. With reference to the valuation model of Chapters 5 and 6, the current bond rate is denoted here as $b$ (and not $b^*$) for simplicity of exposition.
3. A complete discussion of interest-rate risk is available in Chapters 18 and 19.
4. The focus has been on maturity mismatch. A similar reasoning applies to currency mismatch.
5. Complete coverage of the measurement of liquidity risk is provided in Chapter 21.
6. The U.S. subprime crisis is discussed in Chapters 15, 16, and 21.
7. Covered bonds (bonds collateralized by specific assets) are discussed in Chapter 16.
8. Note that this reasoning assumes that the bank's debt is short term. If the bank's debt is long term, the cost of existing debt is fixed and taking a safe asset onboard will result in a wealth transfer to the debt holders of the bank (this is known as the *debt overhang* effect). Debt holders benefit because they keep the fixed coupon rate, while funding a less risky bank.
9. An alternative example would have been to keep the risk and overall cost of bank debt constant. Investing in a AAA-rated asset would reduce the risk of debt in the first stage. To keep the risk constant, it would be necessary, in a second stage, to reduce equity funding. Logically, the marginal funding of the AAA-rated asset, while keeping the overall cost of debt constant, would demand negative equity funding. The author

has never met a bank yet that uses negative equity funding in computing the cost of funds of a very safe asset. Note that the bias is most likely
to occur in the case of a very safe asset. If a bank invests in a risky asset
(risky relative to the rating of its debt), most banks correctly increase
the economic capital allocation to keep the risk of their debt constant.

10. There is a slight approximation in the tax penalty. Given the equity
cushion of \$2, the expected marginal cost of debt funding should be
slightly less than the expected return on the AAA-rated asset, 5 percent
(Merton, 1974; Cooper and Davydenko, 2007). The cost of debt of
debt should be $5\% - \mu$, $\mu$ denoting a very small percentage figure,
and the *advanced* economic profit on the loan is equal to

$$(1 - 0.4) \times (5.5\% - 5\%) \times 100 - 0.4 \times (5\% \times 100)$$
$$+ 0.4 \times (5\% - \varepsilon) \times 98$$

11. With reference to the previous note, the tax shield on debt should be
slightly smaller, as the cost of debt should be less than the return on
assets of 5 percent. As stated in Chapter 6, this result is fully consistent
with the adjusted present value (APV) approach used in corporate
finance to evaluate investment projects. It first evaluates projects as if
they were unlevered, adding back the benefits of the debt interest tax
shield separately [Brealey et al. (2006)].

12. The risk premium on corporate bonds is discussed in Chapter 6.

13. Securitization is discussed in Chapter 16.

14. This section, being a bit more technical, can be skipped without a loss
of continuity.

15. Rate stickiness is discussed in the context of deposit pricing in
Chapter 11. A similar reasoning applies in the case of other products
with rigid pricing, such as credit card loans [Ausubel (1991)].

16. Note that for simplicity, the relation ignores the change in the deposit
rate needed to collect the extra dollar of deposits. The complete
mathematics of deposit pricing in a multiperiod setting is given in
Chapter 11.

17. Note that since the first equation must be equal to the second, it
would be possible to compute a cost of equity $R_s$ that is compatible
with the risk-adjusted return on corporate bonds $b^{**}$.

# Deposit Pricing and Repurchase Agreements

The separation theorem discussed in Chapter 10 allows the separation of the deposit and loan pricing decisions. Each one must be evaluated based on the interbank market rate. This is convenient, as it allows bank managerial issues to be discussed one after the other. In this chapter, several tools that are useful for deposit pricing are covered first. Next, an alternative source of funds, the repurchase agreement (repo) market, is introduced. A discussion of loan pricing and loan-loss provisions will follow in subsequent chapters.

## DEPOSIT PRICING, FROM GRAPHIC EXPOSITION TO ELASTICITY-BASED PRICING

The separation theorem states that the optimal volume of deposits will be such that the incremental cost is equal to the exogenous market rate $b$.

The incremental or marginal cost (see Figure 11.1) represents the cost of raising an extra unit of deposits. It is upward-sloping. There are several explanations for this. For example, the bank may need to open new, expensive branches in remote areas of the country in order to attract more deposits. Or, in the context of deposit pricing, it may need to raise the deposit rate further to attract new investors. In the Figure 11.1, the optimal volume of deposits, $D^{OPT}$, is at the point where the marginal cost of deposits is equal to the exogenous market rate $b$. There is no reason to raise more deposits than this, as the incremental cost would be higher than the funding rate available in the interbank market. And there is no reason to raise fewer deposits, as the marginal cost would be less than the market rate at which the money can be invested.

Incremental cost of deposits = interbank rate $b$

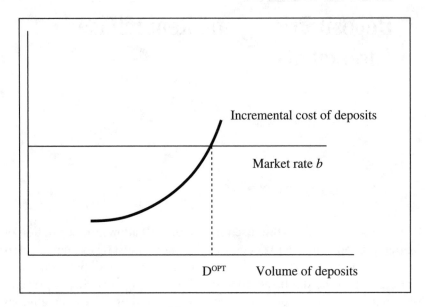

**Figure 11.1**  Microeconomics of deposit pricing.

This result can be made operational by computing an explicit mathematical relation for the incremental cost of deposits. In the first step, the reserve requirement with central banks and any operational expenses are ignored. They will then be introduced.

### Elasticity-Based Pricing

Consider that the amount of deposits $D$ supplied to the bank is positively related to the deposit rate offered by the bank, $D(d^+)$. To increase the volume of deposits by one dollar, the deposit rate will be increased slightly.[1]

Intuitively, the incremental cost of raising one extra dollar of deposits has two parts: the cost of the extra dollar $(d \times 1)$ and the additional cost for the existing deposits resulting from an increase in the deposit rate $[D \times (\Delta^+ d / \Delta^+ D)]$. It can be shown (proof in Appendix A of this chapter) that the incremental cost of raising one extra dollar is given by a very simple expression, with $\varepsilon$ representing the deposit supply price elasticity:

$$\text{Incremental cost} = d \times (1 + \varepsilon^{-1})$$

Price elasticity in economics represents, by definition, the ratio of the percentage increase in volume to a percentage increase in price. In the context of deposits, it gives the ratio of the percentage increase in volume to a percentage increase in the deposit rate:

$$\text{Elasticity} = \frac{\Delta D/_D}{\Delta d/_d} = \frac{\text{percentage increase in volume of deposits}}{\text{percentage increase in deposit rate}}$$

For example, if the deposit volume is expected to increase from $100 to $115 when the deposit rate increases from 10 percent to 11 percent, the elasticity would be calculated as follows:

$$\text{Elasticity} = \frac{\Delta D/_D}{\Delta d/_d} = \frac{15/_{100}}{0.01/_{0.10}} = \frac{15\%}{10\%} = 1.5$$

In this example, an elasticity of 1.5 indicates that the volume of deposits increases by 15 percent for a relative increase in the deposit rate of 10 percent.[2]

So, the golden rule for deposit pricing states:

Incremental cost of deposits = incremental return[3]

$$d \times (1 + \varepsilon^{-1}) = b$$

Rearranging the terms gives a mathematical expression for the optimal deposit rate:

$$d^{\text{optimal}} = b \times \frac{1}{\left(1 + \dfrac{1}{\varepsilon}\right)}$$

For example, with an elasticity of 1, the deposit pricing rule is

$$d^{\text{optimal}} = b \times \frac{1}{\left(1 + \dfrac{1}{\varepsilon}\right)} = b \times \frac{1}{1 + \dfrac{1}{1}} = b \times \frac{1}{2} = b \times 0.5$$

In this case, the deposit rate is equal to 50 percent of the market rate. This implies that an increase in the market rate of 1 percent will lead to an increase in the deposit rate of 0.5 percent. Quite remarkably, this relationship has been observed empirically in many countries. A study at the European Central Bank on the *pass-through* effect—that is, the impact of a market-rate increase on retail deposit rates—has observed a 50 percent pass-through for demand and savings deposits, a quite stable relationship over time.[4] A pass-through of 0.5 is consistent with a deposit volume elasticity of 1.

## Deposit Pricing with Reserve Requirement and Operational Expenses

Next, the corporate tax rate $t$, reserve requirements with central banks $R$ (yielding no revenue, $R = r \times D$), and variable operating expenses (OE%) as a percentage of deposits are introduced. The balance sheet is as follows, with $r$ designing the reserve requirement[5]:

| Reserves $R = r \times D$ | Deposits $D$ |
|---|---|
| Market assets $B = (1 - r) \times D$ | |
| (Bonds, interbank) | |

At the optimum level,

After-tax marginal cost of deposits = after-tax marginal return
$$(1 - t)[d \times (1 + \varepsilon^{-1}) + 0E\%] = (1 - t)[b \times (1 - r)]$$

The marginal cost is increased by the existence of variable operating expenses. In the presence of a reserve requirement, the part of the dollar of deposits that is available for investment is $1 \times (1 - r)$. It can be seen that the corporate tax factor cancels out, as it affects both the marginal cost and the marginal return.

Rearranging the terms gives a deposit pricing rule:

$$d^{optimal} = [b \times (1 - R) - OE\%] \times \frac{1}{\left(1 + \dfrac{1}{\varepsilon}\right)}$$

The pricing rule requires four pieces of information: the matched-maturity market rate, the reserve requirement, the percentage operating expenses, and the price elasticity. The last of these is definitely the hardest one to estimate. This is discussed next.

### Estimating Deposit Volume Elasticity

Leaving aside the use of a crystal ball, three methods can be used to estimate elasticity:

1. Historical statistical regression
2. Interviews with branch managers
3. Backing out implicit elasticity

#### Historical Regression
The first approach is to rely on historical regression. Collecting historical data on volume of deposits, GNP, the deposit rate offered by the bank,

deposit rates offered by competitors, the rates offered on competing products, the level of marketing expenses, and the number of branches, the following relation for the volume of deposits observed at time $t$, $D_t$, can be postulated as

$$D_t = D_t(\text{constant, GNP}_t, d_{\text{own bank } t}, d_{\text{competitor } t}, r_{\text{competitive product } t}, \text{marketing expenses}_t, \text{number of branches}_t)$$

A convenient functional form is a multiplicative one:

$$\text{Volume of deposits} = D_t = \text{constant} \times \text{GNP}^{\alpha_0} \times d_{\text{own rate}}{}^{\alpha_1} \times d_{\text{competitor } t}{}^{\alpha_2}$$
$$\times b_{\text{competitive product } t}{}^{\alpha_3} \times \text{marketing expenses}_t{}^{\alpha_4}$$
$$\times \text{number of branches}_t{}^{\alpha_5}$$

A regression package allows the use of historical data to estimate the regression coefficients $\alpha_i$. The main advantage of the multiplicative form is that the regression coefficients $\alpha$ are precisely the elasticity parameter (proof in Appendix B of this chapter).

On the retail market, market shares are notoriously sluggish. It takes some time for a deposit-rate increase to produce its full effect. It is thus necessary to distinguish between short-term and long-term price elasticity. The functional form used for the deposit volume is therefore

$$\text{Volume of deposits} = D_t = \text{constant} \times \text{GNP}^{\alpha_0} \times d_{\text{own rate } t}{}^{\alpha_1} \times d_{\text{competitor } t}{}^{\alpha_2}$$
$$\times b_{\text{competitive product } t}{}^{\alpha_3} \times \text{marketing expenses}_t{}^{\alpha_4}$$
$$\times \text{number of branches}_t{}^{\alpha_5} \times D_{t-1}{}^{\alpha_6}$$

The short-term elasticity is the parameter $\alpha_1$, and the long-term elasticity, when all lag effects have taken place, is $\alpha_1/(1 - \alpha_6)$.

## Interviews with Branch Managers

Two disadvantages of the regression approach are the difficulty of identifying all relevant variables and the implicit assumption that the relationship is stable over time. A more forward-looking approach is to interview branch managers who have a very deep knowledge of their clients. Ask the question: if the bank increases the deposit rate, what will be the impact on volumes of deposits? Although very qualitative, this approach should not be dismissed, as there is a wealth of knowledge in bank branches.

## Backing Out Implicit Elasticities

The third approach starts with observing the deposit rate currently offered by the bank. The deposit pricing formula given earlier can then be used to back out the *implicit elasticity* used by the bank. This starts a discussion as to whether the "backed-out" elasticity is a reasonable figure, in line with expectations and regression estimates.

## Pricing Deposits with Undefined Maturities[6]

In the previous discussion, the relevant maturity for the marginal return is the maturity of the deposit product. A two-year deposit should be priced against the two-year matched-maturity rate. In the discussion of the fund transfer price, the case of demand deposits, for which the *contractual* maturity (very short, as they are withdrawable on demand) was very different from the effective *economic* maturity, was mentioned. More precisely, dynamic considerations had to be taken into account to reflect the impact of the current volume of deposits on future volumes and interest margins. Pricing decisions must take the impact on future margins into account.

Consider the case where the volume of deposits in Year 2, $D_2(.)$, is a function not only of the deposit rate paid in that period, $d_2$, but also of the deposit rate paid in Year 1, $d_1$.

The present value of profit will be maximized over two years:

$$\text{Maximum present value of profits} = (b_1 - d_1) \times D(d_1) + \frac{(b_2 - d_2) \times D(d_1, d_2)}{1 + b_2}$$

$$\frac{\partial \text{Profit}}{\partial d_1} = (b_1 - d_1) \times \frac{\partial D_1}{\partial d_1} - D_1(d_1) + \frac{(b_2 - d_2)}{1 + b_2} \times \frac{\partial D_2}{\partial d_1} = 0$$

$$(b_1 - d_1) - \frac{D_1 \times d_1}{D_1' \times d_1} + \frac{(b_2 - d_2) \times D_2'}{(1 + b_2) \times D_1'} = 0$$

$$d_1 \times (1 + \eta^{-1}) = b_1 + \frac{(b_2 - d_2) \times D_2'}{(1 + b_2) \times D_1'}$$

or

$$d_1 \times (1 + \eta^{-1}) + \frac{d_2}{(1 + b_2)} \times \frac{\partial D_2}{\partial D_1} = b_1 + \frac{b_2}{1 + b_2} \times \frac{\partial D_2}{\partial D_1}$$

$$d_1 \times (1 + \eta^{-1}) + \frac{d_2 \times \alpha}{1 + b_2} = b_1 + \frac{b_2}{1 + b_2} - \frac{(1 - \alpha)b_2}{1 + b_2} = c + \frac{c}{1 + b_2} - \frac{(1 - \alpha)b_2}{1 + b_2}$$

with $\alpha$ = persistence factor and $c$ = fixed coupon on a 2–year bond

The marginal cost has two parts: the marginal cost of one extra dollar of deposits this period (the same as before, with the elasticity being the short-term elasticity) and the present value of the cost for the next period as a result of the lag effect. Similarly, the marginal return has two parts: the revenue from interbank loans this period and the present value of the revenue from interbank loans in the next period as a result of the lag effect (identical to the present value of a fixed-coupon bond reduced by the decay factor, $1 - \alpha$, effect). As discussed in Chapter 10 for the fund transfer price in a multiperiod setting, this illustrates the need to analyze the shape of the yield curve in pricing deposits.[7] Single-period profit maximization (even if a fixed coupon rate is used as the transfer price) is unlikely to lead to an optimal solution.

Next, some specific conditions that are sufficient to ensure that single-period maximization leads to an optimal solution are analyzed.

### When Is the Long-Term Bond Rate Used in a Single-Period Maximization an Optimal Transfer Price?

As it was reported earlier that banks often use a long-term fixed rate as a transfer price and evaluate the profitability of a value center over one year, questions arise concerning the conditions needed to make this an optimal transfer price leading to correct pricing decisions.

Consider the case where the deposit rate in Year 2 is identical to that in Year 1 ($d_2 = d_1$) and where the deposit base in Year 2 is identical to that in Year 1 ($D_2 = D_1$).

$$\text{Maximum net income} = (1 + b_2) \times (b_1 - d_1) D_1(d_1) + (b_2 - d_1) \times D_1(d_1)$$
$$= [(1 + b_2)(b_1 - d_1) + (b_2 - d_1)] \times D_1(d_1)$$

$$\frac{\partial \text{Net income}}{\partial d_1} = -(1 + b_2 + 1) D_1 + [(1 + b_2)(b_1 - d_1) + b_2 - d_2] \frac{\partial D_1}{\partial d_1}$$
$$= 0$$
$$= -(1 + b_2 + 1) D_1 / D_1 + [(1 + b_2) b_1 + b_2 - (1 + b_2 + 1) d_1]$$
$$= 0$$
$$= -(1 + b_2 + 1) d_1 \, \eta_D^{-1} + [(1 + b_2) b_1 + b_2 - (1 + b_2 + 1) d_1]$$
$$= 0$$
$$(1 + b_2 + 1) \times (1 + \eta_D^{-1}) d_1 = (1 + b_2) b_1 + b_2 = (1 + b_2) c + c$$
$$= c(1 + 1 + b_2)$$

The last relation between fixed the coupon rate and forward rates is given in Appendix C of Chapter 10. The relation states that the future value of marginal costs over two periods is equal to the future value of revenue over two periods.

This leads to the optimal pricing rule, equivalent to myopic one-period pricing over one period using the coupon bond rate as the transfer price:

$$d_1^{optimal} = \left[(1 + b_2 + 1)c\right] \times (1 + \eta_D^{-1})^{-1} \times \frac{1}{(1 + b_2 + 1)}$$
$$= c \times (1 + \eta_D^{-1})^{-1}$$

Thus, the practice of assigning a long-term transfer price to core, stable deposits is, in the case of myopic one-year profit maximization, correct if the deposit rate is fixed in the future and the deposit base is stable, that is, if the economic maturity of these deposits is indeed totally equivalent to that of a long-term fixed-rate deposit. If these conditions are not met (in particular, if there is a decay factor with deposits or if the deposit rate in Year 2 can be adjusted), then the one-period maximization using the fixed-rate transfer price $c$ is unlikely to be optimal.

## When Is the One-Period Short-Term Bond Rate Used in a Single-Period Maximization an Optimal Transfer Price?

A second (obvious) case of optimal single-period optimization is the case in which what happened in Year 2 is independent of what happened in Year 1. In that case, the one-period optimization discussed in the first part of this chapter should be done, using the transfer price for that period:

$$\text{Maximum net income} = (1 + b_2) \times (b_1 - d_1)D_1(d_1) + (b_2 - d_2) \times D_2(d_2)$$
$$d_1^{optimal} = b_1 \times (1 + \eta_D^{-1})^{-1}$$
$$d_2^{optimal} = b_2 \times (1 + \eta_D^{-1})^{-1}$$

## REPURCHASE AGREEMENTS (REPOS)

A source of funds used as an alternative to regular bank deposits is the repo market.

A repurchase agreement (repo) is an agreement between two parties whereby one party sells a security (bond) to another party with an agreement to buy it back at a specific date in the future at a price that is fixed today.

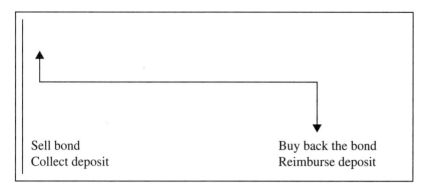

**Figure 11.2** Cash inflows and outflows on repos and deposits.

From a funding perspective and a cash flow perspective, a repo is very similar to a bank deposit, as shown in Figure 11.2. At the time it sells the bond, the bank receives cash (as it does when it collects deposits). At maturity, the bank buys back the bond at a price that was fixed at the start of the transaction, incurring a cash outflow just as it would if it had to pay back a deposit.

So a repo is just another way of raising money. If the cash flow pattern, cash inflow followed by cash outflow, is similar to that of a deposit, it raises the question of why the repo market exists. The first reason for the origin of the repo market was regulation of bank deposit rates. When deposit rates were regulated, banks would use the unregulated repo market to offer an effective higher deposit rate. But that reason has ceased to exist, as deposit pricing has been deregulated around the world. The main reason for the repo market today is related to credit risk and to what would happen if the bank were to go into bankruptcy. Beyond deposit insurance, bank depositors would have a claim only on the assets of the defaulting bank and could incur severe losses. In the case of a repo, if the bank fails to honor its commitment to buy back the bond, the holder of the bond still owns it and is affected only if there is a drop in the market value of the bond at maturity date. A repo is equivalent to a deposit collateralized by the bond.

## CONCLUSION

The separation theorem allows an exclusive focus on deposit pricing.[8] Loan pricing is discussed in the next chapter. Useful results from microeconomics help to identify an optimal pricing rule. As expected, the estimate of deposit volume elasticity will drive the interest margin. When depositors are concerned with the solvency of the bank, collateralized deposits or *repos* are issued.

## APPENDIX A: THE MARGINAL COST OF DEPOSITS

Given that total funding cost $= d \times D$ and total revenue $= b \times D$, the optimal volume is at the point where marginal cost equals marginal revenue:

$$\text{Marginal cost} = \text{marginal revenue}$$
$$(d \times \Delta D) + (\Delta d \times D) + (\Delta d \times \Delta D)$$
$$= b \times \Delta D$$

where $(\Delta d \times \Delta D) = 0$ for small (infinitesimal) changes

$$(b - d) \times \Delta D - \Delta d \times D = 0$$
$$(b - d) - d \times \Delta d / \Delta D \times D/d = 0$$
$$(b - d) - d \times \varepsilon^{-1} = 0$$
$$d \times (1 + \varepsilon^{-1}) = b$$

$$d = b \times \left(1 + \frac{1}{\varepsilon}\right)$$

## APPENDIX B: MULTIPLICATIVE FUNCTIONAL FORM FOR DEPOSIT VOLUME AND ELASTICITY

$$D = \text{constant} \times d^{\alpha}$$
$$\text{Log } D = \log \text{ constant} + (\alpha \times \log d)$$

$$\frac{\partial \log D}{\partial \log d} = 1.5 = \text{elasticity } (N) = \frac{\text{percentage increase in deposits } (D)}{\text{percentage increase in deposit rate } (d)}$$

Proof:

Let $D = D(d)$ and $d = D-1(D)$ (the inverse function). Then

$$\frac{\partial \log D}{\partial d} = \frac{1}{D} \times \frac{\partial D}{\partial d} \qquad \partial \log D = \frac{1}{D} \times \partial D = \text{percentage increase in } D$$

$$\frac{\partial \log d}{\partial D} = \frac{1}{d} \times \frac{\partial d}{\partial D} \qquad \partial \log d = \frac{1}{d} \times \partial d = \text{percentage increase in } d$$

## EXERCISES FOR CHAPTER 11

1. You are being asked to price deposits so as to maximize the profit of the bank, knowing that the estimated price elasticity of deposits is equal to 1.5. The average return on the assets of the bank is 12 percent, the current interbank rate is 10 percent, variable operating expenses linked to deposits are 1 percent, the corporate tax rate is 40 percent, and the reserve requirement regulation works as follows: for each dollar of deposits received, you must invest 0.2 dollar in a zero-interest-bearing account at the central bank (20 percent reserve ratio).

2. You are being asked to price one-year-to-maturity deposits so as to maximize the profit of the bank, knowing that the estimated price elasticity of deposits is equal to 2. The current interbank rate yield curve is as follows: the three-month rate is 8 percent, the six-month rate is 8.5 percent, and the twelve-month rate is 9 percent. Variable operating expenses linked to deposits are 2 percent, the corporate tax rate is 40 percent, and the reserve requirement regulation works as follows: for each dollar deposit received, you must invest 0.3 dollar in an interest-bearing account at the central bank (30 percent reserve ratio). The interest paid by the central bank on this account is 5 percent. The central bank uses these balances to finance the country's public deficit.

### Notes

1. Since this chapter is concerned with pricing deposits, the volume of deposits is increased by raising the deposit rate. Additional tools that are not discussed in this chapter would include the opening of additional branches or increased marketing expenses.
2. Note that a more precise calculation would be to divide the deposit volume increase (15) by 107.5 (the midpoint between 100 and 115), and the deposit rate increase (0.01) by 0.105, again the midpoint.
3. In this chapter, the market rate (interbank, bond) is used as the incremental return on deposits. In case of liquidity constraints, the deposit fund transfer price identified in Chapter 10 should be used.
4. Gropp et al. (2007).

5. Because of the separation theorem, this chapter focuses exclusively on deposits, leaving aside the loan portfolio.
6. This is a more advanced section that can be skipped without loss of continuity.
7. Another case of dynamic consideration is when the deposit rate is fixed for a few quarters to facilitate a marketing campaign. Again, the shape of the yield curve must be taken into account (Dermine, 1984, and Hannan and Berger, 1991).
8. As discussed in Chapter 10, if the conditions needed for the separation theorem are not verified, the profit on deposits and loans should be maximized jointly.

# CHAPTER 12

# Capital Regulation (Basel I), Economic Capital Allocation, and Loan Pricing I (the Equity Spread)

This chapter begins by introducing the international capital regulations known as Basel I. Next, the implications of capital regulation for loan pricing are derived.

## BIS CAPITAL REGULATION (BASEL I)

The medium-size German bank Bankhaus Herstatt defaulted on June 26, 1974, at the end of the business day. Some of the bank's counterparties had irrevocably paid deutsche marks to the bank before its license was withdrawn. These counterparties were expecting to receive U.S. dollars in New York that same day. However, the termination of the bank took place at 10:30 a.m. New York time, prompting Herstatt's correspondents to suspend all outgoing U.S. dollar payments. This left U.S. counterparties with losses exceeding $600 million.

Following the default of Herstatt, central bankers, who meet regularly at the Bank for International Settlements (BIS)[1] in Basel, Switzerland, started negotiations to ensure that international banks had a minimum level of capital. This led to the creation of the Basel Committee of Banking Supervision (BCBS),[2] a committee of senior bank supervisors that was put in charge of designing international capital regulations. The view was that, in integrated international banking markets, domestic regulators might be too lenient with domestic banks in the interest of making them more competitive. This could lead to competitive deregulation and a too low level of bank capital in the world. To prevent this, an international agreement on capital was needed to create a level playing field.

The agreement was reached in 1988 after 14 years of negotiation. The minimum capital ratio is as follows:

$$\frac{\text{Capital}}{\text{Risk-weighted assets}} = \frac{\text{Capital}}{\text{RWA}} \geq 8\%$$

This is known as the BIS ratio or the *Cooke* ratio (Peter Cooke, head of banking supervision at the Bank of England, was the chairman of the Basel Committee in 1988). More recently, it is also referred to as the Basel I ratio, to distinguish it from Basel II, a revision of the original regulation that is discussed in the next chapter. Although the Basel Committee has no legal power to control the implementation of the agreement, it has such a high level of authority that no country would dare to apply more lenient rules. While the BIS ratio was originally applicable to international banks only, it has had a great impact around the world. For example, the European Commission has adopted a similar capital regulation that applies to all banks in the European Union, and the World Bank and the International Monetary Fund have exerted pressure on emerging countries to apply similar regulations.

There are three components of the BIS ratio: the definition of capital, the definition of risk-weighted assets (RWA), and the minimum level of 8 percent.

## Capital

Banks quickly started to lobby for a favorable definition of capital, one that would allow them to pursue leverage. Recall the discussion in Chapter 9 on the determinants of the return on equity, one of them being the leverage ratio. The outcome of the negotiation was that BIS capital would include two parts, Tier 1 and Tier 2, defined as follows:

### Tier 1 Capital

- Paid-in capital: equity issued by the bank.
- Retained earnings: accumulated profits that have not been paid out as dividends.
- Perpetual noncumulative preference shares; *noncumulative* means that if a preferred dividend is passed, it will not be paid in following years.
- Hybrid Tier 1: hybrid Tier 1, a rather recent instrument that is limited to a maximum of 15 percent of Tier 1 capital, is a debt

instrument with tax-deductible interest; it must obey various constraints imposed by the central bank.

- General (disclosed) reserves: those created by appropriations of retained earnings.
- Minus goodwill (in the context of an acquisition, goodwill refers to the difference between the purchase price of assets and the book value of the purchased company at the time of an acquisition).

## Tier 2

### Upper Tier 2

- Reevaluation of premises: when the market value of fixed assets is different from the value reported in the books
- Undisclosed reserves: those created by appropriations of retained earnings
- General provisions (up to 1.25 percent): provisions held against presently unidentified losses
- Unrealized gains on securities (at 45 percent) when the market value of financial assets is different from the value reported in the books
- Hybrid (perpetual subordinated debt)

### Lower Tier 2

- Subordinated debt (with a maximum of 50 percent of Tier 1). To qualify fully, the debt must have a maturity longer than five years.

The sum of Tier 1 and Tier 2 capital is reduced by any equity participation in other banks. This last rule was to prevent one bank from buying equity issued by another bank, resulting in zero net equity inflow into the banking system.

Not all central banks were pleased with this definition of capital. The Federal Republic of Germany formally expressed a reservation in the accord, recorded as footnote 3 in the Basel I Capital Accord (July 1988): "One member country, however, maintains the view that an international definition of capital should be confined to core capital elements and indicated that it would continue to press for the definition to be reconsidered by the Committee in the years ahead." At the date this is being written, 20 years later, the agreement on the definition of BIS capital has not yet been reviewed.

## Risk-Weighted Assets (RWA)

The intention was to start better capturing the risk inherent in bank activities, both on- and off-balance sheet. At the time of the accord, 1988, trading risk was not so important, so the focus was on credit risk. Central banks wanted to measure not only the risk on assets booked on the balance sheet, but also the credit risk arising from off-balance sheet transactions, such as guarantees and derivatives.

### Weights for On-Balance Sheet Assets

- *Cash and OECD government securities*: 0 percent. Cash refers essentially to reserves with central banks.
- *Interbank (OECD)*: 20 percent. This type of loan has a low risk weighting because of the very low number of bankruptcies of OECD financial institutions at the time.
- *Mortgages*: 50 percent. Mortgages have a low risk weighting, as real estate collateral allows for good recoveries at the time of default.
- *Loans*: 100 percent. All other assets were weighted at 100 percent, whatever their maturity or degree of default risk.

### Off-Balance Sheet

Off-balance sheet risk arises from two types of transaction: guarantees and derivatives.

#### Guarantees and Associated Credit Conversion Factors

1. Direct credit substitutes (standby letters of credit): 100 percent

   *In a standby letter of credit, the bank guarantees that it will stand by, or reimburse, a lender if a third-party borrower cannot meet its obligations.*

2. Short-term self-liquidating trade-related contingencies: 20 percent

   *In international trade, these are bank guarantees of payment to a company exporting a good.*

3. Asset sales with recourse: 100 percent

   *This refers to the sale of loans to a third party by banks. "Recourse" means that the bank guarantees the repayment of the loan, thus keeping the entire credit risk.*

4. Note issuance facilities (NIF): 50 percent

   *This arrangement is much used in the commercial paper market. Commercial paper is short-term bonds issued by corporations. In a NIF, the bank guarantees that it will lend to the corporation if the corporation is unable to issue commercial paper, for example, because liquidity has dried up.*

### Forex–Interest-Rate–Equity Contracts

In a derivatives contract,[3] a party promises a counterparty that it will buy or sell an asset at some date in the future for a price that is fixed today, the exercise price. If the counterparty defaults, the bank can still buy or sell the asset, but at the price prevailing in the market at that time. The risk resulting from a counterparty default is the risk of having to replace the contract at unfavorable terms.

Most banks use the *current exposure method* to measure counterparty risk. It involves two parts: the loss if the bank had to purchase a new derivative at unfavorable terms today, and the additional potential loss resulting from a further move in market prices (*add-on*).

### Current Exposure Method

Credit risk = replacement cost ("marking to market") + potential future credit exposure ("add-on")

Table 12.1 lists the percentages used to calculate the add-on.

### Minimum Capital Ratio of 8 Percent

The minimum 8 percent capital ratio has become a standard around the world, imposed also by the World Bank and the IMF. Thus, the question of where the number 8 came from arises. Several years ago, the author had the privilege of asking Peter Cooke the origin of the 8 percent ratio, hoping to receive a set of complex papers with formulas. Big smile from Peter Cooke: "8 percent is the result of negotiation." BIS rules have to be adopted unanimously by the members of the BIS. Some central banks wanted a larger figure, and others thought that this level of capital was already difficult to meet; a compromise was reached at 8 percent. (Bankers from China have an alternative, more appealing argument for using 8 percent: in that

**TABLE  12.1**

Potential Future Credit Exposure (percentage applied to notional principal)

| Residual Maturity | Interest Rate | Forex + Gold | Equity |
|---|---|---|---|
| Less than one year | Nil | 1% | 6% |
| One year to five years | 0.5% | 5% | 8% |
| Over five years | 1.5% | 7.5% | 10% |

country, the number 8 is a symbol of prosperity![4]) So, let us not forget: the
8 percent capital ratio is the outcome of negotiation.

## An Example: The Capital Ratio at
## Royal Bank of Canada, October 2007

Tables 12.2 and 12.3 report, for illustration, information on risk-weighted
assets and capital ratios at the Royal Bank of Canada.

**TABLE 12.2**

Risk-Weighted Assets at Royal Bank of Canada, October 2007

| Risk-Adjusted Assets (C$ millions) | Balance Sheet Amount or Credit Equivalent Amount | Risk Weights (Average) | Risk-Adjusted Balance |
|---|---|---|---|
| **Balance sheet assets** | | | |
| Cash and deposit with banks | 16,107 | 18% | 2,852 |
| Securities: | | | |
| Issued or guaranteed by Canadian or other OECD governments | 16,858 | — | 52 |
| Other | 161,591 | 6% | 9,495 |
| Residential mortgages | | | |
| Insured | 27,994 | 1% | 355 |
| Conventional | 81,713 | 40% | 32,885 |
| Other loans and acceptances | | | |
| Issued or guaranteed by Canadian or other OECD governments | 32,577 | 17% | 5,651 |
| Other | 171,422 | 69% | 118,723 |
| Other assets | 92,100 | 11% | 10,487 |
| | 600,362 | | 180,500 |
| **Off-balance sheet financial instruments, credit instruments** | | | |
| Guarantees and standby letters of credit | 19,758 | 60% | 11,807 |
| Documentary and commercial letters of credit | 100 | 78% | 78 |
| Securities lending | 36,187 | 3% | 962 |
| Commitments to extend credit | 21,954 | 85% | 18,752 |
| Liquidity facilities | 4,826 | 98% | 4,746 |
| Note issuances and revolving underwriting facilities | — | — | — |
| | 82,825 | | |
| Derivatives | 57,973 | 25% | 14,457 |
| **Total off-balance sheet financial instruments** | 140,798 | | 50,802 |
| **Total specific and general market risk** | | | 16,333 |
| **Total risk-adjusted assets** | | | 247,635 |

Source: Annual Report, Royal Bank of Canada.

A few observations stand out. Table 12.2 includes information on both on-balance sheet assets and off-balance sheet financial instruments. Balance sheet assets of $600,362 million are equivalent to $180,500 million in risk-weighted assets. The off-balance sheet financial instruments credit equivalent amount is made up of two categories: credit instruments ($82,825 million) and derivatives ($57,973 million). The total risk-weighted balance for off-balance sheet instruments is $50,802 million. Total specific and general market risk ($16,333 million) refers to risk arising from trading positions (discussed in Chapter 20). Total risk-adjusted assets add up to $247,635 million.

Information on regulatory capital follows in Table 12.3.

**TABLE 12.3**

Regulatory Capital and Capital Ratios at Royal Bank of Canada, October 2007

| Tier 1 Capital (C$ millions) | |
|---|---:|
| Common equity | 22,272 |
| Noncumulative preferred shares | 2,344 |
| Trust capital securities | 3,494 |
| Other noncontrolling interest in subsidiaries | 25 |
| Goodwill | (4,752) |
| | **23,383** |
| **Tier 2 Capital** | |
| Permanent subordinated debentures | 779 |
| Nonpermanent subordinated debentures | 5,473 |
| General allowances | 1,221 |
| Trust capital securities (excess over 15% of Tier 1) | — |
| Trust subordinated notes | 1,027 |
| Accumulated net unrealized gain on available-for-sale equity securities | 105 |
| | **8,605** |
| **Other Deductions from Capital** | |
| Investment in insurance subsidiaries | (2,912) |
| Other | (505) |
| **Total capital** | **28,571** |
| **Capital Ratios** | |
| Tier 1 capital to risk-adjusted assets | 9.4% |
| Total capital to risk-adjusted assets | 11.5% |
| Assets-to-capital multiple | 19.9 times |

Source: Annual Report.

The bank's investment in insurance subsidiaries is deducted from capital. The Tier 1 ratio of 9.4 percent and the total capital ratio of 11.5 percent substantially exceed the BIS minimums of 4 percent and 8 percent, respectively. This could be the result of more stringent regulation imposed by Canadian regulators (Office of Superintendent for Financial Institutions) or management's wishing to hold excess capital to meet market expectations.[5]

## BASEL I AND LOAN PRICING: THE EQUITY SPREAD

At about the time the Basel I rules were implemented around the world, the shareholder value movement was becoming popular. It led banks to analyze the implications of capital regulations for loan pricing.

With reference to the discussion of corporate financial goals in Chapter 9, a loan transaction will break even when the present value of the transaction is just equal to the amount of equity invested. In that case, there is no value creation and no value destruction:[6]

Breakeven loan pricing rule:
Equity invested = present value of net cash flows

To analyze the implications of the BIS capital regulation for loan pricing, consider a simple, but powerful example of a loan with one year to maturity:

| Loan: 100 | Interbank debt: 92 (4%) |
|---|---|
| | Subordinated debt: 2.67 (4.75%) |
| | Equity: 5.33 |

The loan of $100 is funded with interbank debt of $92, subordinated debt of $2.67, and equity of $5.33. Subordinated debt (a maximum of 50 percent of Tier 1 equity, according to BIS rules) and equity add up to the 8 percent BIS ratio. The corporate tax rate is 40 percent. The interbank rate is 4 percent, the rate on subordinated debt is 4.75 percent, and the cost of equity to value dividends is 9 percent. The interbank debt is chosen over financing with retail deposits because the fund transfer price discussion called for a matched-maturity market rate. A cost of equity of 9 percent implies a risk premium of around 5 percent over the interbank rate, a reasonable figure.

The breakeven rule can then be applied to compute the loan breakeven rate, $R$:

Equity = present value of dividend

Value of transaction $= 5.33$

$$= \frac{(1-0.4)\times(R\times100 - 4\%\times92 - 4.75\%\times2.67) + 100 - 92 - 2.67}{1.09}$$

The numerator represents the dividend that could be paid out of the transaction. It has two parts: the profit after tax and the reimbursement of principal on the one-year loan net of the debt.

Solving this relation leads to a breakeven loan rate $R$ of 4.61 percent. Compared to the 4 percent interbank rate, it implies a breakeven spread of 0.61 percent. It should be noticed that the computation of the after-tax profit did not take charges for credit risk[7] or for operational expenses into account. The spread of 0.61 percent is entirely the result of financing the loan with some equity. This spread is called the *equity spread*. This is intuitive; as soon as the bank begins using equity, it needs to create a profit to ensure a minimum return to shareholders.

There are two reasons for the origin of the *equity spread:* the first is that equity is expensive (9 percent), but the second and more important reason is that, unlike the cost of debt, the cost of equity is not tax-deductible.

### Equity Spread vs. Actual Spreads Observed in Banking Markets

When banks began estimating a breakeven equity spread, they realized that the figure was substantially higher than the actual spreads of 10 to 30 basis points observed on corporate loans to large international companies. And the difference was even more substantial when additional expenses — expected loan-loss expense and operating expenses — were taken into account. As competition prevented the banks from raising the interest rates on loans, this result led to a strategic review at many banks, with at least six strategic options being discussed.

### Strategic Options for Operations in Fiercely Competitive Corporate Markets

#### Exit

Because of the very low margin and inability to generate satisfactory returns for shareholders, the bank can decide to exit the loan market.

#### Fund Loans with Cheaper Retail Loans

The example uses an interbank loan and subordinated debt, priced on competitive markets. Some have argued that a bank could use cheaper retail deposits. There are problems with this argument, as the separation theorem shows that maximization of profit calls for the use of the marginal fund transfer price, the market rate. There is no need to cross-subsidize loans with low-cost deposits. It would be better to simply invest deposits in the interbank markets than to grant loans with too low margins.

### Evaluate the Entire Customer Relationship

Some have correctly argued that the loan pricing example was focused exclusively on the cash flows generated by the loan. Often, banks will reduce spreads on loans when they expect additional sources of revenue, such as fees earned on M&A, cash management services, and other such services. Indeed, what matters is that the total customer relationship creates value. In practice, banks evaluate loans on a stand-alone basis and then decide whether lower margins are acceptable in view of the additional business that can be generated as a result of the loan.

### Securitize Loans

The emergence of the equity spread is the result of equity funding. Investment banks have quickly advised banks to take the loans off the balance sheet. They can do this by advising corporation to issue bonds or commercial paper rather than borrowing from the bank. Banks earn a fee for underwriting bonds, but do not have the asset on their balance sheet and a costly equity requirement. The alternative is to lend money as a first step and then securitize the loans, that is, sell them to investors. Securitization is discussed in Chapter 16.

### Search for Innovative Source of Capital

One of the main reasons for the emergence of the equity spread is that the cost of equity, unlike the cost of debt, is not tax-deductible. Banks have lobbied for the ability to substitute various types of debt securities for equity. First, Tier 2 capital, which includes subordinated debt, was recognized as part of the BIS capital definition. Second, and more recently, banks have been allowed to include innovative Tier I capital securities within Tier 1 (up to 1.25 percent of RWA). The key characteristic of these instruments is that their cost, an interest expense, is tax-deductible. To qualify as Tier 1, they must adhere to specific restrictions on maturities.

### Allocate Risk-Based Economic Capital

Since they began working with the regulatory capital of 8 percent, banks have been increasingly dissatisfied with the fact that the weighting for loans (100 percent) does not recognize the riskiness of loans properly. Banks started to allocate *economic capital* to loans based on the actual

**TABLE  12.4**

Equity Spread (%)*

| | BIS | | | | | | | |
|---|---|---|---|---|---|---|---|---|
| Tax | 1% | 2% | 3% | 4% | 6% | 8% | 10% | 12% |
| 0% | 0.04 | 0.07 | 0.11 | 0.14 | 0.22 | 0.29 | 0.36 | 0.43 |
| 20% | 0.05 | 0.1 | 0.15 | 0.20 | 0.31 | 0.41 | 0.51 | 0.61 |
| 30% | 0.06 | 0.12 | 0.18 | 0.25 | 0.37 | 0.49 | 0.62 | 0.74 |
| 40% | 0.08 | 0.15 | 0.23 | 0.30 | 0.46 | 0.61 | 0.76 | 0.91 |
| 50% | 0.1 | 0.19 | 0.29 | 0.38 | 0.58 | 0.77 | 0.96 | 1.15 |

* The cost of debt is 4 percent, cost of subordinated debt is 4.75 percent, and cost of equity is 9 percent. The BIS capital requirement is met two-thirds with equity and one-third with subordinated debt.

riskiness of the loans. This has major strategic implications, as Table 12.4 shows explicitly.

Table 12.4 shows the equity spread, that is, the margin necessary to reward shareholders (this is in addition to expected credit losses and operating expenses) for several combinations of the corporate tax rate and the BIS capital ratio. The formula used to calculate the spread is identical to that used for the one-year loan example. For instance, for a corporate tax rate of 40 percent and a BIS capital ratio of 8 percent, the equity spread is 0.61 percent.

Several observations stand out. The first one, not a surprise, is that, because of differences in the corporate tax level in different countries, the field is not level, even with the common BIS capital ratio. For example, with a BIS capital ratio of 8 percent, the equity spread falls from 0.61 percent to 0.41 percent as the corporate tax rate falls from 40 percent to 20 percent. The second is that the application of an 8 percent BIS capital ratio leads to a breakeven equity spread of 0.61 percent in the 40 percent tax world. The signal created incentives to search for loan transactions with high margins—often with credit risk that would materialize only years later. Bankers remembered that the 8 percent capital ratio was a result of a negotiation, not intended to be applied to each individual loan transaction. A process of economic capital allocation followed, with the capital being allocated according to the riskiness of the loan. The specific process for allocating economic capital will be discussed later. But the strategic implications of economic capital allocation need to be analyzed directly. If you can convince the CFO that a short-term loan to a top-rated client is very safe and that you need to allocate only 2 percent of BIS capital, the equity spread falls to 0.15 percent, making actual loans in a competitive market profitable. Several international banks that had migrated their loan portfolio to high-margin business because of the 8 percent BIS ratio moved their portfolio back to safe clients once they were willing to allocate a lower economic capital to safe clients.

So, how is economic capital allocated to businesses?

## ECONOMIC CAPITAL ALLOCATION

The process of economic capital allocation is based on a simple business principle. Capital is necessary to absorb losses and to reduce the risk of financial distress for a company and the destruction of value that would result because of the loss of clients or suppliers. An alternative explanation is that economic capital is needed to reduce the risk borne by depositors to a minimal level. Economic capital can be thought of as money invested in risk-free Treasury bills that can absorb eventual losses with some degree of confidence.[8] So, intuitively, an activity with very stable cash flows can be highly leveraged, that is, financed with a large amount of debt and little equity. At the opposite extreme, an activity with volatile cash flows would be financed with a larger amount of equity.

The graph in Figure 12.1 reports the quarterly frequency of loan losses observed in the past on loans within a specific risk category. That is, after historical data on loan losses for loans within a particular category have been collected, the number of quarters (frequency) in which low loan losses have been observed and the number of quarters in which high loan losses have been observed are counted.[9]

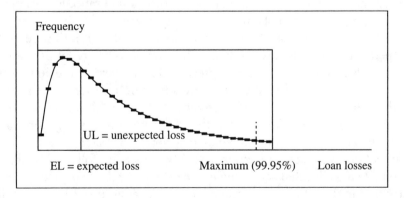

**Figure 12.1** Expected loss (EL) and unexpected loss (UL).

A first observation is that the distribution of loan losses is not symmetrical, but instead is highly skewed to the left. This is intuitively plausible, as there are many quarters in which the economy is doing well, with relatively low loan losses, and only a few quarters with really bad recessions and large loan losses. From a statistical point of view, this makes credit risk very special because it is not possible to rely on symmetrical statistical distributions, such as the widely used normal bell curve. More complex statistics, discussed in Chapter 22, will be needed. After computing the frequency of loan losses, it is possible to compute the expected loss (EL), which is what the bank expects to lose on average over the business cycle. This expected loss should be included in the credit spread in pricing the loan. If the actual loss turns out to be below the expected loss, the loan is turning a profit. However, a problem arises if loan losses start to exceed the expected loss. Indeed, when that happens, the bank starts to lose money on the loan, with losses exceeding the margin. Therefore, the part of the distribution to the right of the expected loss represents a loss situation for the bank, which must be covered by capital. This is often referred to as unexpected loss (UL); however, this term is not well chosen because, in practice, losses will often exceed the expected loss. Using simpler language, it can be said that economic capital should cover the *potential loss* on a transaction. This reasoning was applied to loans, but it has wide applicability and could be applied to market risk or to operational risk.

This leaves a last question. How much of the loan-loss distribution should be covered by economic capital, as equity is known to be costly? This decision is going to be related to the risk of default that a bank is willing to face. For instance, in its 2007 annual report, the Dutch ING Group states that it allocates economic capital with a degree of confidence of 99.95 percent. Technically, that means that there is a risk of 0.05 percent that losses could exceed the bank's capital.[10] The choice of 0.05 percent was driven by rating agencies and the AA rating that the bank wanted to maintain.

This reasoning for economic capital allocation is very similar to what has been done in the insurance industry for decades. For example, in life insurance, the average number of people in a segment of the population who are dying is measured. This allows the company to calculate the life insurance premium. The volatility of the death figures is then analyzed to calculate the reserves necessary to cover risk in case the life insurance premiums are exhausted.

Around the world, banks and consultants have been busy allocating economic capital to different bank businesses. Although historical data collection and statistics are useful, this is still an art, and judgment must be exercised. There are two reasons for this. First, historical data may not incorporate periods of volatility. Second, history is not always a good guide for the future. For instance, in western Africa in 1994, banks experienced losses of 25 percent on their loan portfolios. Is this type of mismanagement likely to be repeated in the future when there has been a major upgrade in central bank controls? A further difficulty, to be discussed in Chapter 23, is that part of the risk will disappear in a portfolio. An adequate allocation of capital needs to incorporate the benefits of diversification.

### Economic Capital vs. Regulatory Capital

As banks applied the economic capital model to drive strategy and to price loans, they began to be uncomfortable because, at the end of the day, they still had to meet their own central bank's capital requirements. A safe loan may demand only a small allocation of economic capital, but the central bank would still require 8 percent capital. This was of particular concern for banks with capital levels close to the regulatory ratio. They knew that adding a new loan would imply an increase in regulatory capital of 8 percent. A lobbying process began, with the goal of altering the BIS capital rules to make them closer to economic capital allocation. Helped by significant progress in measuring credit risk, this led to a major reform, the Basel II capital regulation. This is the subject of the next chapter.

## CONCLUSION

To ensure a fair and level playing field and solvent banks, the Basel Committee of Banking Supervision introduced the 8 percent BIS ratio in 1988. In the 1988 Basel I Accord, crude measures of credit risk for on- and off-balance sheet assets were used. As equity is costly, banks started to review their loan pricing strategy to ensure an adequate return to shareholders. This led to the discussion of how much economic capital had to be allocated to fund loans. The larger the economic capital allocation, the larger the equity spread.

## APPENDIX: RETAIL LOAN PRICING AND LOAN PRICE ELASTICITY

On the retail market (consumer loans and credit card loans), the bank wants to take into account the price elasticity of clients, as was done with deposit pricing. Intuitively, if price elasticity is low, as is the case with credit card business, the rate charged on the loan will be high.

As was true for deposit pricing, profit will be maximized when the after-tax marginal return of lending an additional unit is equal to its after-tax marginal cost. Let

$R$ = contractual loan rate

$t$ = corporate tax rate

%EL = expected loss (bad debt) as a percentage of principal (include any tax shield)[11]

%OE = variable operating expenses as a percentage of principal

$i$ = interbank funding rate

$R_s$ = cost of equity

D/loan = percentage of debt financing

E/loan = percentage of equity financing

$\varepsilon$ = loan demand elasticity (a negative figure, as an increase in the loan rate will reduce loan demand)

Incremental return[12]      = incremental cost

$(1 - t) \times R \times (1 + \varepsilon^{-1})$   $= (1 - t) \times (i \times D/\text{loan} + \%\text{OE}) + \%\text{EL} + R_s \times E/\text{loan}$

$$R = \left[ i \times \frac{\text{debt}}{\text{loan}} + \%\text{OE} + \frac{\%\text{EL}}{1-t} + \left( \frac{R_s}{1-t} \times \frac{\text{equity}}{\text{loan}} \right) \right] \times \left( \frac{1}{1 + \dfrac{1}{\varepsilon}} \right)$$

The first term in the brackets is similar to the weighted average cost of capital (WACC) used in standard corporate finance (see Chapter 8), except that it includes, in addition to cost of debt and cost of equity, the operating expenses and expected loss related to the loan. A word of caution: as discussed in Chapter 10, the assumption that the marginal cost of funding is the market rate needs to be verified. In the event of liquidity constraints, the fund transfer price needs to be adapted.

## EXERCISES FOR CHAPTER 12

1. Here is the balance sheet of a bank. Compute the Tier 1 capital ratio, the Tier 2 ratio, and the overall BIS capital ratio.

| Assets | | Liabilities and Shareholder's Equity | |
|---|---|---|---|
| Reserves with central bank | 60 | Demand deposits | 750 |
| Mortgage loans | 525 | Term deposits | 450 |
| Corporate loans | 450 | Interbank deposits | 370 |
| Interbank loans | 375 | Subordinated debt | 25 |
| Government bonds | 195 | Equity | 55 |
| Fixed assets | 45 | | — |
| Total | 1,650 | Total | 1,650 |

2. The account manager of AlphaBank wants to know the minimum rate that can be quoted on a one-year-to-maturity loan of 100 million without losing money (the breakeven rate). You have the following information:

- Maturity: one year.
- Expected losses on loans are 1.5 percent. That is, when lending $100, the expected loss (probability of default × loss) is $1.5. The expected loss incorporates the tax shield resulting from reporting a loss.
- The cost of debt is 12 percent, and the cost of equity is 17 percent.
- There is, by regulation, an 8 percent equity requirement ($E/L = 0.08$).
- The corporate tax rate is 30 percent.

3. The corporate account manager of AlphaBank wants to know the minimum rate (the breakeven rate) that can be quoted on a one-year-to-maturity loan of $100,000. You have the following information:

- The cost of interbank debt is 12 percent, and the cost of equity is 17 percent.
- There is, by regulation, an 8 percent BIS capital requirement. It can be met by a combination of equity (5.3 percent) and subordinated debt (2.7 percent). The cost of subordinated debt is 12.75 percent.
- Expected losses (EL) on loans are 1.5 percent. That is, when lending $100, the expected loss (probability of default × loss) is $1.5. The expected loss incorporates the tax shield resulting from reporting a loss.
- The corporate tax rate is 30 percent.

# Notes

1. The Bank for International Settlements was created in 1919, after World War I, to facilitate transfer payments between Germany and other European countries. It evolved into the central bank of central banks.
2. It consists of senior representatives of bank supervisory authorities and central banks from Belgium, Canada, France, Germany, Italy, Japan, Luxembourg, the Netherlands, Spain, Sweden, Switzerland, the United Kingdom, and the United States. The secretariat of the BCBS is located in the building of the Bank for International Settlements, but the BCBS is formally independent of the BIS.
3. Derivatives are discussed in Chapter 25.
4. Unrelated to banking, but a symbol of prosperity: 08/08/08 was the date chosen for the opening of the Olympic Games in Beijing (August 8, 2008)!
5. Flannery and Rangan (2002).
6. In standard corporate finance jargon, the net present value of the loan would be said to be equal to zero. The calculation of a breakeven loan rate is useful for a corporate banker entering into a price negotiation with a client. In retail lending, the banker might want to take price elasticity into account, as was done for deposits. This is discussed in the appendix to this chapter.
7. A more complete discussion of credit risk pricing is presented in Chapter 14.
8. An alternative and more stringent definition of economic capital [Merton and Perold (1993); Van Deventer et al., (2005)] is that it is the value of a put option, the ability of depositors to sell the asset (position) at a strike price equal to the promised reimbursement of the debt. Notice that, ignoring counterparty risk on the seller of the put, this reduces the credit risk borne by depositors to zero.
9. The example is based on the use of historical loss data. The Moody's-KMV approach, which allows the measurement of credit risk with an option-type methodology, is presented in Chapter 15.
10. A banker representing U.S. investors who are active in Indonesia told the author that if he had to allocate capital for a 99.95 percent confidence level, he would need so much capital that he would be out of business. The only alternative was to operate with a smaller level of confidence, such as 90 percent, and a larger risk of default.
11. Expected loss and the related tax shield are defined in Chapter 15.
12. The proof that the marginal return on a loan is equal to $R \times (1 + \varepsilon^{-1})$ is similar to that given for marginal cost of deposits in Appendix A of Chapter 11.

# CHAPTER 13

# Capital Regulation (Basel II)

Chapter 12 introduced the international Bank for International Settlements (BIS) capital regulations, Basel I. These were progressively applied around the world. However, there was a major weakness with the original BIS ratio: all loans—whatever their maturity or their degree of risk—received an identical risk weighting of 100 percent. So, to better relate bank capital to actual risk, a major review took place, leading to revised capital regulations, known as Basel II.[1] First presented in 1999, they were finalized in June 2004.

## BASEL II: THE THREE PILLARS

The key insights of this 239-page document, "International Convergence of Capital Measurement and Capital Standards," are discussed in this chapter. For a complete analysis, the document can be downloaded from the BIS Web site (www.bis.org/bcbs). The Basel II regulations will be applied in many countries, with the first application having occurred in Europe in 2008. In the United States, any form of capital reduction from the requirements of Basel I will be phased in between 2009 and 2011.

Basel II includes three pillars.

### The First Pillar: Minimum Capital Requirements

This defines the methodology that will be applied to measure the minimum amount of capital needed to run a bank. These capital requirements are the subject of this chapter.

### The Second Pillar: Supervisory Review Process

This sets out a series of key principles that have to be reviewed by banking supervisors who are in charge of controlling the soundness and solvency of banks. In particular, supervisors have to ensure that the internal risk management systems and internal capital adequacy assessment process (ICAAP) set up by banks are adequate.

## The Third Pillar: Market Discipline

This defines the disclosure requirements for the types and amounts of risk that banks actually take. The hope is that public disclosure of information on risk will reinforce private market discipline, as prudent investors will choose to divest their holdings in risky banks.

This chapter focuses on the first pillar, minimum capital requirements. Two practical questions concerning this pillar were, first, whether the minimum capital ratio would still be set at 8 percent, and second, what would be the name of the new Basel II capital ratio. The answer to the first question is positive. The minimum capital ratio remains at 8 percent, although the calculation of risk-weighted assets is changing. As to the second question, at the time of this writing, the world banking markets had not made up their mind about the name of the revised capital ratio. This is possibly because of the difficulty of attributing the merits of Basel II to one person only. William McDonough, president of the Federal Reserve Bank of New York, was chairman of the Basel Committee during the early years of negotiations. Jaime Caruana, governor of the Bank of Spain, was the chairman of the committee in June 2004, when the accord was approved. In the absence of a recognized name, this chapter will call it the Basel II capital ratio.

## THE BASEL II CAPITAL ADEQUACY REGULATION

The minimum amount of capital required by regulators will be calculated as follows:

Minimum capital $\geq 8\% \times$ risk-weighted assets (RWA)

This is similar to the calculation for Basel I. What is new is that the risk-weighted assets include a revised measure of credit risk. Moreover, they also include a measure of operational risk. The capital charge for trading risk, to be discussed in Chapter 20, is identical to that of Basel I.

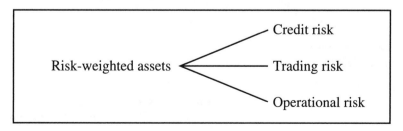

**Figure 13.1** Three types of risk-weighted assets.

The two components of bank capital discussed in Chapter 12, Tier 1 and Tier 2, remain basically unchanged. It is not that central banks were totally satisfied with this complex definition of capital, but rather that they were busy enough with devising a new formula to measure capital adequacy. An important change, however, is that the capital ratio will be applied both at group level on a consolidated basis and also at the level of each subsidiary.[2]

## CREDIT RISK WEIGHTING

Two approaches to computing risk-weighted assets are being proposed. The first is a *standardized approach* that relies on external ratings—that is, ratings given by rating agencies, such as Moody's, Standard & Poor's, or Fitch IBCA. The second approach, which has received the most attention all over the world, is the *internal ratings–based (IRB) approach* (available with two options: *foundation* or *advanced*). Supervisory authorities will decide which banks qualify for the IRB approach. Those that do not qualify for this approach or that choose not to use it will apply the standardized approach.

### The Standardized Approach

The standardized approach is very similar to the original Basel I calculation. However, instead of assigning an identical weighing of 100 percent to all loans, the weighing will be related to the riskiness of the transaction, as identified by the ratings of external rating agencies. The ratings systems of three major international rating agencies, Moody's, S&P, and Fitch IBCA, are given in Appendix A to this chapter. An example for corporate loans is given in Table 13.1.[3]

For example, a loan to a corporate client that is rated $A^+$ would be weighted at 50 percent. This implies that the capital charge on a loan of $100 would be calculated as follows:

$$\text{Capital} \geq 8\% \times (\$100 \times 50\%) = \$4$$

**TABLE 13.1**

External Ratings and Risk Weights

| | AAA–<br>AA⁻ | A⁺–A⁻ | BBB⁺–<br>BBB⁻ | BB⁺–<br>BB⁻ | Below<br>BB⁻ | Unrated |
|---|---|---|---|---|---|---|
| **Corporate** | 20% | 50% | 100% | 100% | 150% | 100% |

From the perspective of the banking community, this is progress, as a safer $A^+$ loan will receive a lower capital charge. Remember that under Basel I, the capital charge would have been $8, calculated with a weighting of 100 percent that was identical for all loans. However, the bankers from many countries were not fully satisfied with the standardized approach. For one thing, for loans to unrated corporations, the weighting is 100 percent, identical to that under Basel I. As in many countries of the world (such as those in Africa, Asia, Europe, Latin America, or Australasia), many corporations are unrated, so the standardized approach would not have helped banks to adjust their capital ratios to the actual riskiness of their loan portfolios. Thus, BCBS devised a second approach, the internal ratings–based approach.[4]

### The Internal Ratings–Based Approach

The BCBS makes an additional distinction between the *foundation* and the *advanced* IRB approaches. Since the key insights can be discussed with the *foundation IRB* approach, this chapter will focus on that approach. Later, the benefits of using the *advanced* approach will be indicated.

The estimation of an acceptable capital ratio for credit risk is a very difficult task. Remember that capital is needed to cover losses in very bad times. As historical data on credit losses are not readily available, and as, even for time periods for which data are available, there may have been very few bad recessions during those time periods, BCBS could not rely on historical data to compute a minimum capital ratio. Instead, it relied on recent progress in statistics.

Under the IRB approach, banks have to calculate themselves the probability (likelihood) of default of a corporate client over a one-year horizon. That is, if they lend to a client today, what is the probability of the borrower's defaulting in one year's time? This probability of default is referred to as the PD. In the case of retail loans, a frequency of default can be calculated for a portfolio of loans. Once the PD has been estimated, a formula devised by BCBS is applied to calculate the capital charge. Here is the magic formula for the case of large corporate loans.[5]

The terms used in this formula are

PD = one-year probability of default
LGD = loss given default = 45% (for senior, unsecured claims)
$M$ = maturity
$b$ (PD) = maturity adjustment
$R$ = correlation between defaults
N(.) = cumulative standard normal distribution
IN(.) = inverse cumulative standard normal distribution

$$\text{Capital} = \left\{ 45 \times N \left[ \frac{\text{IN(PD)}}{\sqrt{1-R}} + \frac{\sqrt{R} \times \text{IN}(0.999)}{\sqrt{1-R}} \right] - 45 \times \text{PD} \right\}$$
$$\times \left[ \frac{1 + (M - 2.5) \times b(\text{PD})}{1 - 1.5 \times b(\text{PD})} \right]$$

with

$$\text{Correlation } R = 0.12 \times \frac{1 - e^{-50 \times PD}}{1 - e^{-50}} + 0.24 \times \left[ 1 - \left( \frac{1 - e^{-50 \times PD}}{1 - e^{-50}} \right) \right]$$

and

Maturity adjustment $= b(\text{PD}) = [0.11852 - 0.05478 \times \ln (\text{PD})]^2$

To apply the capital charge formula using the IRB *foundation* approach, two pieces of data are needed: the probability of default, PD, and the maturity of the loan, M. Estimation of the probability of default will be discussed in Chapter 15.

A formula that can calculate the required capital charge for credit risk is a recent achievement in the field of finance. It is the result of the pioneering work of Oldrich A. Vasicek. Trained as a mathematician, this Czechoslovakian left his country when the Soviet tanks rolled into Prague in August 1968. A San Francisco–based bank, Wells Fargo, offered him a job in its management science department, allowing Vasicek to apply his skills to the evaluation of credit risk. The formula appears complex, as it includes a cumulative normal distribution, an inverse cumulative normal distribution, and correlation between credit risks. Do not be impressed by the mathematics, but rather focus on the structure. The formula (see Figure 13.2) includes four pieces: an assumption about losses incurred in the case of default (LGD = loss given default), a safety factor, a credit spread, and a maturity factor.

## LGD
The first term, $45, the loss given default, refers to the assumption about the amount that the bank would lose in the event of default. When a borrower defaults, the bank is unlikely to lose everything, as it will send powerful individuals (usually former football or rugby players or lawyers) to seize the assets of the borrower. The estimate of $45, based on historical data, applies to senior, unsecured loans.

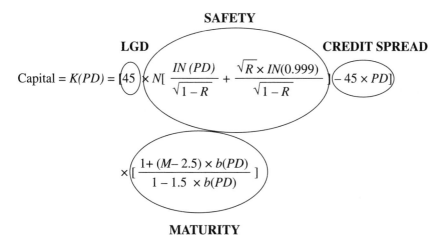

**Figure 13.2** Basel II credit risk formula.

## Safety

As you are expert in statistics, it will be easy to explain the safety factor. Imagine that your bank grants 1,000 loans and that each of these loans has an identical probability of default next year of 1 percent. A 1 percent risk of default is often observed on loans to small and medium-sized enterprises (SMEs). Moreover, add the important assumption that the risks of default are *statistically independent*, meaning that the occurrence of default of one loan is completely unrelated to whether or not other loans default.

Question: if you grant 1,000 loans, how many of the loans in your portfolio will have defaulted one year from now? Answer: 10 loans, that is, 1 percent of your portfolio of 1,000 loans. In this example, the frequency of defaults is identical to the probability of default.

However, in real life, the estimation of the number of loans that will go into default is more complicated. The reason is that the default risks are not independent. Although each loan has a 1 percent probability of default on average over a business cycle, if the economy goes into a recession, it is likely that more than 1 percent of the loans will default at the same time. In designing the capital regulations, this was the key challenge. In the event of a bad recession (with 99.9 percent confidence under Basel II), how many loans could go into default at the same time? This is exactly what the safety factor calculates.[6] The calculated safety factor is given in Table 13.2. For the case of loans with a PD of 1 percent, for example, the safety factor is calculated at 14.03 percent. This implies that the capital charge will be large enough to cover losses if up to 14.03 percent of the loan portfolio goes into default.

## Credit Spread

In the negotiations, the banks argued that they were already charging a credit spread, an interest margin, to cover the expected losses on loans (PD × LGD). As a consequence, the amount of capital necessary to cover potential losses in the event of a big recession should take into account that part of the losses will be covered by these credit spreads. In the end, BCBS agreed to deduct credit spreads from the potential losses.

## Maturity

One of the intents of BCBS was to follow market practice, such as using a one-year horizon to measure the probability of default. However, for loans with longer maturity, the risk is not only default, but also the possibility of a downgrade and loss of value during a recession. This is what the maturity factor is taking into account. The factor is again based on empirical historical data.

Table 13.2 indicates, for illustration, the capital required for a loan of $100 for three PDs (0.03 percent, 1 percent, and 2 percent) and two maturities (2.5 years and 1 year). The components of the formula are given for the 2.5-year case. The safety factor was calculated with a standard spreadsheet, as this tool is needed to calculate the cumulative and inverse cumulative standard normal distributions.

**TABLE 13.2**

Basel II: Capital Required for Credit Risk (Loan of $100)

| PD (%) | LGD | Safety (%) | Credit Spread (PD × LGD) | Maturity Factor (M = 2.5 Years) | Capital (M = 2.5 Years) | RWA (M = 2.5 Years) | Capital (M = 1 Years) |
|---|---|---|---|---|---|---|---|
| 0.03% | $45 | 1.38% | $0.0135 | 1.91 | $1.16 | $14.44 | $0.61 |
| 1% | $45 | 14.03% | $0.45 | 1.26 | $7.39 | $92.32 | $5.86 |
| 2% | $45 | 19.03% | $0.90 | 1.20 | $9.19 | $114.875 | $7.66 |

For a loan with a one-year PD of 1 percent and a maturity of 2.5 years, the capital required for a loan of $100 is equal to:

$$\begin{aligned}
\text{Capital}_{PD} = 1\% &= (\text{LGD} \times \text{safety} - \text{PD} \times \text{LGD}) \\
&\quad \times (\text{maturity factor}) \\
&= (\$45 \times 0.1403 - 0.01 \times \$45) \times 1.26 \\
&= \$7.39
\end{aligned}$$

The formula allows us to calculate the capital required to finance a loan. However, as the banking community was used to the 8 percent BIS ratio and risk-weighted assets (RWA), additional mathematical gymnastics are needed.

Risk-weighted assets = capital × 12.5 (with 12.5 equal to $^1/_8$ percent)

In the case of a 1 percent PD, the RWA is $7.39 × 12.5 = $92.32, and the capital is

Capital 8% × risk-weighted assets 8% × $92.32 = $7.39

This is a curiosity of Basel II. You first calculate the capital required to finance a loan, then you calculate the risk-weighted assets and then you calculate the capital again! All this for the beauty of preserving the 8 percent capital ratio!

Notice the impact of the maturity. For a loan of $100 with a PD of 1 percent, the capital falls from $7.39 to $5.86 when the maturity falls from 2.5 years to 1 year. As equity is expensive, this implies that the *equity spread*, discussed in Chapter 12, will be larger for loans with longer maturity.

In the *advanced IRB* approach, banks will be able to estimate the loss given default (LGD) themselves. Around the world, specialists are busy developing databases for PD and LGD.

It was mentioned that BCBS has allowed banks to deduct the spread priced into the loans from the potential loss in the event of a recession. The argument was that risk was partly covered by the credit risk spread. In return, BCBS has asked banks to verify that all eligible provisions for credit risk be sufficient to cover expected losses on the loan portfolio. A shortage of provisions would be deducted equally from Tier 1 and Tier 2 capital, while an excess of provisions could be added to Tier 2 capital (up to a maximum of 0.6 percent × risk-weighted assets). Methods for evaluating provisions for credit risk are discussed in Chapters 14 and 15.

## Trading Risk

As already mentioned, the capital charge for trading risk will be discussed in Chapter 20.

## Operational Risk

In addition to a better measure of credit risk, a second major innovation in the Basel II framework is to include a capital charge for *operational risk*. This refers to the risk of loss resulting from inadequate or failed internal processes, people, and systems or from external events. It includes legal risk—that is, potential losses resulting from lawsuits. Here is one of many examples. On May 14, 2001, a trader for an investment bank in London keyed in the wrong number of shares on his trading screen. The mistake meant that a sell order on a basket of shares worth a reported $30 million turned into one valued at ten times that. The London stock market index, FTSE 100, fell by 2.2 percent when the trade was made. To preserve its reputation, the investment bank was forced to compensate those of its clients who suffered from the error.

There are two main approaches to calculating capital requirements for operational risk that banks can consider: a *standardized* approach and an *advanced measurement approach* (AMA).

### Standardized Approach

This is simple. The capital charge is simply a multiple of the gross revenue from an activity, averaged over the last three years (see Table 13.3). With

**T A B L E   13.3**

Capital Charge for Operational Risk (Capital = Beta × Gross Income)

| Business Lines | Beta Factors |
| --- | --- |
| Corporate finance | 18% |
| Trading and sales | 18% |
| Retail banking | 12% |
| Commercial banking | 15% |
| Payment and settlements | 18% |
| Agency services | 15% |
| Asset management | 12% |
| Retail brokerage | 12% |

reference to Chapter 4, gross revenue or gross income is the sum of net interest margin and noninterest income (such as fees).

Capital beta factor $\times$ average gross income of last 3 years

For example, in the case of retail banking, the capital is calculated as follows:

Capital$_{retail}$ 12% $\times$ average gross income of last 3 years

Again, the risk-weighted assets for operational risk are equal to

$$RWA_{operational\ risk} = capital \times 12.5$$

To be complete, it should be mentioned that banks can use a simplified version of the *standardized* approach, the so-called basic indicator approach (BIA). In this case, a single parameter of 15 percent is applied to the aggregated gross income of the bank.

### Advanced Measurement Approach (AMA)

A disadvantage of the standardized approach is that it is the same for all banks, whether or not they have good control of their operational processes. So, to encourage banks to have better control of operational risk and thus benefit from a lower capital charge, banks can estimate themselves statistically what their worst operational losses could be, using a confidence level of 99.9 percent. This requires estimating two factors: the number (frequency) of operational losses over a year, and the potential magnitude of these operational losses. The measurement of operational risk relies on techniques developed in the fields of statistics, insurance mathematics, and engineering. For example, techniques developed in hydrology to assess the height of a dam to prevent worst-case flooding are applied to estimate worst-case operational losses.[7] Some of these operational risk models are presented in Chapter 26.

### Model Validation

Under the IRB approach for credit risk or the advanced measurement approach for operational risk, banks are be allowed to measure the risks, such as the PD, themselves. To encourage banks to provide an adequate measurement of risks, central banks will supervise the validity of the models that banks use. This is done in part by comparing the predictions of the models with actual realized losses. The validation of risk measurement models raises a further question: who will supervise the fiercely independent central banks? "Who will guard the guards?" (Juvenal, in *Satires*).

## CONCLUSION

The Basel II capital regulation attempts to measure better the potential losses that could occur with a confidence level of 99.9%. It covers three sources of risk: credit risk, trading risk, and operational risk. As is always the case with risk management models, one should ensure that the model captures properly the distribution of actual risks. Two additional pillars of Basel II concern the need for effective supervision by public authorities and an adequate disclosure of information.

## APPENDIX A

### Long-Term External Ratings*

| Moody's | S&P | Fitch IBCA |
|---|---|---|
| AAA | AAA | AAA |
| AA1 | AA+ | AA+ |
| AA2 | AA | AA |
| AA3 | AA− | AA− |
| A (1, 2, 3) | A | A |
| BAA (1, 2, 3) | BBB (+, , −) | BBB (+, , −) |
| BA (1, 2, 3) | BB (+, , −) | BB (+, , ms) |
| B (1, 2, 3) | B (+, , −) | B (+, , −) |
| CAA (1, 2, 3) | CCC (+, , −) | CCC (+, , −) |
| CA | CC | CC |
| C | C | C |

\* The ratings in the superior part of the table are *investment grade*. Those in the bottom part are *speculative grade*.

### Short-Term External Ratings*

| Moody's | S&P | Fitch IBCA |
|---|---|---|
| Prime–1 | A–1 | F1 |
| Prime–2 | A–2 | F2 |
| Prime–3 | A–3 | F3 |
| Not prime | B | B |
| | C | C |
| | D | D |

\* The ratings in the superior part of the table are *investment grade*. Those in the bottom part are *speculative grade*.

## APPENDIX B: DERIVATION OF THE BASEL II FORMULA

This discussion follows the parsimonious approach given in Repullo and Suarez (2004). An alternative presentation that is consistent with Merton (1974) and Vasicek (1987, 2002) is given in Chapter 22, on credit risk diversification.

A bank is lending money to many firms, $i = 1 \ldots N$. The success or default of a firm $i$ is determined by a latent random variable $X_i$, defined as the sum of three terms:

$$X_i = \mu_i + \sqrt{\rho_i}\, F + \sqrt{(1 - \rho_i)}\, \varepsilon_i$$

where

$\mu_i$ = the expected value of $X_i$

$F$ = a single risk factor that affects all firms (a standardized normally distributed variable)

$\rho_i$ = a measure of the exposure of the firm to the systematic risk factor $F$

$\varepsilon_i$ = an economic shock specific to the firm (normally and independently distributed with mean of 0 and standard deviation of 1).

$F$ is referred to as the systematic risk factor, $\rho_i$ as the factor loading, and $\varepsilon_i$ as a firm-specific or idiosyncratic shock. In this section, loans are assumed to be homogeneous, so the subscript $i$ will be deleted for the expected value $\mu$ and the correlation $\rho$. In a homogeneous loan portfolio, it can be shown that $\rho$ is the correlation between the latent variables for firms $i$ and $j$. $F$ can be interpreted as the inverse of an economic index. A high value implies a recession (large probability of default), and a low value implies an expansion (low probability of default). The case of default and no default is given by the following rule:

No default if $X_i < 0$
Default if $X_i > 0$

If there is a default, everything is lost. The goal is to measure the percentage of loans going into default. If there is some recovery on the defaulted loans, the amount at risk in the case of default would be the loss given default (LGD).

Then, let

$N$ = cumulative normal distribution
$IN$ = inverse cumulative normal distribution

Taking a specific value for the systematic factor $F$, the conditional probability of default of the homogeneous firm, PD, can be computed. A conditional probability of an event is the probability given that another event (in this case, a specific value for the systematic factor $F$) has materialized.

$$PD\,(F) = \Pr\,(X_i > 0)$$

$$= \Pr\left(\varepsilon_i > -\frac{\mu + \sqrt{\rho}\,F}{\sqrt{(1-\rho)}}\right)$$

$$= N\left(\frac{IN\,(PD) + \sqrt{\rho}\,F}{\sqrt{(1-\rho)}}\right) \quad (1)$$

The last result follows from properties of the symmetrical cumulative normal distribution:

Probability $(\varepsilon_i > -c) = N(c)$
$PD = \Pr(X_i > 0) = \Pr\,(X_i - \mu > -\mu)$
$\qquad = N(\mu)$
$\mu = IN(PD)$

Since the idiosyncratic terms $\varepsilon_i$ are independent, if the number of loans in the portfolio is very large,[8] it is possible to rely on the Law of Large Numbers to ensure that the conditional frequency of default in a loan portfolio is equal to the probability of default for a given factor $F$. Credit VAR, the maximum loss that will be seen in a loan portfolio with $\alpha$ degree of confidence, can be calculated by selecting a large value for the systematic risk factor $F$, the $\alpha$ quantile of its distribution. The $\alpha$ quantile is, by definition, the value of a variable such that $\alpha$ percent of the observations lie below this value.

Probability of default ($\alpha$ confidence level for factor $F$)
$= $ default frequency ($\alpha$)
$= $ credit $-$ VAR ($\alpha$)
$$= N\left[\frac{IN\,(PD) + \sqrt{\rho}\,IN(\alpha)}{\sqrt{(1-\rho)}}\right]$$

Basel II fixes capital to cover loan losses with a $\alpha$ confidence level of 99.9 percent.

This is the formula used to compute the safety factor in the Basel II formula.

## EXERCISES FOR CHAPTER 13

1. Using a standard PC spreadsheet for a loan of $100 with a probability of default of 2 percent and a maturity of two years, compute the Basel II correlation factor $R$, the safety factor, the spread, the maturity factor, the capital requirement, and the risk-weighted assets.
2. Basel II will soon be implemented in your country. As a member of the board in charge of reviewing the application of the credit risk component of Basel II, which parameters would you want to check to ensure that the Basel II capital requirement provides the appropriate amount of economic capital needed to run your bank?

### Notes

1. A chronological discussion of the BIS capital regulations would mention the 1996 market risk accord, a capital addendum for trading risk. As this accord is not affected by the Basel II revision, it will be presented in Chapter 20 in the discussion of trading risk.
2. A second change concerns the treatment of *general provisions*. This is discussed later in the chapter.
3. See the Basel 2 document for a complete analysis of the weightings for different types of transactions.
4. The United States might allow some banks to use a Basel I-A approach that somewhat follows the Basel II standardized approach. In the United States, the Federal Deposit Insurance Corporation applies an additional regulation on the *leverage ratio*, or Tier 1 capital to unweighted balance sheet assets. The Federal Deposit Insurance Corporation Improvement Act (FDICIA) of 1991 introduced a closure rule that is triggered when the leverage ratio falls below 2 percent [Eisenbeis and Kaufman (2006)]. After the U.S. subprime crisis, which affected its very large banks, Switzerland's Federal Banking Commission has decided to impose a similar leverage ratio.
5. BCBS considers six categories of corporate loans, with slightly modified formulas for each. For more complete information, see the Basel II document. In the formula, a PD of, for example, 1 percent, has to be entered as 0.01.

6. Two different proofs of the safety factor formula are given: one in Appendix B of this chapter, and a second in Chapter 22, on credit risk diversification.
7. One of these theories is known as the extreme value theory.
8. Regulators refer to *infinitely granular* loan portfolios.

CHAPTER 14

# Loss Given Default and Provisions on Nonperforming Loans

In the Basel II internal ratings–based (IRB) approach, a formula is used to compute capital adequacy. One of its inputs is a measure of the loss given default (LGD). That is, at the time of default, what is the expected loss on a nonperforming loan? A directly related issue is the estimate of provisions on nonperforming loans that should be recognized by the bank in its financial statements at the time of default and after the default date. Estimates of loss given default and provisions on nonperforming loans are discussed in this chapter. The following chapter argues that provisions should also be calculated on performing loans.

## PROVISIONS ON NONPERFORMING LOANS: ARE YOU AN OPTIMIST OR A PESSIMIST?

Determining provisions for loan losses, that is, a reduction of profit resulting from nonperforming loans, is one of the most difficult accounting issues in banking. In many of the banking crises of recent years (Japan, Thailand, China, Crédit Lyonnais in France, and the 2007 U.S. subprime crisis), loan-loss provisions had been underreported, with the result being that bank capital was overestimated.[1]

To illustrate the nature of the difficulty, consider a loan of $100 with two years to maturity and contractual annual interest of 9 percent. The contractual interest on other bonds with similar risk is also 9 percent.

| Year | | |
|---|---|---|
| 0 | 1 | 2 |
| | 9 | 109 |

The fair value of the loan is equal to

$$\text{Value of the loan} = \frac{9}{1.09} + \frac{109}{1.09^2}$$
$$= 100$$

Now imagine that there is information that the interest of \$9 will not be paid next year, but that the second year's cash flow will be paid. The value of the loan could then be computed as follows:

$$\text{Value of the loan} = \frac{0}{1.09} + \frac{109}{1.09^2} = 91.74$$

The provision for credit risk would be

$$100 - 91.74 = 8.26$$

However, an optimistic banker might argue that the delay in payment is the result of a short-term liquidity problem and that in the second year the missed interest of \$9 will be paid with accrued interest: $9 \times (1.09)$. In this case, the fair value of the loan becomes

$$\text{Value of the loan} = \frac{0}{1.09} + \frac{(9 \times 1.09) + 109}{1.09^2} = 100$$

The optimist banker would argue that there is no need to make any provision for loan loss. Making provisions for nonperforming loans is difficult because it requires forecasting future cash flow recoveries on distressed loans. In 1982, the former CEO of Citigroup, Walter Wriston, famously stated that there was no need to make provisions for loans to Latin American countries, such as Brazil or Mexico, on the grounds that these countries were merely experiencing short-term liquidity problems and that the missed interest payments would be made at a later date. History proved him to be wrong, and American and European banks had to recognize large losses in the late 1980s. In Japan in the 1990s and in China early in the second millennium, it was common for banks to lend money to technically bankrupt companies, keeping them afloat and avoiding the need to recognize any provisions.

This chapter first introduces the accounting rules that banks use to recognize loan-loss provisions and then proposes an objective, data-based methodology to determine provisions for nonperforming loans.

## CRITERIA FOR NONPERFORMING LOANS

The criterion used for the classifying a loan as "nonperforming" is critical for studying recovery rates and provisions, as a different classification would lead to different results. There are three definitions that are used:

1. A loan is classified as *doubtful* as soon as "full payment appears to be questionable on the basis of the available information."
2. A loan is classified as *in distress* as soon as a payment (interest and/or principal) has been missed. In many countries, a loan must be classified as nonperforming when interest or principal has not been paid for more than 90 days.
3. A loan is classified as *in default* when a formal restructuring process or bankruptcy[2] proceeding is started.

This chapter uses the second definition, that is, it classifies a loan as "in default" as soon as a payment is missed.[3]

## ACCOUNTING FOR NONPERFORMING LOANS

Banks use four methods for dealing with nonperforming loans:

- Accrual of interest
- Nonperforming loan
- Specific provisions
- Direct charge-off

These methods will be described next.

### Accrual of Interest

Consider the previous example, where an interest payment of $9 is missed at the end of Year 1. The original loan of $100 was funded with debt of $92 priced at 7 percent.

The accrual of interest method works as follows: although the interest has not been paid, the accountant takes her pen, recognizes interest income of $9 in the income statement (also called the profit and loss account), and increases the loan in the balance sheet by $9.

| Balance Sheet | Income Statement |
|---|---|
| $\Delta^+$ Loans = 9 | Interest income = 9 |
| | − Interest expense = −6.44 (= 92 × 7%) |

The accrued interest of $9 is recognized in the profit and loss account, even though the bank has received no payment. This can be interpreted as follows: it is as if the bank had loaned an extra $9 to the borrower, and the borrower had used the money to pay the interest of $9. The accrual of interest method is the best of all worlds for bankers. It is magic! No interest is paid, but the financial reports show that everything is normal. No pain! Nothing to see in the account! In 1983, accrual of interest on Latin American loans represented 33 percent of the profit of large American banks, and dividends were paid just as if everything were normal — there was simply a short-term liquidity problem.

To prevent banks from deceiving investors or regulators by abusing the accrual of interest method, accounting rules were made more stringent. A *nonperforming loan* category was created.

### Nonperforming Loans (NPL)

In most countries, loans are transferred to a nonperforming category when a payment of interest or principal has been due for more than 90 days. In that case, the accounting rules work as follows. First, the banks are no longer allowed to recognize interest income in the income statement (although they still face interest expense on debt financing). Second, banks must disclose information on nonperforming loans by creating a special loan category in the balance sheet.

| Balance Sheet | Income Statement |
|---|---|
| $\Delta-$ Loans $= -100$ | Interest income $= 0$ |
| $\Delta+$ Nonperforming loans $= +100$ | $-$ Interest expense |
|  | $= -6.44 \, (= 92 \times 7\%)$ |

So, when a loan is nonperforming, pain is showing because there is no interest income, but no provision for credit risk has yet been recognized. The next move entails the recognition of an expected loss and provision for credit risk.

### Specific Provisions: Two Steps

The creation of specific provisions involves two steps. In the first one, the expected loss on the loan is evaluated. It is an expected loss because the collateral has not yet been realized, because the tax implications are not yet fully confirmed, or because the outcome of the bankruptcy proceedings is not yet known. Suppose, for example, that only $70 of the principal of $100 is expected to be recovered. This implies an expected loss given default of 30. An expense, a provision[4] for nonperforming loans, is recognized in the income statement, and in the balance sheet, the *gross* loan of $100 is reduced by the provision of $30 to create a *net* loan value of $70.

## Step 1: Provisions

<u>Balance Sheet</u>    **Income Statement**

Gross loans $= 100$   Interest income $= 0$

$-$ Provision $= -30$  $-$ Interest expense $= -6.44$ ($92 \times 7\%$)

Net loans $= 70$      $-$ Provision $= -30$

A few years later, there is a restructuring of the loan, or the bankruptcy proceedings are closed, and the loan is now evaluated for certain at $60. The bank can now proceed with the write-off; that is, it can recognize the correct value of the asset, making a last income statement adjustment if necessary.

## Step 2 Write-Off

<u>Balance Sheet</u>    **Income Statement**

Loan $= 60$      $-$Value adjustment $= -10$

For completeness, a fourth method of accounting for credit risk is presented.

### Direct Charge-Off

The *direct charge-off* method collapses the previous two steps into one. This will occur only if the loss given default can be evaluated very rapidly. For instance, if the LGD is known to be $40,

<u>Balance Sheet</u>    **Income Statement**

Loan $= 60$      Charge-off expense $= -40$

Around the world, banking authorities are enforcing the 90-day rule for nonperforming loans. However, this still leaves the large problem of making adequate provisions for loans. In many countries, a standard practice has been for the bank to first compute the annual profit without provisions. If the results were very good, large provisions would be created. However, if the results were poor, only small provisions would be created. The objective was to attempt to stabilize reported accounting earnings. The philosophy was that stable reported earnings would contribute to confidence in the banking system and to financial stability. The danger, of course, was that during recessions, banks would be reporting provisions that were too low and overreporting the level of equity, leading to the danger of paying larger dividends than the banks could afford. In other countries, banks were reporting reserves based on the average actual realized loss rates of the last five years. This took away some discretionary power, but it could also imply that if the previous four years had been very good, the provisions for loan losses would be too low during a recession. If market participants and analysts understood that the reported amount of equity was overstated, there could be a risk of a crisis of confidence in the banking system. In recent years, there has been a worldwide convergence on the view that increased transparency and reporting of actual losses contribute to increased accountability of management, since managers cannot not rely on the massaging of loan-loss provisions and accounting numbers. Increased accountability would lead to increased confidence in and stability of the banking system.

So, a search is on for more objective methods of determining loan-loss provisions. The next section presents such a method.

## PROVISIONS FOR NONPERFORMING LOANS: A MORTALITY-BASED APPROACH[5]

There are two methodologies that can be used to estimate expected recovery on distressed loans and to calculate loan-loss provisions:

1. The price of the loan at the default date, defined most frequently as the trading price one month after the default. This approach has been used in studies of recoveries on corporate bond defaults.
2. The discounted value of future cash flows recovered after the default date.

In some countries, such as the United States, there is a liquid market for distressed loans, so that the price of loans at default dates can be observed and the loss given default or the provision can be evaluated by finding the difference between the principal and the market price. A similar liquid market exists for distressed corporate bonds. However, in many countries, there is no such liquid market for distressed loans, so that it is necessary to estimate the value of future expected recovered cash flows.

If a bank has access to the history of cash flows recovered on loans after default, it can study the time distribution of recovery. This section applies the mortality approach discussed in the studies by Altman (1989) and Altman and Suggitt (2000). It must be noted that these studies applied the mortality approach to measure the percentage of bonds or loans that

**TABLE 14.1**

Cash Flow Recovery on Nonperforming Loans: An Example

|  | December 2000 | December 2001 | December 2002 | December 2003 |
|---|---|---|---|---|
| Loan outstanding (before cash payment) | 100 | 110 | 66 | 44 |
| Cash payment | 0 | 50 | 26 | 14 |
| Loan balance (after cash payment) | 100 | 60 | 40 | 30 |

defaulted $n$ years after origination. The application of mortality to loan recovery rates examines the percentage of a bad and doubtful loan that is recovered $n$ months after the default date.

To define the concepts used to measure the loan recovery rate and the appropriate provisions on impaired loans, it is, for expository reasons, useful to refer to a simple example. Formal definitions of concepts are presented in the appendix to this chapter. Consider a representative loan of $100 that entered the default category in December 2000. The subsequent payments on this loan are shown in Table 14.1, assuming, for expository convenience, that all payments take place at the end of the year, with a final payment in December 2003. The contractual interest rate is 10 percent.

The next sections present a methodology for calculating appropriate provisions at the time of default and changes in provisions several years after the default date.

### Loan-Loss Provisions at the Time of Default

The *marginal recovery rate* at December 2001, $MRR_1$, is defined as the proportion of the loan outstanding in December 2001 that is being paid one period (in the example, one year) after default:

$$MRR_1 = \text{cash flow paid}_1/\text{loan balance}_1$$
$$= 50/110 = 5/11$$

The *percentage unpaid loan balance* after the payment in December 2001, $PULB_1$, is defined as the proportion of the December 2001 loan balance that remains to be paid one period after default:

$$PULB_1 = 1 - MRR_1 = 1 - 5/11 = 6/11$$

The marginal recovery rate and the percentage unpaid loan balance at December 2002, two periods after default, can also be defined:

$$MRR_2 = \text{cash flow paid}_2/\text{loan}_2 = 26/66$$
$$PULB_2 = 1 - MRR_2 = 1 - 26/66 = 40/66$$

And the *cumulative recovery rate* in December 2002 for a loan defaulting in December 2000, $CRR_{0,2}$, is defined as

$$
\begin{aligned}
CRR_{0,2} &= 1 - (PULB_2 \times PULB_1) \\
&= 1 - (40/66 \times 6/11) = 1 - 240/726 \\
&= (1 - 40/121) = 81/121 \\
&= (81/1.1^2)/100 = 66.9\%
\end{aligned}
$$

Similarly, a *marginal recovery rate*, $MRR_3$, a *percentage unpaid loan balance*, $PULB_3$, and a *cumulative recovery rate*, $CRR_{0,3}$, can be calculated at December 2003:

$$MRR_3 = \text{cash flow paid}_3/\text{loan}_3 = 14/44$$
$$PULB_3 = 1 - MRR_3 = 1 - 14/44 = 30/44$$
$$
\begin{aligned}
CRR_{0,3} &= 1 - (PULB_3 \times PULB_2 \times PULB_1) \\
&= 1 - (30/44 \times 40/66 \times 6/11) = 1 - 7,200/31,944 \\
&= 1 - 30/133.1 \\
&= 103.1/133.1 = (103.1/1.1^3)/100 = 77.5\%
\end{aligned}
$$

The *cumulative recovery rate* at time $T$ on a loan balance outstanding at time 0, $CRR_{0,T}$, represents the proportion of the initial defaulted loan that has been repaid[6] (in present value terms) $T$ periods after default.

Finally, the *loan-loss provision*, $LLP_0$, on a loan balance outstanding at the default date, December 2000, is defined as

$$LLP_0 = 1 - CRR_{0,3} = 1 - 0.775 = 22.5\%$$

This percentage, 22.5 percent, represents the percentage of the loan (interest included) that will not be recovered in the future. Once the cumulative recovery rate on individual loans has been computed, an arithmetic average cumulative recovery rate for the sample of loans can be calculated. Alternatively, it is possible to compute a principal-weighted average recovery rate that will take the size of each loan into account. A comparison of the sample weighted cumulative recovery rate with the average of recovery rates on individual loans will be indicative of a size effect.

The provision estimate can be used to determine the loss given default, a parameter that is required in the advanced internal ratings–based approach of Basel II (see the discussion in Chapter 13).

Therefore, historical data on recovery of bad loans provide an objective basis for calculating provisions at the time of default.

### Dynamic Provisions after the Default Date

Once provisions at the time of default have been calculated, a second question will arise: how should these provisions evolve after the default date. Intuition tells you that at the time of default, there is still some hope that the loan will be paid back, especially if the borrower in fact had a short-term liquidity problem. But several years after default, the probability of being repaid diminishes. Again, historical data on recoveries can help to define a *dynamic provisioning* schedule.

Moving forward, it is possible to define a *cumulative recovery rate*, $CRR_{1,3}$, on the loan balance outstanding at December 2001 (one year after default), and a dynamic *loan loss provision*, $LLP_1$, on the loan balance outstanding at December 2001. These are defined as

$$CRR_{1,3} = (1 - PULB_3 \times PULB_2) = 1 - 30/44 \times 40/66 = 58.7\%$$
$$LLP_1 = 1 - CRR_{1,3} = 41.3\%$$

In a similar manner, the *cumulative recovery rate*, $CRR_{2,3}$, and the dynamic *loan-loss provision*, $LLP_2$, on a loan balance outstanding at December 2002 (two years after default) are defined as

$$CRR_{2,3} = (1 - PULB_3) = 1 - 30/44 = 31.8\%$$
$$LLP_2 = 1 - CRR_{2,3} = 68.2\%$$

Knowledge of marginal recovery rates over time on a portfolio of distressed loans thus allows the calculation of a dynamic provisioning schedule. In this example, provisions would start at 22.5 percent at the time of default and rise to 68.2 percent of the outstanding loan balance two years after default.

## CONCLUSION

Provisions on nonperforming loans are not easy to estimate because they require a forecast of future recovered cash flows. Too often, banks have used loan-loss provisions to smooth reported income. However, the provisioning issue is far more important than capital regulation. Indeed, if provisions are not correct, the book value of equity will not represent the correct net worth of the bank, and the best methods of capital regulation will be defeated, as they will be relying on erroneous equity figures. Historical data on recovered cash flows provide a basis for a more objective approach to calculating provisions on nonperforming loans. The measurement of provisions, the loss expected at the time of distress, is directly related to the estimate of loss given default (LGD), the parameter needed to apply the Basel II advanced internal ratings–based approach.

## APPENDIX: RECOVERY CONCEPTS

For an individual loan $I$ that is in default, four concepts are defined, with $t$ denoting the number of periods after the initial default date 0:

$MRR_{i,t}$ = marginal recovery rate in period $t$
  = cash flow$_I$ paid at the end of period $t$/loan$_I$
  outstanding at time $t$

$PULB_{i,t}$ = percentage unpaid loan balance at the end of period
  $t = 1 - MRR_{i,t}$

The cumulative recovery rate evaluated from the default date 0 until infinity, $CRR_i,0,\infty$, and the loan-loss provision, $LLP_i,0$, are equal to

$CRR_i,0,\infty$ = cumulative recovery rate $\infty$ periods after the default =

$$1 - \prod_{t=1}^{\infty} PULB_{it,}$$

$LLP_I,0$ = loan-loss provisions = $1 - CRR_I,0,\infty$

For the sake of presentation, the loan-loss provision was calculated on a loan balance outstanding at the default date, 0. In a more general dynamic provisions setting, the provision can be calculated on a loan balance outstanding at any date $n$ after the default date. For instance, the cumulative recovery on loan balances outstanding 4 or 13 months after the default date can be computed. The loan-loss provisions at the time of default represent the loss given default, a parameter needed to apply the Basel II internal ratings–based approach.

## EXERCISE FOR CHAPTER 14

1. Some historical information on loan balances and cash flows recovered on nonperforming loans (at the date of December 2005) is given in the following table. The interest rate on loans is 5 percent, and the balance outstanding on December 2008 ($23.15) will not be recovered.

| | December 2005 | December 2006 | December 2007 | December 2008 |
|---|---|---|---|---|
| Loans outstanding | 100 | 105 $(100 \times 1.05)$ | 73.5 $(70 \times 1.05)$ | 34.65 $(33 \times 1.05)$ |
| Cash payment | 0 | 35 | 40.5 | 11.5 |
| Loan balances (after payment) | 100 | 70 | 33 | 23.15 |

Compute the following (rounding of numbers should be done at the first decimal):

a. The marginal recovery rates (MRR) on this sample of loans in the years 2006, 2007, and 2008.

b. The percentage unpaid loan balances (PULB) on this sample at December 2006, December 2007, and December 2008.

c. The cumulative recovery rates (CRR) on a loan outstanding at December 2005 over one year, two years. and three years.

d. Based on the information provided by this sample, compute a dynamic provisioning schedule for loan outstanding balances at the time of distress, one year after distress, and two years after distress.

## Notes

1. "The official estimate of bad loans held by the top 15 Japanese banks in 2001 rose to 20,700 bn (4% of gross domestic product). Analysts say that the real figure could be seven times this amount." (*Financial Times*, December 13, 2001.)
2. The word *bankruptcy* originates from the Latin words *banca rotta*, meaning "rotten bench."
3. For the sake of comparison, the definition of default adopted by the Basel Committee is as follows (Basel Committee, 2004, p. 92): "A default is considered to have occurred with regard to a particular obligor when either or both of the two following events have taken place:
   a. The bank considers that the obligor is unlikely to pay its credit obligations to the banking group in full, without recourse by the bank to actions such as realizing security (if held).
   b. The obligor is past due more than 90 days on any material credit obligation to the banking group. Overdrafts will be considered as

being past due once the customer has breached an advised limit or been advised of a limit smaller than current outstandings."

4. American banks use the term *loan-loss allowance* or *loan-loss reserve*, while international banks often refer to *provisions*.

5. This section draws on Dermine and Neto de Carvalho (2005, 2006, and 2008).

6. It can be seen that 103.1, in $CRR_{0,3}$, is the future capitalized value of interim cash flow recovered $[103.1 = (50 \times 1.1^2) + (26 \times 1.1) + 14]$.

# CHAPTER 15

# Loan Pricing II, Loan-Loss Provisions on Performing Loans, and Estimates of Probabilities of Default

This chapter focuses on two related issues: loan pricing and determining loan-loss provisions for performing loans. This is followed by the presentation of four methods for estimating probabilities of default. As will be shown, similar methodologies and data sets provide guidance for both pricing loans at origination and determining loan-loss provisions for performing loans.

## LOAN PRICING AT ORIGINATION DATE

An introduction to loan pricing was given in Chapter 12. It showed that financing loans with equity would require a profit and an *equity spread* to satisfy shareholders. This chapter introduces credit risk explicitly.

Consider the following loan pricing example. In this example, the cash flows will be discounted at the bank's overall cost of equity. As argued in the bank fundamental valuation model in Chapter 6, it would be preferable to discount at a specific risk-adjusted discount rate. This will be done next.

Consider the following example of a loan with two years to maturity:

- A $100 fixed-rate loan with two years to maturity (interest is paid at the end of the year and the principal at maturity)
- A corporate tax rate of 40 percent
- A fixed interbank rate of 10 percent for the first year and 10 percent for the second year
- Cost of equity of 15 percent
- Equity (economic capital) funding: 6 percent; interbank funding: 94 percent

- Probability of default in Year 1: 0 percent; probability of default in Year 2: 3 percent
- Recovery of $60 in case of default [i.e., loss given default (LGD) = $40]

Admittedly, the last three pieces of information are difficult to estimate. But they must be estimated in order to avoid *crystal ball* pricing. The funding structure will be guided by economic capital allocation, based on unexpected or potential loss. Estimates of the probability of default over time will be discussed at the end of the chapter. Finally, a methodology for estimating the loss given default was discussed in Chapter 14.

Two issues will be addressed, as illustrated in the following timeline. First, at the origination date when the loan is granted, what should the breakeven rate $R$ be? Second, a year later, when the interest is being paid on a loan that still has one year to maturity, should a provision be recognized?

| Origination Date, | Year 1 | Year 2 |
|---|---|---|
| Breakeven rate $R$ | Interest income $R$ − provisions (?) | Maturity date of the loan |

### Loan Pricing at Origination Date: Foundation Approach with Discounting at the Overall Cost of Equity

The breakeven loan interest rate, $R$, is such that the discounted value of expected cash flows is equal to the initial equity investment of $6:

$$
\begin{aligned}
\text{Equity} = 6 = {} & \frac{(R \times 100 - 10\% \times 94) \times (1 - 0.4)}{1.15} \\
& + \frac{0.97 \times [R \times 100 \times (1 - 0.4) + 100] + 0.03 \times (60 + 0.4 \times 40)}{1.15^2} \\
& - \frac{94 \times 10\% \times (1 - 0.4) + 94}{1.15^2}
\end{aligned}
$$

There is no risk of default in Year 1, so the cash flow is the after-tax interest margin.

The expected cash flows from the loan in Year 2 have two parts: the expected revenue in the case of no default, and the recovery ($60) plus the tax shelter created by the losses in the case of default (40 percent × $40).[1] The expected cash flows are discounted at the overall cost of equity, 15 percent.

The breakeven loan rate, $R = 11.62$ percent, will capture implicitly the funding structure, the probability of default, the expected losses arising from default, and the cost of equity of the bank. As the bank fundamental valuation model recommended the use of specific risk-adjusted discount rates to value loans, the next section presents a pricing model with a risk-adjusted discount rate for the same loan.

### Loan Pricing at Origination Date: Advanced Approach with Discounting at a Risk-Adjusted Discount Rate

Consider the previous example, but assume that information on the expected return on corporate bonds with similar risk is available:

- A $100 fixed-rate loan with two years to maturity (interest paid at the end of the year and the principal at maturity)
- A corporate tax rate of 40 percent
- An expected return on similar-risk (zero-coupon) corporate bonds with one year and two years to maturity of 10.20 percent and 10.31 percent, respectively.
- A fixed interbank rate of 10 percent for the first year and 10 percent for the second year
- Equity (economic capital) funding: 6 percent; interbank funding: 94 percent
- Probability of default in Year 1: 0 percent; probability of default in Year 2: 3 percent
- Recovery of $60 in case of default (i.e., loss given default = $40)

Following the bank fundamental valuation model of Chapter 6, the expected cash flows on the loans are evaluated at the expected return on corporate bonds, while the funding flows are discounted at the current cost of debt available to shareholders (assumed in this example to be identical to the bank's cost of debt, or 10 percent). The breakeven loan interest rate, $R$, is such that the discounted value of expected cash flows is equal to the initial equity investment:

$$\text{Equity} = 6 = \frac{R \times (1 - 0.4)}{1.102}$$
$$+ \frac{0.97 \times [R \times (1 - 0.4) + 100] + 0.03 \times [(60 + 0.4 \times 40)]}{1.1031^2}$$
$$- \frac{94 \times 0.10 \times (1 - 0.4)}{1.1} - \frac{94 \times 0.10 \times (1 - 0.4) + 94}{1.1 \times 1.1}$$

The breakeven loan rate, $R = 11.62$ percent, will capture implicitly the funding structure, the probability of default, the expected losses arising from default, and the expected return on corporate bonds.[2]

## The Triple Cost of Credit Risk

Bankers often asked if this approach doesn't penalize credit risk too many times. Indeed, credit risk affects the breakeven rate in three ways: an expected loss reduces the expected cash flows, economic capital is needed to cover an unexpected loss, and a risk-adjusted discount rate is used to evaluate cash flows. The answer is *no*, this approach does not penalize credit risk too many times. To make a parallel with the standard corporate finance techniques discussed in Chapter 8, the evaluation of any investment requires an evaluation of the expected free cash flows (in the case of a loan, cash flows adjusted for expected loss), a funding structure (in the case of a loan, the economic capital needed to cover an unexpected loss), and a risk-adjusted discount rate that represents the expected return available to shareholders on similar-risk investments. This includes a risk premium to satisfy risk-averse investors.

A separate but related issue concerns the creation of fair credit risk provisions over the life of the asset.

## FAIR PROVISIONS FOR PERFORMING LOANS

As discussed in Chapter 14, the issue of determining fair provisions for credit risk is a very important one in banking. The first reason for this concerns the estimate of a bank's solvency and the need to measure its equity properly. Instead of waiting for problems to occur, it is preferable to recognize the loss of value of assets early so that the bank can reduce dividends and/or increase its equity base. The second issue concerns the creation of proper incentives inside a bank. If provisions for performing loans are not recognized early, there could be a myopic temptation to go into high-risk–high-margin lending to show very good profit and performance early, especially when rewards and bonuses are linked to performance. So, to reduce this bias, early provisions should be created to reduce the apparent profit. Whatever the reason, solvency or risk-adjusted performance evaluation, there is a need for a sound methodology for determining appropriate loan-loss provisions for performing loans. This section argues that the value-based model allows a fair level of provisions to be created, fully consistent with finance theory.

Consider the example of the previous loan, priced at 11.62 percent. At the end of Year 1, the interest has been collected, and the issues are concerns about the calculation of loan-loss provisions and the evaluation of the loan officer's performance.

To clarify, the time structure of the transaction is as follows:

| Origination Date | Year 1 | Year 2 |
|---|---|---|
| Loan origination | Interest income: | Maturity date |
| (priced at 11.62 percent) | 11.62 − provisions (?) | of the loan |

For the sake of the example, imagine that one year later, the parameters remain unchanged:[3]

- A $100 fixed-rate loan with two years to maturity (interest, 11.62 percent, paid at the end of the year, and principal paid at maturity)
- A corporate tax rate of 40 percent
- Cost of equity = 15 percent
- A fixed interbank rate of 10 percent for the second year
- Equity funding: 6 percent; interbank funding: 94 percent
- Probability of default in Year 2: 3 percent
- Loss given default: $40 (i.e., recovery of $60 in the event of default)

A mark-to-market approach is followed, recognizing the change in the fair net value of the loan, that is, the change in the value of the loan net of the value of the debt.

$$\text{Provisions} = \Delta \text{ net loan value} = \Delta \text{ (value of loan} - \text{value of debt)}$$

$$
\text{Net loan value}_{\text{end of Year 1}} = \frac{0.97 \times [100 + 11.62 \times (1 - 0.4)] + 0.03 \times [(60 + 0.4 \times 40)]}{1.15}
$$
$$
- \frac{94 \times 0.10 \times (1 - 0.4) + 94}{1.15}
$$
$$
= 5.57
$$

Since the net value of the loan is $5.57 at the end of Year 1, when it was $6 million at the beginning, the provision is calculated as the change in net value over the year:

$$\text{Provision} = 6 - 5.57 = 0.43$$

The *risk-adjusted* profit on the loan and the economic profit (EP) are calculated as follows:

$$\text{Profit} = \text{after-tax interest margin} - \text{provision}$$
$$= (1 - 0.4) \times (11.62 - 10\% \times 94) - 0.43$$
$$= 1.33 - 0.43 = 0.90$$

$$\text{Economic profit} = \text{profit} - \text{cost of allocated equity}$$
$$= 0.90 - (6 \times 15\%) = 0$$

The economic profit in this example is zero.[4] This is to be expected, as the loan rate, R, of 11.62 percent was chosen because it was the breakeven loan rate that would give shareholders the minimum required return on their investment. It can be seen that the methodology used to calculate the fair provision is identical to that used to price loans. It is based on fundamental valuation principles.

On a technical note, and contrary to common belief, the creation of provisions can be seen in Year 1, although the probability of default remained unchanged (at 3 percent). The intuitive reason is that a part of the high breakeven rate of 11.62 percent is needed to cover the expected cost of default in Year 2. Of course, the level of provision would increase further if, in the event of a recession looming, the estimate of the probability of default and/or the estimate of the recovery were being revised.

It is necessary to clarify the conceptual difference between the loan-loss provisions just proposed and the practice of some banks of computing provisions as the present value of expected losses. This last measure is related to the change in net value, but it includes only the expected losses, whereas the change in the market value of the loan net of debt takes pricing into account. The argument here is in favor of the change in market value, as not only is it consistent with value-based finance, but it also provides a common methodology for evaluating performances across the bank on a mark-to-market basis.[5]

Both this chapter and Chapter 14 have emphasized the great importance of making provisions for credit risk, whether in order to measure the bank's solvency or to permit a sound evaluation of performance. A clarification is needed to distinguish among provisions that must be recognized in the financial statements by the auditing profession and the stock exchange regulator, provisions recognized by tax authorities, and provisions needed internally to evaluate the risk-adjusted performance of a business unit. In many countries, banks are allowed to recognize provisions only on well-identified problem loans. Provisions on performing loans are not recognized in the income statement. The reason is that the parameters for estimating these provisions can be manipulated. In the author's view, at a minimum, provisions on performing loans should be recognized internally to measure the performance of a loan department correctly. Remember that if no provision is recognized, there is a danger that the department will move into high-margin (and higher-risk) lending. Provisioning is not only an issue of evaluation of equity and solvency, but also an issue of measurement of performance and incentives. It is the author's view that tax authorities, stock exchange regulators, and auditing firms should also recognize provisions on performing loans. If the Basel Committee of Banking Supervision (BCBS) accepts the internal model of banks and their ability to calculate the probability of default and loss given default, there is no reason why this should not be applied as well in accounting for tax authorities or for financial reporting.

The Basel II regulations presented in Chapter 13 and the current chapter on loan pricing and provisioning demand the calculation of probability of default. The next section presents several methodologies that banks use to estimate the risk of default.

## ESTIMATES OF PROBABILITY OF DEFAULT

There are four methods that banks use to estimate the probability of default (PD) on loans: statistical regression based on the bank's historical loan database, frequency of default on corporate bonds observed by rating agencies, risk-neutral probability of default implied in corporate bond spreads, and the KMV expected default frequency (EDF).

### Bank's Own Data (Historical)

Banks collect historical data on loans in a particular category. These data include the characteristics of the borrowers. Discriminant analysis, or estimation of the probability of default with a statistical regression, can then be applied.

### Discriminant Analysis

This technique has been used extensively by a pioneer in credit risk analysis, Professor Ed Altman. The analyst searches for key variables, such as, in the retail consumer loan market, the number of years of employment or the number of years of marriage, to discriminate between *high-quality* borrowers and *low-quality* borrowers. For two discriminatory variables, this can be represented on the graph presented in Figure 15.1. The $X_i'$ refer to performing loans, while the *dots* refer to nonperforming loans. A diagonal line separates them, discriminating between the good loans and the bad loans. The statistical technique is called *discriminant analysis*.[6]

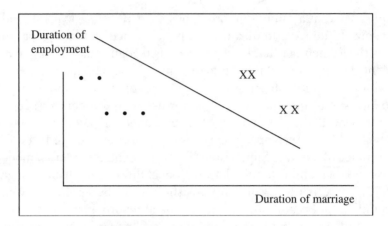

**Figure 15.1** Discriminant analysis: an example.


### Statistical Regression

An alternative to discriminant analysis is to estimate the probability of default. Defaulted loans in the historical database are assigned a value of 0, while performing loans are assigned a value of 1. The following regression[7] is then run on historical loan data—for instance, the data for corporate loans:

$$\text{Probability of default} = \text{PD (equity/asset, current asset ratio,}$$
$$\text{cash flow/debt service, \ldots)}$$

### Rating Agencies' Data (Corporate Bonds; Historical)

A second method for estimating the probabilities of default relies on data collected by rating agencies for rated corporate bonds.

For example, Table 15.1 reports the proportion of U.S. corporate bonds that fell into distress (missed a payment) several years after the origination date. These are *pooled* data, meaning that all bonds issued over the period 1971–1991 are pooled, or grouped together, into one data set.

The publication of these data had a major impact on the banking industry. For AAA-rated transactions, there was no surprise, as the risk of default is small. But for B-rated transactions, five years after origination, the rate of distress increases to 25 percent. Many banks are still using the data from rating agencies as a proxy to estimate the risk of default on corporate loans.

Moody's, on its Web site (www.moodys.com), reports similar data by annual cohort. Instead of pooling several years of data into one data set,

**TABLE  15.1**

Cumulative Mortality (Financial Distress) Rates (%) for Bonds with Ratings
Observed at Origination Date, 1971–1991

| Rating | Year 1 | Year 2 | Year 3 | Year 5 | Year 7 | Year 9 |
|--------|--------|--------|--------|--------|--------|--------|
| AAA | 0 | 0 | 0 | 0 | 0.17 | 0.17 |
| AA | 0 | 0 | 1.09 | 1.52 | 1.71 | 1.79 |
| A | 0 | 0.19 | 0.45 | 0.93 | 1.08 | 1.49 |
| BBB | 0.1 | 1.1 | 1.51 | 2.72 | 3.96 | 4.09 |
| BB | 0 | 0.91 | 4.53 | 8.97 | 14.02 | 14.02 |
| B | 1.72 | 6.31 | 14.9 | 25 | 30.09 | 35.54 |
| CCC | 1.55 | 16.16 | 26.01 | 35.4 | 38.85 | NA |

Source: Standard & Poor's.

the distress data are presented year by year. This has the advantage of
allowing the volatility of these parameters year by year to be studied. As an
illustration, Tables 15.2A and B report cumulative distress figures for two
years: bonds issued in 1993 and bonds issued in 1995.

Data on mortality rates by cohort allow the volatility of these rates to
be analyzed. For example, the five-year mortality rate for bonds rated B at
origination was 20.01 percent for the 1993 cohort and 18.32 percent for
the 1995 cohort.

**TABLE  15.2A**

Cumulative Mortality (Financial Distress) Rates for Bonds Issued in 1993

| | Year 1 | Year 2 | Year 3 | Year 5 | Year 7 | Year 9 |
|--------|--------|--------|--------|--------|--------|--------|
| AAA | 0 | 0 | 0 | 0 | 0 | 0 |
| AA | 0 | 0 | 0 | 0 | 0 | 0 |
| A | 0 | 0 | 0 | 0 | 0 | 0.59 |
| Baa | 0 | 0 | 0.25 | 0.25 | 1.13 | 3 |
| Ba | 0.55 | 0.55 | 2.63 | 4.66 | 7.16 | 12.6 |
| B | 5.71 | 9.9 | 15.27 | 20.01 | 27.54 | 37.73 |
| Caa–C | 28.57 | 28.57 | 42.18 | 50.44 | 50.44 | 75.22 |

Source: Moody's.

**TABLE 15.2B**

Cumulative Mortality (Financial Distress) Rates for Bonds Issued in 1995

|       | Year 1 | Year 2 | Year 3 | Year 5 | Year 7 | Year 9 |
|-------|--------|--------|--------|--------|--------|--------|
| AAA   | 0      | 0      | 0      | 0      | 0      | 0      |
| AA    | 0      | 0      | 0      | 0      | 0      | 0      |
| A     | 0      | 0      | 0      | 0      | 0.39   | 0.4    |
| Baa   | 0      | 0      | 0      | 1.29   | 3.14   | 3.9    |
| Ba    | 0.69   | 0.94   | 2.05   | 6.43   | 11.57  | 15.67  |
| B     | 4.8    | 7.32   | 10.18  | 18.32  | 32.89  | 43.74  |
| Caa–C | 11.57  | 19.52  | 19.52  | 30.78  | 55.62  | 68.3   |

Source: Moody's.

Tables 15.2A and B give information on the likelihood of a bond's falling into distress. This is not yet a loss, as a restructuring could take place or some assets could be realized in a bankruptcy proceeding. The rating agencies have also provided data on the value (price in the market) of corporate bonds that are in distress to serve as a market estimation of the losses given default.

### Current Margin on Corporate Bonds and Credit Derivatives

The observation of spreads on corporate bonds and credit derivatives[8] allows the implicit recovery of the probability of default used to price the bond. However, to calculate this, it is necessary to make assumptions about the recovery rate. For example, consider a bond with one year to maturity:

Principal: $100
Coupon: 10 percent
Risk-free rate: 9 percent
Current price: $99.4
Loss given default: $45

It is possible to recover implicitly the probability of default ($\pi$) that would be observed in a risk-neutral world with zero risk premium:

$$\text{Price} = \text{present value of expected cash flows}$$
$$= 99.4 = \frac{(1-\pi) \times (110) + (\pi \times 55)}{1.09}$$

It can be verified that the probability of default is equal to 3 percent. This is referred to as the *risk-neutral probability of default* (RNPD), as no risk premium was added to the discount rate. To the extent that the risk premium for credit risk is positive, the risk-neutral probability of default will overstate the actual probability of default. Risk-neutral probabilities of default are used extensively to price corporate bonds and credit derivatives.[9]

The fourth and last approach has received a very large amount of attention worldwide.

### Moody's KMV Expected Default Frequency (EDF)

The KMV model is directly inspired by option theory (KMV, 2002). It assumes that the value of a company's assets follows a lognormal distribution. At a minimum, asset value takes a value of zero, and it can potentially take a very high value (see Figure 15.2). As discussed in Chapter 3, a lognormal distribution implies that the (instantaneous) return on an asset, $r_A$, follows a normal distribution with standard deviation of return $\sigma_A$.

$$A_t = A_0 \times e^{r_A \times t}$$

In theory, a firm goes bankrupt when the value of its assets falls below the contractual amount of its debt. The probability of default is the area below the debt contractual obligation, that is, the probability that assets falls below the debt, X. Intuitively, the probability of default will be related to two factors: the distance between the current value of the assets $(A_0)$ and the debt contractual obligation (X), and the volatility of return of the asset.

The application of the option pricing framework to estimate credit risk and probability of default demands some approximation.

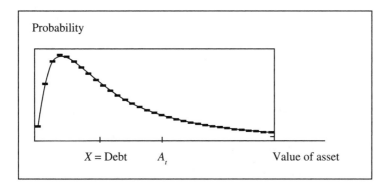

**Figure 15.2**  Probability distribution of end-of-period value of asset.

First, the current value of the assets has to be approximated. It is estimated to be the sum of the current value of equity and the book value of debt.

Second, the volatility of the return on assets has to be estimated. Here, the first step is to compute the volatility of return on shares. Next, a corporate finance formula is applied to deleverage and translate the volatility of return on shares into the volatility of return on assets.

$$\sigma_E = \frac{V_A}{X} \times N(d_1) \times \sigma_A$$

and

$$d_1 = \frac{\ln\left(\dfrac{V_A}{X}\right) + \left(r + \dfrac{1}{2}\sigma_A^2\right) \times T}{\sigma_A \sqrt{T}}$$

where $X$ = promised reimbursement on debt

$T$ = time to maturity of debt

$V_A$ = value of assets of company

$r$ = instantaneous risk-free rate $[= \ln(1 + R)]$

(See the appendix to Chapter 1 for conversion of a rate compounded once a year, $R$, to an instantaneous rate $r$ compounded continuously.)

$N()$ = cumulative normal distribution

It is then possible to compute the *distance to default*, that is, the number of standard deviations required to bring the company to a default point over the specific time horizon (Kealhofer, 2003). It can be viewed as a volatility-adjusted measure of leverage. It is the distance between the log of the expected value of the asset and the log of the debt obligation divided by the standard deviation of asset return.

$$DD(T) = \frac{\ln\left(\dfrac{V_A}{X}\right) + \left(\mu - \dfrac{1}{2}\sigma_A^2\right) T}{\sigma_A \sqrt{T}}$$

If the lognormal distribution was a perfect representation of reality, the mathematics of the lognormal curve could be used to compute the probability of default, that is, the area below the bankruptcy point:

Probability of default $= N(-DD) = 1 - N(DD)$

However, to get closer to the empirical bankruptcy data, KMV uses the following approach.

First, it is necessary to fix the bankruptcy threshold, which is an "ad hoc point" between short-term and long-term debt. Vassalou and Xing (2004) and Duffie et al. (2007) use short-term debt plus half of long-term debt.

The final step is to link the calculated distance to default to the bankruptcy database. That is, in KMV's extensive database, all firms with a similar distance to default are identified, and the number of defaulted firms one year later is observed. KMV can then obtain a linkage between the distance to default (DD) and the probability of default, which it calls EDF, the expected default frequency. Table 15.3 shows the correspondence between EDF (basis points) and different ratings (Crouhy et al., 2000).

**TABLE  15.3**

Correspondence between Ratings and Expected Default Frequencies (EDF)

| EDF (Basis Points) | S&P | Moody's |
|---|---|---|
| 2–4 | > AA | >AA2 |
| 4–10 | AA–A | A1 |
| 10–19 | A–BBB$^+$ | Baa1 |
| 19–40 | BBB$^+$–BBB$^-$ | Baa3 |
| 40–72 | BBB$^-$–BB | Ba1 |
| 72–101 | BB–BB$^-$ | Ba3 |
| 101–143 | BB$^-$–B$^+$ | B1 |
| 143–202 | B$^+$–B | B2 |

After a rapid success, KMV, which was cofounded by Oldrich Vasicek (the V in KMV), was bought out by the external rating agency Moody's and became Moody's KMV.[10]

While banks use four approaches to estimate the probability of default (bank historical data, historical data from rating agencies, risk-neutral probability of default, and KMV EDF), the 2007 experience of the British bank HSBC shows that this exercise is far from science.

## CREDIT RISK ASSESSMENT: THE 2007 CASE OF HSBC HOLDING PLC AND HOUSEHOLD FINANCE CORP[11]

HSBC, a 142-year-old London-based bank with operations in 76 countries and territories, got into the U.S. consumer finance business in 2003 with the $14 billion purchase of Household Finance Corp., a large subprime lender based in Prospect Heights, Illinois. HSBC saw Household as a way to diversify beyond Europe and Asia, and it viewed subprime mortgage lending as being a far less competitive business than lending to more creditworthy customers. Subprime borrowers are those with a limited or poor credit history. These loans are sometimes referred to as *ninja* loans (loans to borrowers with no income and no job or assets). Moreover, as discussed in Chapter 6, low interest rates in the United States had increased margins on retail consumer loans as a result of interest-rate stickiness.

After the deal was announced, Household's then chief executive, William Aldinger, bragged that Household employed 150 Ph.D.s who were skilled at modeling credit risk. Household had developed a system for assessing consumer lending risk called Whirl (Worldwide Household International Revolving Lending System), which it used to underwrite credit card debt and to collect from consumers in the United States, United Kingdom, Middle East, and Mexico.

When the real estate market was booming in recent years, subprime loans were hotly demanded by Wall Street banks and other investors, thanks to the higher interest rates that subprime borrowers paid. This competitive market prompted HSBC and others to seek riskier loans from less creditworthy customers. Some of these mortgages were originated by HSBC branches, but a large part were purchased on the secondary markets.

In February 2007, the percentage of HSBC mortgages that were more than 60 days past due was climbing. HSBC added $1.8 billion to its 2006 bad debt provisions for Household, now called HSBC Finance. This brought the pretax profit of the group down to $2.3 billion.

Mortgage lenders typically base their calculations of a borrower's creditworthiness on credit ratings known as FICO scores, which are generated by Fair Isaac Corporation of Minneapolis. FICO scores measure the credit risk of individual borrowers based on a statistical analysis of their credit files. They are used to assess applicants for credit cards, auto loans, and fixed-rate mortgages, among other things. But the ability of FICO scores to predict the performance, during a weakening housing market, of second-lien loans[12] taken out by subprime borrowers had not yet been put to the test. The same was true of adjustable-rate mortgages (ARMs) to subprime borrowers at a time of now rising interest rates. "What is now clear is that FICO scores are less effective or ineffective when lenders are granting loans in an unusually low interest rate environment," Douglas Fint, a director of HSBC Finance, told investors last December. A spokesman for Fair Isaac says that the company simply provides credit scores, and it is up to lenders to decide how to use them. HSBC doubled, to 875, the number of employees in Tampa and nearby Branton who contact customers about missed payments and try to work out payment plans. That operation was running seven days a week.

Subprime loan losses reported by HSBC in February 2007 marked the start of the U.S. subprime crisis.[13]

## CONCLUSION

Significant methodological progress has been made in pricing credit risk to ensure value creation for shareholders. There are four methods that banks use to estimate the probability of default. Related tools can be used to calculate loan-loss provisions on performing loans. In evaluating performance, these must be taken into account to give lenders the right incentives. If these tools are ignored, there is a danger of biasing the loan portfolio toward long-maturity loans with high margins and high credit risk.

## APPENDIX: LOAN VALUATION: DISCOUNTING EXPECTED CASH FLOWS VS. DISCOUNTING CONTRACTUAL CASH FLOWS

The standard valuation approach is to discount the expected cash flows from a loan at the expected rate available on the market. An interpretation of present value was given in Chapter 1. The present value represents a "cash equivalent": investors are indifferent between holding the asset or buying another one in the market because holding either of the two assets will generate identical expected future cash flows.

This approach has been used to value expected dividends or, as in this chapter, to value loans.

To value loans and corporate bonds, the market sometimes uses an alternative approach (see Appendix A to Chapter 19 for the valuation of floating-rate bonds). The value is the present value of *contractual* cash flows discounted at the *contractual rate* (often referred as the *yield*) on an asset. The contractual rate refers to the promised interest on a loan, which will be paid only if the counterparty is not in distress.

Although the two methods (value of expected cash flows and value of contractual cash flows) should yield an identical value, it is preferable to be consistent with the standard finance valuation framework and compute the value of expected cash flows at an expected return. The reason is that the logic of discounting is the ability to invest at some expected return.

The mathematical relationship between the two approaches (discounting expected cash flows and discounting contractual cash flows) helps to bring clarity.

Consider a one-year loan with a probability of default (PD) and a recovery in case of default (REC, tax shield included). The discount rate to use to evaluate the expected cash flow is the risk-free rate plus a risk premium (RP).

It can be seen that the discount rate that should be used for discounting *contractual* cash flows must include the risk-free rate, a risk pre-

$$\text{Value of loan} = \frac{(1-\text{PD}) \times [100 \times (1+R)] + \text{PD} \times \text{REC}}{1 + R_f + \text{RP}}$$

$$= \frac{100 \times (1+R) - \text{PD}[100 \times (1+R) - \text{REC}]}{1 + R_f + \text{RP}}$$

$$= \frac{100 \times (1+R) - EL}{1 + R_f + \text{RP}}$$

where EL = expected loss

$$\text{Value} \times \left(1 + R_f + RP + \frac{EL}{\text{value}}\right) = 100 \times (1+R)$$

$$\text{Value of loan} = \frac{100 \times (1+R)}{1 + \lambda}$$

where $\lambda = 1 + R_f + RP + \dfrac{EL}{\text{value}}$

mium, and the expected loss premium. Thus, the two methods for valuing risky loans or risky corporate bonds (discounting expected cash flows and discounting contractual cash flows) are equivalent if the proper discount rate is used.

## EXERCISES FOR CHAPTER 15

1. Price the following loan of $100 with two years to maturity. The probability of default in Year 1 is 0 percent, and the probability of default in Year 2 is 10 percent. Given the low seniority of the loan, only $40 would be recovered in the event of default. The loan is funded with 95 percent interbank debt (at a cost of 9 percent) and 5 percent equity. The corporate tax rate is 30 percent. You can use a constant shareholders' cost of funds of 10 percent to answer the following two questions:

    **a.** How much interest would you charge on the loan?

    **b.** Given that the full interest is paid in Year 1 and that the probability of default in Year 2 is revised downward to 5 percent, how much economic profit[14] would you accrue to the loan department at the end of the first year?

2. Would you accept or reject the following loan proposal?

    **a.** A loan of €100,000 with two years to maturity carries an interest rate of 8 percent. It is funded with debt of €95,000 and equity of €5,000. Principal on the loan of €50,000 and debt of €47,500 are to be paid at the end of the first year, with the balances outstanding being paid at the end of the second year. Interest on outstanding balances is paid at the end of Years 1 and 2. The probability of default in Year 1 is 0 percent, and that in Year 2 is 2 percent. The loan is guaranteed by collateral that is likely to have a value of €20,000 in Year 2.

    Given that the estimated cost of equity for the bank is 9 percent, that the interbank rate is 6 percent (flat yield curve), that the corporate tax rate is 40 percent, and that the bank chooses a financial structure of 5 percent equity and 95 percent interbank funding, would you accept the loan proposal priced at 8 percent?

    Show your calculation.

    **b.** Assume that the loan has been granted and that the interest of 8 percent and the principal payment of €50,000 have been paid on time at the end of the first year.

    How much loan-loss provision do you create at the end of the first year, assuming that the information remains unchanged, with the exception that the expected value of the collateral will be zero in case of default?

3. Would you accept the following loan of $100 priced at an annual rate of 14 percent?

    The maturity is two years, with interest paid at the end of the year and the principal at maturity. The cost of equity is 15 percent, and the corporate tax rate is 40 percent.

    In the first year, the loan is funded with equity of $6 and interbank debt of $94 (interbank rate = 10 percent). In the second year, the loan is funded with equity of $4 and interbank debt of $96 (interbank rate = 10 percent). The probability of default is 0 percent in Year 1 and 5 percent in Year 2, with a recovery of $40.

a. Do you accept the loan priced with an interest rate of 14 percent?

b. Assuming that the loan is priced at 14 percent, calculate the economic profit (EP) for the first year, assuming that all parameters are unchanged at the end of Year 1.

4. Would you lend $100 for two years at an annual interest rate of 18 percent (interest paid at end of the year, and reimbursement of principal at maturity), given that you have the following information.

The bank wants an average return on equity of 14 percent on its overall activities. Of a population of 100 similar loans, it is expected that on average 5 would default in Year 1 and another 5 would default in Year 2. That is, on average, only 90 would repay their loan completely. Given the low seniority of the loan, nothing would be recovered in the event of default. The expected return on similar-risk corporate bonds is 10 percent, while the interbank rate is 9 percent. The bank wishes to fund its loan with 6 percent equity and 94 percent debt. The corporate tax rate is 40 percent. If the borrower defaults in Year 1, the bank will repay the principal on interbank funding immediately.

5. Compute the one-year risk-neutral probability of default (RNPD) on the following bond with one year to maturity:

Principal: 100; coupon: 12 percent; current price: 98; risk-free rate: 10 percent; recovery: 45.

## Notes

1. Bankers are often surprised that the loss given default that is applicable to the tax shield is the difference between the loan principal ($100) and the recovery ($60). The interest on the loan is not included. A more explicit calculation of the net cash flow recovered in case of default is as follows: with $L$ = loan principal, $R$ = interest on loan, $t$ = corporate tax rate, recovery = cash flow recovered, and LGD = loan principal – recovery, the result is

Net after-tax cash flow collected on loan in the event of default
= contractual cash flow on loans – loan losses – tax
(calculated on interest net of loss)
= $(R \times L + L) - (R \times L + L - \text{recovery})$
$- \{t \times [R \times L - (R \times L + L - \text{recovery})]\}$
= recovery + $t \times (L - \text{recovery})$ = recovery + $(t \times \text{LGD})$

2. This loan pricing approach is referred to as economic value-added in lending (EVAL). It allows calculation of the breakeven rate on a loan transaction [Dermine (1995, 1998)].

3. The provision will be evaluated with an overall cost of equity of 15 percent. A similar exercise can be done with the expected return on corporate bonds.

4. With reference to Chapter 10 on value centers and performance evaluation, it is necessary to choose a measure of economic profit based on realized EP (the example given here), on expected EP, on average realized EP, or on benchmarked EP. The objective is to separate good luck (expansion in the economy and lower probability of default) from good management skills.

5. Since June 2000, the Bank of Spain has introduced a mandatory statistical (dynamic) provision on performing loans based on expected losses.

6. Note that some countries prohibit the use of some variables, such as race or sex, in credit risk evaluation. From an economic (although not political) perspective, it is not clear if these measures against discrimination produce the desired results. Indeed, measures that reduce the ability of banks to screen credit risk will either reduce loan availability or raise interest margin to cover the higher risk.

7. As probabilities of default are in the interval 0 to 1, it is not possible to use standard ordinary least-squares (OLS) regression; a technique, such as probit-type regression, that constrains the dependent variable to the interval [0, 1] must be used (Lando, 2004).

8. Credit derivatives are discussed in Chapter 25.

9. The loan was valued by discounting the expected cash flows. An alternative approach discussed in the appendix to this chapter is to discount the *contractual* cash flows.

10. Creditgrades (www.creditgrades.com) was set up by large international banks and investment banks to calculate the probability of default and CDS spreads. It essentially builds on KMV with a stochastic default barrier.

11. *Wall Street Journal*, February 8–9, 2007.

12. A second-lien loan is a second mortgage loan taken by a borrower that is subordinated to the first mortgage in the event of the borrower's default.

13. The U.S. subprime crisis is also discussed in Chapters 16, 21, and 25.

14. With reference to Chapter 9, the question refers to *realized* economic profit.

# CHAPTER 16

# Securitization

## ASSET-BACKED SECURITIES, COLLATERALIZED DEBT OBLIGATIONS, AND STRUCTURED INVESTMENT VEHICLES

Over the years, banks have developed a number of techniques for selling loans to investors. This process is called *securitization*. Bank loans are transformed into securities, which are sold to investors. As mentioned in Chapter 12, one of the economic reasons for this process is to remove the loans from the balance sheet so as to avoid the costly BIS capital requirements. The purpose of this chapter is first to introduce the securitization process. As this process is costly, the various economic benefits of securitization are evaluated. Next, recent developments in the markets are introduced: collateralized debt obligations (CDOs), synthetic CDOs, and single-tranche CDOs. Finally, the chapter presents the case of structured investment vehicles (SIVs), which were the source of a worldwide liquidity crisis in 2007.

## THE SECURITIZATION PROCESS

Securitization involves the transformation of loans into securities, with the resulting asset-backed securities (ABSs) being sold to investors. These include both individuals and institutional investors such as mutual funds, pension funds, hedge funds, life insurance companies, and other banks.

Potential investors may be worried about the quality of the loans being sold by the bank. This problem is very similar to the one that is seen in the used-car market, where the buyer is afraid of receiving a lemon. Economists refer to this as a situation of *asymmetric information*, with the seller knowing much more about the characteristics of the loans being sold than the buyer does. A process has to be put in place to reassure the investors and to reduce the asymmetric information problem.

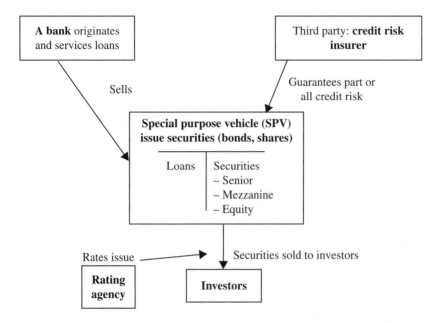

**Figure 16.1** The securitization process.

So, to reassure investors about the quality of the loans, two additional parties are involved in securitization: a credit risk insurer and a rating agency. The general mechanism of the securitization process is shown in Figure 16.1.

The sale of loans to investors is done through a separate corporate entity called a *special-purpose vehicle (SPV)*, also called a *special-purpose entity (SPE)*. The SPV can be viewed as a distinct corporate structure, a bankruptcy-remote vehicle that buys the loans from the bank. In order to finance this acquisition, it issues securities (bonds or shares[1]), which are sold to investors. These securities are referred to as *asset-backed securities*, since their value is derived from the value of the assets in the portfolio.

Usually, the originating bank continues to service the loans (for a fee), and the net cash flows generated by the loans are passed to investors through the SPV.

To reassure investors, a third party steps in, promising to guarantee part or all of the credit risk on the loans. For instance, in the United States, two government-sponsored enterprises (GSEs), the Federal National Mortgage Association (Fannie Mae) and the Federal Home Loan Mortgage Corporation (Freddie Mac), were created to facilitate the sale of mortgages by savings banks.[2] In many countries, institutions of this type do not exist, but private institutions or the skillful design of securities have facilitated securitization. As an example, European reinsurance companies, such as Swiss Re, have offered to guarantee credit risk. One of the reasons that reinsurance companies have entered the credit risk arena is not only their expertise in actuarial science and statistics, but also the diversification benefits of a new asset class. Risk diversification is discussed in Chapters 22 and 23.

An example of a skillful design of securities is the deal done by the French bank Crédit Lyonnais in 1989, one of the first of this type in Europe. To free equity and finance growth, the bank, led by its CEO, Jean-Yves Haberer, wanted to sell 35,000 consumer loans worth 2 billion French francs (FF) (around € 300,000). Advised by the American investment bank Bear Stearns, Crédit Lyonnais created an SPV (a *fonds commun de créances*) funded by two types of securities: Tranche A for FF1.75 billion, and Tranche B for FF0.25 billion (see Figure 16.2). The difference between the two tranches was that Tranche B was subordinated to Tranche A. That is, holders of Tranche A were promised a return (similar to that of a bond). The cash flows earned on the pool of loans were first used to make payments to the holders of Tranche A. What was left was used to remunerate the holders of Tranche B. The set of contractual terms governing the payout of interest and principal payments on the portfolio of the SPV is called a *waterfall*.

A AAA rating was awarded to Tranche A, which was sold to retail investors. The size of Tranche B, with FF0.25 billion, was deemed adequate to protect the holders of Tranche A. As there was no interest from the market, Tranche B remained on the balance sheet of Crédit Lyonnais. The result was that an asset of FF2 billion had been replaced by an asset of FF0.25 billion on the bank's balance sheet. The bank argued successfully

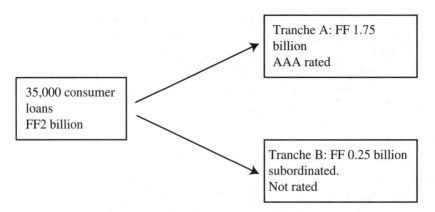

**Figure 16.2** Securitization: an example.

with the French regulator that the Basel I 8 percent ratio should be applied only to the FF0.25 billion asset on the balance sheet, not on the FF2 billion. While the ruling met the letter of the BIS regulations, it clearly did not meet its spirit, as any observer can recognize that Tranche B, being subordinated, absorbed most of the credit risk on the FF2 billion loan portfolio.[3] Later, the Basel ruling was changed, requiring a much higher capital charge (100 percent) for subordinated structures of this type.

In many countries, laws have had to be passed to permit the securitization of loans without the explicit consent of retail borrowers.[4]

In the Crédit Lyonnais example, there were two classes of securities, Tranches A and B. In many cases, there can be several types of securities, including both rated and unrated tranches. The rating of each tranche is determined by its priority with regard to receipt of the cash flows generated by the securitized assets. The senior notes, typically rated from AAA to A, have the highest-priority claim on the cash flows. The mezzanine tranches, typically rated BBB to B, have a claim on the cash flows that is subordinated to that of the senior notes. The rating is based on the probability of receiving the contractual interest and principal on the note. The last tranche is the equity in the ABS, which has a residual claim on cash flows after the other tranches have been paid. It is commonly referred to as the *equity tranche*. Generally, the senior notes will be about 92 percent of the deal and the mezzanine notes 4 percent, with about 4 percent of equity (Goodman, 2002). This implies that losses of from 0 to 4 percent of the total portfolio are borne by equity holders, losses of from 5 to 8 percent are borne by mezzanine securities, and losses above 8 percent are borne by senior notes. The endpoints of each interval are called the *attachment points*. For a reference portfolio of $1,000, a stylized ABS could be represented as shown in Table 16.1 (Basel Committee, 2005; adapted by the author).

**T A B L E   16.1**

Stylized Hypothetical CDOs

| Tranche | Attachment Points | Notional Amount | Credit Rating | Spread (Basis Points) |
|---------|-------------------|-----------------|---------------|-----------------------|
| Senior | 10–100% | $920 | AAA | 30 |
| Mezzanine | 3–10% | $40 | BBB | 100 |
| Equity | 0–3% | $40 | Not rated | 460 |
| Overall portfolio | 0–100% | $1,000 | A | 50 |

In the example in Table 16.1, the overall is made up of $1,000 in loans that are rated A. For each single loan, the probability of default is very small, 0.06 to 0.10 percent, according to the rating agencies' default tables (see Chapters 13 and 15). Intuitively, it can be seen that the risk borne by the senior, mezzanine, and equity tranches is related to the likelihood that many loans will default at the same time, or, in other words, to the correlation across defaults. In addition, the risk is affected by the probability of default and recovery rate assumptions. This is discussed in Chapter 22, on credit risk diversification, and Chapter 25, on credit derivatives.

## THE ECONOMICS OF SECURITIZATION

Securitization is costly, as several parties are involved: auditors, lawyers, rating agencies, and third-party insurers. In view of the costs, a bank needs to evaluate the economic benefits of securitization, a business model referred to as the *originate to distribute* (OTD) model. Six types of benefits have been identified.

### Liquidity and Resolution of the Asymmetric Information Problem

If markets were perfect, with complete information freely available, securitized assets would be redundant, as investors could buy the underlying securities directly. As mentioned earlier, however, asymmetric information between the holder of the loans and the buyers reduces liquidity in the loan sales market. The securitization process contributes to reducing the asymmetric information problem, especially when the bank keeps the equity tranche on its books (Duffie and Garleanu, 2001). Banks that face liquidity constraints[5] can sell their loans to access new sources of liquidity. Given the growth of pension funds and life insurance companies to provide retirement benefits to an aging population, the demand for securitized assets has grown rapidly in many countries.

### Timing of Profit Recognition

If the interest margin on the loan, net of credit risk, is attractive, the loan can be sold to the SPV at a price higher than the principal, creating a capital gain for the bank. This can accelerate the timing of profit recognition, with a positive impact on the return on equity in the short term. This is *cosmetic*, as it simply represents an acceleration of profit recognition. Instead of reporting the positive margin over the life of the loan, the bank reports a capital gain early; in principle, this gain is identical to the present value of the net margin. Moreover, the bank keeps a part of the revenue on the loan. Indeed, it retains a fee for servicing the loan.

## Freeing the Equity

This has been the argument used most by investment banks and consultants advising banks. Selling the assets reduces the need for expensive equity funding and the *equity spread,* discussed in Chapter 12. Alternatively, the equity that has been freed can be used to fund new loans. This last argument assumes either capital rationing (a bank's inability to issue fresh equity to fund growth) or that securitization is a cheaper way to access equity to fund new loans. This has been the way American savings banks with a limited equity base have been able to finance mortgages.

However, Basel II is changing the relevance of this "free the equity" argument in a fundamental way. Indeed, for safe loans, the ones that are easiest to securitize, the capital requirement will be less than 8 percent, meaning that securitization will free much less capital than it did under the Basel I capital rule of 8 percent.

## Management and Diversification of Credit Risk

A bank that has too large an exposure to a country or to a business sector can sell assets to better diversify its credit risk. Credit risk diversification is discussed in Chapter 22.

## New Asset Classes

Institutional investors are able to access investments in loans indirectly, through investment in rated securities, when direct holdings of unrated loans would be prohibited.

## Cheaper Funding Cost

The author has seen the following case. A monoline credit card company operating in the United Kingdom was securitizing 85 percent of its credit card–related loans. The argument was that this provided a *cheaper funding* cost for the bank. Two funding options were available. First, the company could keep the loans on its balance sheet, funded partly with certificates of deposits issued in the market (as the company does not have a deposit base) and partly with equity. The second option was to securitize the loans and sell them to investors.

This bank claimed to have a gross lower funding cost of 15 basis points (0.15 percent) before securitization expenses. To better visualize

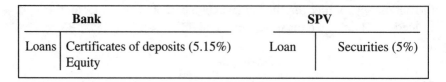

| Bank | | SPV | |
|---|---|---|---|
| Loans | Certificates of deposits (5.15%) | Loan | Securities (5%) |
| | Equity | | |

**Figure 16.3**  Balance sheet finance vs. securitization.

the case, assume that the holders of certificates of deposits would demand
5.15 percent when holders of securitized loans would be satisfied with a
5 percent return (see Figure 16.3).

At first glance, this story seems to violate a fundamental principle in
economics and finance, the *law of one price*. This law states that two goods
or services with identical characteristics should command the same price.
If the loans are identical[6] under the two options, on-balance sheet funding and securitization, how can the pricing of the securities differ by 15
basis points? Furthermore, the cost of bank debt should, in theory, be
slightly lower, as bank debt is protected partly by the equity of the bank,
whereas securities holders, in an SPV, bear the entire credit risk.

The CFO of the bank explained the source of the lower funding cost.
According to him, those who are lending to the bank absorb the entire
enterprise risk of the bank: not only credit risk, but also liquidity risk, interest-rate risk, and operational risk.[7] Because lenders are not fully informed
(a case of asymmetric information between the bank and the market), they
charge the bank a higher cost of funds. To avoid this expensive funding
cost, the bank securitized the assets. This argument has received some
backing from institutional fund managers, such as pension funds and life
insurance companies, who, the author is told, prefer to buy specific asset
classes, such as securitized credit card loans, rather than the entire risk of a
bank. So, the last argument is that securitized loans are an efficient way to
fund a bank whenever asymmetric information is an issue.[8]

*Warning:* It is necessary to be very careful that the perceived lower
funding cost of the securitized assets does not increase the funding cost
of the assets remaining on the balance sheet. For example, this would be
the case if the bank is securitizing safe assets. As the riskier assets left in
the bank would command a higher funding cost, the net benefits of
securitization will not always be as large as they sound. The marginal
benefits of securitization have to be examined carefully. They will, in
most cases, include two parts: the lower funding cost of the securitized
assets and the impact on the funding cost of the assets remaining on the
balance sheet.

Common acronyms or terminology related to securitization have emerged: CBOs, CLOs, CDOs, synthetic securitization, single-tranche CDOs, and covered bonds. They are discussed next.

## DEVELOPMENTS IN THE ABS MARKET

In this section, several types of asset-backed securities offered in the market are discussed.

1. *Collateralized bond obligations (CBOs)*. These are securities issued by a special-purpose vehicle (SPV) or a special-purpose entity (SPE) that holds actual bonds (Goodman, 2002).
2. *Collateralized loan obligations (CLOs)*. These are securities issued by a special-purpose vehicle (SPV) or a special-purpose entity (SPE) that holds actual loans.
3. *Collateralized debt obligations (CDOs)*. These are securities issued by a special-purpose vehicle (SPV) that holds actual loans or other debt obligations.
4. *"Squared CDOs" or structured finance CDOs (SF CDOs)*. These securities package parts of other securitizations, such as slices of other CDOs (Hu, 2007).
5. *ABS CDOs*. These are collateralized debt obligations backed by pools of asset-backed securities (ABSs), including residential and commercial mortgage-backed securities (RMBSs and CMBSs) (Basel Committee, 2008a).

All of these instruments are referred to as *cash* CDOs, in contrast to the *synthetic* CDOs in the following list:

1. *Synthetic securitization*. A structure whereby a credit derivative (insurance) is used to transfer the credit risk associated with a portfolio of loans into a special-purpose vehicle (SPV), which then issues securities whose performance depends on the portfolio of these loans. This structure was first created in 1997 by Swiss Bank Corporation (Goodman, 2002). In this case, the loans remain on the balance sheet of the bank. This is particularly attractive if the borrowers do not want the loans to be transferred to a third party, or if the bank does not want to make it public that it is transferring the credit risk to a third party. Credit derivatives, which are essentially a form of credit guarantee, are discussed in Chapter 25. In the synthetic securitization reported in Figure 16.4, the bank pays a credit insurance premium to the SPV. In return, the SPV

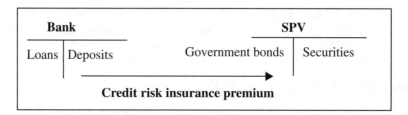

**Figure 16.4** Synthetic securitization.

guarantees the credit risk on the loans. That is, in the event of a loan default, it makes a payment to the bank.

In the example in Figure 16.4, the credit guarantee was directly between the bank and the SPV. Often, there will be a third party in between. The example represents the case of a *funded* synthetic CDO. That is, when the SPV was created, investors paid the principal on their tranches, which was invested in government bonds or AAA-rated corporate bonds that were used as collateral. Any default would cause a write-down of principal of the relevant tranche. Synthetic CDOs with *unfunded* tranches are also common. An example was BISTRO, offered by JPMorgan in 1997 (BISTRO means broad index secured trust offering). Unfunded tranches are structured as swaps with no up-front payment. Investors in those tranches receive periodic spread payments and are required to make a payment when a default affects their tranches. Because unfunded tranches rely on investors' ability to make payments to the CDO, they create a counterparty risk.

2. *Single-tranche CDOs.* In the previous discussion of cash and synthetic CDOs, it was assumed that investors had funded all the tranches: senior, mezzanine, and equity. The creator of the CDO is a broker, an arranger, as the risk is borne by the holders of the various tranches. In a single-tranche CDO, a dealer issues a specific single tranche (defined by specific attachment points, for example, 3 percent to 7 percent) to investors who want it, and manages the risk of the issue (Smithson, 2004). The value of the CDO tranche is the expected value of the fee leg minus the expected present value of the contingent leg (Gibson, 2004). This is discussed in Chapter 25, on credit derivatives.

3. *Covered bonds* (sometimes referred to as *on-balance sheet securitization*). This is debt of a bank that is collateralized by

assets (mortgages). These securities are known in Germany as *Pfandbriefe*, in Spain as *cedulas hipotecarias*, and in France as *obligations foncières*. They are used to fund a mortgage portfolio. In the case of covered bonds, the assets remain on the balance sheet, so that the regular BIS capital regulations apply. The bonds are collateralized by the assets. Bondholders are protected first by the equity of the bank and then, in the event of default, by the value of the collateral. In this case too, cheaper funding may be more apparent than real if other junior investors (not protected by the collateral) start to charge higher interest rates. Although market participants refer to covered bonds as on-balance sheet securitization, this is actually a form of collateralized financing with no impact on capital, since the assets and the credit risk remain on the balance sheet (Packer et al., 2007).

## THE 2007 SAGA OF STRUCTURED INVESTMENT VEHICLES (SIVS)

Chapter 15 related the story of Household Finance Corp. (now Household International), the U.S. consumer finance subsidiary of HSBC. Because it was exposed to the U.S. subprime mortgage loan market, it was forced to announce a first series of large credit risk provisions in February 2007. But more bad news followed. On June 19, 2007, Bear Stearns, the U.S. investment bank, offered to provide $1.5 billion in loans to help rescue a money-losing fund run by its asset management unit. The fund was called the High-Grade Structured Credit Strategies Enhanced Leverage Fund. On August 6, the French bank BNP-Paribas suspended trading in and the valuation of three funds because illiquidity in the market made it impossible to value these funds.[9] This was the starting point of the SIVs problem.

A structured investment vehicle (SIV) is a special-purpose vehicle. Banks had used these vehicles extensively to fund their booming mortgage and consumer loan portfolios. A common characteristic of these SIVs was that long-term assets were funded by the issuance of short-term securities. These short-term securities were part of the so-called asset-backed commercial paper (ABCP) market. As with regular SPVs, several tranches were issued. In this case, the risky equity and mezzanine tranches were sold to investors, while banks sometimes retained the highly rated AAA senior tranches on their books.

The holders of these securities were running three types of risk. There was the regular credit risk if defaults in the mortgage market started to rise. There was a correlation risk, as the value of the securities was related to credit risk correlation.[10] And there was a liquidity risk if the SIVs were unable to redeem the short-term paper through a new issue of paper, that is, if the liquidity in the ABCP market were to dry up.[11] The liquidity risk was often mitigated by the sponsoring bank's providing a liquidity backup guarantee to refinance the SIVs, if needed (Basel Committee, 2008a).[12] Notice that the inability of an SIV to redeem the short-term paper would be a cause of default, with the owners of the securities taking over the assets of the SIV (the mortgage loans), launching a possible fire sale of mortgages to access cash.

The problem that Bear Stearns faced originated in this maturity mismatch and a liquidity squeeze in the short-term ABCP market. Investors, fearing the worst for the mortgage market and unable to value the risk correctly, decided to withdraw from the market. For market regulators and central banks, there was a fear of default and massive sale of mortgages, with the result that a drop in value would itself affect the value of other SIVs that were marked to market.

In December 2007, Citigroup took onto its balance sheet $58 billion of debt from seven troubled investment funds. As will be discussed again in Chapter 21, on liquidity risk, the U.S.-based SIV credit crisis created a major liquidity squeeze around the world, as banks began holding cash, anticipating the need to refinance the SIVs, and as market participants started to worry about the solvency of some financial institutions.

Six solutions to resolve the liquidity crisis were proposed. Some of them came from regulators, others from private market participants:

1. Create a superfund that would lend to the cash-drained SIVs. Such an initiative was discussed in the United States at the initiative of U.S. Treasury Secretary Henry Paulson, and also in France.[13] The limited supply of funds available from investors prevented the success of this initiative.
2. As was done in Canada,[14] freeze the reimbursement of SIVs and replace the short-term paper with long-term floating-rate notes. This is similar to the case of a restructuring of a company's liabilities at a time of financial distress.
3. As was done by Bear Stearns and Citibank, discussed earlier, let the sponsoring bank refinance the SIVs. The consequence was new assets on the bank's balance sheet, with a negative impact on its capital ratio.
4. Allow banks to access central bank lending collateralized by the assets.

5. Allow banks to swap (exchange) government bonds for illiquid assets with the central bank. This was done in the United States and the United Kingdom.

6. A private solution, originating from the restructuring of real assets, was to work in two steps. The first step was to auction the assets of SIVs to evaluate their fair value. In a second step, the assets would be repackaged into new funds. The acceleration of the crisis did not allow this plan to be implemented.

Heads of CEOs of major financial institutions started to roll in 2007 and 2008: Peter Wuffli and Marcel Ospel at the Swiss UBS, Chuck Prince at Citigroup, Stan O'Neal at Merrill Lynch, and Ken Thompson at Wachovia. In March 2008, JPMorgan agreed to buy the investment bank Bear Stearns, which was facing a liquidity crisis. The purchase was facilitated by a $29 billion loan by the Federal Reserve, with repayment contingent on the performance of risky assets. For the first time since the 1929 crisis, the Federal Reserve stepped in to facilitate the rescue of an investment bank.

This was going to be only the start of public interventions. Merrill Lynch was acquired by Bank of America in September 2008, just before the investment bank Lehman Brothers filed for bankruptcy. The world of insurance was also affected. American International Group Inc. (AIG) accepted a loan of $85 billion from the Federal Reserve in return for surrendering 79.9 percent control to the government. The reason for public intervention[15] was the fear that a default by a large financial player would generate heavy losses for its counterparties[16] and, even more, uncertainty, as this opaque world would need time to sort itself. Of the five largest investment banks, only two were left: Morgan Stanley and Goldman Sachs, and both of them applied for bank holding company status. This implied a change in regulatory framework, from the Securities and Exchange Commission (SEC) to the Federal Reserve. The change of status allows the two banks to collect retail deposits, easing a liquidity problem.[17]

Finally, in the United States, Treasury Secretary Henry Paulson proposed to Congress the creation of a fund of $700 billion (the Troubled Assets Relief Program, or TARP) to buy back toxic assets from financial institutions, the largest public intervention since the Great Depression in 1929.[18] In the European Union, leaders from different countries decided in October 2008 to follow a British strategy in repairing the liability and equity sides of their banks. Public money was injected to buy preferred shares issued by banks, and public guarantees were granted not only to retail deposits, but also to new interbank funding and debt issues. Similar public capital injections were observed in the United States. In 2009, President Obama introduced the Private-Public Investment Program (PPIP) to buy toxic or legacy assets from banks. The objective was to restore confidence and liquidity in the banking system.

The collapse of the SIVs market has raised a very large debate about the proper functioning of capital markets and the need for regulators to step in. Some of these issues include the following:

- Were investors properly informed about the risks attached to these securities? For example, the Norwegian city of Narvik,[19] located north of the Arctic Circle, was invited to subscribe to these securities without proper notice of the risk.

- Was there a conflict of interest inherent in the work of rating agencies? On the one hand, they are paid by the banks to rate the SIVs, and, on the other hand, they are supposed to provide investors with accurate information on risk. There is a conflict of interest because banks hope for a good rating to make it easier for them to sell loans to investors.

- Should central banks enforce higher capital ratios on securitization, as experience has shown that some of the risk is returning to the balance sheet of sponsoring banks at the time of a recession?

- Should regulators allow the development of a large market in securities that are difficult to value, creating the risk of a potential liquidity crisis? Indeed, it was pointed out in Chapter 4 that a key service of banks is to hold loans that are difficult to value and to engage in a risk-sharing service by providing low-risk deposits. Should liquidity transformation be performed primarily by regulated banks that benefit from access to central banks' liquidity, or can it be performed by other unregulated market participants?.

## CONCLUSION

Over the years, banks have evolved from an *on-balance sheet* financing model to an *originate to distribute* model. The reasons for selling loans are many: from reducing costly capital financing to better diversification of credit risk. To convince investors to buy the assets and hold the credit risk, sophisticated securitization techniques have been used. Recent problems with structured investment vehicles have called to investors' attention the need to care about liquidity risk and the fact that there is a limit to the originate to distribute model.

## EXERCISES FOR CHAPTER 16

1. Identify four potential economic benefits resulting from the securitization of loans.

2. Investment banks have convinced banks to issue *covered bonds* to ensure a lower funding cost. The cost of covered bonds is cheaper because these bonds are collateralized by some of the bank's assets. That is, in the event of bank default, the holders of covered bonds have first claim on some of the assets.

   Do you accept the argument that covered bonds provide cheaper financing to banks, or do you have some reservations? Explain.

### Notes

1. Since the cash flows—interest and principal—are coming from the loans, the securities issued by the SPV have cash flow characteristics very similar to those of bonds.

2. Government-sponsored enterprises (GSEs) were created by the U.S. Congress. As a result of their exposure to the U.S. mortgage crisis, Fannie Mae and Freddie Mac were bailed out in September 2008, when the U.S. government placed them into "conservatorship," taking effective control of them.

3. Unfortunately for Crédit Lyonnais and for the French taxpayers, the equity that had been freed by securitization was used to finance growth and hazardous loans, leading to a public bailout package of FF160 billion (€ 24 billion) in 1993.

4. New terminology has had to be created in many languages. For example, the French commission on economic and financial terminology for the Finance Ministry has translated the term *securitization* as *titrisation*.

5. Liquidity risk, which can arise from too small a base of stable deposits, is discussed in Chapter 21.

6. In many securitizations, the loans being securitized are safer than the average credit risk on the balance sheet, and they are sometimes protected by a layer of guarantees. In the case of the monoline credit card issuer, the credit risk of the securitized pool of loans was identical to that of the bank.

7. Interest-rate, liquidity, and operational risks are discussed in Chapters 18 to 26.

8. A similar argument is used to explain project finance, the creation of a special vehicle to finance long-term infrastructure projects [Brealey and Habib (1996)].

9. These funds were reopened on August 28, 2007, with very limited losses for investors. (BNP-Paribas communiqué.)

10. Credit risk correlation is discussed in Chapter 22.

11. Value creation in the presence of liquidity risk is discussed in Chapter 21.

12. The net Basel I regulatory capital arising out of securitization accompanied by a liquidity backup line was smaller than the regulatory capital for a loan booked on the bank's balance sheet. This is an example of unintended regulatory arbitrage.

13. *Wall Street Journal*, December 14, 2007.

14. *Financial Times*, December 14, 2007.

15. The economics of bank regulation and public intervention is discussed in Chapter 28, an extra chapter not found in this book but available online at www.mhprofessional.com/bankvaluation.

16. Counterparty risk and the techniques used to contain it are discussed in Chapter 24.

17. Liquidity risk is discussed in Chapter 21.

18. The Emergency Economic Stabilization Act of 2008.

19. *Financial Times*, November 24, 2007.

# PART THREE

# Risk Management

# CHAPTER 17

# Risk Management in Banking: An Overview

The first two parts of the book were concerned with the valuation of banks and with deposit and loan pricing. The third part focuses on the evaluation and management of risk. An identification of the sources of risk in banking is followed by a discussion of the economics of corporate risk management and the need for sound governance.

## RISKS IN BANKING

At least 15 sources of risk can be identified in banking. They can be grouped into six major categories: credit, market, liquidity, operational, regulatory, and strategic risks. A comprehensive and possibly joint management of these sources of risks is referred to as enterprisewide risk management (ERM).

- Credit risk
  - Retail and corporate credit risk
  - Counterparty risk
  - Settlement risk
  - Environmental risk
  - Country risk
- Market risk
  - Interest-rate risk
  - Foreign exchange risk
  - Equities
  - Commodities
- Liquidity risk
- Operational risk

- ○ Execution risk
- ○ Model risk
- ○ Fraud
- ○ Legal risk
- Compliance risk
- Regulatory risk
- Strategic risk

## Credit Risk

*Credit risk* refers to the failure of a retail, corporate, or institutional borrower to make payments of interest and/or principal on a loan or on derivative transactions on time.

*Counterparty risk* refers to a particular type of credit risk in which the borrower is a financial institution.

*Settlement risk* (sometimes referred to as *Herstatt* risk)[1] is a particular type of counterparty risk. It refers to the risk involved in trading securities, foreign exchange, or commodities. A time difference in settlement dates could imply that one party has already delivered the asset before the payment is completed.

*Environmental risk* is a type of credit risk in which the guarantee on a loan contract may force the bank to hold real assets with some environmental liability.

*Country or sovereign risk* refers to the potential losses that could arise when a country that is facing a severe economic crisis takes actions that are detrimental to the bank (such as nationalization, increases in taxes, or capital controls).[2]

## Market Risk

*Market risk* refers to the loss of revenue resulting from adverse movements in interest rates, foreign exchange, and the prices of securities or commodities. With regard to interest-rate risk, a distinction must be made between the banking book and the trading book. Because of accounting rules, the banking book is accounted for on a historical cost basis (i.e., assets and deposits are recorded at acquisition cost). The banking book generates net interest income (net interest margin), which is recorded in the income statement. The first source of interest-rate risk is therefore the volatility of the net interest income. The trading book is marked to market, either at actual market prices, when these are available, or at calculated *fair* present values. The change in the value of the trading book is also recorded in the income statement. A second source of interest-rate risk is the impact of interest rates on the value of the trading book.

## Liquidity Risk

*Liquidity risk* refers to a shortage of cash resulting from a loss of bank deposits, unexpected drawdowns on loan commitments, or margin calls on trading transactions. A second source of liquidity risk is sales of assets leading to large price movements.

## Operational Risk

*Operational risk*, in its widest definition, includes every risk other than credit, market, and liquidity risks. It is the risk of loss resulting from inadequate or failed internal processes, people, and systems or from external events. It includes legal risk, or potential losses resulting from lawsuits. More specifically, operational risk includes the following:

- *Execution risk* refers to losses resulting from data entry errors[3] or computer failures.
- *Model risk* refers to losses incurred when the mathematical modeling of financial instruments does not match the movements in actual market prices.
- *Fraud* refers to outright stealing of value by employees or clients.
- *Legal risk* involves unexpected losses resulting from legal liabilities.
- *Compliance risk* refers to the failure of a bank to comply with relevant laws, regulations, internal policies and procedures or ethical standards.

## Regulatory Risk

*Regulatory risk* refers to the losses arising from an unexpected change in regulations, such as more stringent capital requirements. A change in tax regime could also be included here.

## Strategic Risk

*Strategic risk* refers to the risk that a new entrant, firm, or product will change the type of competition prevailing in banking markets.

Sometimes, a specific loss (such as a trading or credit loss) can generate a fall in the market value of a bank's shares that is much larger than the original loss. This is often explained by a loss of confidence in the bank's management. The "blowing up" of an initial loss arising from credit, market, liquidity, or operational risks is referred to as *reputational risk*. It is particularly acute in banking because of the *opacity* of bank operations. Given the very large number of transactions, sometimes booked through foreign subsidiaries, and the holding of nontraded instruments, it is very difficult for an outsider to verify the quality of a bank's management. A reported loss can be interpreted as a signal of bad management quality, which explains the amplified fall in market value. As one banker put it: take risks, but avoid risk. He meant that the business of banks is to face many sources of risk but that it is necessary to avoid a single source of risk that can lead to a large loss, triggering a loss of confidence in the management of the bank.

## THE ECONOMICS OF RISK MANAGEMENT

Chapters 9 and 12 argued that costly economic capital was needed to cover unexpected losses so as to reduce the risk of bank default. An alternative to funding with economic capital is hedging risks, which can also be costly. So a practical question concerns the extent to which a bank should hedge risks. In a world with perfect information and complete markets, corporate firms, such as banks, should allocate resources to manage only those risks that cannot be controlled by shareholders (nontradable risk). According to this view, perfectly informed shareholders could manage a large series of market risks (tradable risk) themselves. For instance, a bank's exposure to interest-rate risk or to foreign exchange risk could be managed by shareholders themselves, who can take, if they so wish, an offsetting hedging position. Control of market risk by banks demands a justification. Five motivations for corporate risk management have been advanced in the literature (e.g., Santomero, 1995, or Froot and Stein, 1998): managerial self-interest, nonlinearity of taxes, cost of financial distress, capital market imperfections, and funding with short-term deposits. These are discussed next.

First, *managerial self-interest* refers to the fact that managers, having a significant fraction of their permanent employment income attached to the firm, cannot diversify risks adequately. Managers' risk aversion will lead to risk mitigation or to a higher level of funding with costly capital. Risk reduction could be the least costly alternative.

Second, the *nonlinearity of taxes* means that losses may not be fully tax-deductible and that large profits could be taxed at a higher rate. In this case, a reduction in profit variance leads to a reduction in expected tax payments.

Third, the *cost of financial distress* refers to the loss of value that results from the bank's being in a situation of financial distress. In banking, this could imply a loss of clientele or a loss of a profitable banking license (the "charter value"). In such a case, a first loss precipitates the bank into a situation of distress. This triggers additional losses, possibly much greater than the initial one. Again, management will compare the cost of higher funding with equity to the cost induced by risk reduction.

Fourth, costs may arise from *capital market imperfections*. Because of imperfect (asymmetric) information, banks may find it costly to raise external funds through the issuance of bonds or equity. In such a context, losses could lead to a lower equity level (less internal funds available) and the missing of profitable investment opportunities because of the higher cost of external financing. Stabilization of profit can reduce the need for expensive external financing and lead to the realization of profitable investments. An alternative explanation of the resources spent on risk control is linked to reputational risk, discussed earlier. Because of opacity, investors cannot evaluate whether a reported loss is the result of bad luck or of inferior management quality. In this context, stabilization of profit and risk control prevents a loss of value.

Fifth, as discussed in Chapter 4, a specific function of banks is to offer *short-term deposits* that are withdrawable on demand. An implication is that banks are subject to the risk of bank runs, that is, depositors running to the bank to withdraw their deposits. As banks finance illiquid assets, such as loans, this creates a liquidity risk. Confidence in the banking system is key. One way to create such confidence for depositors and reduce the risk of a bank run is to report stable profit. Risk management helps greatly in reducing the volatility of earnings.

So, even in the absence of bank regulation, there are several economic motivations for the control of risks in a bank.

## RISK GOVERNANCE

An observer of the banking world can be stunned by the repetition of large losses incurred by large international banks. In 1989, British Midland Bank lost £290 million on its fixed income portfolio. The share price collapsed by 45 percent as a result of a loss of confidence, and the bank was taken over by HSBC. Another example involves the loss of £860 million by a 28-year-old derivatives trader, Nick Leeson, at the British merchant bank Barings. In January 2008, the French bank Société Générale (SocGen) announced a loss of 4.9 billion francs as a result of unauthorized trading. Estimates of loan losses resulting from the U.S. subprime crisis range, at the time of this writing, from $500 billion to $1 trillion.

## CONCLUSION

Banks face many sources of risk. The main ones are credit risk, market risk, liquidity risk, and operational risk. To avoid financial distress and the resulting loss of value, banks must compare the cost of funding with equity to the cost or loss of revenue induced by a change of positions needed to reduce risk. The many accidents observed over the years in so many countries call attention to the need for proper risk governance in banks.

History repeating itself in so many countries is a sign that the governance of risks needs to be greatly improved. At the very top, some board members with an understanding of risk management should ensure that risks are properly identified and measured and that an acceptable risk level has been set. As discussed in Chapter 9, the evaluation of performance and the design of bonus schemes should not create a bias toward excessive risk taking. Performance evaluation must take into account not only the short-term, but also the long-term impact of a position. It should not be based on realized earnings, as this often creates a call option payoff (profit with an eventual bonus if there is good fortune, with the bank or the country facing the loss if there is a bad draw), but either on ex ante expected earnings or on average earnings over a longer period. The risk management function should be independent of the commercial units. Last but not least, there is a need for character, the courage not to follow the herd, as people have so often done during periods of rapid credit expansion. It is the courage to finance every year the cost of a risk department to reduce the probability of rare events with large loss severity.

### Notes

1. See the discussion at the beginning of Chapter 12.
2. An example of country risk is what happened in Argentina on January 6, 2002, when the Parliament approved the end of the currency-board system (a one-to-one parity between the peso and the U.S. dollar). A key measure of the plan was to convert the banks' dollar loans into pesos at a one-to-one exchange rate, while deposits were converted at 1.4 pesos to the dollar. This created a large and unexpected currency mismatch between assets and liabilities, which increased even further in 2003. As the peso plunged to 3.18 pesos to the dollar, 180,000 depositors filed lawsuits against the decree. On March 5, 2003, the Supreme Court ruled that the conversion of deposits to pesos was illegal, allowing depositors to claim dollars. *The Economist*, March 8, 2003.
3. See the discussion in Chapter 13.

# CHAPTER 18

# The Control of Interest-Rate Risk on the Banking Book, Part 1: The Earnings at Risk

As discussed in Chapter 4, one of the fundamental functions of banks is to help in the sharing of risks in the economy. For instance, depositors may prefer deposits denominated in euros, while a corporation may prefer to borrow in U.S. dollars. Or a depositor may prefer to have a variable-rate deposit, whereas a borrower prefers to raise funds on a fixed-rate basis. The offering of products that meet the needs of the market creates inherent risks of mismatching that are borne by the bank. Market risk refers to the impact of the movements of interest rates, exchange rates, equity prices, and commodity prices on the profitability of banks. The coming three chapters study the evaluation of interest-rate risk for a bank.

Before proceeding with a discussion of the management of interest-rate risk, it is important to remember some key accounting rules in banking. They have a major impact on the way to look at this source of risk.

## ACCOUNTING IN BANKING: THE BANKING BOOK VS. THE TRADING BOOK

In accounting for bank transactions, accountants distinguish two major categories of transactions.

The first set, recorded in the *banking book*, includes transactions such as loans or deposits, which are recorded at historical cost. For instance, a five-year fixed-rate deposit of $1 million will be recorded at a value of $1 million, and its value will remain constant over the next five years. Similarly, a loan of $1 million is booked at its historical cost. Interest income on assets and interest expense on deposits are recorded in the income statement, generating a net interest margin. What is important to keep in mind, and is often confusing for those coming from a trading environment, is that the change in the fair value of the asset or deposit does not show up in either the balance sheet or the income statement.

**Banking book:**

- Balance sheet: transactions are recorded at historical cost (changes in value are not reported).
- Income statement: interest income minus interest expense = net interest margin.

The second set of transactions is recorded in the *trading book*. These transactions include trading of derivatives or assets that are marked to market. That is, every day, the value of the book is calculated, and changes in value are taken into account in the income statement. To calculate the value, the bank uses market prices for traded instruments, or estimates the fair value using present value techniques.[1]

**Trading book:**

- Balance sheet: transactions are recorded at current fair value.
- Income statement: net interest margin plus the change in value of the trading book is recorded.

The distinction between the banking book and the trading book becomes a bit blurred when the accounting treatment for holdings of bonds and derivatives used for hedging purposes are considered. That has been clarified recently by the International Accounting Standards Board and the International Financial Reporting Standards (IFRS). Three categories of bonds are recognized.

The *investment portfolio* includes bonds that the firm intends to hold until maturity. In several countries, these are included in the banking book and booked at historical cost (a footnote at end of the annual report will usually give information on the current value of the investment portfolio). Changes in market value of these bonds are not reported in the balance sheet or the P&L.

*Treasury securities* are bonds that are being traded in the very short run. These bonds are recorded in the trading portfolio and are marked to market. Capital gains or losses are directly reported in the income statement.

*Available-for-sale (AFS)* securities is a hybrid category, as there is no intention to trade them in the short term, but they are unlikely to be held until maturity. For this category, a special treatment applies. The capital gain or loss is not taken through the income statement, but instead is taken directly to the equity in the balance sheet. That is, the bonds are marked to market in the balance sheet, and a gain or a loss affects the equity of the bank directly. Available-for-sale securities are usually part of the banking book because a change of value does not affect the income statement.

The appendix to this chapter discusses the accounting treatment of derivatives used for hedging purposes.

The accounting treatment just discussed, the *banking book* versus the *trading book*, has a major impact on the way banks look at interest-rate risk. A twofold approach is used here. First, since some transactions reported in the *banking book* create a net interest margin in the income statement, the impact of interest-rate risk on a bank's net interest margin will be analyzed. Second, since transactions in the trading book are marked to market, the focus will be on the impact of interest rates on the value of the trading book.

From an organizational viewpoint, the control of interest-rate risk in a bank is performed by two separate departments. The asset and liability management (ALM) group usually focuses on interest-rate and liquidity risks on the banking book, while a trading risk department focuses on interest-rate risk on the trading book. Both departments report to the chief risk officer (CRO). This and the following chapter analyze the management of interest-rate risk on the banking book. Next, the measurement of risk on the trading book will be presented.

## THE MEASUREMENT OF INTEREST-RATE RISK ON THE BANKING BOOK: THE EARNINGS AT RISK (EAR)

The income statement of a representative bank, the Royal Bank of Canada, was introduced in Chapter 4. In the year 2007, it reported a net interest income of Can\$7,532 million and a total noninterest revenue (fees, trading profit) of Can\$14,930 million. Although the second source of revenue, fee income, has increased over the years, the net interest income of most banks continues to be a very substantial part of revenue. Therefore, a great deal of emphasis is placed on the control of the net interest margin.

To evaluate the impact of a change in interest rates on the net interest margin of a bank, banks compute a repricing gap table, also called an interest-rate-sensitivity table. First, the time scale is broken into discrete time buckets, for instance, quarters[2]: 1, 2, and so on. Second, looking at the current balance sheet, the stock of assets and debt that will be repriced (have its interest income or expense adjusted) during a specific time interval in the future if there is an immediate movement in the interest yield curve is measured. For example, assuming a change in the yield curve this evening, a one-quarter Treasury bill and a floating-rate

**T A B L E   18.1**

Repricing Gap Table

| | Rollover Date or Nearest Interest-Rate Adjustment Date (Can$ million) | | | | | |
|---|---|---|---|---|---|---|
| | Sight up to 3 Months | > 3 Months, < 6 Months | > 6 Months, <1 Year | 1 to 5 Years | Over 5 Years | Non-interest-sensitive |
| **Assets** | 270, 959 | 16,813 | 21,375 | 115,831 | 35,893 | 139,475 |
| Loans | | | | | | |
| Bonds | | | | | | |
| Other assets | | | | | | |
| **Liabilities** | 331,496 | 25,721 | 26,344 | 67,256 | 20,754 | 128,775 |
| Deposits | | | | | | |
| Bonds | | | | | | |
| Derivatives | | | | | | |
| **Repricing gap** | −60,537 | −8,908 | −4,969 | 48,575 | 15,139 | 10,700 |
| **Cumulative gap** | −60,537 | −69,445 | −74,414 | −25,839 | −10,700 | 0 |

Source: Royal Bank of Canada, annual report, 2007.

loan that is repriced every quarter would be slotted into the one-quarter bucket. A five-year fixed-rate bond would be slotted into the five-year bucket. Table 18.1 shows a representative repricing gap table.

Assuming that the rollover (reinvestment of the assets) takes place over a quarter,[3] a positive cumulative gap indicates that there will be a net excess of assets to reprice in the coming quarter, while a negative cumulative gap indicates that there will be an excess of deposits to reprice. In the case of an increase in the interest-rate curve, a positive cumulative gap will help the bank to increase its net interest margin, while a negative cumulative gap will generate a reduction in net interest margin.

With reference to Table 18.1, the negative gaps run by the Royal Bank of Canada for periods up to one year imply that the bank would benefit from a fall in interest rates. For instance, focusing on the first quarter on-balance sheet gap of −Can$60,537, this means that a fall in interest rates will reduce revenue on assets of Can$270,959, but will reduce the funding cost on liabilities of Can$331,496. Since, in the first-quarter gap, the amount of deposits coming due for repricing is larger than the amount of assets coming due for repricing (as is the case when there is a negative gap), a fall in interest rates will improve the bank's net interest margin. The meaning of the cumulative gap in Quarter 2, at the bottom of the table, is as follows. If interest rates at the end of the second quarter fall, the bank benefits twice: the previous net gap of Can$60,537 has to be repriced with a lower funding cost, and, in addition, during the second quarter there is a negative gap of $8,908 to reprice. The two gaps can be aggregated to form the cumulative gap of $-$Can$69,445 for the second quarter: a negative cumulative gap indicates that, as far as repricing in the second quarter is concerned, there is a surplus of deposits over assets to reprice.

To summarize, a reading of the cumulative gaps allows the impact of changes in interest rates on the net interest margin in the coming quarters to be evaluated.

This can be expressed formally. Define the current curve of forward rates as $R_1, R_2, R_3. . .$ Considering the balance sheet of the bank at a specific date $t$, the stock of assets and debt that will be repriced (have their interest income or expenses adjusted) is measured at time $t + I$ ($I = 1$ to N), giving, respectively, $A_{t+I}$ and $D_{t+I}$, if there is an instantaneous movement in the yield curve at time $t + \varepsilon$. Formally, the change in the net interest margin at time $t + n$ for a change in the forward rate $\Delta R_{t+n}$ is equal to

$$\Delta \text{ Net interest margin}_{t+n} = \sum_{i=1} A \times \Delta R_{t+n} - \sum_{i=1} D \times \Delta R_{t+n}$$

$$= \sum_{i=1}^{n} (A_{t+i} - D_{t+i}) \times \Delta R_{t+n}$$

$$= \text{cumulative gap}_{t+n} \times \Delta R_{t+n}$$

Banks have introduced the powerful concept of earnings at risk (EAR) to indicate the potential impact of an adverse change in interest rates on the income statement for a particular quarter:

$$\text{Earnings at risk}_{t+n} (\text{EAR}_{t+n}) = \Delta \text{ net interest margin}_{t+n}$$
$$= \text{cumulative gap}_{t+n} \times \Delta R_{t+n}$$

Once a repricing gap table has been prepared, an immediate question concerns the relevant change of interest rate ($\Delta R_{t+n}$) that should be chosen to measure earnings at risk. This refers to the calculation of the relevant volatility to use in measuring the earnings at risk.

## VOLATILITY OF INTEREST RATES ($\Delta R$)

Before calculating the volatility of interest rates, that is, the relevant change of interest rates to use in measuring earnings at risk, it is first necessary to decide what the relevant *holding* or *defeasance* period is.

In the case of the Royal Bank, if interest rates start to increase, the ALM group will not simply watch and take a loss, but it can take action to reduce the size of the gap. The term *defeasance* is quite explicit. It refers to the number of days needed to close, or *square*, a position without having a material impact on market prices. Clearly, this will vary from bank to bank and from country to country. For a well-known bank, a small gap in a liquid market can be closed very rapidly, perhaps in a few hours. However, if a bank has a large gap or is not so well known, it can take several days to close the gap. As an example, banks measuring risk on the trading book in OECD countries often use a one-day holding period to report risk to senior management. The presumption is that they can use a very liquid derivatives market to close the gaps. An immediate implication of this is that the measure of earnings at risk that is reported is relevant only if the bank can indeed reduce the gap rapidly. As will be discussed later, central banks, concerned that liquidity could dry out rapidly in periods of shocks, are forcing banks to measure trading risk with a 10-day holding period.

Once the defeasance or holding period has been decided, banks can estimate volatility. Two methods are available: calculation of historical volatility or calculation of implied volatility.

### Historical Volatility

This calculation proceeds in three steps:

1. Collection of historical data on interest rates. Statistics suggest that as many data as possible should be used, but only data that refer to an economic environment similar to the current one. In practice, banks use one or two years of data.
2. Calculation of changes in interest rates ($\Delta R$). This is where the *defeasance* period kicks in. If it is one day, changes in interest rates are measured over intervals of one day (from January 2 to January 3, from January 3 to January 4, and so on). These changes are likely to be small. If the defeasance period is a month (from January 2 to February 1, and so on), changes of interest rates over a longer period would be computed. In this case, bigger rate changes would be expected.
3. Calculation of a histogram, that is, a graph that reports the frequency of interest-rate changes that have been observed (See Figure 18.1.)

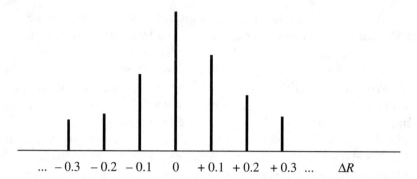

... −0.3  −0.2  −0.1   0   +0.1  +0.2  +0.3 ...        $\Delta R$

**Figure 18.1** Histogram of interest-rate changes.

The histogram aims to represent the probability distribution of interest-rate changes. A normal curve is often used as an approximation of the true underlying probability distribution because, as is discussed here, it greatly eases the calculation of risk.[4]

If it were possible to calculate the earnings at risk with a very large shock that captures all observations, most analysts would agree that this measure of risk would be very conservative, as the probability of a very big shock is very small. So around the world, bankers have adopted a pragmatic approach to reporting risk.

A first measure of risk is a shock to interest rates covering 99 percent of cases.[5] This uses the 99 percent quantile as the value $X$ of a random variable such that the cumulative distribution $F(x < X) = 99$ percent. That is, the $\alpha$ quantile is, by definition, the value of a variable such that $\alpha$ percent of the observations lie below this value.

$$\text{EAR} = \text{gap} \times \Delta R_{99\%}$$

In the special case of a normal curve, it takes 2.33 standard deviations ($\sigma$) to reach 99 percent, and the measure of risk becomes

$$\text{EAR} = \text{gap} \times (2.33 \times \sigma)$$

A measure of risk with 99 percent confidence indicates that there is a 1 percent probability that the EAR underestimates the potential loss.[6]

A second measure of risk involves the measure of risk for rare big shocks (often referred to as a "stress" or an "event" scenario), which is an attempt to measure risk for those cases in the 1 percent interval.

$$\text{EAR}_{t+n}\text{,stress} = \text{cumulative gap}_{t+n} \times \Delta R_{t+n}\text{,stress}$$

Designing stress scenarios is often an art, because few large shocks have been observed in recent history. In practice, banks conduct various exercises, such as the worst shock of the last 100 days and the worst shock of the last 20 years. If historical data provide the psychological comfort of precision, they should not prevent a more forward-looking approach, as the use of historical data is like driving a car looking only in the rearview mirror. Data from countries with higher volatility can be useful, or advanced statistics techniques can also be used to estimate relevant large shocks.[7]

### Simulation Model

The repricing gap table provides a first tool for measuring the interest-rate risk on a bank's banking book. It must be completed with the use of a simulation model for several reasons. First, such a table gives only information on the current structure of assets and liabilities. It ignores the dynamic changes in volumes of business over time. Indeed, the volumes of future loans or deposits could be affected by a movement in the yield curve. For instance, the volume of corporate demand deposits and retail consumer loans is likely to decrease when interest rates tighten up.

Second, the earnings at risk calculation implicitly assumes that interest rates on assets and liabilities will adjust by the same percentage change as the change in the market yield curve. It ignores the interest-rate elasticity, which could be very different from 1. This is particularly true in the retail market, with savings deposits or consumer loans. It is, indeed, well known that some deposit rates and credit rates can display a fairly low elasticity. For instance, as discussed in Chapter 11, the so-called pass-through rate in the retail market—that is, the impact on retail deposit rates of a market rate change of 1 percent—is close to 0.5 in many countries. In general, the absence of perfect co-movement between two interest rates in the same bucket is referred to as *basis risk*. In order to take into account the impact of a change of interest rates on future volumes of business and the imperfect correlation between some interest rates, simulation models have been developed (Platt, 1986). Although Monte Carlo simulations could in principle generate thousands of scenarios, banks usually consider only a few scenarios (around a dozen) that take into account several movements in the market yield curve and various responses of volumes or interest rates.

Finally, various products can have embedded options. A classical example is the prepayment option on a fixed-rate long-term mortgage. Although, the loan is unlikely to be prepaid in a rising rate environment, this would not hold true if interest rates were decreasing. As is the case with options, the symmetry between the effect of an increase in interest

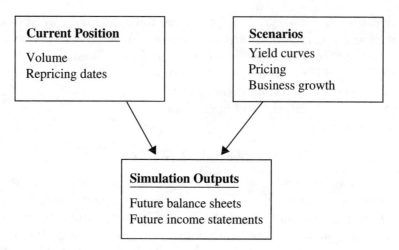

Figure 18.2  Simulation model.

rate and that of a decrease is lost. Simulation of prepayment under various interest-rate scenarios can help to capture this complexity.[8]

The structure of a simulation exercise can be represented graphically, as shown in Figure 18.2.

A simulation model works in three steps. First, the bank calculates the repricing gap table. The next step is to design a series of economic scenarios that incorporate assumptions about the shape of the yield curve and the sensitivity of rates and volumes to changes in interest rates. In the final step, the income statement is simulated for each of these scenarios. The objective is to limit the volatility of profit.[9]

## COMMON PITFALLS WITH THE MEASUREMENT OF INTEREST-RATE RISK

Several weaknesses of repricing gaps and bank simulation models have been identified (Dermine, 1991 and 1993).

1. Repricing gaps most often ignore the payment of interest/coupons and taxes. Fixed-income instruments should be treated as a series of zero-coupon instruments with different maturity dates.
2. Most often, floating-rate assets and deposits are slotted into the first-quarter gap. This ignores the fixed spread on the floating rate, which creates the equivalent of a fixed-rate annuity (Dermine, 1991, and Chapter 19).
3. Last but not least, the treatment of equity is inappropriate. Indeed, equity is most often slotted into the last bucket

(non-interest-sensitive), as if its cost were not sensitive to interest rates. This is correct from an accounting and net interest income perspective, as the cost of equity is not included in the income statement. However, from a finance perspective, the correct measure of profitability should be an economic profit, which takes away from net income the opportunity cost of equity. As the estimate of the cost of equity is based on the current return available on risk-free government bonds, it must be concluded that the cost of equity is interest-sensitive, and therefore that equity should be included in the first bucket.[10] Therefore, economic profit at risk (EPAR) should be used rather than earnings at risk (EAR):

$$\text{Economic profit at risk (EPAR)} = \Delta \text{ economic profit}$$
$$= \Delta \, (\text{profit} - \text{cost of allocated equity})$$
$$= (\text{gap} \times \Delta R) - (\text{equity} \times \Delta R)$$

If equity is partly invested in fixed assets or investments, these fixed assets or investments could be included in the first bucket with an underlying assumption that an interest-rate increase fueled by inflation will lead to capital gains on fixed assets and investments. However, here is another case where simulation with different scenarios would be useful. Indeed, there are well-known instances in which interest-rate increases driven by hawkish, restrictive monetary policy have led to lower inflation, recession, and a drop in the value of real estate and investment.

## CONCLUSION

One source of risk is the impact of a change in the market interest rates on the bank's profitability. As the *banking book* (loans and deposits) is often recorded at historical cost, it produces a net interest margin. The control of earnings at risk (EAR) refers to the control of the net interest margin, which, despite the importance of fee income, is still a significant part of gross revenue for many banks. Banks measure volatility at two levels of confidence: for 99 percent confidence and for larger *stress* scenarios.

## APPENDIX: ACCOUNTING FOR DERIVATIVES

The general principle (SFAS 133 and IAS 39) is that derivatives have to be marked to market, with changes in their value being recorded in the income statement.[11] Exceptions to this rule involve "hedge accounting." The issue is as follows. If an asset or liability that is on the balance sheet is hedged economically (meaning that a change in the value of the asset is offset by an adverse change in the value of the derivative), it would appear reasonable that the profit in the income statement should not be affected by a change of value in the derivative. Indeed, successful hedging should minimize the volatility of income. However, since assets and liabilities are booked at historical cost on the banking book, and since, according to the general rule, derivatives are marked to market, a situation could arise in which a loss of value in a derivative reduces profit, while a capital gain on a fixed-income loan is not reported because of the historical accounting rule for the banking book. This would result in accounting income volatility, although, on a value basis, the bank is fully hedged. To prevent this, specific rules have been designed for hedge accounting.

## Hedge Accounting

Two accounting rules are involved:

1. *Fair value hedge.* The changes in value of both the asset and the derivative go through the income statement. In the case described previously, a hedged instrument would create zero volatility in reported profit.

2. *Cash flow hedge* (for example, a fixed-rate loan). Divide the results of the hedge into an "ineffective" and an "effective" part. The reason for the existence of an ineffective part is that the instrument used for hedging does not match the characteristics of the hedged asset perfectly. The ineffective part goes to the income statement, while the effective part goes to a special account in equity. Profit or loss is recognized in the income statement when the cash flow of the asset affects it.

A very important consideration is that the exception for hedge accounting applies only to *micro* hedges, or hedges that are applied to specific transactions. It does not apply to *macro* hedges, or hedges used for aggregated positions (such as a cumulative gap in the repricing bucket). Macro hedges must be marked to market, with immediate impact on the income statement.

## EXERCISES FOR CHAPTER 18

1. The information given here is for the repricing bucket of Lisbank. For simplification, the time interval is one year.

|  | Year 1 | Year 2 | Year 3 and on | Total |
|---|---|---|---|---|
| Assets | 100 | 80 | 20 | 200 |
| Deposits | 120 | 10 | 40 | 170 |
| Equity | 30 |  |  | 30 |
| Simple gap | −50 | 70 | −20 |  |
| Cumulative gap | −50 | +20 | 0 |  |

Given that the volatility of interest rates is 2 percent (= two standard deviations) and that stress scenarios of 4 percent interest-rate changes have been observed in the past, write a report to the ALM committee evaluating the interest-rate risk incurred by Lisbank from an earnings at risk (EAR) perspective.

2 Bank Zeta is collecting high-interest-rate savings deposits. In Legoland, it is paying a rate of 3 percent at a time when the interbank rate is 2 percent. Its financial strategy is to "ride the yield curve." The bank is benefiting from an upward-sloping yield curve, so that the deposits are invested in long-term fixed-rate assets that carry a higher interest rate, 3.8 percent.

A hedge fund manager advises Bank Zeta that it should follow an even more profitable strategy: invest in similar long-term assets, but fund them on the short-term interbank market (with a lower cost of funds of 2 percent).

Question: Why does Bank Zeta borrow funds at 3 percent instead of borrowing them at 2 percent?

## Notes

1. U.S. GAAP distinguishes among three levels of market participants' assumptions, which depend on the use of observable market inputs when determining fair-value estimates: *Level 1* contains instruments with quoted market prices in active markets, *Level 2* includes observable market inputs for similar or related instruments, and *Level 3* includes unobservable, entity-specific inputs.

2. The length of the time bucket—a quarter—is arbitrary, being chosen for expository convenience. In a very volatile environment, banks should work with finer buckets (daily or weekly).
3. Note that the one-quarter rollover at the one-quarter forward rate is not a restrictive assumption. Indeed, the rollover of two quarters at a two-quarter rate is, by definition of the six-month forward rate, equivalent in present value terms to a series of one quarter rollovers (see Chapter 2). Of course, the cash flow and net interest margin in any particular quarter would be affected by the choice of the reinvestment strategy, but not by their present value.
4. An alternative to using historical data to estimate the volatility of interest rates is to back out the implicit volatility from the price of interest rate options (Figlewski, 1997).
5. Some banks use 95 percent, others use 97.5 percent.
6. If the distribution is not normal, we can rank the rate changes in decreasing order. A crude estimate of the 1 percent confidence level for a series of 500 observations is the fifth largest rate change. A more sophisticated approach (Hull, 2007) involves modeling the tail of the distribution with the power law. See our discussion of power law and extreme value theory in Chapter 26.
7. Extreme value theory is discussed in Chapter 26 on operational risk. A review of volatility forecasts can be found in Figlewski (1997). Discussion of stress testing can be found in Longin (2000), Hull (2007), or in Committee on the Global Financial System (2001). N. Taleb (2007) refers to as "black swans" these rare, large shocks that might never have been observed in the past.
8. Prepayment options on mortgages are discussed in Fabozzi (1995 and 1997).
9. Replicating asset portfolios that immunize against cash flow volatility are discussed in Chapter 19.
10. One observes here an inconsistency in bank practice. Many banks control the impact of interest rates on the net interest margin (ignoring the cost of equity capital), while they evaluate internally the performance of business units on the basis of economic profit which is the net of the cost of equity capital.
11. The European Union has accepted most of IAS 39. The main exception includes the hedging of core (demand, savings) deposits. Several countries, such as France, allow banks not to report the change in value of derivatives in their equity.

CHAPTER 19

# The Control of Interest-Rate Risk on the Banking Book, Part 2: The Economic Value at Risk

The focus on the impact of a change in interest rates on the net interest margin and the income statement is understandable, as bank analysts focus very much on ROE and earnings per share (EPS) as measures of performance. But these measures create a risk of myopia if management focuses only on short-term profits. Following the savings and loan association (S&L) crisis in the United States in the early 1990s, increasing attention has been focused on the impact of interest-rate changes on the economic value of the equity of a bank. This is the second approach to the measurement of interest-rate risk on the banking book.

A review of the S&L crisis helps to explain the introduction of a second measure of risk. The economic value at risk and duration tools are introduced next.

## THE SAVINGS AND LOAN ASSOCIATION CRISIS

American savings banks, the S&Ls, specialized in financing the mortgage market. Short-term retail savings deposits were invested in long-term fixed-rate mortgages. The reason for setting the pricing on a fixed-rate basis may be questioned. However, it reflected market habits or preferences of borrowers in the United States, with very similar preferences being observed in some other countries, such as Germany, France, and Belgium. Interestingly, other countries, such as Great Britain and Spain, are used to variable-rate financing. A representative balance sheet of an S&L is as follows:

| Fixed-rate mortgage loans: 100 | Deposits: 95 |
| | Equity:5 |

The mortgages were booked at their historical acquisition cost. Since these mortgages were funded with short-term deposits, S&Ls were running a large maturity mismatch. When Paul Volcker, chairman of the Board of Governors of the Federal Reserve, decided in 1979 to push interest rates up to 15 percent to eradicate inflation, the present value of the mortgages went down, say to $80. The savings bank was technically in default, as the value of its assets was substantially below the value of its debt, $95. However, since the assets were recorded in the books at the historical value of $100, the S&Ls were reporting a positive accounting value of equity, which allowed them to continue operations. To compound the problem, some S&Ls invested in risky junk bonds marketed by Michael Milken, ending up a few years later with very large losses.[1] When the U.S. Congress finally decided to bail out the industry at a cost of $300 billion, it required a change in regulation concerning interest-rate risk. Instead of focusing on the short-term earnings at risk, regulators had to focus on the economic value of the bank, that is, the difference between the fair value of its assets and its liabilities:

Economic value = value of assets − value of liabilities

A bank would be solvent as long as the value of its assets exceeded the value of its liabilities. A new measure of interest-rate risk was introduced: the economic value at risk.

## ECONOMIC VALUE AT RISK

When the economic value of the equity of a bank is defined as the difference between the value of its assets and the value of its debt, it is necessary to calculate the impact of a change in interest rates on the economic value (EV) of equity:[2]

Economic value of equity = value of assets − value of debt

The impact of a change in interest rates on the economic value of the bank is then computed to obtain the economic value at risk (EVR):

EVR = Δ economic value of equity = Δ value of assets − Δ value of debt

To perform this calculation, the impact of a change in interest rates on the value of an asset must be evaluated. The concept of duration was introduced to measure the value sensitivity.

### Duration

Although duration is often introduced for the case of a flat yield curve with short-term rates that are identical to long-term rates, the *adjusted duration*

**TABLE 19.1**

Bond Pricing

|  | Year 1 | Year 2 | Year 3 |
|---|---|---|---|
| Cash flow | 10 | 10 | 110 |
| Zero coupon rate | 10% | 11% | 12% |
| Discounted cash flows | $\dfrac{10}{1.10^1}$ | $\dfrac{10}{1.11^2}$ | $\dfrac{110}{1.12^2}$ |

Price = 95.503

concept for a more general case of a non-flat yield curve is introduced here. The case of a flat yield curve is then just a special case.

Consider the example in Table 19.1.

As discussed in Chapter 1, the current price of the bond is the present value of future cash flows, each one discounted at the relevant zero coupon rate. In Table 19.1, the yield curve is upward-sloping, rising from 10 percent to 12 percent. The value of the 10 percent fixed-coupon bond is equal to 95.503.

The adjusted duration of the bond is calculated as follows:

Adjusted duration

$$= \frac{\left(1 \times \dfrac{10}{1.10^1} \times \dfrac{1}{1.10}\right) + \left(2 \times \dfrac{10}{1.11^2} \times \dfrac{1}{1.11}\right) + \left(3 \times \dfrac{110}{1.12^3} \times \dfrac{1}{1.12}\right)}{95.5} = 2.4356$$

Intuitively, the *adjusted duration* is a weighted measure of the life of the bond. Although the maturity is three years, some cash flows are received earlier. Each year (Year 1, Year 2, and Year 3) is multiplied by the present value of the cash flow as a percentage of the price and by the interest factor.

Note that this definition of the adjusted duration differs slightly from the standard duration formula. The standard duration formula is defined as

$$\text{Standard duration} = \frac{1 \times \dfrac{10}{1.10^1} + 2 \times \dfrac{10}{1.11^2} + 3 \times \dfrac{110}{1.12^3}}{95.5} = 2.7246$$

The standard duration is the weighted average life of an asset, with the weights applied to each year being the discounted cash flows for that year.[3] In the special case of a flat yield curve ($R_1 = R_2 = R_3 = R$), the result is the following relation:

$$\text{Adjusted duration} = \text{standard duration} \times \frac{1}{1 + R}$$

The adjusted duration concept allows the more general case of a non-flat yield curve to be discussed directly. The adjusted duration given here is widely used, as it allows easy calculation of the change in the value of the bond for a parallel shift in interest rates, $\Delta R$:[4]

$$\Delta \text{ Price} = -\text{price} \times \text{adjusted duration} \times \Delta R$$

or

$$\frac{\Delta \text{ Price}}{\text{Price}} = -\text{adjusted duration} \times \Delta R$$

The duration thus measures the percentage change in the price of the asset for a change in the interest rate of 1 percent.

In the previous example, for a shift of the curve of 1 percent, the result is

$$\Delta \text{ Price} = -95.503 \times 2.4356 = -2.326$$

To verify that the formula works, in Table 19.2, the bond is reevaluated given an upward move of the curve of 1 percent.

For a parallel shift in interest rates of 1 percent, the price falls from $95.503 to $93.217. The reduction in price is

$$93.217 - 95.503 = -2.286$$

**TABLE 19.2**

**Bond Pricing**

|  | Year 1 | Year 2 | Year 3 |
|---|---|---|---|
| Cash flow | 10 | 10 | 110 |
| Zero coupon rate | 11% | 12% | 13% |
| Discounted cash flows | $\dfrac{10}{1.11^1}$ | $\dfrac{10}{1.12^2}$ | $\dfrac{110}{1.13^2}$ |
| Price = 93.217 | | | |

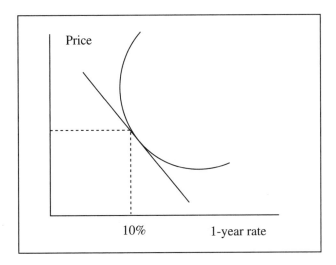

**Figure 19.1** Bond pricing and convexity.

Thus, the duration formula is only an approximation, as the effective drop in price following an interest-rate increase of 1 percent ($2.286) is smaller than that predicted by the duration formula ($2.326).

The origin of the approximation can be identified easily on a graph that links a bond price to interest rates. For simplicity (as there are three different zero coupon rates in this example), the bond price is related to a move in the one-year rate (with other rates being unchanged). (See Figure 19.1.)

As a result of the mathematics of discounting, the relationship between the bond price and the interest rate follows a curve, a convex line. The duration formula is a linear approximation (the tangent or first derivative in mathematics) that assumes that the relationship is a straight line. It can be seen that when interest rates are pushed up by 1 percent, the straight-line duration formula overstates the true drop in price, as the convexity of the curve reduces the fall in value.

The duration approximation is widely used in measuring risk on a bond or swap portfolio. As the size of the approximation error is related to the magnitude of the change in interest rates, it is always necessary to be careful with linear approximation when volatility is high.[5] In the management of interest-rate risk, banks often use the concept of *basis point value* (BPV) or *DV01*. This measures the change in value for a parallel shift of the interest-rate curve by 1 basis point.

Two useful properties of the adjusted and standard durations are

1. The adjusted duration of a portfolio of assets is equal to the weighed average adjusted duration of each asset, with the weights being the current value of each asset as a percentage of the portfolio.
2. The standard duration of a zero coupon asset is equal to its maturity.

Based on this discussion of duration as a measure of the change of value of an asset, the concept can now be applied to a change in value of the equity of a bank.

### Economic Value at Risk

Letting $A$ and $D$ refer to the current value of assets and debt and $Du_A$ and $Du_D$ refer to the adjusted duration of asset and debt, and applying the duration formula to the change in value of assets and debt, the result is

$$\Delta EV = (-A \times Du_A \times \Delta R) - (-D \times Du_D \times \Delta R)]$$

$$\Delta EV = -A \times \left( Du_A - \frac{D}{A} \times Du_D \right) \times \Delta R$$

$$\frac{\Delta EV}{EV} = -\frac{A}{EV} \times \left( Du_A - \frac{D}{A} \times Du_D \right) \times \Delta R$$

The last expression gives a very useful summary measure of interest-rate risk, that is, the percentage change in the value of the equity of a bank for a change in interest rates. It is the product of three factors: the leverage (assets over economic value), the duration mismatch between assets and liabilities, and the change in the interest rate. Although the adjusted duration applies only to a parallel shift in the yield curve, it can easily be extended to different twists in the yield curve through a *vector duration* approach (Chambers, Carleton, and McEnally, 1988) or a value at risk approach, which will be discussed in Chapter 20.

Since 1994, the United States has had a capital regulation on interest-rate risk. All banks must compute the impact of a parallel shift in interest rates of 1 percent on the economic value of the bank. As long as the change in EV does not exceed 25 percent of the bank's equity, no additional capital is required. If it does exceed 25 percent, the risk must be covered by additional equity. Since 1994, lobbying took place at the Basel Committee of Banking Supervision to impose a similar capital regulation around the world. Currently, no capital charge is calculated in the first pillar of Basel II for a mismatch on the banking book. The main reason was that there was no common agreement on which methodology to use to measure interest-rate risk, EAR or EVR, or on how to deal with deposits with undefined maturities (discussed later in the chapter). However, in the second pillar (the supervisory review), banking supervisors are invited to evaluate the impact of a parallel shift of 2 percent on the economic value of a bank. It should not exceed 20 percent of the sum of Tier 1 and Tier 2 capital. The absence of explicit capital regulation of interest-rate risk on the banking book is a significant weakness of the Basel II accord, as this source of risk is often substantially larger than market risk on the trading book (see Chapter 20).

## THE CASE OF UNDEFINED MATURITIES: APPLICATION OF THE FRANCHISE VALUE MODEL

The economic value at risk approach applies quite well to assets and deposits with well-defined maturities, such as bonds, loans, or term deposits. However, banks are often funded with deposits with undefined maturities, such as demand and savings deposits. On contractual terms, these deposits have a short maturity. Nonetheless, many of these deposits have an effective longer maturity, as they are stable. These are called *core* deposits. In managing the interest-rate risk of a bank, a practical question concerns the effective maturity or duration of these deposits. In the case of a retail bank, this is a fundamental question, as these deposits are a substantial part of its funding.

Which duration should be applied to demand deposits: the short contractual one, or a longer effective one, and if the latter, how much longer? It is in part because of a lack of a clear established methodology to measure the duration of these liabilities that the BCBS did not include (yet) a capital charge for a mismatch on the banking book. The bank valuation framework presented in Chapters 5 and 6 allows an answer to this question.[6]

The duration of deposits is defined indirectly. It is equal to the duration of bonds needed to neutralize to zero the impact of a change of interest rates on the value of a bank. Ignoring operating expenses, consider the following balance sheet, with deposits $D_0^*$ invested in bonds:

Bonds $B_0^*$ Deposits $D_0^*$
The value of equity is equal to[7]

$$\text{Market value of equity}_0 = [B_0^* - D_0^*] + \frac{(1-t) \times (b_1^* - d_1^{**}) \times D_1^*}{1 + b_1^{**}}$$

$$+ \frac{(1-t) \times (b_2^* - d_2^{**}) \times D_2^*}{(1 + b_1^{**}) \times (1 + b_2^{**})} + \cdots$$

The first term is the liquidation value. Since deposits have a very short maturity, the value of deposits will be equal to the book value $D_0$. And the change in the liquidation value of deposits ($\Delta D_0$) following an increase in interest rates will be equal to zero.

Hedging requires the change in the market value of equity to be equal to zero:

$$\Delta \text{Market value of equity}_0 = (\Delta B_0^\circ - 0)$$

$$+ \Delta \left[ \frac{(1-t) \times (b_1^\circ - d_1^{\circ\circ}) \times D_1^\circ}{1 + b_1^{\circ\circ}} \right.$$

$$\left. + \frac{(1-t) \times (b_2^\circ - d_2^{\circ\circ}) \times D_2^\circ}{(1 + b_1^{\circ\circ}) \times (1 + b_2^{\circ\circ})} + \cdots \right]$$

$$= 0$$

$$\Delta \text{Market value of equity}_0 = (-B_0^\circ \times \text{adjusted duration} \times \Delta R - 0)$$

$$+ \Delta \left( \frac{(1-t) \times (b_1^\circ - d_1^{\circ\circ}) \times D_1^\circ}{1 + b_1^{\circ\circ}} \right.$$

$$+ \frac{(1-t) \times (b_2^\circ - d_2^{\circ\circ}) \times D_2^\circ}{(1 + b_1^{\circ\circ}) \times (1 + b_2^{\circ\circ})} + \cdots \left. \right)$$

$$= 0$$

It is possible to solve this equation to find the adjusted duration of bonds that immunizes the market value of equity. An increase in interest rates will reduce the value of the bond, but, in most countries, an increase in interest rates will increase the franchise value of deposits because of the well-documented inelasticity or rigidity of deposit rates (see Chapter 11 or Dermine and Hillion, 1992). Intuitively, the greater the stability of deposit rates and volumes of deposits, the longer the duration of assets that will neutralize the impact of an interest-rate increase can be. This indirect approach allows the computation of the implicit duration of nonmaturing deposits. Data inputs demand a forecast of the volume of deposits and interest margins under several interest-rate-curve scenarios.

Obviously, the smaller the franchise value or its sensitivity to the interest rate, the smaller is its relevance to the measurement of interest-rate risk. This "imperfect market" approach to the measurement of interest-rate risk was applied in the case of deposits. It can be extended to any asset or debt with a franchise value.[8]

**TABLE  19.3**

Volume of Deposits Required at Varying Interest Rates

| Interest Rate | Demand Deposits in Year 1 | Demand Deposits in Year 2 |
|---|---|---|
| 8% | 135.71 | 142.86 |
| 6% | 150 | 152.86 |
| 10% | 132.86 | 138.57 |

## Numerical Example

Consider the case of demand deposits that pay, because of regulation, 0 percent. Operating expenses are equal to 3 percent of deposits, and the corporate tax rate is 30 percent. The current level of interest rates is a flat yield curve at 8 percent. What is the adjusted duration of assets that ensures a zero interest-rate risk? As shown in Table 19.3, it is necessary to forecast the volume of deposits under 8 percent, 6 percent, and 10 percent scenarios. For simplicity, assume that the bank lives for two years.

| | |
|---|---|
| Assets: 135.71 | Deposits: 135.71 |

A drop in the market rate from 8 percent to 6 percent will make the 0 percent deposits relatively more attractive, generating a higher volume. In reverse, an increase in the market rate to 10 percent will make the deposits less attractive.

First, the market value of equity is computed under the three interest-rate regimes, assuming in the first step that the adjusted duration of the assets is zero. In a second step, it is necessary to search for the adjusted duration of assets that ensures hedging of the market value of equity.

$$
\begin{aligned}
\text{Market value of equity}_{8\%} &= 135.71 - 135.71 \\
&\quad + \frac{(1 - 0.3) \times (8\% - 0\% - 3\%) \times 135.71}{1.08} \\
&\quad + \frac{(1 - 0.3) \times (8\% - 0\% - 3\%) \times 142.86}{1.08^2} \\
&= 8.685
\end{aligned}
$$

$$\text{Market value of equity}_{6\%} = 150 - 150$$
$$+ \frac{(1-0.3) \times (6\% - 0\% - 3\%) \times 150}{1.06}$$
$$+ \frac{(1-0.3) \times (6\% - 0\% - 3\%) \times 152.86}{1.06^2}$$
$$= 5.829$$

$$\text{Market value of equity}_{10\%} = 132.86 - 132.86$$
$$+ \frac{(1-0.3) \times (10\% - 0\% - 3\%) \times 132.86}{1.10}$$
$$+ \frac{(1-0.3) \times (10\% - 0\% - 3\%) \times 138.57}{1.10^2}$$
$$= 11.53$$

### Hedging a Reduction in Interest Rates from 8 Percent to 6 Percent

$$\Delta \text{ Market value}_{6\%-8\%} = 5.829 - 8.685 = -2.856$$

The market value drops by $2.856 when the interest rate goes down from 8 percent to 6 percent. This is the result of a reduction in the franchise value. The much lower interest margin is not compensated for by an increase in the volume of deposits. To hedge the market value of equity, a capital gain is needed to compensate for the drop in the franchise value. Next, the adjusted duration of assets that will generate the appropriate capital gains on assets when interest rates go down from 8 percent to 6 percent is computed.

$$\Delta \text{ Asset value}_{6\%-8\%} = 2.856 = -100 \times \text{adjusted duration} \times (-2\%)$$

$$\text{Adjusted duration}_{6\%-8\%} = 2.856/(100 \times 0.02) = 1.428 \text{ years}$$

An adjusted duration of 1.428 years for the assets will hedge the market value of the equity of the bank. Indirectly, this calculation has determined the implicit duration of demand deposits for the case of an interest-rate decrease: 1.428 years.

A similar reasoning can be applied to an increase in interest rates from 8 percent to 10 percent. In that case, it can be verified that the franchise value is going up. A capital loss on assets must be accepted when interest rates increase.

## Hedging an Increase in Interest Rates from 8 Percent to 10 Percent

$$\Delta \text{ Market value}_{10\%-8\%} = 11.53 - 8.685 = 2.843$$

$$\Delta \text{ Asset value}_{10\%-8\%} = -2.843 = -100 \times \text{adjusted duration} \times (2\%)$$

$$\text{Adjusted duration}_{10\%-8\%} = 2.843/(100 \times 0.02) = 1.42 \text{ years}$$

Note that in this example, as in real life, the symmetry between the case of an interest-rate decrease (adjusted duration of 1.428 years) and the case of an interest-rate increase (adjusted duration of 1.42 years) is not perfect. The ALM committee will decide which side to hedge, or can use interest-rate options[9] to hedge both sides perfectly.[10]

## THE CASE OF UNDEFINED MATURITIES: THE OTS MODEL

The U.S. Office of Thrift Supervision (OTS) has developed its own model for computing the value of savings deposits (Office of Thrift Supervision, 2000). It is based on the discounted value of cash flows linked to deposits; these include interest payments, deposit reimbursements, and new deposits. The model incorporates behavioral assumptions concerning the relationship between market yield, deposit rates, and deposit volumes. The effective duration is based on the percentage change in the value of deposits for a 1 percent move in the yield curve. Since the franchise valuation model is also based on the discounted deposits (discussed in Chapter 5), it implies that

$$\begin{aligned}
\text{Value of deposits}_{OTS} &= \text{liquidation value of deposits}_0 \\
&\quad - \text{franchise value of deposits} \\
&= D_0^{\circ} - \frac{(b_1^{\circ} - d_1^{\circ}) \times D_1^{\circ}}{1 + b_1^{\circ}} - \frac{(b_2^{\circ} - d_2^{\circ}) \times D_2^{\circ}}{(1 + b_1^{\circ}) \times (1 + b_2^{\circ})} - \cdots
\end{aligned}$$

The durations given by the franchise approach discussed earlier and by the OTS model should be identical. An advantage of the franchise model is that it is explicit about the deposit margins and volumes assumed each year in the franchise value.

## CASH FLOW IMMUNIZATION AND REPLICATING PORTFOLIOS

As discussed earlier, there are several ways to construct an asset portfolio with a desired duration. It would be possible to buy an asset with zero coupon or to build a mix of short- and long-duration assets. If each asset portfolio had an identical duration, hedging the economic value at risk, this would not imply that the cash flow (net interest margin) in each period would be immunized. For example, if a three-year zero coupon asset were bought, a change in interest rates tomorrow would have no impact on interest income in the first two years. But, if a mix of one-year-duration and five-year-duration assets were bought, a change in interest rates would have a positive impact on interest income rapidly. Banks that want to immunize their cash flows design a *replicating* portfolio. It works as follows.

- Step 1: Design a base-scenario forecast of interest expenses.

**Year 1**              **Year 2**              **Year 3**                    . . .
Interest expenses$_1$  Interest expenses$_2$  Interest expenses$_3$

- Step 2: Raise the interest ($\Delta R$) and forecast the new interest expenses.
  The revised interest expenses include the change in the interest rate plus, eventually, the impact of a change in volumes.

**Year 1**              **Year 2**              **Year 3**                    . . .
New interest            New interest            New interest
expenses$_1$            expenses$_2$            expenses$_3$

- Step 3: Calculate the change ($\Delta$) in interest expenses with respect to the base-scenario.

**Year 1**              **Year 2**              **Year 3**                    . . .
$\Delta$ Interest       $\Delta$ Interest       $\Delta$ Interest
expenses$_1$            expenses$_2$            expenses$_3$

- Step 4: Design a replicating asset portfolio.
  A *replicating* asset portfolio yields a change in interest revenue for $\Delta R$ identical to the change of interest expenses. This is often achieved with zero coupon bonds or swaps.[11] The replicating asset portfolio allows the immunization of cash flows and net interest margins. As was very much the case with the simulation models discussed in Chapter 18, this will work only if the assumptions about the impact of a change in market interest rates on the rate and volume of deposits prove to be correct.

## MANAGING INTEREST-RATE RISK

Two approaches can be used to hedge interest-rate risk, commercial and market-based. A commercial approach involves choosing maturities or repricing dates for loans and deposits to ensure matching. If this approach can be undertaken, it is often very costly, as the restrictions on maturity and repricing terms can reduce profitability. Indeed, in some countries, consumers are used to fixed-rate loans and short-term deposits. If a bank wished to switch from fixed-rate lending to variable-rate lending, its margins might suffer. For this reason, banks prefer to use financial instruments available on the capital markets to manage their interest-rate exposure. They can run an opposite mismatch on the interbank market or use financial derivatives, such as forward rates agreements (FRAs), financial futures, interest-rate options, or swaps.[12] With regard to the use of derivatives, an additional difficulty has arisen concerning the accounting treatment of derivatives. This was discussed in the appendix to Chapter 18.

Interest-rate risk on the banking book is monitored and managed at three levels in a bank. At the level of the board of directors, some members will be in charge to ensure that risk is properly identified and measured and that a risk appetite level is set. That is, these board members determine the maximum earnings at risk or economic value at risk that is acceptable. Below the board level, the asset and liability committee (ALCO) puts the risk measurement and fund transfer price system in place. This committee is made up of very senior executives: the CEO; heads of business units such as retail, corporate, or treasury; chief economist; chief risk officer; and heads of accounting and control.

The ALCO usually meets once a month to review the recommendations made by the asset and liability management (ALM) unit. ALM specialists, often sitting often close to the Treasury Department, analyze the economic situation and business developments so as to develop a maturity structure proposal for the ALCO.

## CONCLUSION: INTEREST-RATE RISK—A MULTIHEADED HYDRA MONSTER

As discussed in the last two chapters, interest-rate risk can take various forms. It can affect the net interest margin of the bank, a significant component of the gross income reported in the income statement. It can affect the economic value of the bank and the fair value of future cash flows. Also, it can directly affect the book value of equity and the regulatory capital needed to fund operations. For example, a change in the value of the "available-for-sale" securities will, under IFRS, directly affect the equity of the bank, but not its income statement. The risk officer in charge of controlling interest-rate risk must therefore simultaneously monitor the impact of interest rates on net interest income (and the income statement), on the economic value of the bank, and on the amount of regulatory capital. Skill will be needed not only to balance these three indicators, but also to report risk to the senior management of the bank in a clear manner. The risk manager and the ALCO should direct their attention primarily to the second indicator of risk (impact on economic value), while keeping an eye on the other two indicators. The reason is that the economic value is the present value of both short-term and long-term cash flows.

## APPENDIX A: DURATION OF FLOATING-RATE SECURITIES

In this chapter, duration has been applied to fixed-income instruments. But a bank also finances floating-rate assets. Thus, the duration of floating-rate assets is a natural question. A numerical example is followed by a formal model.

### Numerical Example

On June 30, 2008, consider an asset with $2^1/2$ years until maturity that is repriced every January 2 (that is, the coupon paid at the end of the year is equal to the one-year rate observed on January 2, 2008).

Question: What is the duration of the bond?

The common answer is that the duration of a floating-rate instrument is the time until the next repricing, six months in this example. The logic is as follows: when the bond is repriced early next year, its value at that time will be the *par value* (because, at that time, it will be paying the current rate). So, on June 30, 2008, the bond is similar to a short-term fixed-rate asset with a maturity/duration equal to the time until the next repricing date. On June 30, the bond would have a duration of six months.

This is often the correct answer, but not always. When the floating coupon on the bond at the time of repricing is not the same as the discount rate, then the duration can differ from the time until repricing. This is illustrated in the following example.

On June 30, consider a $2^1/2$-year bond that is repriced once a year in January. Three sets of interest rates are given:

1. The risk-free forward rate curve (4 percent for the first six months, followed by 9 percent and 10 percent).
2. The forward contractual rate on a *new* loan = risk-free forward rate + 6 percent.

3. The contractual rate on the *current* loan = risk-free forward rate + 2 percent. The discrepancy between the spread on the existing loan (2 percent) and on the new loan (6 percent) can be caused by a change in credit or liquidity risk. The next coupon, to be paid in December (already fixed since last January), is 10 percent.

$f_i$ = risk-free forward rate in period $i$ (June: 4%; December: 9%; December: 10%)

$f_i + p_i$ = forward contractual rate on a new risky loan (with $p_i$ = annual credit risk spread = 6 percent)

$c_i$ = annual contractual floating coupon[13] on an existing loan = $f_i + 2$ percent

$c_0$ = first annual coupon to be paid next December (already fixed) = 10 percent

$$\text{Price} = \frac{10}{1.07} + \frac{1}{1.07} \times \left( \frac{11}{1.15} + \frac{112}{1.15 \times 1.16} \right) = 96.75$$

Note:

Coupon of 10, fixed last January; discount rate = 4% + 6%/2
Coupon of 11 = 9 + 2; discount rate of 15% = 9% + 6%
Coupon of 12 = 10 + 2; discount rate of 16% = 10% + 6%

To enable the duration of a floating-rate loan to be computed, use the following trick: rewrite the annual coupon as $c_i = (f_i + 6\%) + (2\% - 6\%)$

$$\text{Price} = \frac{10}{1.07} + \frac{1}{1.07} \times \left( \frac{15-4}{1.15} + \frac{116-4}{1.15 \times 1.16} \right)$$

$$= \frac{10+100}{1.07} + \frac{1}{1.07} \times \left( \frac{-4}{1.15} + \frac{-4}{1.15 \times 1.16} \right)$$

$$= 96.75$$

Price = value of short-maturity (time until repricing) asset + PV of differences in spreads on coupon and discount rates

If $\Delta R = 1\%$ (1/2 percent over six months),

$$\text{Price} = \frac{10+100}{1.075} + \frac{1}{1.075} \times \left( \frac{-4}{1.16} + \frac{-4}{1.16 \times 1.17)} \right) = 96.38$$

$$\frac{\Delta \text{Price}}{\text{Price}} = \frac{96.38 - 96.75}{96.75} = -0.00387 = -0.387 \times 1\%$$

In this case (where the spread on the coupon is lower than the spread on the discount rate), the duration (0.386) is less than 0.5 year, the time until repricing.

### Valuation of Floating-Rate Assets

The next step is to formalize the valuation of floating-rate bonds.
Definitions:

$R_i$ = spot zero coupon risk-free rate in Year $i$
$f_i$ = risk-free forward rate in Year $i$
$f_i + p_i$ = current risk-adjusted forward rate
= current contractual return (with $p_i$ = annual risk spread)
$c_i$ = annual floating coupon in Year $i = a + (b \times f_i)$
$c_0$ = first annual coupon (already fixed)
$F$ = principal

$$\text{Price} = \frac{c_0}{1 + R_1 + p_1} + \frac{1}{1 + R_1 + p_1} \sum_{i=2}^{N} \frac{c_i F}{\prod_{i=2}^{N}(1 + f_i + p_i)} + \frac{F}{\prod_{i=2}^{N}(1 + f_i + p_i)}$$

Rewrite the annual coupon as $c_i = (f_i + p_i) + [a - p_i + f_i \times (b - 1)]$

$$\text{Price} = \frac{(1 + c_0)F}{1 + R_1 + p_1} + \frac{1}{1 + R_1 + p_1} \sum_{i=2}^{N} \frac{[a - p_i + f_i \times (b - 1)] \times F}{\prod_{i=2}^{N}(1 + f_i + p_i)}$$

The floating-rate bond is the sum of two assets: a short-term (time until repricing) zero coupon bond plus the discounted value of the differences between the contractual return on the asset and the return on a new asset. The case of $b = 1$ is the one presented in the numerical example.

## APPENDIX B: DURATION AND CONVEXITY

As was stated in the chapter, the duration formula provides a linear approximation of the relationship between the price of the bond and the movement of interest rates. In reality, the relationship is a convex curve. To obtain a better approximation of the impact on price of a change in interest rate, it is possible to incorporate a convexity factor. The presentation assumes a flat yield curve, $R$.

$PVCF_t$ = present value of cash flow received at time $t$

$n$ = number of years until maturity

$$\Delta \text{ Price} = (-\text{price} \times \frac{\text{standard duration}}{1+R} \times \Delta R) + (\text{price} \times \frac{Cx}{2} \times \Delta R^2)$$

with

$$Cx = \text{convexity} = \frac{1 \times 2 \times PVCF_1 + 2 \times 3 \times PVCF_2 + \cdots n \times (n+1) \times PVCF_n}{(1+R)^2 \times \text{price}}$$

## APPENDIX C: THE RELEVANT MATURITY OF THE TRANSFER PRICE AND THE HEDGE

It is argued that the choice of the relevant maturity for the transfer benchmark rate depends on each specific application: pricing the product, selecting the hedge instrument, or evaluating a branch performance ex post. Consider the case of deposit collection, a representative case. Similar reasoning can apply to retail loans.

1. *Maturity of the transfer price for pricing.*

   It was argued in Chapter 11 that, although the maturity of a deposit could be quite short, a lag in the supply of deposits and/or interest-rate rigidity would require using some average of the current and forward market rates as a transfer price. Therefore, with regard to pricing, the choice of a longer-term benchmark rate has to be justified either by a lag or by interest-rate "stickiness."

2. *Effective duration of deposits.*

   This chapter showed that the effective duration of a deposit would be longer than the contractual maturity whenever an increase in the interest rate increased the value of the franchise on deposits. In this case, it is imperfectly competitive markets (the source of the interest margin and the franchise value) that drive the choice of the appropriate duration of the hedge instrument. A simple example is the case of demand deposits with very low or no interest. As the franchise on these deposits is usually much higher in countries with high interest rates, the duration of demand deposits is much longer than the contractual short-term maturity. It must be noticed that the maturity used for pricing could differ from the maturity used for hedging. Indeed, if repricing occurs frequently and if there is no lag, the duration applicable for pricing should be close to the maturity of the product. However, the duration used for hedging could be much longer, if the franchise value increases with the level of interest rates.

3. *Transfer price for ex post evaluation of performance.*

A golden rule in management accounting to evaluate a value center is to choose a transfer price that leads to value creation decisions. As a transfer price for deposits (or loans), a branch should be given the relevant market rate used for pricing (i.e., an average of the current and forward rates whenever there are lags or rigid rates, as discussed in Chapter 11). The transfer price must reflect the marginal profit of new business. However, the use of the current rate (or an average of the current and forward rates) implies that a low-interest-rate environment will often lead to very low performance for a branch that collects retail deposits. The reason for this is that interest margins on deposits are usually much lower in a low-interest-rate environment. It would be somewhat unfair to penalize the branch manager for this low performance, especially when the bank, as a whole, can be hedged with the purchase of longer-duration assets and capital gains created in a declining-rate environment. In short, in a declining-interest-rate environment, who should get the benefits of the hedge? The retail branch or the bank? Although a formula could be devised to return the benefits of the hedge to the branch, we take the view that the value-center system should reflect the true current marginal profitability based on the current rate (ignoring the benefits of the hedge). The implication is that the profitability of a deposit-gathering branch is likely to be correlated with the level of interest rates. In our view, branch performance should be evaluated vis-à-vis a "benchmark performance level," not in absolute terms. In a low-interest-rate environment, the benchmark level of performance should be adjusted downward to recognize that the "normal benchmark" profit will be lower.

## EXERCISES FOR CHAPTER 19

1. Economic value (EV) at risk

| Value of Assets: 10 billion | Value of debt: 9.5 billion |
|---|---|
|  | Value of equity: 0.5 billion |

A bank has assets valued at $10 billion and debt valued at $9.5 billion. Given that the duration of assets is two years, that the duration of the debt is one year, and that the interest-rate level is 5 percent, calculate the economic value of equity at risk (as a percentage of the current value of equity) for a parallel shift in the yield curve of 2 percent.

2. A slightly simplified balance sheet of Alpha-Direct, the Internet bank of Alpha Group, is as follows:

| Total assets: €100 billion (Duration 3 years) | Savings deposits: €98 billion (Duration: 0.5 year) |
|---|---|
| | Equity: €2 billion |

In the second pillar, Basel II recommends that the change in economic value of a bank should not exceed 20 percent of BIS capital (Tier 1 + Tier 2) for a 2 percent parallel interest-rate move. To simplify (as Tier 1 is more or less equal to 50 percent of BIS capital), that says that the change in economic value cannot exceed 40 percent of Tier 1.

The percentage of economic value (EV) at risk of Alpha Direct could be calculated as follows:

$$\Delta EV/EV = -(A/EV) \times [Du_A - (D/A) \times Du_D] \times \Delta R$$
$$= -(100/2) \times [3 - (98/100) \times 0.5] \times 0.02 = -251\%$$

As a consultant invited by Alpha-Direct to defend its case with the bank supervisor, how do you justify the mismatch and the percentage economic value at risk of 251 percent?

3. It is often said that it is not possible to hedge the economic value of equity and profitability at the same time. Consider the following example:

| Asset (duration 2 years): 100 | Debt (duration 2 years): 100 |
|---|---|
| Asset [duration 1 day (overnight)]: 10 | Equity: 10 |

In this case, $\Delta$ asset value = $\Delta$ debt value (and $\Delta$ economic value = 0), but the repricing gap is positive. An increase in interest rates will increase net interest margin and profit.

Is it true that the bank has to choose to hedge either economic value or profit? Explain your answer.

4. In IAS 39, the International Accounting Standards Board (IASB) proposed to require firms to mark to market most derivatives instruments. Hedge accounting (according to which a derivative contract does not need to be marked to market if

and only if it is used to hedge an instrument that is not marked to market) would be very severely restricted. According to the original IASB proposal, hedge accounting for deposits that are payable on demand (such as demand or savings deposits) would not be allowed. This was opposed by French bankers, among others, who want to apply hedge accounting for derivatives used to hedge their deposits payable on demand. They argue that mark-to-market accounting will increase the volatility of their income statements and balance sheets and, according to the *Financial Times* (February 9, 2004) "Jacques Chirac, French President, last year, claimed that IAS 39 could have nefarious* consequences for Europe's economies."

In the context of the bank fundamental valuation model, do you agree or not with the viewpoint of the French bankers who demanded an exception? That is, do you think that derivatives that are used to hedge deposits payable on demand should not be marked to market, meaning that the profit or loss on the derivative instrument could be accrued (recognized) over a long period of time?

* According to the *Oxford English Dictionary*, *nefarious* means "wicked, iniquitous."

## Notes

1. This strategy is known as a "gamble for resurrection." A last resort risky gamble is taken in hopes of turning the situation around.
2. In the first step, the franchise value is ignored. This is introduced later.
3. Note that the sum of the weights divided by the price adds up to 1 for the standard duration. These factors do not add up to 1 for the adjusted duration because of the multiplication by the interest factors in the numerator.
4. Appendix A to Chapter 20 shows how to adapt the framework for non-parallel shifts in the yield curve, the so-called *vector duration* approach.
5. The adjusted duration formula has been introduced for a fixed-rate asset. Appendix A of this chapter discusses how to compute the duration of a floating-rate asset.
6. This approach generalizes the results of Dermine (1985a, 1987).
7. With reference to the fundamental valuation formula, there is no tax penalty, as, every year, financial assets are assumed equal to financial liabilities.

8. Application of this methodology to other assets and stochastic yield curves can be found in O'Brien et al. (1994), O'Brien (2000), Hutchinson and Pennacchi (1996), or Jarrow and van Deventer (1998). Notice that the franchise value must be computed on an after-tax basis, something that is often missing in the literature.
9. Options are discussed in Chapter 24.
10. Appendix C of this chapter shows that effective maturities for non-maturing products have to be used for pricing, for hedging, and for assessment of performance ex post. For each of these applications, an effective maturity must be chosen, as it can vary from application to application.
11. Swaps and financial derivatives are discussed in Chapter 24.
12. Off-balance sheet derivatives are discussed in Chapter 24.
13. This example follows common practice in valuing the contractual cash flows of the asset at the current contractual rate on new loans. An alternative, consistent with the valuation model, would be to value the expected contractual cash flows of the asset at an expected return on new loans (see the discussion in the Appendix to Chapter 15).

# CHAPTER 20

# Value at Risk in the Trading Book: The Aggregation of Risks

So far, the impact of a change in interest rate on the earnings or economic value of the bank has been considered. The reality is much more complex, however, as even in a one-currency bank, there will be several interest rates along the yield curve. A multinational bank will face movements of interest rates in different currencies, as well as foreign exchange risk. In short, a bank is facing a multitude of sources of risk. Each source of risk, or specific earnings at risk, needs to be identified:

- Risk related to a change in the short-term rate in U.S. dollars
- Risk related to a change in the long-term rate in U.S. dollars
- Risk related to a change in interest rates in the euro
- Risk related to a change in currency parity between the U.S. dollar and the euro
- Risk related to commodity prices, equity prices, and so on

Practical questions arise: When a bank faces multiple sources of risk, how is total risk measured? How can risks be aggregated into a single measure of total risk?

Two parties were interested in the measurement of total risk. First, the banks were starting to allocate economic capital to trading units to measure risk-adjusted performance. As discussed previously, a bank's economic capital is allocated to cover potential losses. So, banks were searching for an aggregate measure of the total risk assumed by a trading unit. Second, after the creation of the 1988 Cooke ratio (Basel I), central banks wanted to add a complement to the accord to cover trading risk. To apply a capital regulation for trading risk, there was again a need for a measure of total risk when trading units are involved in many markets: bonds, equities, and commodities. This is the issue discussed in this chapter.

How it is possible to move from the measurement of risk for a single source of risk to the measurement of total aggregated risk?

The historical development of this issue can be traced to the measurement of trading risk. Remember from the discussion in Chapter 18 that accountants make a distinction between the banking book and the trading book. A key accounting characteristic of the trading book is that it is marked to market every day and that changes in the value of the book are reported in the income statement. Therefore, a loss of value in the trading book will reduce the bank's profit. This source of risk is referred to as *value at risk*, known as VAR. It applies exclusively to the trading book, whereas the term *economic value at risk* (EVR) is applied to the banking book. As central banks came to focus on VAR, the issue of multiple sources of risk arose rapidly in the context of the trading book. However, it should be recognized that the aggregation of risks applies to earnings at risk as well when a bank is operating in different markets around the world, or when a bank would like to aggregate earnings at risk related to the various buckets in a repricing gap table. This chapter focuses on aggregation of risks in the trading book.

## AGGREGATION OF RISKS: AN EXAMPLE

First, consider a simple example to illustrate the nature of the issue. A trading book (as shown in Table 20.1) includes two positions: an asset whose cash flows of $100 and $80 will be paid with certainty at the end of Year 1 and Year 2, and a liability whose cash flows of $80 and $100 will be paid with certainty at the end of Year 1 and Year 2.

Since this is a trading position, the value of the position is computed, with the net cash flow of $20 in Year 1 being valued at the one-year-to-maturity zero coupon bond rate $R_1$, and the cash flow paid in Year 2, $-\$20$, being discounted at the two-years-to-maturity zero coupon

**TABLE 20.1**

Trading Book

|  | Year 1 | Year 2 |
|---|---|---|
| Cash inflow from asset | +100 | +80 |
| Cash outflow from debt | −80 | −100 |
| Net cash flow | +20 | −20 |

rate $R_2$. The matching of the maturity of the zero coupon rate with the timing of the cash flows was discussed in Chapter 2.

$$\text{Value of trading position} = \frac{+20}{1+R_1} + \frac{-20}{(1+R_2)^2}$$

For instance with $R_1 = 9$ percent and $R_2 = 12$ percent, this position is valued at

$$\text{Value of position} = \frac{+20}{1.09} + \frac{-20}{(1.12)^2} = 18.349 - 15.944 = 2.405$$

The risk to the bank, from an income statement perspective, is that a movement in the interest-rate curve could change the value of that position. This source of risk is referred to as the value at risk, or VAR.

Since the cash flows in this example are risk-free and known with certainty, there are two sources of value at risk:

- Changes in the one-year-to-maturity rate $R_1$ $(\Delta R_1)$
- Changes in the two-years-to-maturity rate $R_2$ $(\Delta R_2)$

A first proposal, Proposal 1, to measure the total value at risk is to look at the sum of the VARs.

### Proposal 1: The Sum of Key VARs

Since the first cash flow is positive ($+\$20$, an asset), an increase in the interest rate $(\Delta^+R_1)$ would reduce the present value of the first cash flow. To measure the first source of value at risk, one possibility would be to analyze the historical volatility of the one-year rate and evaluate the impact on value of an increase in the interest rate with, say, 99 percent confidence. The impact on value of a change of 1 percent in a specific maturity rate is known as *key-rate duration*. Each rate along a yield curve is a key rate, as a change in that rate will affect the value of a position. With reference to this terminology, *key VAR* is the impact on value of a change in a specific rate with 99 percent confidence.

### First Source of Risk: Change of Value $(\Delta^+R_1)$ = key VAR $(\Delta^+R_1)$

For a 99 percent volatility of 1.5 percent—that is, the one-year rate $R_1$ increasing from 9 percent to 10.5 percent—the value of the first cash flow is equal to

$$\text{Value of first cash flow} = \frac{+20}{1.105} = 18.1$$

and

$$\text{Key VAR } (\Delta^- R_1) = |18.1 - 18.349| = 0.249$$

Similarly, the impact of a change in interest rate on the value of the second cash flow can be analyzed. Since it is negative ($-\$20$, a liability), a reduction in the two-year rate ($\Delta^- R_2$) would increase the value of the liability.

**Second Source of Risk: Change of Value $(\Delta^- R_2)$ = key VAR$(\Delta^- R_2)$**
Similarly if the 99 percent confidence level for the two-year rate is 0.5 percent, the value of the second cash flows moves to

$$\text{Value of second cash flow} = \frac{-20}{(1.115)^2} = -16.087$$

and

$$\text{Key VAR}(\Delta^+ R_2) = |-16.087 - 15.944| = 0.143$$

A natural proposal for measuring the total risk incurred is to recognize that there are two sources of risk and to take the mathematical sum of these risks, the sum of the key VARs:

$$\text{Total VAR} = \text{key VAR}(\Delta^+ R_1) + \text{key VAR}(\Delta^- R_2) = 0.249 + 0.143 = 0.392$$

Using Proposal 1, the measure of total risk would be the potential loss of value resulting from an adverse change in the one-year maturity rate (with 99 percent confidence), augmented by the potential loss of value resulting from an adverse change in the two-year maturity rate (with 99 percent confidence). Total VAR (0.392) represents 16.32 percent of the original value of the position (0.392/2.405).

This method of calculation is simple and intuitive: total risk is the sum of all the individual risks. However, a trader would quickly object that in this example, the bank would lose $0.392 only in the event of very bad luck: both of the two interest rates moving in an adverse direction, with the one-year rate going up (reducing the value of the first positive cash flow, an asset) and the two-year rate going down (increasing the value of the debt obligation resulting from a negative cash flow). Proposal 1 is a very conservative, *worst-worst*-case measure of risk that implicitly assumes that the bank is losing on all fronts at the same time. The trader would argue that one- and two-year interest rates rarely go in opposite direction, that is, with one of them going up while the other one is going down. Most of the time, they move in parallel, displaying a high degree of correlation. If either central banks or banks were simply taking the sum of all the risks, the measure of total risk would be so large that banks would be forced to reduce their trading positions and profits. As a result, banks started to search for more "reasonable" measures of aggregate risk. Two such measures are the *twist in the yield curve* (also called *vector duration* or *scenario analysis*) approach and the application of modern portfolio theory.

### Proposal 2a: Twist in the Yield Curve or Vector Duration

The *twist in the yield curve* approach, or *vector duration* approach, proposes a general measure of duration that applies to any type of changes in the yield curve, parallel or nonparallel. Chapter 19 introduced the duration formula, a measure of the change in value of a fixed-income asset in the event of a parallel shift in the yield curve. This approach is now generalized to any type of change or twist in the curve. Consider the previous example of the trading position:[1]

|                       | Year 1 | Year 2 |
|-----------------------|--------|--------|
| Cash flow from asset  | +100   | +80    |
| Cash flow from debt   | −80    | −100   |
| Net cash flow         | +20    | −20    |

$$\text{Value of position} = \frac{+20}{1.09} + \frac{-20}{(1.12)^2} = 18.349 - 15.944 = 2.405$$

The position is the sum of two positions, the present value of the two cash flows. The first position is a one-year zero coupon asset with a standard duration of one year. The second position is a two-year zero coupon debt with a duration of two years.[2] Applying the duration formula discussed in Chapter 19 to each cash flow separately gives

$$\Delta \text{ Total value} = \left( -\text{price}_1 \times \frac{\text{duration of first cash flow}}{1+R_1} \times \Delta R_1 \right)$$

$$+ \left( -\text{price}_2 \times \frac{\text{Duration of second cash flow}}{1+R_2} \times \Delta R_2 \right)$$

$$\Delta \text{ Total value} = \left( -18.349 \times \frac{1}{1.09} \times \Delta R_1 \right)$$

$$+ \left[ -(-15.944) \times \frac{2}{1.12} \times \Delta R_2 \right]$$

Now define:

$$\Delta R_2 = \alpha \Delta R_1$$

The parameter $\alpha$ will allow the type of change, or twist in the yield curve, to be captured. Representative $\alpha$s include

- $\alpha = 1$. This is a parallel shift. One-year and two-year rates move up and down in parallel. This was the case presented in Chapter 19.
- $0 \leq \alpha \leq 1$; for example, $\alpha = 0.5$. In this case, a change of 1 percent in the one-year rate is accompanied by an increase of 0.5 percent in the two-year rate. This can happen when strict monetary policy pushes up short-term rates, with longer-term rates increasing by less.
- $\alpha \leq 0$; for example, $\alpha = -0.33$. In this case, an increase in the one-year rate is accompanied by a decrease in the long-term rate because the market anticipates a recession or a drop in interest rates. This is the case of an inversion in the yield curve. Proposal 1 (the conservative worst-worst case) was assuming $\alpha = -0.5/1.5 = -0.33$.

The intuitive explanation is that the elasticity parameter $\alpha$ allows the capture of different movements, or twists in the yield curve, with the parallel shift ($\alpha = 1$) being a special case. Playing with the mathematics leads to

$$\frac{\Delta \text{ Total value (VAR)}}{\text{Value}} = -\frac{\left(1 \times 18.349 \times \frac{1}{1.09}\right) + \left[2 \times (-15.944) \times \frac{1}{1.12} \times \alpha\right]}{2.405} \times \Delta R_1$$

This can be recognized as the adjusted duration formula discussed in Chapter 19, that is, a weighted average maturity of the position, except that the elasticity parameter $\alpha$ has been introduced. For example, for the three special cases just discussed ($\alpha = 1$, $\alpha = 0.5$, and $\alpha = -0.33$), a vector of value sensitivities for the case of a 1 percent increase in the one-year rate $R_1$ can be obtained:

| Elasticity $\alpha$ | VAR/Value |
|---|---|
| $\alpha = 1$ | 4.84% |
| $\alpha = 0.3$ | 3.45% |
| $\alpha = -0.33$ | 10.91% |

With the yield curve twist or vector duration approach, the focus is on a few twists described by the parameters $\alpha$. For each one, the value at risk is computed. In this approach, the term correlation is not being used. Rather, what is being looked at is various potential shifts or various scenarios, with the parallel shift being a special case. A risk manager will ensure that the VAR for each scenario is acceptable. This approach has the advantage of transparency. Members of the ALCO can easily recognize the types of twist that have been tested and can always ask for more. Moreover, a statistical technique, principal component analysis (PCA), is available to identify the types of $\alpha$ that should be looked at.

An alternative to the *vector duration* approach is the application of modern portfolio theory.

### Proposal 2b: Application of Modern Portfolio Theory

The alternative proposal that has received a great deal of attention worldwide is the application of modern portfolio theory (MPT) to the problem at hand. Developed in 1959 by two future Nobel Prize winners (Harry Markowitz and James Tobin), the theory was first applied to the holding of stocks. Buying one stock is risky, as its price can go either up or down, but if you buy several stocks, diversification will help to reduce your risk, as a loss on one stock is expected to be offset in part by a gain on another stock. Modern portfolio theory provides the mathematics to measure total risk, incorporating the diversification benefits. Although the problem at hand, interest-rate risk, is different from the risk of holding stocks, the mathematical abstraction is similar. There are several sources of risk (shares or interest rates), and the problem is how to measure total risk.

Applying modern portfolio theory to the problem at hand,

$$\Delta \text{ Total value} = \left( -\text{price}_1 \times \frac{\text{duration of first cash flow}}{1 + R_1} \times \Delta R_1 \right)$$

$$+ \left( -\text{Price}_2 \times \frac{\text{duration of second cash flow}}{1 + R_2} \times \Delta R_2 \right)$$

$$\Delta \text{ Total value} = \left( -18.349 \times \frac{1}{1.09} \times \Delta R_1 \right) + \left[ -(-15.944) \times \frac{2}{1.12} \times \Delta R_2 \right]$$

$$= -16.834 \times \Delta R_1 + 28.471 \times \Delta R_2$$

To compute the volatility of profit (one standard deviation of potential change in value) requires two steps:

1. Step 1. Calculate the variance (the square of the volatility of total risk).

The variance formula is as follows, with $R_1$ and $R_2$ denoting two random variables, $a$ and $b$ denoting the fixed coefficients, $\sigma_R 1$ being the standard deviation of $R_1$, $\sigma_R 2$ being the standard deviation of $R_2$, and $\rho_{R1,R2}$ being the correlation between $R_1$ and $R_2$:

$$\text{Variance } (a \times R_1 + b \times R_2) = \sigma_{\text{total risk}}^2$$
$$= (a^2 \times \sigma_{R1}^2) + (b^2 \times \sigma_{R2}^2) + (2 \times a \times b \times \rho_{R1,R2} \times \sigma_{R1} \times \sigma_{R2})$$

In the previous case, with $\sigma_{R1} = 0.006$, $\sigma_{R2} = 0.002$, and $\rho_{R1,R2} = 0.6$, the variance is

$$\text{Variance } (16.834 \times R_1 + -28.471 \times R_2) = \sigma_{\text{total risk}}^2$$
$$= (16.834^2 \times 0.006^2) + (-28.471^2 \times 0.002^2) + [2 \times 16.834 \times$$
$$(-28.471) \times 0.6 \times 0.006 \times 0.002]$$
$$= 0.0065$$

2. Step 2. Calculate the standard deviation, that is, the volatility of total risk:

$$\sigma_{\text{total risk}} = \sqrt{\text{variance}} = \sqrt{0.0065} = 0.081$$

It can be seen that the total risk, with diversification included, of 0.081 is less than the sum of each risk, the worst-worst case:

$$\text{Total risk}_{\text{worst case}} = 16.834 \times 0.006 + 28.471 \times 0.002 = 0.158$$

Note that the worst-worst case in the example discussed here[3] corresponds to the case with the one-year rate $R_1$ going up and the two-year rate $R_2$ going down, consistent with a correlation of $-1$. Once the standard deviation has been calculated, it can be multiplied by 2.33 to obtain a measure of aggregate risk with 99 percent confidence.

Figure 20.1 shows the normal curve with confidence intervals

## ESTIMATION OF VAR

Three statistical methods can be used to evaluate value at risk: parametric methods, historical simulation, and Monte Carlo simulation.[4]

### Parametric Method (Variance-Covariance Method)

In the parametric approach, first the gaps or the adjusted duration and then the volatility of interest rates and correlations are estimated. An underlying assumption is that the payoffs are a linear function of the random variable. This is a fair approximation for bonds and futures

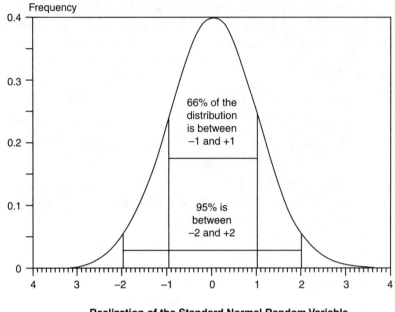

Figure 20.1 Normal curve.

Source: Jorion, 2007.

(excluding the convexity discussed earlier), but it is not adequate for options, which exhibit nonlinear payoffs. As a consequence, alternative tools have been developed.

## Historical Simulation

In a historical simulation, the first step is to compute vectors of changes in interest rates (exchange rates, commodity prices,. . .) observed in the past. For example, if daily VAR is being measured, a vector is a column with the observed interest-rate changes during a specific day in the past. There will be as many vectors as there are historical observations. Then, the vector of interest-rate changes is applied to the current portfolio to calculate the change in value. Repeating this for each vector of past price changes gives a distribution of simulated changes. It is then possible to calculate VAR at some confidence level. The advantage is that with this method it is not necessary to assume linearity.

## Monte Carlo Simulation

A Monte Carlo simulation begins with an assumed variance-covariance matrix. It is then possible to create interest-rate changes consistent with the variance-covariance matrix. Once the vectors of price changes have been created, it is then possible to apply each vector to the current portfolio to simulate a change of value. As in the previous case, a distribution of simulated changes in value is obtained.

## CONDITIONAL VAR

A weakness of the VAR measure is that it gives the probability that a loss could exceed a certain number, but it does not say by how much it could exceed that number. For instance, a one-day $VAR_{99\%}$ of $10 million says that there is a 1 percent probability that a loss over one day could exceed $10 million. But a trader could create a position that has a low 1 percent probability of a very big loss (Hull, 2006). This could be easily achieved by selling an out-of-the-money option.

Conditional VAR (CVAR) is the (conditional) expected loss for losses beyond the VAR level [also called "expected shortfall (ES)," "tail VAR," and "beyond VAR"]. It shows the expected loss, conditional on being behind the confidence interval.

For a normal distribution at the 99 percent confidence level, with $\alpha = 99$ percent,

$$\text{Expected shortfall}_\alpha \ (ES_\alpha) = \frac{e^{-(1/2)\times(\#\sigma_\alpha)^2}}{(1-\alpha)\sqrt{2\pi}} = \frac{e^{-(1/2)\times 2.326^2}}{0.01\sqrt{2\times 3.1415}} = 2.67$$

Expected shortfall = 2.67 (equivalent to VAR at 99.6% confidence level)

An advantage of the CVAR measure is that it meets the *coherence* properties demanded for risk measures by Artzner et al. (1999):

- *Monotonicity.* If a portfolio has lower returns than those on another portfolio for every state of the world, its measure of risk should be greater.
- *Translation invariance.* If an amount of cash (Treasury bill) $K$ is added to a portfolio, that portfolio's risk measure should go down by $K$.

- *Homogeneity.* Changing the size of a portfolio by a factor of lambda while keeping the relative amount of positions in the portfolio the same should result in the risk measure's being multiplied by lambda.
- *Subadditivity:* The risk measure of two portfolios after they are merged should be no greater than the sum of their risk measures before they were merged. This condition states that diversification should either reduce risk or keep it constant.

## THE CASE OF LONG-TERM CAPITAL MANAGEMENT

Long-Term Capital Management (LTCM) was an American hedge fund created in 1994. Using the legal form of a limited liability partnership, it raised funds from wealthy individuals and institutional investors, such as banks and pension funds.[5] Because it targeted wealthy clients, it was unregulated. The presumption is that wealthy individuals should be able to assess the risk of investment correctly. Some of the 16 founding partners were well known: John Meriwether (a former bond trader at the U.S. investment bank Salomon Brothers), David Mullins (former vice chairman of the Federal Reserve Board), Myron Scholes (winner of the Nobel Prize), and Robert Merton (winner of the Nobel Prize). Its first three years were a great success, with $ROE_{1995,1996}$ of 40 percent and $2.7 billion returned to investors in 1997. The mystery was large, as the fund did not have to disclose its investment strategy. Information revealed at a later date showed that the fund was highly leveraged:

### LTCM Balance Sheet (1998)

|                               | Debt:   $120 billion |
|-------------------------------|----------------------|
|                               | Equity: $ 5 billion  |
| Total assets: $125 billion    | Total:  $125 billion |

This represents only the on-balance sheet assets, as off-balance sheet transactions were large. Money was essentially borrowed from banks, with the loans being collaterized by the assets.

The asset allocation strategy that LTCM followed is called *market-neutral arbitrage, relative value,* or *convergence arbitrage.* It did not attempt to forecast interest-rate movements, something that is very hard to do. Instead, it was betting that pairs of interest rates would get closer to one another, that there would be a convergence of interest rates. A few of these positions included

- Italian lira interest rate–deutsche mark rate: 1.7 percent. At that time, it had not yet been decided whether or not Italy would adopt the euro, with some Germans expressing reluctance to take on board some "club Med" countries with large public deficits.

- U.S. mortgage bond rate–U.S. Treasury bonds: 2 percent. The view was that the prepayment option did not justify such a large spread.
- Russian GKO rate–U.S. T-bill rate: 10 percent. GKOs are local-currency (ruble) Treasury bills in Russia. This was a period of rapidly declining inflation in Russia and a booming economy, with large amounts of foreign investment in Moscow. The view was that convergence would continue.

Of course, each of these positions was risky, but calculating the volatility of the spreads and the very low correlations, as each of these markets was fairly independent, the risk manager concluded that an equity of $5 billion was enough to cover risk with 99 percent confidence.

On August 17, 1998, in a surprise move, Russian President Yeltsin announced a moratorium on the Russian GKOs — a very rare event, as countries usually do not default on local-currency bonds. On September 20, 92 percent of LTCM's equity had been wiped out. Following the "Russian crisis," world markets jumped into safe assets, U.S. Treasury bonds and German bonds (a classic flight to quality at a time of uncertainty). This resulted in a large increase in spreads, technically a surprising and unwelcome increase in correlation.

On September 23, Bill McDonough, then president of the Federal Reserve Bank of New York, corralled representatives of 14 leading banks into the Fed's office at 33 Liberty Street in Manhattan's financial district and urged them to bail out the ailing hedge fund. Banks were "invited" to invest $3.6 billion for 90 percent of LTCM's equity. The fear was that in the event of default, the lenders would liquidate the collateral and that the sale of billions worth of bonds would create a meltdown of the capital market. By the end of September 1998, the founding partners' 1997 stake of $1.6 billion was worth $30 million.

It is left to the reader to decide whether the failure of LTCM was the result of bad *management* or bad *luck* (after all, wealthy shareholders do not mind chipping in a few million in risky leveraged transactions). What was certainly bad management was the behavior of some of the banks, which had lent money without any understanding of LTCM's strategy. As a sign of good governance and accountability, the CEO of United Bank of Switzerland was dismissed by the board.

A consequence of the LTCM debacle was severe criticism of modern portfolio theory. Although the mathematics is correct, there is a danger that the measurement of total risk misses the reality when changes and increases in correlation make historical measures obsolete. And those critics pointed out that increases in correlation often happen at the worst times: at times of large shocks, when diversification would be most needed.

The critics cannot be ignored. Applying common sense, this leads to two messages:

1. Diversification of risks, and its associated reduction of aggregated total risk, is often a reality.
2. Measures of risk must include not only a 99 percent confidence interval, but also stress scenarios incorporating changes in correlation.

## BASEL MARKET RISK AMENDMENT

In the 1988 Basel I Cooke ratio, the emphasis was on capturing, even if imperfectly, credit risk, including counterparty risk. Trading activities were relatively limited at the time. However, once the task was done, the Basel Committee on Banking Supervision (BCBS) started to work on a complement to the accord that would capture trading risk. This includes the risk arising out of trading debt securities, equity shares and related derivatives, foreign exchange, and commodities. Note that part of the risk, the loss arising out of a default by a counterparty, was included in the Basel I accord. Market risk refers to losses caused by movements in market prices, interest rates, foreign exchange, or commodity prices. The BCBS reached an agreement on a capital charge for market risk in 1996 (Basel Committee, 1996),[6] with the implementation date being the end of 1997. The market risk amendment (MRA) remains in force with Basel II.

### Internal Model

Although the regulation provides for a standardized approach, with a measure of risk being prescribed by central banks,[7] the focus of attention was on the idea that banks, if authorized by their regulators, would be allowed to use their own methodology to measure risks. This is known as the *internal model* approach. While the BCBS was at first reluctant to recognize the risk reduction produced by diversification across markets, in the end, it allowed banks to choose their methodology, with four caveats:

1. *Confidence: 99 percent.* VAR must be measured with a confidence level of at least 99 percent.
2. *Historical data.* Volatility would need to be measured using at least one year of data.

3. *Holding period: 10 days.* Central banks that are not convinced that trading positions could be closed in 1 day (the standard defeasance or holding period used by OECD banks for trading risk) can ask banks to measure risk with a 10-day holding period. That is, if a bank is sitting on a portfolio for 10 days, what would be the VAR with 99 percent confidence? Obviously, this is larger than if the bank keeps the portfolio for only 1 day. Redesigning their systems to measure risk over a 10-day holding period would have proved costly for banks, so instead, they were allowed to use a statistical formula that translated 1-day risk into 10-day risk: $\sigma_{daily} \times \sqrt{10}$. While the formula is easy to use, it is statistically valid only in the case of no autocorrelation of prices, which means that what happened yesterday in a market provides no information concerning what will happen tomorrow. Although this condition has not been validated empirically, the BCBS has allowed the use of the formula.

4. *Backtesting.* Finally, ex post (the day after trading), banks would compare their actual realized results with the VAR measure. If the results exceeded the VAR too often, the banks would be penalized for not being able to measure risk correctly.

The BIS capital for trading risk is given by the following formula:

$$\text{BIS capital} = \max(3 \times \text{VAR}_{-1}, 3 \times \text{average VAR}_{60days})$$

$\text{VAR}_{-1}$ refers to the VAR observed yesterday. As central banks were afraid that banks would close their trading risk on the announcement of their visit, banks also have to measure the average VAR over the last 60 days, $\text{VAR}_{60days}$. Finally, the multiplicative factor 3 was the result of a negotiation. Banks were allowed to use their own model, incorporating the expected benefits of diversification. In return, the measure of risk was grossed up by a factor of 3 to recognize instability in correlation and intraday trading risk, which can be much larger than the end-of-the-day trading risk measured by the regulator. The backtesting penalty mentioned earlier consists of increasing the factor beyond 3 for banks that are unable to measure their risk with a satisfactory degree of confidence.

The market risk accord is a historical landmark. For the first time in banking history, banks were allowed to measure the risk by themselves. In the past, the measure of risk was always imposed by the central bank. As central banks had responded positively to the use of the internal model, the banks decided to ask for more, that is, to be allowed to use more leverage so that they could compete against securities firms subject to nonbank regulations. This is reflected in a new definition of capital eligible to meet the market risk capital regulation:

Tier 1.

Tier 2 (subordinated debt, maturity > 5 years).

Tier 3 (subordinated debt, maturity > 2 years, < 250 percent of Tier 1). Since it has a shorter maturity, it is less costly than Tier 2. Tier 2 + Tier 3 must be less than 250 percent of Tier 1.

This implies that BIS capital of $350 for trading risk, for example, could be met with $100 of Tier 1 equity (28.6 percent) and $250 of subordinated debt (71.4 percent). The persistent lobbying of banks to reduce the use of Tier 1 equity is another proof of the perceived higher cost of equity funds.

## REPORTING VAR

Up until 1995, banks did not disclose VAR in their annual reports. The U.S. firm Bankers Trust was the first to report its VAR in its 1994 annual report, published in March 1995. The bank voluntarily disclosed its VAR because of the following situation. In early 1994, interest rates in the United States went up. As Bankers Trust had a reputation for incurring trading risk, its counterparties were concerned about the impact of the rate increase on its financial condition. Since they had no access to information (a case of opacity), they decided to take conservative measures, substantially reducing their counterparty trading limits with Bankers Trust. As a result, Bankers Trust experienced a severe liquidity crisis, as it was unable to find counterparties in the market. So, to reduce the opacity and reassure the market that it was measuring risk every day and that the size of its VAR was acceptable, Bankers Trust published information on VAR in its 1994 annual report.

For illustration, Figure 20.2 shows the 2007 VAR published in the annual report of the Royal Bank of Canada.

The bank reports a VAR with 99 percent confidence and for a one-day holding period, as well as the realized daily profit or loss. The average VAR over the year was Can$21 million. It includes the diversification effect across markets. Exceptional reporting is observed on the last day of October, with a loss of Can$340 million. This includes an exceptional writedown of Can$357 related to the U.S. subprime crisis. As the graph shows, with the exception of the last trading day, there were very few days with a loss exceeding the VAR measure.

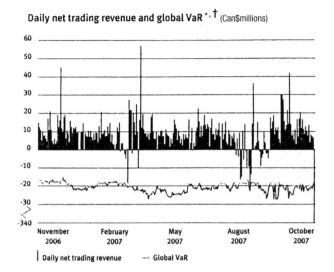

**Daily net trading revenue and global VaR** [*, †] (Can$millions)

| November 2006 | February 2007 | May 2007 | August 2007 | October 2007 |

| Daily net trading revenue    --- Global VaR

\* Trading revenue on a taxable equivalent basis excluding revenue related to consolidated VIEs.
† The $357 million writedown on the valuation of U.S. subprime RMBS and CDOs of ABS was included on October 31, 2007.

**Figure 20.2** Value at risk (99 percent) and realized trading revenue.
Source: Royal Bank of Canada, annual report, 2007.

## CONCLUSION

Banks measure risk, the potential (unexpected) loss that can occur, with a confidence level. In a situation where there are multiple sources of risk (interest rate, foreign exchange, commodity prices, equities), questions arise as to how to aggregate the risks and how to measure global risk. The intuition is that there must be some effect from diversification, somewhat reducing total risk. Modern portfolio theory provides an elegant tool for incorporating the benefits of diversification, but common sense demands that the bank stress-test changes in correlation. In a landmark ruling in 1996, the Basel Commitee (BCBS) has allowed banks to use their own internal risk models to measure trading risk.

## APPENDIX A: TWIST-ADJUSTED DURATION FOR A THREE-YEAR BOND

Consider a three-year bond with cash flows $CF_1$, $CF_2$, and $CF_3$:

| 0 | 1 | 2 | 3 |
| Cash flows | $CF_1$ | $CF_2$ | $CF_3$ |

$$\Delta \text{ Price} = -\frac{CF_1}{1+R_1^{1}} \times \frac{1}{1+R_1} \times \Delta R_1 - \frac{CF_2}{(1+R_2)^2} \times \frac{2}{1+R_2} \times \Delta R_2$$

$$-\frac{CF_3}{(1+R_3)^3} \times \frac{3}{1+R_3} \times \Delta R_3$$

Define

$$DCF_1 = CF_1/(1+R_1)^1$$
$$DCF_2 = CF_2/(1+R_2)^2$$
$$DCF_3 = CF_3/(1+R_3)^3$$
$$\Delta R_2 = \alpha \times \Delta R_1$$
$$\Delta R_3 = \beta \times \Delta R_1$$

$$\Delta \text{ Price} = -\text{price} \times \left[ \frac{\left(1 \times \dfrac{DCF_1}{1+R_1}\right) + \left(2 \times \dfrac{DCF_2}{1+R_2} \times \alpha\right) + \left(3 \times \dfrac{DCF_3}{1+R_3} \times \beta\right)}{\text{price}} \right] \times \Delta R_1$$

The change in price is the product of three terms: the price, a twist-adjusted duration, and the change in the one-year rate.

## APPENDIX B: MODERN PORTFOLIO THEORY APPLIED TO THE MEASUREMENT OF INTEREST-RATE RISK

Define $R_1$ and $R_2$ as interest rates of different maturities (currencies), $\sigma_{R1}$ and $\sigma_{R2}$ as the standard deviation of these rates, $\rho$ as the correlation between the interest rates, and $a$ and $b$ as the changes in value of two assets[8] for a 1 percent increase in interest rates.

If interest rates $R_1$ and $R_2$ move, the revenue on the portfolio will be given by the following relation:

$$\text{Revenue} = (a \times \Delta R_1) + (b \times \Delta R_2)$$

The total risk of such a position can be expressed by the standard deviation $\sigma_{aR1 + bR2}$, the square root of the variance (Var), calculated as follows:

$$\begin{aligned}
\text{Var}(aR_1 + bR_2) &= a^2 \text{ Var}(R_1) + b^2 \text{ Var}(R_2) + (2 \times a \times b \times \rho \times \\
&\quad \sigma_{R1} \times \sigma_{R2}) \\
&= [a^2 \text{ Var}(R_1) + b^2 \text{ Var}(R_2)] + 2 \times a \times b \times 1 \times \\
&\quad \sigma_{R1} \times \sigma_{R2} - 2 \times a \times b \times (1 - \rho) \times \sigma_{R1} \times \sigma_{R2}) \\
&= (a\sigma_1 + b\sigma_2)^2 - [2 \times (1 - \rho) \times a \times \\
&\quad b \times \sigma_{R1} \times \sigma_{R2}]
\end{aligned}$$

Four implications follow from the last relation:

1. Total risk (the standard deviation, $\sigma$) will be the sum of the risks on each single component $(a\sigma_1 + b\sigma_2)$ only in the case in which the two interest rates are perfectly correlated $(\rho = 1$, the case of a parallel shift in the yield curve):

$$\text{Risk} = \sigma_{aR1+bR2} = a\sigma_1 + b\sigma_2 \text{ if } \rho = 1$$

Note that the parameters $a$ and $b$ refer to the actual amounts, not the absolute values.

2. A condition for aggregation of positions $(a + b)$ is a perfect correlation of interest rates $(\rho = 1)$ and identical standard deviations $(\sigma_1 = \sigma_2 = \sigma)$:

$$\text{Risk} = (a + b) \times \sigma$$

3. In the other cases $(\rho \neq 1)$, the sum of the two components could over- or underrepresent the true measure of risk, depending on the signs of $a$, $b$, and the correlation $\rho$:

$$\sigma_{aR1+bR2} \begin{array}{l} < a\sigma_1 + b\sigma_2 \\ > a\sigma_1 + b\sigma_2 \end{array} \quad \begin{array}{l} \text{if } \rho < 1 \text{ and } a, b > 0 \text{ (or } a, b < 0) \\ \text{if } \rho < 1 \text{ and } a \text{ or } b < 0 \end{array}$$

4. The practice of summing the worst case for each of the two positions (technically, $|a|\sigma_1 + |b|\sigma_2$) will in most cases overstate total risk. It is a measure of a *worst-worst*-case scenario.

## EXERCISES FOR CHAPTER 20

1. Compute the overall earnings at risk (with one standard deviation) on the following international money market book, taking into account that the correlation between the dollar and euro interest rates is 0.6. Since the bank is based in Germany, the banking books are denominated in euro.

| Gap* (Million €) | | % Volatility ($\sigma$) |
|---|---|---|
| USD | 60 | 0.0030 |
| Euro | -30 | 0.0020 |

* Gap = assets − deposits.

2. If you want to report to management the overall earnings at risk in the absence of diversification benefits, what number would you report?

3. Value at risk (VAR) reports a measure of risk with 99 percent confidence. If you are responsible for risk management, are you

satisfied with a VAR report, or do you wish to see more
information? What are your additional information needs?

## Notes

1. This is a general approach. It could have been applied to a bond with
   any maturity. In Appendix A of this chapter, the mathematics for a
   bond with three years to maturity is shown.
2. The standard duration for a zero coupon asset is equal to its maturity
   (Chapter 19).
3. Taking $2.5 \times$ total risk (to obtain the rate move of 1.5 percent and
   $-0.5$ percent discussed earlier), the total risk is equal to $2.5 \times$
   $0.158 = 0.395$, very close to the actual 0.392 discussed in the text.
   The discrepancy is the result of the duration approximation.
4. Jorion (2007) or Crouhy et al. (2001).
5. A more detailed analysis of the LTCM saga is developed in Edwards
   (1999) and Jorion (2000).
6. The amendment was slightly updated in 2005. Following up on the
   U.S. subprime crisis, the Basel Committee (2008c) released a proposal
   for charging capital for incremental risk (IRC). It is intended to address
   a number of perceived shortcomings in the current VAR framework:
   default risk, credit risk migration, and, first and foremost, the lack of
   liquidity in several markets.
7. The standardized approach is a "building block" approach that measures
   total risk as the sum of individual risks. That is, it ignores the potential
   benefits of diversification. It makes a distinction between general risk
   (such as loss of value resulting from a general movement in interest rates)
   and specific risk (idiosyncratic risk that an individual debt or equity
   security moves by more than the general market in day-to-day trading).
8. The analysis is done for a trading book (marked to market at its current
   value). If the analysis refers to the net interest margin on the banking
   book, the $a$ and $b$ would represent the repricing gaps.

# CHAPTER 21

# Liquidity Risk and Value Creation

In Chapter 4, it was stated that two of the five main functions of a bank are to lend money to mitigate problems of asymmetric information and to provide insurance. One type of insurance is liquidity insurance, ensuring that depositors or borrowers are able to withdraw money on demand. This chapter first discusses the measurement and management of liquidity risk. Next, it clarifies the debate on the value creation resulting from selling liquidity insurance.

## LIQUIDITY RISK: MEASUREMENT AND MANAGEMENT

Liquidity risk for a bank arises because cash withdrawals cannot be met at low cost by a *fire sale* (sale on short notice) of illiquid loans. Because of asymmetric information between the seller and the buyer, the sale of an illiquid loan on short notice would result in a sharp reduction in the loan's value. In addition, banks must have enough liquidity on a day-to-day basis to cover the payments made through the central bank's clearing system, such as Fedwire in the United States or Target[1] for the European Central Bank. This liquidity consists of

1. Expected incoming transfers from other banks
2. Borrowing from other banks
3. Balances with the central bank
4. Sale of marketable assets
5. Discount window borrowing from the central bank

A representative statement of a bank's cash flows is first presented. It allows an understanding of the various sources of a bank's cash inflows and outflows. A discussion of the measurement of liquidity risk follows. The consolidated statement of cash flows shown in Table 21.1 is that of the Royal Bank of Canada for the year ended October 31, 2007.

**TABLE 21.1**

Consolidated Statement of Cash Flows (Can$ Million)

**Cash Flows from Operating Activities (Can$ million)**

| | |
|---|---|
| Net income from continuing operations | 5,492 |
| Adjustments to determine net cash from (used in) operating activities | |
| Provision for credit losses | 791 |
| Depreciation | 434 |
| Business realignment payments | (38) |
| Future income taxes | (147) |
| Amortization of other intangibles | 96 |
| Gain (loss) on sale of premises and equipment | (16) |
| (Gain) loss on loan securitization | (41) |
| (Gain) loss on sale of available-for-sale securities | (63) |
| (Gain) loss on sale of investment securities | — |
| Changes in operating assets and liabilities | |
| Insurance claims and policy benefits liabilities | (54) |
| Net change in accrued interest receivable and payable | (28) |
| Current income taxes | 1,034 |
| Derivative assets | (28,856) |
| Derivative liabilities | 29,916 |
| Trading securities | 9,623 |
| Net change in brokers and dealers receivable and payable | (317) |
| Other | 1,647 |
| **Net cash from (used in) operating activities from continuing operations** | 19,473 |
| **Net cash flows from (used in) operating activities from discontinued operations** | — |
| **Net cash from (used in) operating activities** | 19,473 |
| **Cash Flows from Investing Activities** | |
| Change in interest-bearing deposits with banks | (1,379) |
| Change in loans, net of loan securitizations | (39,569) |
| Proceeds from loan securitizations | 8,020 |
| Proceeds from sale of available-for-sale securities | 7,565 |
| Proceeds from sale of investment securities | — |
| Proceeds from maturity of available-for-sale securities | 18,784 |
| Proceeds from maturity of investment securities | — |
| Purchases of available-for-sale securities | (24,097) |
| Purchases of investment securities | — |
| Net acquisitions of premises and equipment | (706) |
| Changes in assets purchased under reverse repurchase agreements | (4,935) |
| Net cash from (used in) acquisitions | (373) |

*(Continued)*

| | |
|---|---:|
| **Net cash from (used in) investing activities from continuing operations** | (36,690) |
| **Net cash from (used in) investing activities from discontinued operations** | — |
| **Net cash from (used in) investing activities** | (36,690) |
| **Cash Flows from Financing Activities** | |
| Change in deposits | 17,831 |
| Issue of RBC Trust Capital securities | — |
| Issue of subordinated debentures | 87 |
| Repayment of subordinated debentures | (989) |
| Issue of preferred shares | 1,150 |
| Redemption of preferred shares for cancellation | (150) |
| Issuance costs | (23) |
| Issue of common shares | 155 |
| Purchase of common shares for cancellation | (646) |
| Sales of treasury shares | 208 |
| Purchase of treasury shares | (133) |
| Dividends paid | (2,278) |
| Dividends/distributions paid by subsidiaries to noncontrolling interests | (59) |
| Change in obligations related to assets sold under repurchase agreements | (4,070) |
| Change in obligations related to securities sold short | 6,436 |
| Change in short-term borrowing of subsidiaries | (145) |
| **Net cash from (used in) financing activities from continuing operations** | 17,374 |
| **Net cash from (used in) financing activities** | 17,347 |
| Effect of exchange rate changes on cash and due from banks | (332) |
| **Net change in cash and due from banks** | (175) |
| Cash and due from banks at the beginning of the year | 4,401 |
| **Cash and due from banks at the end of the year** | 4,226 |

Source: Royal Bank of Canada, annual report, 2007.

The annual consolidated statement of cash flows starts with the net income of Can$5,492 million reported in the consolidated income statement discussed in Chapter 4. It then takes into account all the non-cash items included in the income statement, such as depreciation and provision for credit losses. Finally, it takes into account the cash flows linked to investing and financing activities. In banking, there are two items that require a clarification: *accrued interest* receivable and payable, and the *float*.

Interest income (expense) is generally recognized (accrued) as income (expense) over time, even if it has not yet been paid. The following accounting relations have to be used to compute the actual net cash flows related to interest accruals:

Accrued interest receivable (payable)$_T$ = accrued interest receivable (payable)$_{T-1}$ + interest income (expense) accrual$_T$ – interest income (expense) actually paid$_T$

The stock of accrued interest receivable (payable) at a specific date is equal to the stock of interest receivable (payable) a year earlier, plus the interest accruals for the year, minus the interest actually paid during the year. This relation allows the cash inflows (outflows) linked to interest accruals to be calculated:

Cash inflow (outflow)$_T$ = interest income (expense) accrual$_T$ – $\Delta$ accrued interest receivable (payable)

Net cash flows$_T$ = net interest accrual margin$_{2007}$ – $\Delta$ accrued interest receivable + $\Delta$ accrued interest payable

In the RBC example, for instance, the net change in accrued interest receivable and payable created a negative cash flow of Can$28 million.

The second cash flow item to discuss is the *float*. The practice of many banks is to credit (debit) deposit accounts several days after (before) the bank has actually received (paid) the cash. At any time *t*, the float is a non-interest-bearing source of funds that represents the volume of deposits that have been debited "early" or paid "late" to clients because of the "value date" system. Therefore, an increase in the float, an item that banks typically do not disclose, represents an additional source of available cash.

An annual consolidated statement of cash flows was presented to identify the various sources of cash inflows and outflows. To control liquidity—i.e., to ensure that they have cash available on a day-to-day basis to meet various commitments, such as payments of interest, reimbursement of deposits, margin requirements, or payment of taxes—banks use an instrument very similar to the repricing gap table, except that the concern now is the amount of cash flowing in or out over a particular, very short time interval (see Table 21.2). One such table is constructed for a "normal" time, in which a large proportion of deposits that are withdrawable on demand, remain with the bank. These are referred to as *core* deposits. A second exercise is done for a "stress" time, during which the outflow of deposits is much larger.

**TABLE 21.2**

Liquidity Profile: An Example

| | Cash Flow Gap (daily, weekly, . . .) for Normal Times (Can$ Million) | | |
|---|---|---|---|
| | Day 1 | Day 2 | Day 3 . . . |
| Interest accrual income | 44.1 | 46.2 | |
| − Interest accrual expense | −29.7 | −28.3 | |
| −/+ Margin calls | −1,000 | −1,000 | |
| − Operating expense | −20.9 | −22 | |
| − Tax | −3.9 | −3.9 | |
| + Δ Assets ("normally" maturing) | 76.71 | 78.3 | |
| − Δ Deposits ("normally" maturing) | −15,000 | −1,000 | |
| − Δ Assets (new commitments) | −90.41 | −93 | |
| + Δ Deposits (new flows) | 3,000 | 2,000 | |
| − Δ Accrued interest receivable | −0.44 | −0.44 | |
| + Δ Accrued interest payable | 0.74 | 0.74 | |
| + Δ Float | −0.82 | 0.83 | |
| + Marketable assets | 12,000 | | |
| Net cash flows | −1,024.62 | −21.57 | |
| Cumulative net cash flows | −1,024.62 | −1,046,19 | |

If the cumulative cash flow is positive, there is no liquidity problem. If it is negative, the bank will be forced to borrow on the interbank market or at the discount window of the central bank. An alternative is to sell assets. To avoid market disruptions when banks have too large a call for liquidity, central banks have put caps on the size of the cumulative cash outflows. For instance, the Financial Services Authority (FSA) in the United Kingdom requires all banks to report all cash flows on the maturity ladder for periods of up to six months. Mismatch guidelines are set for cumulative periods of up to eight days and up to one month. Typically, these would be zero and minus 5 percent of the deposit base, respectively.[2]

## Cash Flow Gaps for Stress Scenario

A similar exercise is conducted for the case of a severe liquidity shock, such as a run on bank deposits or the inability of some clients to repay their loans. Under such extreme stress circumstances, a bank needs enough liquidity to survive for a few days (for example, the requirement is five days in the United Kingdom), during which period the banking industry or the national central bank is expected to intervene. Two historic examples of central banks' contingency liquidity plans include the plan for the century date change, Y2K (Drossos and Hilton, 2000), and the liquidity provision following the September 11, 2001, attacks on the World Trade Center and the Pentagon (McAndrews and Potter, 2002). The physical disruptions had left some banks unable to execute payments to other banks, resulting in an unexpected shortfall for those other banks. To meet this liquidity problem, discount window loans rose from about $200 million to $45 billion on September 12, 2001. The 2007 liquidity crunch related to the crisis in structured investment vehicles (SIVs) is discussed later in the chapter.

In forecasting cash flow gaps for normal times and stress scenarios, an approach similar to that used for the measurement of interest-rate risk can be adopted. That is, it is possible to analyze the volatility of cash flows and measure the cash flow gap with a 99 percent confidence interval or, for the case of a stress scenario, in the 1 percent risk zone. As is discussed later in this chapter for the case of the British bank Northern Rock, the design of liquidity stress scenarios is an art that requires identification of both the market circumstances — bank-specific or systemic — that could lead to a liquidity squeeze and the magnitude of the resulting cash shortage.

In addition to forecasting net cash flows, banks monitor various indicators such as the loan-to-deposit ratio, contingent liquid assets to short-term deposits, and diversification of funding sources.[3]

### Deposit Taking and Loan Commitment: A Natural Hedge?

As discussed in Chapter 4, one of the services that banks provide is to offer liquidity. This occurs on both sides of the bank balance sheet. Some types of deposits are withdrawable on demand, while with loan commitments, banks must be ready to lend to borrowers on demand. Both types of services can therefore, in principle, dry up the liquidity of banks. However, if these two types of liquidity are not correlated, diversification (discussed in Chapter 23) will occur, and this will reduce the need for the bank to hold costly liquid assets. The benefits of diversification are of the same nature as those discussed in Chapter 20 in the context of trading risks and value at risk (VAR). The intuitive understanding of the benefit of diversification in the management of liquidity risk is as follows. At times of uncertainty in capital markets (especially the short-term commercial paper market or the bond market), corporations turn to banks as sources of funds. A period of uncertainty in capital markets is also a time during which worried investors move part of their savings back into safer deposits. Thus, an inflow of deposits partly compensates for an outflow of bank money linked to loans. A natural hedge is provided in a stress period, when it is most needed.[4]

## THE 2007 SIVS GLOBAL LIQUIDITY CRUNCH: FROM THE UNITED STATES TO KAZAKHSTAN AND NORTHERN ROCK

Structured investment vehicles (SIVs) were introduced in Chapter 16, which dealt with securitization. In short, these are special-purpose vehicles financing loans (often real estate mortgages) through the issue of securities tranches (senior notes, often rated AAA; mezzanine subordinated notes; and junior equity tranches). To reduce the funding cost, some SIVs were funded with short-term notes, referred to as asset-backed commercial paper (ABCP). The assumption was that, at the redemption date of the short-term notes, new notes would be issued to refinance the SIVs. In many cases, the banks sponsoring the SIVs had provided backup credit line guarantees, promising to lend money to the SIVs if they could not refinance themselves in the market.

When fears of losses on subprime mortgages started to materialize in February 2007 with a loss announcement by Household International, a U.S. subsidiary of HSBC, liquidity in the commercial paper market dried up. The U.S. asset-backed commercial paper market went down by $400 billion, from $1,200 billion in July 2007 to $800 billion in December 2007. In December 2007, Citigroup announced that it was putting $58 billion of assets back on its balance sheet. This unexpected buildup of assets not only affected Citigroup's capital ratio, but also created the need for funding. A capital infusion of $7.5 billion came from the Abu Dhabi Investment Authority (ADIA) (representing 4.9 percent of the bank's capital).

Aware of the potential need to put assets back on their balance sheets, banks started to borrow early, creating tension in the interbank market. The spread between the rate on the three-month LIBOR interbank market and that on a risk-free three-month Treasury bill (the TED spread) increased to 200 basis points (bp) from a normal range of 50 bp, an example of *basis* risk with a spread on two identical-maturity securities changing. To stem this panic, concerted action by central banks on December 12, 2007 (the Federal Reserve for the United States, the European Central Bank for the European Union, the Bank of England for the United Kingdom, the Bank of Canada, and the Swiss National Bank), resulted in an increase in lending to the banking sector. On December 18, the ECB announced that it had lent €350 billion to 390 financial institutions.[5]

What is remarkable in this crisis is how a real estate problem in one country, the United States, created a herdlike increase in credit risk aversion around the world and a scramble for bank liquidity (Fender and Hördahl, 2007). On December 12, 2007, President Nursultan Nazarbayev of Kazakhstan pledged to prevent the collapse of the country's banking sector. Kazakh banks had borrowed voraciously on foreign capital markets to fund a six-year consumer boom driven by windfall oil earnings.[6] The fear of credit risk had suddenly dried up the international sources of funds.

In Great Britain, a bank, the Newcastle-based Northern Rock, nearly collapsed as a result of the liquidity squeeze. Northern Rock is a specialized mortgage lender, the fifth-largest mortgage company in the United Kingdom, with a 10 percent market share in 2007. With an ROE of around 23 percent in 2005 and 2006, the bank had been expanding its mortgage activities rapidly, relying on securitization of mortgages to fund its portfolio. When the liquidity crisis hit on August 9, 2007, the bank found itself with a large book of mortgages on its balance sheet that it had planned to securitize. Its strategy had been to rely on market-based interbank funding for the short term, until the next securitization deal. Moreover, it had to help refinance its SPV Granite, which was funded in part with short-term securities.[7] About 70 percent of its funds came from the wholesale market rather than depositors.[8]

With the credit squeeze, interbank money started to dry up as well, as the market understood that, among British banks, Northern Rock was a likely candidate to suffer from liquidity risk. One of the reasons for the market to be worried was that the governor of the Bank of England, the former Professor Mervyn King, had stated that the Old Lady (the Bank of England) would to not come to the rescue of imprudent banks.

Short of money, Northern Rock called on the Bank of England for emergency funding on September 13. When the news hit the market,[9] worried depositors rushed to take their deposits from the bank, a first in recent British banking history. Since deposit insurance covered only 100 percent of the first £2,000 and then 90 percent of the next £33,000, depositors had reason to take their money away to safety. A few days later, on September 17, given fears that the bank run could spill over to other mortgage banks (such as Alliance & Leicester, the eighth-largest bank; Bradford & Bingley; and HBOS), the chancellor of the exchequer, Alistair Darling, offered a 100 percent guarantee to all depositors of Northern Rock to stem the run. This was an extraordinary U-turn, with the fear of a spillover to other banks and a threat to overall financial stability overwhelming the argument in favor of market punishment that had been put forward a few days earlier. On October 1, 2007, the United Kingdom's

Financial Services Authority (FSA) announced a change in the deposit insurance system to 100 percent coverage of the first £35,000.

On September 23, it came out that Northern Rock intended to press ahead with a dividend payout to its shareholders.[10] Under pressure from regulators and members of Parliament, a decision to scrap the dividend was made on September 25, 2007. By October 5, three weeks after Northern Rock went to the Bank of England for support, it owed nearly £11 billion, equal to 45 percent of its June deposit base. By November 2, it owed £23 billion.[11] A permanent run on deposits implies a transfer of the franchise value of deposits to other banks, making the rescue even more difficult.

In December, the colorful entrepreneur Sir Richard Branson was competing against a private equity group, Olivant, to take over the Rock. With the loss of much of the bank's deposit franchise, the value of the shares had fallen from £8.6 in July to £0.86 in December. In the end, in February 2008, the British government decided to nationalize Northern Rock.

Matt Ridley, the chairman of Northern Rock,[12] said of the situation:

> Sir, with the benefit of hindsight, you describe Northern Rock's business model as "dangerous" ("The Bank That Failed," September 22). Northern Rock's strategy was at all times transparent to the market and to regulators. Our lending was and is prudent. We have half the industry average of arrears and no subprime loans. To manage liquidity risk, our funding is deliberately diversified, both geographically and between four funding streams—retail, wholesale, securitisation and covered bonds. Of the non-retail funding, less than 20% has a shorter term than the average three-year duration of a mortgage on our balance sheet.
>
> We were repeatedly advised that liquidity in wholesale markets depended on lending quality: good loans would continue to attract funding when bad loans began to default. Instead, from August 9th, liquidity has dried up across all the wholesale markets, making no distinction between loans of different quality, for much longer than even the most extreme forecast. In America and Germany, where many subprime loans have ended up on the banks' balance sheets, the liquidity crisis has been managed smoothly, whereas in Britain, with low arrears, a bank with a high-quality loan book nonetheless found itself in a situation where its retail depositors temporarily felt threatened.
>
> While we have welcomed the measures which the British authorities have put in place to reassure depositors, this should not hide the fact that in Britain, it was general liquidity that was the problem, rather than specific lending.

On October 16, the bank's chief executive Adam Applegarth told a parliamentary committee, "If the bank had been able to access ECB funding, which is not made public, then a retail run on the bank could have been avoided."

The lesson of Northern Rock is exceptional in that the liquidity squeeze was created not by bad loans, but by an external event. The bank was penalized for not ensuring its liquidity needs (until the next securitization run, plus the refinancing of its Granite SPV) and for being different (having a higher liquidity risk).

The following tale helps to understand the source of liquidity risk,

"Two young man were running, followed by a tiger. The first one, who was a bit slow, asks: "Why do you run so fast? You cannot outrun a tiger." The answer from the second one was, "Correct, but I will outrun you" (meaning that you will be eaten by the tiger, who possibly will then not run after me). Similarly, in a systemic liquidity crisis, you do not want to appear to be the weak bank, a black sheep, as you will be the first victim. Adequate liquidity is a relative concept that demands that a bank have as much liquidity as other banks to avoid being singled out by the market. As liquidity risk can be affected by an external factor, the position of other banks, liquidity benchmarks given by the central bank or the banking industry appear to be needed.

Following up on the world liquidity crisis, the Basel Committee for Banking Supervision (2008b) published revisions of its principles on liquidity risk management. In addition to a general call to banks and supervisors to establish a degree of liquidity risk tolerance, to put into place an information system to monitor liquidity risk in "normal" and "stress" times, and to ensure the adequacy of a contingency liquid assets buffer, the principles do not propose quantitative liquidity guidelines on gaps, a contingency liquidity buffer, or capital, a sign that the international banking community has not reached yet a consensus on these parameters.

## LIQUIDITY INSURANCE AND VALUE CREATION

As discussed in Chapter 4, another service that banks provide is liquidity insurance. This section clarifies the debate on the extent of the value creation resulting from investment in illiquid assets. A market misconception needs to be clarified first.

It is often stated in the press that an upward-sloping yield curve (discussed in Chapter 2) is good for banks. Borrowing at a short-term rate that is lower than the long-term rate at which banks invest yields a positive interest margin. This type of position is also reported as a "cash and carry" trade: borrow and hold the asset. The misconception[13] comes from the fact that the market is looking only at the short-term interest margin. As discussed in Chapter 2, a positive yield curve implies that the market expects a higher yield in the next period. If this is this case, since the coupon on the long-term asset is fixed, the interest margin will fall in the second period.

First, consider the case of *liquid risk-free bonds*. The funding of illiquid assets is then considered.

In this first case, the liquid bonds can be sold quickly, without adverse market movement, if needed. Defining $R_i$ as a zero coupon rate, $R_i^c$ as a fixed coupon on a bond with maturity $i$, and $f_2$ as the forward rate in Year 2 (equal to market expectation + an eventual maturity risk premium), the result is

$$(1 + R_2)^2 = (1 + R_1) \times (1 + f_2)$$
$$\frac{100 \times R_2^c}{1 + R_1} + \frac{100 + 100 \times R_2^c}{(1 + R_1) \times (1 + f_2)} = 100$$

Borrowing money at the short-term rate to invest in a two-year risk-free bond does not create any value (when the maturity risk premium is taken into account). It is only when it is possible to beat the market expectation that value can be created.

For example:

Year 1         Year 2          Year 3
$R_1 = 2\%$    $f_2 = 3\%$    $f_3 = 5\%$

Consider a three-year bond with a fixed coupon of 3.293 percent. This is a case of an upward-sloping yield curve, with the three-year rate of 3.293 percent being higher than the one-year rate of 2 percent.

$$\text{Value of bond} = \frac{3.293}{1.02} + \frac{3.293}{(1.02) \times (1.03)} + \frac{103.293}{(1.02) \times (1.03) \times (1.05)} = 100$$

Consider a case in which the three-year bond is funded with short-term debt:

| Asset (three years, 3.293%): 100 | Deposits (one year, 2%): 95 |
|---|---|
| | Equity: 5 |

Cash flow in Year 1:

$$3.293\% \times 100 - 2\% \times 95 = 1.393$$

Cash flow expected in Year 2:

$$3.293\% \times 100 - 3\% \times 95 = 0.443$$

Cash flow expected in Year 3:

$$3.293\% \times 100 - 5\% \times 95 + 100 - 95$$
$$= -1.457 + 100 - 95 = 3.543$$

$$\text{Value of equity} = \frac{1.393}{1.02} + \frac{0.443}{(1.02) \times (1.03)} + \frac{3.543}{(1.02) \times (1.03) \times (1.05)} = 5$$

As can be seen, although the upward-sloping curve generates a positive margin in the short term, the value of the equity is equal to $5, the equity invested. There is no value created in this example. With reference to the bank valuation model discussed in Chapter 5, the franchise value is equal to 0, since the funding of the three-year risk-free bond is done at market rate. Value would be created only if the cost of funds turned out to be different from (lower than) the forward rates. This is what hedge funds attempt to do, hoping to "beat the market" with their own interest-rate forecasts. Given that many investors are attempting to beat the market, it is unlikely that there is much value left in playing an upward-sloping yield curve on the risk-free government bond market.

This first strategy has nothing to do with liquidity risk, as the bank was investing in a liquid risk-free asset that could be sold at any moment without affecting market rates. The next case considers the holding of an *illiquid* asset and the value created by banks.

Consider the case of an *illiquid asset funded with short-term funding*.

The illiquidity of the asset could arise from the fact that there is some probability ($\pi$) that the asset will need to be sold at a low price (as a result of illiquidity in the market), or that the funding will have to be done at a rate higher than the forward rate (as a result of illiquidity in the short-term funding market). Whatever its source, the illiquidity risk will give rise to a liquidity risk premium (LRP) that will be priced by the market.

Assume that the liquidity risk (selling at a lower price) becomes an issue in Year 2. Denoting the fixed coupon on an illiquid asset by $R^{c,L}$ and the probability of a fire sale of the asset at a discount by $\pi$ gives

$$\frac{100 \times R_2^{c,L}}{1 + R_1} + \frac{(1 - \pi) \times (100 + 100 \times R_2^{c,L}) + \pi \times \text{liquidation value}}{(1 + R_1) \times (1 + f_2 + \text{LRP})} = 100$$

$$= \frac{100 \times R_2^{c,L}}{1 + R_1} + \frac{100 + 100 \times R_2^{c,L} - \pi \times (100 + R_2^{c,l} \times 100 - \text{liquidation value})}{(1 + R_1) \times (1 + f_2 + \text{LRP})}$$

The expected cash flow in Year 2 is reduced by the expected loss resulting from a sale at a low price. The discount rate in Year 2 is adjusted by a liquidity risk premium if the market is risk averse to liquidity shock (that is, if the market prices that risk).

Consider the previous three-year example.

**Year 1**     **Year 2**     **Year 3**

$R_1 = 2\%$     $f_2 = 3\%$     $f_3 = 5\%$

In Year 3, a liquidity risk is introduced. There is a probability of 15 percent that the asset will have to be sold at a discount of 10 percent. Also assume a 20-bp liquidity risk premium. The coupon on the illiquid bonds will then be 3.853 percent (instead of 3.293 percent).

$$\text{Value of bond} = \frac{3.853}{1.02} + \frac{3.853}{1.02 \times 1.03}$$
$$+ \frac{0.85 \times 103.853 + 0.15 \times (0.9 \times 103.853)}{1.02 \times 1.03 \times 1.052}$$
$$= 100$$

Imagine that the asset is funded with short-term money by a hedge fund.

Cash flow in Year 1:

$$3.853\% \times 100 - 95 \times 0.02 = 1.953$$

Cash flow expected in Year 2:

$$3.853\% \times 100 - 95 \times 0.03 = 1.003$$

Cash flow expected in Year 3:

$$0.85 \times (103.853 - 0.05 \times 95 - 95) + 0.15 \times (0.9 \times 103.853$$
$$- 95 \times 0.05 - 95) = (0.85 \times 103.853 + 0.15 \times 93.468)$$
$$- 0.05 \times 95 - 95$$
$$= 102.2952 - 99.75$$

$$\text{Value of equity} = \frac{1.953}{1.02} + \frac{1.003}{1.02 \times 1.03} + \frac{102.2952}{1.02 \times 1.03 \times 1.052}$$
$$- \frac{99.75}{1.02 \times 1.03 \times 1.05} = 5$$

If liquidity risk is priced properly, there is no value created in this case.[14] Again, the net interest margin is large in Years 1 and 2 because a spread was built into the coupon to reflect the liquidity risk in Year 3. A hedge fund can create value if it correctly identifies that the risk of selling the asset is lower than anticipated (15 percent) or that the discount premium (10 percent) will be lower.

A bank funding the asset could create value for the following reason: if the risk of withdrawals of core deposits is low (because of imperfect correlation of liquidity needs across depositors), the bank can estimate a lower probability of selling the asset. By pooling depositors, banks provide liquidity insurance and create value. For instance, if the probability of selling the asset is 8 percent, yielding in addition a lower liquidity risk premium (10 basis points, for example), the cash flows and value of the equity of the bank become

Cash flow in Year 1:

$$3.853\% \times 100 - 95 \times 0.02 = 1.953$$

Cash flow in Year 2:

$$3.853\% \times 100 - 95 \times 0.03 = 1.003$$

Cash flow in Year 3:

$$0.92 \times (103.853 - 0.05 \times 95 - 95) + 0.08 \times (0.9 \times 103.853 - 95 \times 0.05 - 95) = (0.92 \times 103.853 + 0.08 \times 93.468) - 0.05 \times 95 - 95$$

$$= 103.022 - 99.95$$

$$\text{Value of Equity} = \frac{1.953}{1.02} + \frac{1.003}{1.02 \times 1.03} + \frac{103.022}{1.02 \times 1.03 \times 1.051} - \frac{99.75}{1.02 \times 1.03 \times 1.05}$$

$$= 5.75$$

In this case, the bank creates value. With reference to the bank valuation model discussed in Chapter 5, it implies that there is a franchise value for the asset, since the liquidity-risk-adjusted return on the asset exceeds the rate on other investments available to the shareholders.

Chapter 16, on securitization, discusses the crisis of the *structured investment vehicles* (SIVs) that were funding illiquid assets with short-term commercial paper. It is quite possible that, tempted by high short-term interest margins, the sponsors of the SIVs underestimated and did not properly value the illiquidity risk.

## CONCLUSION

Liquidity risk is inherent in banking activities, as the function of banks is to transform short-term deposits into illiquid loans. Although this is a traditional source of risk, it was generally ignored in many countries as long as a portfolio of liquid assets was present to fund cash outflows. Because of a significant increase in the size of banks' loan portfolios and a reduction in their holdings of liquid assets, liquidity risk has resurfaced in many countries. Banks evaluate net cash flows under both normal and stress circumstances. In addition, they need to monitor their liquidity position relative to that of other banks, so as to avoid being spotted as the black sheep. In evaluating the value created by the funding of long-term and/or illiquid assets, it is necessary to evaluate the discounted value of both short-term and long-term expected cash flows in the event of a possible fire sale of the assets at a discount.

## EXERCISES FOR CHAPTER 21

Here is the current balance sheet of e-Bank. The liquidity risk manager has calculated the liquidity profile for the coming two weeks.

### Balance Sheet

| | | | |
|---|---|---|---|
| Loans | 300,000 | Customers' deposits | |
| Marketable assets | 10,000 | (demand and savings) | 400,000 |
| Bonds | 240,000 | Interbank | |
| (contingency liquid assets— | | (6-month maturity) | 100,000 |
| eligible for discounting at | | | |
| the Central Bank) | | Equity | 50,000 |
| Total | 550,000 | Total | 550,000 |

### Liquidity Profile

| | 1 week | 2 weeks |
|---|---|---|
| Interest income | 1,000 | 1,000 |
| Interest expense | − 700 | − 700 |
| Operating expenses | − 100 | − 100 |

*Cont.*

| | | |
|---|---|---|
| Tax | – 0 | – 0 |
| Reimbursement of principal on loans and bonds | + 30,000 | + 30,000 |
| Estimated amount of lending | – 25,000 | – 35,000 |
| Reimbursement of deposits | – 50,000 | – 10,000 |
| Estimated amount of new deposits | + 10,000 | + 10,000 |
| Marketable assets | +10,000 | |
| Net cash flows | – 24,800 | – 4,800 |
| Cumulative net cash flows | – 24,800 | – 29,600 |

1. The liquidity risk policy of e-Bank is as follows:

   The one-week liquidity gap (which includes the sale of marketable assets) cannot exceed 5 percent of the customers' deposit base.

   The two-week cumulative liquidity gap cannot exceed 10 percent of the customers' deposits.

   Does e-Bank meet the one-week liquidity rule: yes or no?

   Does e-Bank meet the two-week liquidity rule: yes or no?

2. How can e-Bank improve its liquidity position? Suggest a portfolio transaction that will enhance its liquidity.

3. If there were a run on the bank, it is estimated that there would be an additional net cash outflow of $180,000 in the coming five days. Does e-Bank meet the contingency liquidity stress policy, which wants the bank to be able to mobilize assets (in this case, the portfolio of bonds) to survive for one week in the event of a run on its deposits?

## Notes

1. Target stands for "Trans-European Automated Real-Time Gross Settlement Express Transfer system."
2. Hall (1989), *Financial Stability Review* (2000), and *Financial Services Authority* (2007).
3. Some banks refer to the normal case liquidity analysis as *tactical liquidity risk*. Stress scenarios are referred to as *contingency liquidity risk*. In addition, *structural liquidity risk* is the risk that the structural, long-term balance sheet cannot be financed in a timely manner or at a reasonable cost. This calls for long-term measures to ensure an adequate funding profile.

4. The literature includes Kashyap et al. (2002), Gatev et al. (2005), and Gatev and Strahan (2006).
5. *Financial Times*, December 19, 2007.
6. *Financial Times*, December 13, 2007.
7. *Financial Times*, November 20, 2007.
8. *Wall Street Journal*, September 25, 2007; *Financial Times*, September 26, 2007.
9. The governor of the Bank of England stated that covert operation (lending with no public information) was not compatible with British and European laws on corporate transparency (*Wall Street Journal*, September 21, 2007).
10. *Financial Times*, September 23, 2007.
11. *Financial Times*, November 2, 2007.
12. *The Economist*, September 29, 2007.
13. This misconception is widespread. In numerous bank annual reports or reports by bank analysts, one can read the comment that a positive yield curve is helping banks.
14. Note that in the valuation of cash flow in Year 3, we have only applied the liquidity risk premium to the risky asset cash flow.

# Credit Risk Portfolio Diversification: Credit Value at Risk

The evaluation of credit risk on a single transaction is a difficult exercise. It requires the evaluation of the probability of default over time, the loss given default, and a risk-adjusted discount rate. This was discussed in Chapter 15. The evaluation of credit risk on a portfolio of loans is an even more daunting task. Significant conceptual and applied progress has been made in recent years. This has opened the way to the trading of credit risk, to securitization, and to the use of credit derivatives. The purpose of this chapter is to highlight the sources of difficulty in measuring aggregate credit risk on a portfolio of loans and the methodologies that are used. Similar to value at risk (VAR), the *maximum* loss that could be observed on a *trading* portfolio with some confidence level, a new term has been created, *credit VAR*, which is the *maximum* loss that can be observed on a *loan* portfolio with some degree of confidence.

Whenever the mathematics become more demanding, the intuitive explanation is presented first, before the complete presentation.

## THE DIFFICULTY OF MEASURING CREDIT VAR

There are two main reasons why it is difficult to measure the potential loss on a loan portfolio. The first, as indicated in Chapter 12, is that the probability distribution of loan losses is not a normal Gaussian distribution, but is highly skewed. There are many observations with low loan losses when the economy is doing well and a few observations of heavy losses at the rare times of deep recessions. One implication of this skewed distribution is that it is not possible to rely on the mathematics of the normal distribution used in modern portfolio theory to aggregate total risk.

The second reason that the potential loss is difficult to measure in that there are few historical observations to use to estimate potential loan losses at the time of a deep recession. In the context of trading risk, as covered in the discussion of value at risk in Chapter 20, it is customary to use historical simulations to evaluate trading risk on an existing portfolio. That is, the gain or loss on a current portfolio is simulated, using market price changes observed in the past 250 days (which are applied to the current trading portfolio). Historical simulations generate a frequency distribution of gains and losses, from which it is possible to compute the 99 percent quantile and the value at risk. It is not possible to carry out a similar exercise with credit risk because the last 250 trading days might not include a recession at all.

Moreover, even with access to a longer data series, historical observation might not be relevant for the future. For instance, with the creation of the euro in 1999, several European countries voluntarily abandoned the right to devalue their currency. In the event of a local recession, if the common euro-zone monetary policy conducted by the European Central Bank is not accommodating, a recession in the post–1999 euro period could potentially be deeper than recessions was in the pre–1999 legacy currency period (Dermine, 2003). For example, in the past, it was very common for Italy to devalue its currency to help export-oriented companies. This implies that in the euro zone, historical data from before 1999 might not be relevant to assessing current credit risk. Another case is Brazil. Since 1994, the government has introduced a new currency, the *real*, and moved from a high-inflation regime to a low-inflation regime. Again, a shock to the structure of the economy makes historical data irrelevant for predicting future credit losses. To measure credit risk on a portfolio of loans, banks rely on progress in statistics and computer power that allows simulations to measure aggregate loan portfolio credit VAR.

## TWO CATEGORIES OF CREDIT RISK MODELS: THE *MARKED-TO-MARKET* AND *DEFAULT* MODES

There are two main categories of models for measuring aggregate credit risk on a loan portfolio: the *marked-to-market* models and the *default-mode* models.

The marked-to-market models recognize that a change in the value of a loan can arise not only from a default, but also from a downgrade or upgrade of the borrower. For example, Table 22.1 reports data from rating agencies on the frequency of upgrades, downgrades, and default of rated bonds over a one-year horizon. It is called a *migration matrix*.

**TABLE 22.1**

Ratings Migration Matrix (Probability of Moving from One Rating to Another over a One-Year Horizon)

| | One Year | | | | | | | |
|---|---|---|---|---|---|---|---|---|
| Current | AAA | AA | A | BBB | BB | B | CCC | Default |
| AAA | 90.81 | 8.33 | 0.68 | 0.06 | 0.12 | 0 | 0 | 0 |
| AA | 0.7 | 90.65 | 7.79 | 0.64 | 0.06 | 0.14 | 0.02 | 0 |
| A | 0.09 | 2.27 | 91.05 | 5.52 | 0.74 | 0.26 | 0.01 | 0.06 |
| BBB | 0.02 | 0.33 | 5.95 | 86.93 | 5.3 | 1.17 | 1.12 | 0.18 |
| BB | 0.03 | 0.14 | 0.67 | 7.73 | 80.53 | 8.84 | 1.0 | 1.06 |
| B | 0 | 0.11 | 0.24 | 0.43 | 6.48 | 83.46 | 4.07 | 5.2 |
| CCC | 0.22 | 0 | 0.22 | 1.3 | 2.38 | 11.24 | 64.86 | 19.79 |

Source: Crouhy et al., 2000.

As can be seen from Table 22.1, the probability that an A-rated firm will continue to be A-rated in one year's time is very high (91.05 percent). The risk of default is very low (0.06 percent). This again illustrates an observation made earlier: the distribution of credit risk is highly skewed.[1] CreditMetrics (1997), discussed later in the chapter, provides a model for the probability distribution of the changes in the value of a loan portfolio.

The *default-mode* models attempt to measure only the percentage of loans in a portfolio that will go into default. As these models focus only on a specific state of the asset (default) instead of on all the states (upgrades and downgrades), they are less complete than the marked-to-market models. However, pragmatists will argue that parsimony (simplicity) is a valuable quality in modeling and that the number of defaults is the most important issue in measuring credit risk. Credit Risk$^+$ (Credit Suisse, 1997), discussed later in the chapter', is a default-mode model.

The discussion that follows first presents the *asymptotic single risk factor* (ASRF) model to evaluate portfolio credit risk. This model serves as the foundation of the Basel II capital regulation as well as of pricing models for credit derivatives. Next, two issues related to concentration risk, name and sectoral concentration, are identified. Finally, the main characteristics of two widely used credit portfolio models, CreditMetrics and Credit Risk$^+$, are presented.

## THE ASYMPTOTIC SINGLE RISK FACTOR MODEL AND CONCENTRATION RISK

Vasicek (1987, 2002) has developed a model that is widely used to evaluate aggregate credit risk on a portfolio of loans. As mentioned in Chapter 13, this model forms the basis of the Basel II capital charge formula for credit risk. A major merit of this model is its intuitive nature and closed-form solution. That is, it provides a mathematical formula that permits the measurement of aggregate credit risk on a loan portfolio. Just as the option pricing model developed by Black and Scholes (1973) has revolutionized option pricing, the ASRF formula is at the core of any study of the measurement of aggregate credit risk and of the pricing of several types of credit derivative contracts. As will be explained later, the simplicity of the Vasicek model comes at the cost of two significant assumptions: the assumption that there is a very large portfolio of credit exposures (*granularity*) and the assumption that credit risk in the economy is driven by a single risk factor.

As the ASRF model is central to the measurement of credit VAR, a complete proof of the formula is presented. This allows the precise identification of some of the key assumptions of the model.[2]

*Intuition: There are many identical loans in a portfolio. They all have the same average probability of default over a business cycle. If the economy goes into a recession, many loans will default. If the economy is doing well, fewer loans will default. In short, the default probability of each loan is driven by a single risk factor, the economy. It is this risk factor that affects the frequency of default in a loan portfolio.*

Assume that the assets $A_i$ of firm $i$, with current value $A_{i,0}$, are funded with debt with promised reimbursement $B_i$ at maturity (time $T$) and equity. The value of the assets at the maturity of the debt, $A_{i,T}$, follows a lognormal distribution:

$$A_{i,T} = A_{i,0} \times e^{\mu_i T - 0.5\sigma^2 T + \sigma_i \sqrt{T} X_i}$$

The exponent of the exponential function is the instantaneous return on the asset.[3] It incorporates two components: an expected return and the impact of a shock:

$$\text{Instantaneous asset return} = (\mu_i T - 0.5\sigma^2 T) + (\sigma_i \sqrt{T} X_i)$$

where $\mu_i$ = expected annual instantaneous return on the asset
$\sigma^2$ = variance of annual return
$T$ = number of years from today
$X_i$ is a standardized normal variable with cumulative distribution $N(.)$ (with an expected value of 0 and standard deviation of 1)

The variable $X_i$ represents business risk. A high value of $X_i$ is representative of good times for the firm. A low value is indicative of bad times.

## Assumption 1: Single Risk Factor

Next, assume that the business risk variable $X_i$ is itself the sum of two terms:

$$X_i = \sqrt{\rho}\, F + \sqrt{(1-\rho)}\, \varepsilon_i$$

where $F$ is a standardized normal risk factor common to all firms in the portfolio, and $\varepsilon_i$ is a standardized independently distributed normal shock that is specific to firm $i$. This assumption states that the well-being of a firm is affected by two risk factors, a single shock that affects all firms in the economy and an additional shock that is specific (idiosyncratic) to that firm. It is possible to show that the variance of $X_i = 1$, and that $\rho$ is the correlation across pairwise asset returns of different firms. $\rho$ is referred to as the factor loading, to reflect the impact of the single risk factor on the business risk variable $X_i$. This model is known as the asymptotic single risk factor (ASRF) or Gaussian copula[4] model.

In this model, it is assumed that the firm defaults when the value of its assets falls below a threshold value, the promised reimbursement on the debt $B$:

$$\begin{aligned}
\text{Probability of default (PD)} &= P(A_{i,T} < B_i) = P[\ln(A_{i,T}) < \ln(B_i)] \\
&= P[\ln(A_{i,0}) + \mu_i T - 0.5\sigma^2 T + \sigma_i \sqrt{T} \\
&\quad X_I < \ln(B_i)] \\
&= P(X_i < c_i) = N(c_i)
\end{aligned}$$

with

$$c_i = \frac{\ln(B_i) - \ln(A_{i,0}) - \mu_i T + 0.5\,\sigma^2 T}{\sigma\sqrt{T}}$$

$N =$ the cumulative standardized normal distribution

This states that default occurs when a bad economic situation (business factor $X_i$ smaller than $c_i$) brings the value of the firm's assets to too low a level, below the bankruptcy threshold $B_i$.

Denoting by the inverse cumulative normal distribution by IN gives

Probability of default $= P(X_i < c_i) = N(c_i)$

$c_i = \text{IN(PD)}$

Next, remember that the business factor $X_i$ is itself driven by a single economic risk factor $F$. Considering a specific value, $F_\alpha$, for this single risk factor, a probability of default can be calculated, given that the value $F_\alpha$ is observed (conditional probability of default).

Conditional on a specific value $F_\alpha$ for the risk factor $F$,

$$\text{Probability of default} = PD_{|F=F\alpha} = P(X_i < c_i \,|F = F\alpha) = N(c_i)$$
$$= P(X_i = \sqrt{\rho}\, F_\alpha + \sqrt{(1-\rho)}\,\varepsilon_i < c_i)$$

$$PD \text{ (conditional on } F = F_\alpha) = P\left[\varepsilon_i < \frac{-\sqrt{\rho}F_\alpha}{\sqrt{(1-\rho)}} + \frac{c}{\sqrt{(1-\rho)}}\right]$$

$$= N\left[\frac{IN(P_D) - \sqrt{\rho}F_\alpha}{\sqrt{(1-\rho)}}\right]$$

To take a conservative value for the probability of default, assume that the country goes into a very bad recession and choose a very low value for the single risk factor $F$—for instance, a value so low that there is only a 0.1 percent probability of its being worse. That is, take the 0.1 percent quantile of the $F$ distribution. This is given by

$$F_\alpha = IN(0.001)$$

$$PD \text{ (conditional on } F = F_\alpha = IN\,(0.001) = N\left[\frac{IN(P_D) - \sqrt{\rho}F_\alpha}{\sqrt{(1-\rho)}}\right]$$

$$= N\left[\frac{IN(P_D) - \sqrt{\rho}\,IN\,(0.001)}{\sqrt{(1-\rho)}}\right]$$

At this stage, the probability of default, PD, conditional on the single economywide risk factor $F$ taking a value $F_\alpha$ has been calculated. One more step and assumption is needed to obtain the percentage of loans in a portfolio going into default.

## Assumption 2: Granularity of the Loan Portfolio

The second assumption is that there is a very large number of loans in the portfolio (as an order of magnitude, more than 1,000 loans), and that each loan is like a small grain in a bag (therefore the term *granularity*). It is then possible to use the law of large numbers in statistics, which, in this application, states that the realized percentage of loans in default will converge to the probability of default (PD) as the number of loans in the portfolio increases.

Given $F_\alpha$, the frequency of observed firm-specific (idiosyncratic) shocks will match the normal probability distribution, and the percentage of loans for which $X_i < c_i$ (the default case) will be identical to the PD calculated in the previous section.

This formula differs from the Basel II safety factor formula, given by (see Chapter 13)

$$\text{Safety factor}_{99.9\% \text{ confidence}} = N \left[ \frac{\text{IN}(P_D) + \sqrt{\rho}\ \text{IN}(0.999)}{\sqrt{1 - \rho}} \right]$$

To move from the Vasicek formula to the safety factor formula of Basel II, it is necessary to rely on a statistical result that is valid for a symmetrical normal distribution:

$$F_\alpha = \text{IN}(0.0001)$$

Remember that to predict a recession, a low value for the single economywide risk factor—that is, a negative value to the left of the standardized normal distribution—is needed.

$$-F_\alpha = -\text{IN}(0.001) = \text{IN}(0.999)$$

This is the result of the symmetry of the normal distribution. It is a positive value at the far right of the normal distribution.

This yields the credit VAR for the 99.9 percent quantile, the percentage of loans in default with a confidence level of 99.9 percent, that is identical to the Basel II safety factor:

$$\text{Credit VAR}_{99.9\%} = N \left[ \frac{\text{IN (PD)} - \sqrt{\rho}\ \text{IN (0.001)}}{\sqrt{1 - \rho}} \right]$$

$$= \left[ \frac{\text{IN (PD)} + \sqrt{\rho}\ \text{IN (0.999)}}{\sqrt{1 - \rho}} \right]$$

The Vasicek ASRF model permits calculation of the maximum loss on a loan portfolio with some degree of confidence. It is a breakthrough in the measurement of aggregate credit risk on a portfolio of loans.

Two extreme polar cases can be analyzed. A special case is when the business risk, $X_i$, for each firm is independent of that for the others ($\rho = 0$). That is, for each firm, the risk of default is independent of that of all other firms.

In this case the formula collapses into

$$\text{Credit VAR}_{99\%} = N[\text{IN}(PD)] = PD$$

The percentage of loans going into default in a very large portfolio is equal to the probability of default. The general 99.9 percent credit VAR can be interpreted as being equal to the probability of default (PD) plus a term that represents the fact that there will be default clustering at a time of a large recession. This clustering is induced by a positive correlation across asset returns.

Another extreme case is when the risk of default is highly correlated ($\rho$ tends to 1), in which case the frequency of default with a confidence interval of 99.9 percent is either 1 (when the numerator is positive) or 0 (when the numerator is negative).

The credit VAR given here is a loss that is conditional on a specific value for the systematic risk factor $F$. It is possible to compute (see the appendix to this chapter) the unconditional cumulative probability distribution function of the percentage of defaulted loans in a portfolio, $L$. This function is unconditional in that it does not constrain the common risk factor $F$ to take a specific value, but rather incorporates the randomness of that factor. The unconditional probability that the frequency of defaulted loans in a portfolio is smaller than $x$ is given by

$$P(L < x\,;\,\rho\,;\,PD) = N\left[\frac{\sqrt{1-\rho}\ \text{IN}(x) - N(PD)}{\sqrt{\rho}}\right]$$

This probability distribution is highly skewed and leptokurtic (Vasicek, 2002). Figure 22.1 shows the loan-loss distribution for a PD of 2 percent and a correlation of 0.1. It has been drawn with the following probability density function (pdf):

$$f(x,\,PD,\,\rho) = \sqrt{\frac{1-\rho}{\rho}}\cdot e^{\left\{-\frac{1}{2\rho}\left[\sqrt{1-\rho}\,\text{IN}(x) - \text{IN}(PD)\right]^2 + \frac{1}{2}\left[\text{IN}(x)\right]^2\right\}}$$

If the correlation is reduced, there will be less probability of observing large losses, a clustering of defaults. This is apparent from Figure 22.2, in which the correlation has been reduced to 0.02.

Two important assumptions have been made on the way. The first is the assumption of granularity, or an infinitely grained portfolio. This says that there is a very large number of loans in the portfolio. It is thus possible to rely on the law of large numbers and state that the observed frequency of defaults in a portfolio will be identical to the conditional

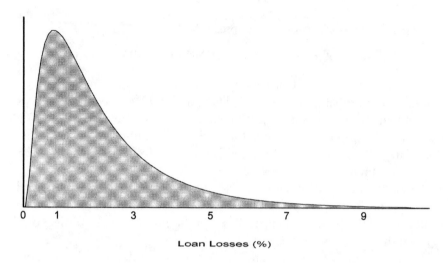

**Loan Losses (%)**

**Figure 22.1** Loan-loss distribution (PD = 2 percent; correlation = 0.1).

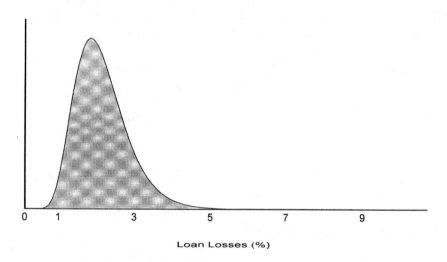

**Loan Losses (%)**

**Figure 22.2** Loan-loss distribution (PD = 2 percent; correlation = 0.02).

probability of default.[5] The second assumption was that the risk factor $X_i$ affecting all firms was made up of two components: a factor that is common to all firms and an idiosyncratic shock that affects only a single firm. This approach is reminiscent of the capital asset pricing model applied to a stock market, where the prices of stocks are affected by systematic risk, or a shock affecting all firms, and unsystematic risk, or shocks affecting individual firms; the latter disappears in a large portfolio. As these two assumptions might not be met in reality, further developments have been made to better capture concentration risk in a loan portfolio.

## EXPANDING THE VASICEK ASRF MODEL TO INCORPORATE NAME CONCENTRATION AND SECTORAL/REGIONAL CONCENTRATION

*Intuition: The Vasicek and Basel II formula relies on two important assumptions: a very large number of loans (more than a thousand) in a portfolio and a single risk factor that affects the risk of default. Clearly, these hypotheses may not be met. First, there could be a portfolio with few loans. Second, there might be more than one risk factor; for example, for an international bank with credit exposure in two countries, there might be a need for two risk factors that drive default: the state of each of the two economies. Therefore, the ASRF model has been expanded to adjust to the real world.*

It can be seen that the measure of credit risk on a portfolio discussed in the previous section misses two possible realistic features: a small number of loans in the portfolio and loans that are affected by different risk factors. Indeed, it is intuitive that lending money to small and medium-sized enterprises (SMEs) in a single region is more risky than lending to SMEs located in different parts of the world. Thus, it is possible to guess that loans can be affected by different risk factors. Both features—few loans and exposure to a single risk factor—refer to concentration of risk, a concept that is related to diversification of risk. With respect to the previous discussion, it is possible to refer to two types of concentration risk: name concentration and regional or sectoral concentration. This terminology captures the problems identified by many banks in history very well: too large an exposure to a single client and too large an exposure to a business sector or to a region. For instance, in Sweden, many large banks received a formal guarantee from the Ministry of Finance in the early 1990s as a result of their exposure to the Scandinavian real estate market.

Banking regulations attempt to limit risk concentration. For example, in the European Union, a directive on large exposure demands that exposure to a single client be less than 25 percent of a bank's capital and that the total of large exposures be less then 800 percent of capital (Dermine, 2003). In the second pillar of Basel II (see Chapter 13), banking supervisors are invited to review the adequacy of risk diversification.

This has led to efforts to incorporate into credit risk models concentration risk arising from these two sources: name concentration and sectoral/regional concentration.

## Name Concentration

Four measures of name concentration or granularity are used to correct the Vasicek asymptotic model. The first three are used in industrial economics to measure the market power of a firm in a market. The last one builds on the credit risk model. These measures are the concentration coefficient ($Cn$), the Gini coefficient, the Herfindahl-Hirschman index (HHI), and the granularity adjustment (GA), simulated or closed-form.

### Concentration Coefficient ($Cn$)

For example, C5 is the ratio of the five largest loans divided by the total loan portfolio. This measure has a handicap: it does not give any information on the other loans in the portfolio.

### Gini Coefficient

To determine the Gini coefficient, plot a graph with the percentage of the number of borrowers (ranked from small to large loan size, from 0 percent to 100 percent) on the $x$ axis and the corresponding percentage of the volume of loans in the portfolio (from 0 percent to 100 percent) on the $y$ axis. For example, for the smallest 10 percent of borrowers, what is their share of loan volumes? An even distribution will fall on the 45-degree line, while an uneven distribution will lie on a curve below the diagonal. The Gini coefficient, $G$, is a measure of the area between the curve and the diagonal:

$$\text{Gini}\,(G) = \int_0^{100} \left[ x - f(x)\,dx \right]$$

A severe drawback of this distribution is that it does not take the number of loans in the portfolio into account. As an extreme example, a portfolio with two loans of \$50 million each would have a Gini coefficient of 0.

### Herfindahl-Hirschman Index (HHI)

This measure of concentration has received a great deal of attention in the antitrust literature. It is a measure of market concentration and market power. Applied to loan portfolios, it is the sum of the squared loan shares in a portfolio (measured in fractions).

Herfindahl-Hirschman index $= \Sigma s_i^2$
with $s_i = \text{loan}_i / \text{total loan portfolio}$

The HHI goes from 0 to 1. A measure close to 1 indicates very high concentration, while a measure close to 0 indicates diversification and granularity (each loan has an infinitesimal share).

A disadvantage of the first three approaches—the concentration coefficient, the Gini coefficient, and the Herfindahl-Hirschman index— is that none of them tells how much risk to add to the Vasicek asymptotic credit VAR calculated for an infinitely grained loan portfolio. Simulated or model-based granularity adjustments (GA) have been proposed.

## Granularity Adjustments (GA)
A granularity adjustment is an *addition* to the asymptotic granular credit VAR measure. Some of these adjustments are based on simulations. Others are based on statistics.

## Monte Carlo Simulations
Balthazar (2004) proposed the following procedure, relying on Monte Carlo simulations.

Assume, as in Vasicek, that the business factor $X_i$ is the sum of two random variables, a single risk factor and a firm-specific factor:

$$X_i = \sqrt{\rho}\, F + \sqrt{(1-\rho)}\, \varepsilon_i$$

where $X_i$ = business shock to asset return

$F$ = the common factor

$\varepsilon_i$ = the idiosyncratic risk

The Monte Carlo simulation has several steps:

- Generate a common factor $F$ and $n$ idiosyncratic variables $\varepsilon_i$, one for each loan in a portfolio of size $n$. This generates $n$ returns for the assets of each firm.
- Define the threshold return as $c_i$ = IN(PD).
- Calculate the number of defaults $(X_i < c_i)$ in the sample.
- Repeat this procedure 100,000 times to get a distribution of the default rate. Compare the 99.9 percent quantile of the credit VAR with that predicted by the ASRF model. This provides an adjustment for the credit VAR.

## Basel II Granularity Adjustment
The first version of Basel II, presented in 2001 (Basel Committee, 2001a, b), included a granularity adjustment to take name concentration into account. It is derived from a Credit Risk+ model (Wilde, 2001). The granularity adjustment was not included in the final Basel II capital

regulation, but banking supervisors are invited in the second pillar to assess the degree of credit risk diversification. The 2001 granularity adjustment works as follows:

1. Divide the loan portfolio into buckets of homogeneous loans with identical PD and LGD, $PD_b$ and $LGD_b$.
2. For each bucket $b$, calculate the systematic risk factor $F_b$. It is equal to the Vasicek safety factor discussed in the Basel II formula reduced by the probability of default. It has the general form $F_b = N[\alpha_1 \ln(PD_b) + \alpha_0] - PD_b$
3. For each bucket $b$, calculate the Herfindahl-Hirschman index $H_b$, the sum of the squared shares of loans in the specific bucket.
4. Calculate averages across the buckets of loans:

$$PD_{av} = \sum_b s_b \times PD_b \qquad \text{with } s_b = \text{loan share in total loan portfolio}$$

$$LGD_{av} = \frac{\sum_b s_b \times PD_b \times LGD_b}{\sum_b s_b \times PD_b}$$

$$F_{av} = \sum_b s_b \times F_b$$

$$n^* = \frac{1}{\sum_b s_b^2 \times H_b}$$

5. Calculate the granularity scale factor (GSF) (Basel Committee, 2001b, paragraph 456): GSF = $(0.4 + 1.2 LGD_{av}) \times [0.76 + 1.1(PD_{av}/F_{av})]$
6. Make a capital adjustment for granularity:[6] capital addition for granularity = $(GSF/n^*) \times$ (total nonretail exposure).

An alternative granularity adjustment is presented in Gordy and Lütkebohmert (2007). In running simulations for German banks' loan portfolios, they found that the capital increase to reflect the granularity adjustment should move from a relative 2 percent for large banks (4,000 loans) to 8 percent for small portfolios (300 loans).

### Business Sector/Regional Concentration

A second limitation of the Vasicek model is the assumption that all asset returns are driven by a single common factor $F$. That is, the credit VAR on a PD = 1 percent loan portfolio concentrated in one region, say the

United Kingdom, is identical to the credit VAR on a PD = 1 percent loan portfolio split between two regions of the world: say the United Kingdom and South Africa. Intuition says that the second portfolio should be less risky because the probability of a simultaneous deep recession in both the United Kingdom and South Africa is likely to be small.

This can be expressed formally in the context of the Vasicek ASRF model.

Consider a large number of firms in sector (or region) s. They have the identical probability of default, $PD_{i,s}$. In the spirit of the asymptotic single risk factor (ASRF) model, default occurs when the asset return falls below a threshold value $c_s$.

The (unconditional) probability of default is

$$PD_{i,s} = P(X_{i,s} < c_s)$$

The asset return is driven by the following process:

$$X_{i,s} = \sqrt{\rho_s} F_s + \sqrt{(1-\sigma_s)}\, \varepsilon_i$$

$F_s$ is the common factor affecting all firms in sector s (the sector s systematic factor), and $\varepsilon_i$ is an independently distributed normal variable that affects only firm i in sector s (the unsystematic risk). The intrasector asset correlation for each pair of borrowers in that sector is $\rho_s$.

Choosing $\alpha_{1\%}(F)$, a low value for the systemic factor at the 1 percent confidence interval, it is possible to compute the conditional probability of default, that is, the probability of default conditional on being in a severe recession. Relying on the law of large numbers, this is also the Vasicek frequency of default, conditional in being in a recession.

$$Credit\ VAR_{s,99\%} = N\left[\frac{IN(P_D) + IN(0.99)\sqrt{\rho_s}}{\sqrt{(1-\rho_s)}}\right]$$

Now, assume that the loan portfolio is split into two sectors, s and r. The first subportfolio is governed by the process $X_s$, described previously, and the second subportfolio is governed by the process $X_r$, as follows:

$$X_{i,r} = \sqrt{\rho_r} F_r + \sqrt{(1-\rho_r)}\, \varepsilon_i$$

$F_r$ is the common factor affecting all firms in sector r (the sector r systematic factor), and $\varepsilon_i$ is an independentlcy distributed normal variable that affects only firm i in sector r (the unsystematic risk).

Applying this information, the marginal credit VAR for the second subsector can be computed:

$$\text{Credit VAR}_{r,99\%} = N\left[\frac{\text{IN}(P_D) + \text{IN}(0.99)\sqrt{\rho_r}}{\sqrt{(1-\rho_r)}}\right]$$

The correlation between the two factors $F_s$ and $F_r$ is denoted by $R_{r,s}$. The sector factors, $F_s$ and $F_r$, are often expressed as a linear function of independent, standard normally distributed factors $F_1, F_2, \ldots, F_f$.

$$Y_s = \sum_{t=1}^{f} \alpha_{t,s} F_t$$

$$\text{with } \sum_{t=1}^{f} \alpha_{t,s} = 1$$

The asset correlation $\omega_{s,r}$ for each pair of borrowers in sectors $s$ and $r$, respectively, can be shown to be equal to

$$\omega_{s,r} = \rho_r \rho_s R_{r,s} = \rho_r \rho_s \Sigma \alpha_{t,s}\, \alpha_{t,r}$$

Assume first that the two sectors are independent, that is, that the correlation between the risk factors, $R_{s,r}$, is equal to zero. The probability of observing credit $\text{VAR}_r$ at the same time as credit $\text{VAR}_s = 1$ percent $\times$ 1 percent $= 0.0001$, that is,[7] 1 in 10,000. The probability of having two bad recessions at the same time, 1 in 10,000, is much less than the probability of having a single recession (1 in 100). In other words, and intuitively, diversification reduces aggregate risk tremendously.

The case of independence of sectoral factors was chosen because the result is intuitively obvious. In real life, sector factors are correlated. It is necessary to simulate various combinations of $X_r$ and $X_s$, such that $P(X_r < c_r, X_s < c_s) = 1$ percent, to compute the aggregate credit VAR for each and to select the maximum aggregate credit VAR. Or, as discussed next, a Monte Carlo simulation can be performed.

For a Monte Carlo simulation, three inputs are needed:

- Loan size in each sector
- Factor loading, $\rho_s$ and $\rho_r$, for each sector, $s$ and $r$
- Correlation across sector factors, $R_{s,r}$

A Monte Carlo simulation allows the determination of a distribution of potential aggregate loan losses.

Each run of the Monte Carlo simulation generates asset returns and a count of the number of defaults. Default occurs when the return on a particular asset is below a threshold $c_i$. This gives a total portfolio loss. This is run 200,000 times to obtain a distribution of losses. Credit VAR can be calculated at the chosen quantile $q$.[8]

Düllmann and Masschelein (2007) have tested the impact of portfolio concentration on the capital of German banks. To illustrate their choice of parameters, they use a unique loading sector $\rho$ of 0.5. This implies a pairwise correlation across intrasector asset returns of $\rho_s \times \rho_r = 0.5 \times 0.5 = 0.25$. Table 22.2 reports the concentration (the Herfindahl-Hirschman index) in the average German loan portfolio and the correlation $R_{r,s}$ between sectoral stock index returns.

Not surprisingly, the authors find that increasing concentration away from the average German loan portfolio can have a significant impact on credit VAR, of the order of 35 percent.[9]

In a review of empirical studies on credit risk concentration, the Basel Committee (2006) observed that sectoral concentration is likely to be a more important issue than name concentration. If name concentration (lack of granularity) can require an increase in capital from 2 to 8 percent, sectoral concentration can require an increase in capital from 20 to 40 percent.

*Warning*: There should be no need to say that sectoral factor loading and correlation across factors are key to getting a good estimation of aggregate credit risk. The impact of correlation and change in correlations will

**TABLE 22.2**

Sectoral Concentration in German Bank Corporate Lending (Herfindahl-Hirschman Index) and Correlation across Sectoral Index Returns

| | Share | A | B | C1 | C2 | C3 | D | E | F | H | I | J |
|---|---|---|---|---|---|---|---|---|---|---|---|---|
| A: Energy | 0% | 1 | 0.5 | 0.42 | 0.34 | 0.45 | 0.46 | 0.57 | 0.34 | 0.1 | 0.31 | 0.69 |
| B: Materials | 6% | | 1 | 0.87 | 0.61 | 0.75 | 0.84 | 0.62 | 0.3 | 0.56 | 0.73 | 0.66 |
| C1: Capital goods | 12% | | | 1 | 0.67 | 0.83 | 0.92 | 0.65 | 0.32 | 0.69 | 0.82 | 0.66 |
| C2: Commercial services | 34% | | | | 1 | 0.58 | 0.68 | 0.4 | 0.08 | 0.5 | 0.6 | 0.37 |
| C3: Transportation | 7% | | | | | 1 | 0.83 | 0.68 | 0.27 | 0.58 | 0.77 | 0.67 |
| D: Consumer discretionary | 15% | | | | | | 1 | 0.76 | 0.21 | 0.69 | 0.81 | 0.66 |
| E: Consumer staples | 6% | | | | | | | 1 | 0.33 | 0.46 | 0.56 | 0.66 |
| F: Health care | 9% | | | | | | | | 1 | 0.15 | 0.24 | 0.46 |
| H: Information technology | 3% | | | | | | | | | 1 | 0.75 | 0.42 |
| I: Telecommunication | 1% | | | | | | | | | | 1 | 0.62 |
| J: Utilities | 7% | | | | | | | | | | | 1 |
| Herfindahl-Hirschman index | 0.18 | | | | | | | | | | | |

Source: Düllmann and Masschelein (2007).

affect the value of credit derivatives, such as CDS index tranches. This is discussed in Chapter 25. Several studies have looked at the correlation across sectors, and have observed that they increase significantly at the time of a recession (de Servigny and Renault, 2002; Das et al., 2006; Das et al., 2005; Duffie et al., 2007). High correlation explains the observation of default clusters.[10]

## TWO REPRESENTATIVE CREDIT VAR MODELS: CREDITMETRICS AND CREDIT RISK[+]

Given the importance of measuring the diversification of a loan portfolio adequately, several models have become popular among banks. Two of the best known are CreditMetrics (1997) and Credit Risk[+] (Credit Suisse, 1997). Their main characteristics follow.[11]

### CreditMetrics (1997)

This model was developed by KMV and a group of banks, under the leadership of the RiskMetrics unit at JPMorgan. It attempts to evaluate the probability distribution of the value of a loan portfolio at the end of the horizon, often one year. It relies on the transition matrix of the rating agencies, which shows the probability of upgrade or downgrade for a particular rating. An example of a transition matrix, shown earlier in Table 22.1, is repeated in Table 22.3.

**TABLE 22.3**

Migration Matrix (Probability of Moving from One Rating to Another over a One-Year Horizon)

| | One Year | | | | | | | |
|---|---|---|---|---|---|---|---|---|
| Current | AAA | AA | A | BBB | BB | B | CCC | Default |
| AAA | 90.81 | 8.33 | 0.68 | 0.06 | 0.12 | 0 | 0 | 0 |
| AA | 0.7 | 90.65 | 7.79 | 0.64 | 0.06 | 0.14 | 0.02 | 0 |
| A | 0.09 | 2.27 | 91.05 | 5.52 | 0.74 | 0.26 | 0.01 | 0.06 |
| BBB | 0.02 | 0.33 | 5.95 | 86.93 | 5.3 | 1.17 | 1.12 | 0.18 |
| BB | 0.03 | 0.14 | 0.67 | 7.73 | 80.53 | 8.84 | 1 | 1.6 |
| B | 0 | 0.11 | 0.24 | 0.43 | 6.48 | 83.46 | 4.07 | 5.2 |
| CCC | 0.22 | 0 | 0.22 | 1.3 | 2.38 | 11.24 | 64.86 | 19.79 |

Source: Crouhy et al., 2000.

Next, the model assumes, like KMV, that the value of the asset (the return on the asset) drives the change in rating. Assuming a normal distribution for the return on the asset, it calculates the number of standard deviations of return that are necessary to move from the current rating (for example, an A rating) to another rating (say, to default status). For instance, it will take 3.24 standard deviations to move an A-rated asset to the default probability area (equal to 0.06 percent).[12]

The next step is to run a Monte Carlo simulation as follows:

- Assuming a variance-covariance matrix of asset returns (with equity returns often used as a proxy), simulate a vector of returns, one for each asset in the portfolio (the return can be converted into the number of standard deviation from the mean).
- Translate each return (number of standard deviations) into a new rating.
- Compute the value of the asset, assuming a known rating-adjusted yield curve.
- Add up the value of each position to obtain the value of the portfolio.
- Repeat this process 100,000 times to simulate the distribution of value of the portfolio.

**T A B L E  22.4**

Rating Migration for an A-Rated Asset

| Rating in One Year for a Currently A-rated Asset | Probabilities of an Upgrade or Downgrade of the Asset in One Year's Time | Threshold (Number of Standard Deviations) |
|---|---|---|
| AAA | 0.09 | 3.12 |
| AA | 2.27 | 1.98 |
| A | 91.05 | −1.51 |
| BBB | 5.52 | −2.3 |
| BB | 0.74 | −2.72 |
| B | 0.26 | −3.19 |
| CCC | 0.01 | −3.24 |
| Default | 0.06 | |

Source: CreditMetrics (1997).

Needless to say, the choice of the variance-covariance matrix and the yield curves used to value the assets will have a major impact on the measurement of aggregate credit risk.

A second model that banks use to aggregate credit risk is Credit Risk$^+$.

## Credit Risk$^+$

A short presentation of the characteristics of Credit Risk$^+$ will be followed by some comments.

In comparison with other credit risk models, two main characteristics of Credit Risk$^+$ are as follows.

### Default Mode

Credit Risk$^+$ belongs to the category of default-mode models. That is, over one year, it measures the percentage of loans that are likely to go into default. As indicated earlier, the default-mode approach is different from the marked-to-market models (such as CreditMetrics), which attempt to measure the change in the value of a loan portfolio as a result not only of default, but also of the downgrading of some counterparties.

### Actuarial Base

Credit Risk$^+$ is inspired by the mathematics of insurance. It observes that, as in the case of life insurance, the probability of the event (default of a borrower) is very small, and that the frequency of default in a loan portfolio varies over the business cycle. This allows a statistical model to be built that computes the potential loss with some confidence level. Key data inputs are the probability of default of the borrower, the volatility of the frequency of default over a business cycle, and the loss given default. This approach can be compared to that of structural models (such as KMV or CreditMetrics), which try to model explicitly what drives default and the correlation across borrowers. Note that although Credit Risk$^+$ does not mention correlation explicitly, the volatility of frequency of default is implicitly related to the correlation across defaults (Gordy, 2000). A large volatility in the observed frequency of defaults is indicative of high correlation across defaults. Finally, Credit Risk$^+$ allows diversification to be studied. If the portfolio can be divided into subsets of loans that are affected by independent, possibly common, factors, the benefits of diversification can then be incorporated.

Assume that there is a portfolio of loans, each with a small probability of default $P_A$, with $\mu$ being the average number of defaults per year.

The probability distribution of the number of defaults during a given time period (say one year) is well represented by a Poisson distribution:

$$P(n \text{ defaults}) = \frac{\mu^n e^{-\mu}}{n!}$$

with $n!$ (read "$n$ factorial") $= 1 \times 2 \times 3 \times \ldots \times n$.

Next, observe that the frequency of default varies over time (this is equivalent to saying that defaults are correlated), with mean $\mu$ and standard deviation $\sigma_{\mu}$.

Next, the portfolio is divided into independent groups, each affected by its own independent factor. This allows reaching a closed-form solution[13] to measure aggregate credit VAR and to measure marginal contribution, that is, the impact on aggregate credit VAR of a change in the portfolio. Marginal risk analysis is discussed in Chapter 23. Additional variation in Credit Risk+ allows each group of loans to be subject to a set of independent, possibly common factors.

Warning: With respect to the application of Credit Risk+, empirical questions arise concerning the estimation of probability of default, the volatility of default frequency, the loss given default, and the classification of loans into independent sectors or factors. The results of Credit Risk+ are particularly sensitive to the volatility parameter and to sector/factor classifications.[14]

With regard to loan portfolios, there is often a question concerning the marginal impact on risk of a new loan in the portfolio. Marginal risk contribution is discussed in Chapter 23.

## CONCLUSION

Significant statistical progress in evaluating credit risk on a portfolio of loans has been made in recent years. Not surprisingly, the magnitude of correlation across factors affecting default at the time of a deep recession will drive the percentage of loans in a portfolio that default. Although the statistical tools are in place, the estimation of correlation parameters is proving difficult, in large part because data on deep recessions are few. As the 2007 subprime crisis indicates, stress testing the correlation assumptions is a must if the degree of credit risk in a portfolio is to be properly assessed.

## APPENDIX: UNCONDITIONAL LOAN-LOSS DISTRIBUTION

The unconditional loan-loss distribution for an infinitely granular homogeneous loan portfolio is calculated in this section. It builds on Vasicek (2002). The discussion starts with the conditional credit VAR formula:

$$\text{Percentage of losses}\,(F = F_\alpha) = x = \text{N}\left[\frac{\text{IN(PD)} + \sqrt{\rho}\,F_\alpha}{\sqrt{(1-\rho)}}\right]$$

This yields

$$\frac{\text{IN(PD)} + \sqrt{\rho}\,F_\alpha}{\sqrt{1-\rho}} = \text{IN}(x)$$

$$F_\alpha = \frac{\sqrt{1-\rho}\,\text{IN}(x) - \text{IN(PD)}}{\sqrt{\rho}}$$

Probability $(\text{loss} < x)$ = probability $(F < F_\alpha) = \text{N}(F_\alpha)$

$$\text{Probability}\,(\text{loss} < x) = \text{N}\left[\frac{\sqrt{1-\rho}\,\text{IN}(x) - \text{IN(PD)}}{\sqrt{\rho}}\right]$$

## EXERCISES FOR CHAPTER 22

To answer Exercises 1 to 4, you must enter the asymptotic single risk factor (ASRF) credit VAR and the unconditional cumulative loan-loss distribution formula into a PC spreadsheet.

1. For a confidence level of 99.9 percent, PD = 1 percent, and correlation = 0.2, compute the credit VAR under the asymptotic single risk factor (ASRF) model.
2. Under the ASRF model for PD = 2 percent and correlation = 0.1, compute the probability that loan losses will be equal to or less than 1 percent of the portfolio.
3. Under the ASRF model for PD = 2 percent and correlation = 0.1, compute the probability that loan losses will be equal to or greater than 5 percent of the portfolio.
4. Under the ASRF model for PD = 2 percent and correlation = 0.3, compute the probability that loan losses will be equal to or greater than 5 percent of the portfolio. Compare your answer to that for Exercise 3. How do you explain the difference?

## Notes

1. Rating agencies were criticized in 2008 for their ratings of tranches of securitizations (see Chapter 16). Some have argued that they should not use the same alphanumeric ranking for securitizations as they use for bond ratings, as credit risk on corporate bonds is different from credit risk on a pool of assets (for which correlation will matter). Rating agencies have argued that they were expressing a view on the probability of default of specific tranches and on expected loss (probability of default times loss given default), but not on the probability of a downgrade or a migration of the tranche to a more risky category. Probability of default should not be confused with probability of migration (Fender et al., 2008).

2. As the mathematics is more demanding, a first reading of the chapter can focus on the intuition summary at the start of each section. An alternative presentation of the asymptotic risk factor model was presented in the appendix to Chapter 13.

3. As discussed in Chapter 1, the instantaneous return is the return over a very small (infinitesimal) time interval.

4. The mathematics of copula is introduced in Chapter 25, on credit derivatives. The intuitive understanding is that it brings together the marginal probability distributions of risky loans with a Gaussian factor.

5. It is interesting to observe that in the case of a portfolio of stocks, it is estimated that a minimum of 15 stocks is necessary to eliminate idiosyncratic risk (Brealey et al., 2006). In the case of credit risk, more than 1,000 loans are needed to ensure the convergence between the conditional probability of default and the observed frequency of defaults. In the case of a portfolio of stocks, the concern is with the average return on the portfolio. Thus, one idiosyncratic shock (good news) is partly compensated by another idiosyncratic shock (bad news). The shocks to returns add up directly. In a credit portfolio, the problem is very different. The analyst is looking at a loan-loss distribution and is interested in measuring the frequency of default with some confidence level. For example, take a loan with a conditional PD of 5 percent (conditional on the economy being in a recession). If there is only one loan in the portfolio, it is not possible, of course, to guarantee that 5 percent of the portfolio will default (with 99.9 percent confidence). In fact, there will be a probability of 5 percent that 100 percent of the loan will default. If there are 100 loans in the portfolio, the observed frequency of default will get closer to 5 percent.

Depending on the single risk factor $F_\alpha$, many loans and observations (draw) of the firm-specific shock $\varepsilon_i$ are needed to ensure that the frequency distribution of $\varepsilon_i$ matches the normal probability distribution.

6. The focus is directly on the adjustment to capital. The 2001 Basel document focuses on the adjustment to risk-weighted assets. Because of the large number of borrowers, the retail loan portfolio is assumed to be granular.

7. When two random variables are independent, the joint probability is the product of the marginal probabilities.

8. An application of this approach to U.S. banks was made by Frye and Pelz (2008). A numerical approximation that avoids Monte Carlo simulation is available in Pykhtin (2004) and in Düllmann and Masschelein (2007).

9. Another useful empirical study on pitfalls in measuring portfolio credit risk is Tarashev and Zhu (2007).

10. Duffie et al. (2007) introduced the concept of *frailty*: default clusters seem to result from unobservable explanatory variables that are correlated across firms.

11. Discussion of other models is available in Saunders and Allen (2002).

12. The normal distribution is discussed in Chapter 3.

13. Credit Suisse (1997) or Crouhy et al. (2000).

14. At a particular bank the author visited, loans were classified into sectors, with each sector being affected by a *single* independent factor. That is, the bank implicitly assumed that the economic forces affecting loan losses in one sector had no impact on loan losses in other sectors. The independence assumption was a key driver of the estimated diversification benefits. Needless to say, these diversification benefits were overstated if the independence across economic factors was not met.

# CHAPTER 23

# Marginal Risk Contribution, Diversification, and Economic Capital Allocation

The application of portfolio theory and the use of simulation models have allowed banks to measure the aggregate risk of a portfolio that has many different sources of risk. The objective is to have a measure of risk that incorporates the risk reduction benefits of diversification. For financial firms with multiple businesses, such as commercial banking, investment banking, and insurance (or with businesses in several countries), a new issue arises: how to measure the risk contribution of a specific business unit, that is, the *marginal risk contribution*. Although the *stand-alone* risk of a business (i.e., the volatility of income or the worst potential loss) can be calculated, it is likely that when the business is integrated into a multibusiness firm, part of the *marginal* risk will disappear through diversification.

A presentation of the mathematical tool is followed by a numerical example and conclusions.

## MATHEMATICS OF MARGINAL RISK CONTRIBUTION

Consider a bank with three businesses: A, B, and C. These could refer to commercial banking, insurance, and investment banking businesses, or to banking businesses in three different countries. The model, being quite general, applies to any sources of risk.

Define:

$A$ = asset position $(A, B, C)$

$R_A$ = return on asset $A$ $(A, B, C)$

$\sigma_A$ = standard deviation of return on asset $A$ $(A, B, C)$

Total portfolio income = $P = R_A \times A + R_B \times B + R_C \times C$

$\sigma_P$ = aggregate total risk = standard deviation of total portfolio income

$\rho_{A,B}$ = correlation between the return on asset $A$ and the return on asset $B$

$\rho_{A,P}$ = correlation between the return on asset $A$ and portfolio income $P$

Then, according to the standard modern portfolio theory formula (Markowitz, 1959), the variance of total portfolio income ($\sigma_P^2$) is equal to

$$\text{Variance of portfolio income } (\sigma_P^2) = A^2 \times \sigma_A^2 + B^2 \times \sigma_B^2 + C^2 \times \sigma_C^2 + 2 \times A \times B \times \rho_{A,B} \times \sigma_A \times \sigma_B + 2 \times A \times C \times \rho_{A,C} \times \sigma_A \times \sigma_C + 2 \times B \times C \times \rho_{B,C} \times \sigma_B \times \sigma_C$$

The standard deviation of portfolio income ($\sigma_P$), a measure of the aggregate risk, is equal to

$$\text{Aggregate risk} = \sigma_P = \sqrt{\text{variance}}$$

The intuitive explanation of the managerial issue is as follows: a bank is composed of three business units. Each one has its own risk, but what matters to the bank is the total risk, that is, the volatility of the portfolio income. The 1959 modern portfolio theory formula allows the standard deviation of total income to be computed. The parameters include the assets invested in the three businesses, the standard deviation of the return on each asset, and the correlation across returns. Historical data can provide a basis for computing these parameters.

So far there may seem to be nothing new, just an application of modern portfolio theory; however, the formula for the variance is not very transparent or easy to understand, because the chain of cross-products makes analyzing the specific risk contribution of each business unit difficult.

Fortunately, there is an alternative formula for the standard deviation of risk on total portfolio income ($\sigma P$) that gives a much more transparent understanding of the sources of total risk and the impact of diversification (see the proof in Appendix A to this chapter):

Aggregate risk = standard deviation of total portfolio income
$$= (A \times \sigma_A \times \rho_{A,P}) + (B \times \sigma_B \times \rho_{B,P}) + (C \times \sigma_C \times \rho_{C,P})$$

This expression of the aggregate risk ($\sigma_P$) is attractive, as the total risk is now the sum of three components: the marginal risks for Businesses A, B, and C.[1]

The term for the marginal contribution of each business is quite intuitive. The marginal risk contribution of each component is the *stand-alone* risk (A $\times$ $\sigma_A$) multiplied by the correlation between the return on this business and the total portfolio income ($\rho_{A,P}$). That is, a business may be risky on its own, but if, when it is integrated into a bank, it shows only a small correlation with the return on the total bank ($\rho_{A,P}$ small), a large part of the risk disappears, thanks to the portfolio diversification effect. In contrast, a business that is highly correlated with the return on the total bank ($\rho_{A,P}$ close to 1) would not benefit much from diversification, and the marginal risk would be close to the stand-alone risk.

Thus, the concept of the *marginal risk contribution* for Business A is equal to

Marginal risk contribution of Business A = (stand-alone risk) $\times$
(correlation with total income)
$$= (A \times \sigma_A) \times (\rho_{A,P})$$

In order to better understand the issues in the measurement of marginal risk, consider a numerical example.

### Numerical Example: From the Global Bank to Individual Business Units

This example looks at a bank with three business units. The objective will be to analyze value creation and the expected economic profit created by the bank and each individual business unit. According to Chapter 9, economic capital should be allocated to each profit center to cover potential losses or unexpected losses (UL). But, as part of the risk will disappear with portfolio diversification, the concept of the marginal risk contribution of a business that recognizes both the risk of a business and the diversification effect will be applied.

Businesses A, B, and C could be commercial banking, investment banking, and insurance, or they could be banking in three different countries. The bank invests $100,000 in assets in each business, with an expected after-tax return of 2 percent for Businesses A and B and 1.2 percent for Business C. The standard deviation of all returns is 10 percent. In real life, historical data could be used to estimate these values. Data also include information on correlation across returns and on the bank's cost of equity.

| Asset (Position) | Expected Return (After Tax) | Standard Deviation ($\sigma$) |
|---|---|---|
| A = 100,000 | 2% | 10% |
| B = 100,000 | 2% | 10% |
| C = 100,000 | 1.2% | 10% |

Correlation ($\rho$): $\rho_{A,B} = 0.7$; $\rho_{A,C} = 0.18$; $\rho_{B,C} = 0.2$
Cost of equity = 10 percent

The analysis of the amount of value creation by the bank will follow three standard steps:

- Step 1: Measure global risk
- Step 2: Allocate economic capital
- Step 3: Compute expected economic profit

## Step 1: Measure Global Risk
The standard 1959 portfolio theory formula is applied.

$$\text{Variance of portfolio income } (\sigma_P^2) = A^2 \times \sigma_A^2 + B^2 \times \sigma_B^2 + C^2 \times \sigma_C^2 + 2 \times A \times B \times \rho_{A,B} \times \sigma_A \times \sigma_B + 2 \times A \times C \times \rho_{A,C} \times \sigma_A \times \sigma_C + 2 \times B \times C \times \rho_{B,C} \times \sigma_B \times \sigma_C$$

$$= 100{,}000^2 \times 0.1^2 + 100{,}000^2 \times 0.1^2 + 100{,}000^2 \times 0.1^2 + 2 \times 100{,}000 \times 100{,}000 \times 0.7 \times 0.1 \times 0.1 + 2 \times 100{,}000 \times 100{,}000 \times 0.18 \times 0.1 \times 0.1 + 2 \times 100{,}000 \times 100{,}000 \times 0.2 \times 0.1 \times 0.1$$

$$= 515{,}998{,}480$$

$$\text{Total risk} = \text{standard deviation of total portfolio income} = \sigma_P$$
$$= \text{square root of variance} = \sqrt{515{,}998{,}480}$$
$$= 22{,}715.6$$

## Step 2: Allocate Economic Capital

With information on the total risk, the standard deviation of total portfolio income, the next step is to decide how much of the downside risk (unexpected losses) should be covered by economic capital. Remember that the logic of economic capital is to have capital available to absorb potential losses and avoid a costly bankruptcy. In this example, economic capital equal to twice the standard deviation of total income will be allocated. The factor 2 was chosen for clarity of exposition. In reality, the factor would probably be higher than 2 in order to provide a higher degree of confidence that losses would not exceed capital.

$$\text{Economic capital } (2 \times \sigma_P) = 2 \times 22{,}715.6 = 45{,}431.2$$

So, in this example, the bank decides to allocate \$45,431.2 to finance the investment in \$300,000 of assets.[2]

With access to the expected return on each asset and to the economic capital allocation, it is now possible to compute, in Step 3, the expected economic profit of the total bank.

## Step 3: Compute Expected Economic Profit

$$\text{Economic profit} = \text{expected return on assets net of a cost of allocated equity}$$
$$= (2\% \times 100{,}000 + 2\% \times 100{,}000 + 1.2\% \times 100{,}000) - (10\% \times 45{,}431.2)$$
$$= 656.88$$

The conclusion is that the overall bank creates value, because the expected economic profit is positive (\$656.88); that is, the expected profit exceeds the cost of the allocated equity. However, it is preferable to go one step further. That is, the economic profit of each business, A, B, and C, should be determined separately. Perhaps the bank would like to pay a bonus to each manager, or perhaps its management would like to be able to discuss strategy, such as to discuss which businesses to expand and which to reduce. Until recently, this was not easy to do because the 1959 formula for the variance involves many cross-products. So, while modern portfolio theory allows the total risk and economic profit of a bank to be measured, it is ill designed for determining the marginal contribution of each business unit. The alternative formula for total risk presented earlier will allow the discussion to be conducted at a business-unit level.

### Value Creation at a Business-Unit Level

First, the formula is applied to allocate risk to each business units. Remember that the marginal risk contribution is the product of stand-alone risk and a correlation between the risk of the business and that of the total bank:

$$\text{Volatility of total portfolio income } \sigma_P = A \times \sigma_A \times \rho_{A,P} + B \times \sigma_B \times \rho_{B,P} + C \times \sigma_C \times \rho_{C,P}$$
$$= 100{,}000 \times 0.1 \times 0.828 + 100{,}000 \times 0.1 \times 0.836 + 100{,}000 \times 0.1 \times 0.608$$
$$= 8{,}276.2 + 8{,}364.3 + 6{,}075.1$$
$$= 22{,}715.6$$

Two observations stand out. The first is that the measure of total risk (\$22,715.6) is identical to that given by the standard 1959 portfolio theory formula. What is new is that the risk can be allocated to Business A ($8,276.2), to Business B ($8,364.3), and to Business C ($6,075.1). Second, the correlation between the return on a business and that of the bank (for example, the correlation between the return on Business A and total portfolio income $\rho_{A,P} = 0.828$) has to be calculated. Indeed, it is usually possible to access or compute correlations between *pairs* of variables (for instance, correlations between banking and insurance income, or between banking and asset management income), but the formula demands the correlation between the return on a business and the total portfolio income. Appendix B shows how to use correlations between pairs of variables to compute the correlation between one variable and the total portfolio income.[3]

With information on the marginal risk contribution of each business, economic capital can be allocated to each business (2 × marginal risk contribution, to use the same factor 2 that was used earlier to keep the example consistent). The expected economic profit of each business can then be computed:

Expected economic profit = expected economic profit of Business A
+ expected economic profit of Business B
+ expected economic profit of Business C

Economic profit = 656.88 = (2% × 100,000) − (10% × 2 × 8,276.2)
+ (2% × 100,000) − (10% × 2 × 8,364.3)
+ (1.2% × 100,000) − (10% × 2 × 6,075.1)
= 344.75 (contribution of A)
+ 327.14 (contribution of B)
− 15.02 (contribution of C)

Mission accomplished. The economic profit of each business has been computed, taking into account both the stand-alone risk of each business and the risk reduction brought about by diversification. Note that the sum of the economic profits adds up to the total economic profit of $656.88, calculated earlier.

The computation of economic profits for separate businesses allows management to reward the managers of profit centers or to discuss strategy. In this example, Businesses A and B generate a positive economic profit, while Business C has a negative economic profit (−$15.02), so it appears tempting to close Business C so as to increase overall economic profit, and ultimately increase the share price.

*Advice*: Before you decide to apply this analysis and close a business, you are strongly advised to redo the calculations to verify that closing the business will indeed generate higher economic profit. Here's a check.

## Closing Business C

Suppose the bank closes Business C and returns the excess equity to the shareholders. They can then invest in the stock market and obtain an expected return with zero value creation or destruction.[4] Value creation will come from the investment in the bank with two businesses only: Businesses A and B. The other parameters are the same.

| Asset (Position) | Expected Return (After Tax) | Standard Deviation ($\sigma$) |
|---|---|---|
| A = 100,000 | 2% | 10% |
| B = 100,000 | 2% | 10% |

Correlation ($\rho$): $\rho_{A,B} = 0.7$
Cost of equity = 10%

As before, the computation of the expected economic profit involves three steps: measure total risk, allocate economic capital, and compute expected economic profit.

### Step 1: Measure Global Risk

The 1959 portfolio theory formula is applied to the case of two businesses, A and B:

$$
\begin{aligned}
\text{Variance of profit } \sigma_P^2 &= A^2 \times \sigma_A^2 + B^2 \times \sigma_B^2 \\
&\quad + 2 \times A \times B \times \rho_{A>,B} \times \sigma_A \times \sigma_B \\
&= 100{,}000^2 \times 0.1^2 + 100{,}000^2 \times 0.1^2 + 2 \\
&\quad \times 100{,}000 \times 100{,}000 \times 0.7 \times 0.1 \times 0.1 \\
&= 340{,}000{,}040
\end{aligned}
$$

$$
\begin{aligned}
\text{Global risk} &= \text{square root of variance} = \sigma_P \\
&= \sqrt{340{,}000{,}040} \\
&= 18{,}439.09
\end{aligned}
$$

### Step 2: Allocate Economic Capital

To keep the example consistent, economic capital equal to twice the standard deviation, or $36,878.18, is allocated.

$$\text{Economic capital} = 2 \times \sigma_P = 2 \times 18{,}439.09 = 36{,}878.18$$

In this example, the excess capital ($45,431.2 − $36,878.18 = $8,553.02) is returned to the shareholders. When they invest it in the stock market, they get just the risk-adjusted return, with no value creation.[5]

### Step 3: Compute Expected Economic Profit

$$\text{Economic profit} = (2\% \times 100{,}000 + 2\% \times 100{,}000) -$$
$$(10\% \times 36{,}878.18)$$
$$= \$312.18$$

It can be seen that a decision to close Business C would in fact reduce the economic profit from \$656.88 to \$312.18. This is a reduction of 52.5 percent of economic profit, although the previous calculation of the marginal economic profit contribution seemed to indicate that dropping Business C would increase economic profit! That's the magic and mystery of portfolio diversification.

Before identifying the sources of the error in logic and rational decision making involved in the recommendation to abandon Business C, the first step is to go with intuition. Experts in portfolio theory and diversification will quickly recognize that, although Business C had a low expected return on assets (1.2 percent vs. 2 percent for Businesses A and B), it had a unique characteristic. While the returns on assets of Businesses A and B were highly correlated (0.7), the correlations between the return on assets for Business C and those for Businesses A and B were low (0.18 and 0.2, respectively). In other words, and intuitively, Business C was a great producer of diversification of risk and reduction in economic capital allocation. Keeping only Businesses A and B onboard, two highly correlated businesses, did not allow the bank to benefit much from risk diversification.

As seen in this example, a business unit can contribute to the bank in three possible ways:

- Expected profit
- Stand-alone risk (the risk of the business by itself)
- Risk diversification

In the example, Business C was a contributor on the third dimension, that of diversification. Before discussing some significant strategic messages from this example, it is first necessary to be more precise about where the recommendation went wrong in the application of the marginal risk contribution formula.

Although the formula for the standard deviation as a sum of marginal risk contributions is mathematically exact, the measure of aggregate risk is not a simple addition of independent components. Indeed, the marginal change in aggregate risk for an increase (decrease) in Business A is not just the *marginal risk contribution* ($\Delta A \times \sigma_A \times \rho_{A,P}$), but also the change in correlation between each business and the total bank ($\rho_{A,P}$, $\rho_{B,P}$, and $\rho_{C,P}$), as a change in one business will change the total bank portfolio $P$. Strategic decisions are thus more complex than meets the eye. The only way to make a logical decision is to analyze several combinations of businesses in search of the one that yields the highest economic profit.

## DIVERSIFICATION, RISK REDUCTION, AND BANK STRATEGY

This example calls attention to five separate issues in bank strategy that are related to diversification and marginal risk contribution.

### Does Diversification Increase Value?

Finance professors have taught for many years that financial diversification per se cannot increase shareholder value for the powerful reason that shareholders can diversify themselves. There is no need for a Spanish company to merge with a British company if shareholders can buy both shares of a Spanish company and shares of a British company. This argument is powerful, leading to a recommendation for focused strategies. Around the world, students at business schools have been taught (or possibly brainwashed into believing?) that diversification is useless. To argue for diversification in banking, the argument must be made that banking is a special industry and that the usual argument that shareholders can diversify themselves does not apply fully in this special case. There are two arguments for this, already discussed in Chapter 17, "Risk Management in Banking." The first one is *opacity*, and the second one is *funding with short-term deposits*. They lead to the same conclusion: stability of income at the firm level is useful, and one way to achieve stability of income at the firm level is diversification.

The opacity argument is that it is difficult for analysts outside a bank to understand the various types of complex transactions and risks that the bank has actually taken. If the bank reports a loss, the market can be confused as to whether this loss is the result of bad luck or bad management. This can lead to reputational risk, a drop in the share price, and shareholder value destruction. Reporting a stable income helps to avoid these problems.[6]

The short-term funding argument is discussed in Chapter 4. A useful service that banks offer to the economy is liquidity insurance, with depositors being able to withdraw funds on demand and borrowers being able to draw on their credit lines. To avoid bank runs and costly fire sales of illiquid assets, it is important to create confidence in the system. Again, stability of income at the firm level helps. It must be emphasized that this stability of income must be achieved within the company, not at the level of a shareholder's portfolio.

Company diversification can help. This does not mean, of course, that a bank should diversify in any direction. It needs to keep a business focus, while achieving diversification.[7]

The debate about the benefits of diversification is an old one. There are two sayings that lead to different conclusions. In reply to the "do not put all your eggs in the same basket" argument, the business-focused American Andrew Carnegie is reported to have said, "Put all your eggs in one basket, and watch the basket." This means that focus can lead to better management, better understanding of the risks, and, in the end, better control. The conclusion here is that financial diversification coupled with focus—which can be achieved in a well-managed decentralized company—can yield both benefits.

### The Correct Measure of Marginal Risk Contribution
### (with and without Business Unit)

Mathematical models such as Credit Risk$^+$ can allow the marginal risk contribution (closed-form solution) to be computed directly. However, in most cases, the marginal risk measure is valid only for small (infinitesimal) changes. As discussed in the example in this chapter, the proper way to evaluate marginal risk or marginal economic profit is to do the calculations with and without a transaction/business unit in the portfolio.

### Incremental Tactical Decisions vs. Strategic Global Portfolio Decisions

Quite often, there is a question concerning whether an additional transaction would increase the value created for shareholders. For instance, does a new loan contribute to value creation? This exercise can be referred to as marginal incremental analysis. It requires the computation of both the additional profit arising from the transaction and the additional risk-based capital needed to back up the incremental risk. In doing this computation, management should be aware that while it may be receiving correct information on whether adding a transaction to an existing portfolio creates additional value (tactical decision), this does not imply that the new portfolio is the best one (strategic decision).

The reason why marginal analysis does not give adequate information on the optimality of a portfolio of activities is as follows. Because of the mathematics of diversification, the incremental risk—that is, the additional risk coming from adding a transaction (and therefore the economic capital allocation) to a portfolio—is related to the other transactions that are already in the portfolio. What is the practical implication of this mathematical result? Here is an example.

Consider an existing portfolio of six loans. A new proposal has come in for Loan 7. It is possible to compute the RAROC and economic profit for Loan 7 and conclude that it creates value. The correct conclusion is that a portfolio with seven loans is better than the initial portfolio with six loans. So far, so good. However, and this is where the difficulty lies, it could very well be that another portfolio with the first five loans and Loan 7 (that is, excluding Loan 6) is even better (the mathematical reason being that the incremental risks measured for Loan 7 or Loan 6 are highly dependent on the existing loans that were in the initial portfolio). It could well be that adding Loan 6 to a portfolio made up of the first five loans and Loan 7 does not create value.

What is the conclusion to be drawn from this tricky mathematical discussion? In real life, people often face marginal incremental decisions. Should a new transaction be added to the portfolio or not? Marginal analysis gives the answer. But, as the previous analysis showed, running marginal analysis case by case can result in a portfolio that might not be the best one. Therefore, in addition to marginal analysis, it is necessary to do an additional exercise: simulate various portfolios to see which one creates the most value. In other words, a *tactical incremental analysis* is needed to ensure that a *new* asset adds value to the existing portfolio. A *strategic* analysis by simulation to find the best portfolio is also needed. The latter gives strategic indications as to the directions (industries or countries) in which to move the loan portfolio.

## Separation Theorem and Diversification

In Chapter 10, fund transfer pricing and the separation theorem were introduced. That is, loans and deposits could be managed independently of each other, with only one reference point: the matched-maturity market rate, an opportunity rate that is available for investment or for funding. That chapter argued that at least two situations could break this simple separation theorem. First, joint operating cost or joint demand for loans and deposits would create a linkage between these businesses. A second argument was that, in the case of liquidity constraints, the volume of loans would be constrained by the availability of core stable deposits. Risk and diversification of risks provide an additional reason for the breakdown of the separation theorem. In fact, academics have observed a positive correlation between loan demand and the supply of deposits at a time of crisis. Investors move to bank deposits for safety, while borrowers, being unable to issue bonds, rely on bank loans. In this case, the joint offering of deposits and loans allows minimization of the need for liquid reserves.[8]

### Risk-Adjusted Performance Measurement (RAPM), Bonuses, and Diversification

Chapter 9 argued for decentralization of the bank into value centers, each with its own income statement and balance sheet. This allowed the computation of a risk-adjusted return on capital (RAROC) or an economic profit, defined as

$$\text{Economic profit} = \text{allocated net income} \\ - (\text{allocated equity} \times \text{cost of equity})$$

In this framework, equity or economic capital was allocated to cover an unexpected or potential loss so as to avoid a costly bankruptcy. Economic profit could be used to assess strategy or to compute rewards or bonuses for managers. As the example in this chapter shows, a practical question arises as to whether the allocation of equity to evaluate risk-adjusted performance should take into account the benefits of diversification. The arguments in favor are that diversification is a reality that leads to risk reduction, that managers should receive a correct signal, and that economic capital allocation should therefore reflect marginal risk contribution, with the benefits of diversification included. The arguments against the inclusion of diversification benefits and in favor of allocating economic capital on a stand-alone basis are that a business unit is not responsible for diversification at the firm level and that its equity allocation should not be affected by positions in other businesses. Accepting the general argument that value-center accounting should deliver the right signal to increase shareholder value, the recommendation here is that the diversification benefits should be taken into account (otherwise some transactions might not take place because of an excessive capital charge). However, in performance evaluation, what really matters is the identification of *superior* performance, which suggests the following calculation:

$$\text{Superior economic profit} = \text{realized economic profit} \\ - \text{benchmarked economic profit}$$

This avoids paying large bonuses to executives who happen to work in a profitable but not very competitive environment[9] or penalizing business units (such as Business C in the example) that show a low economic profit but are useful for diversification.

## CONCLUSION

The tool of marginal risk contribution allows two ideas to be integrated neatly. Risk demands economic capital, but diversification reduces risk. It introduces a joint dimension in management, leading to a call for a proper degree of decentralization and focus, while keeping a healthy degree of financial diversification at group level.

## APPENDIX A: PROOF OF THE MARGINAL RISK CONTRIBUTION FORMULA

Denoting $R_i$ as the return on asset $I$ and $x_i$ as the portfolio share of asset $I$ gives

Portfolio income $P = x_1 \times R_1 + x_2 \times R_2 + \ldots + x_n \times R_n$

Variance (portfolio income) $= \sigma_p^2$

$$\sigma_P^2 = \sum_i \sum_i x_i x_i \operatorname{cov}(R_i, R_j)$$

$$= \sum_i x_i \operatorname{cov}(R_i, P)$$

$$= \sum_i x_i \rho_{i,P} \, \sigma_i \sigma_P$$

$$\sigma_p = \sum_i x_i \, \sigma_i \, \rho_{i,p}$$

## APPENDIX B: COMPUTATION OF CORRELATION BETWEEN THE RETURN ON A SPECIFIC BUSINESS AND THE RETURN ON A PORTFOLIO OF BUSINESSES

Most often, the correlations that are available are those between pairs of returns—for example, the return on insurance business and the return on banking assets. As the marginal risk formula demands the correlation between the return on each business and total portfolio income, here are the formulas for moving from correlations between two businesses (pairwise correlation) to those between one business and the portfolio income.
Define:

$A$ = asset position A (B, C)

$R_A$ = random return on asset A (B, C)

$\sigma_A$ = standard deviation of return $R_A$ on asset A (B, C)

$P$ = total portfolio income $= A \times R_A + B \times R_B + C \times R_C$

$\sigma_P$ = standard deviation of portfolio income

$\rho_{A,B}$ = correlation between the return on asset $A$ and the return on asset $B$

$\rho_{A,P}$ = correlation between the return on asset $A$ and the portfolio income $P$

$\rho_{A,P}$ = covariance $(R_A$, portfolio income$)/(\sigma_A \times \sigma_P)$

with

Covariance $(R_A$, portfolio income) = covariance $(R_A, AR_A + BR_B + CR_C)$
$$= A \text{ covariance } (R_A, R_A) + B \text{ covariance } (R_A, R_B) + C \text{ covariance } (R_A, R_C)$$
$$= A \times \sigma_A \times \sigma_A + B \times \rho_{A,B} \times \sigma_A \times \sigma_B + C \times \rho_{A,C} \times \sigma_A \times \sigma_C$$

Example: Calculate covariance $(R_A$, portfolio income) with

$\sigma_A = 0.1$

$\sigma_P = 22{,}715.63$ (this is calculated using the standard 1959 modern portfolio theory formula)

Covariance $(R_A$, portfolio income) $= A \times \sigma_A \times \sigma_A + B \times \rho_{A,B} \times \sigma_A \times \sigma_B + C \times \rho_{A,C} \times \sigma_A \times \sigma_C$
$$= 100{,}000 \times 0.1 \times 0.1 + 100{,}000 \times 0.7 \times 0.1 \times 0.1 + 100{,}000 \times 0.18 \times 0.1 \times 0.1$$
$$= 1{,}880$$

$$\text{Correlation}(R_A, \text{portfolio income}) = \rho_{R_A,P} = \frac{\text{covariance}(R_A, \text{portfolio income})}{\sigma_A \times \sigma_P}$$

$$= \frac{1{,}880}{0.1 \times 22{,}715.63} = 0.828$$

## EXERCISES FOR CHAPTER 23

The balance sheet of a financial conglomerate can be divided into two main activities: banking and insurance. There are $100,000 of assets in banking and $80,000 in insurance. The expected rate of return on banking assets is 1.5 percent, while that on insurance assets is 1.3 percent. The volatility (standard deviation) of return in banking is 10 percent, while that in insurance is 8 percent. Finally, the correlation between the return on the banking assets and that on the insurance assets is 0.7.

1. Using the traditional modern portfolio theory formula, compute the standard deviation of total income for the financial group.
2. Divide the standard deviation of total portfolio income into two parts: the marginal risk contribution of banking and the marginal risk contribution of insurance.

## Notes

1. This decomposition of the aggregate risk into a sum of components is also referred to as delta VAR or DVAR (Crouhy et al., 2001).
2. To be precise, there are $300,000 of assets funded by debt. The equity of $45,431.2 is assumed to be invested in risk-free Treasury bills. The cost of equity of 10 percent is a cost net of the after-tax return on the Treasury bills. Corporate tax, risk, or imperfect information (cost of external finance) will create a net cost of equity.
3. It can be shown that the correlation between the return on asset A and total portfolio income is identical to the correlation between the return on asset A and the return on the total asset portfolio.
4. Investing in stock creates zero economic value, as the return on the investment is equal to the cost of equity.
5. One question could be why the equity is not invested in other value-creating activities. The answer is that this could be done whether the bank is investing in Businesses A and B or in Businesses A, B, and C. That is, there is no equity rationing.
6. A second argument related to opacity, discussed in Chapter 17, is that avoiding a loss means not having to raise expensive funds on external capital markets.
7. Note that the debate is exclusively on the benefits of financial diversification. Presence in different business segments can be justified by other arguments: joint sales or economies of scope.
8. Liquidity risk is discussed in Chapter 21.
9. The evaluation of performance and the design of bonuses were discussed in Chapter 9.

# CHAPTER 24

# Forwards, Futures, Swaps, and Options: Counterparty Risk

This chapter provides an introduction to some of the widely used financial derivative contracts: forwards, financial futures, swaps, and options. A complete analysis of these instruments requires and has been the subject of complete books.[1] The objective here is to focus on the economics of these off-balance sheet derivative contracts, that is, to understand what services they provide and to highlight the risks associated with them. A discussion of counterparty risk follows.

## FORWARDS

For many years, banks have used forward contracts to hedge risk or to take positions. A *forward contract*, or forward, is an agreement between two parties to buy or sell an asset (a stock, currency, a bond, or a commodity) at a future date (the *delivery date*) at a price that is fixed today (the *exercise* or *strike* price). For example, consider the forward currency contract. You plan to import goods from Great Britain in six months time, and you are afraid that the pound sterling may appreciate. To protect/hedge yourself, you decide to enter into a currency forward contract whereby you will buy the pounds sterling you will need in six months' time at a price that is fixed today. If the pound sterling does appreciate during the six-month period, you are protected or hedged because you will buy the pounds at the exercise price fixed today. The following discussion considers interest-rate derivatives related to the purchase or sale of bonds.

For instance, suppose Alpha Bank agrees today to buy a three-month Treasury bill from Gamma Bank, with delivery next December at a price of $90, fixed today. It is always useful to represent the history of the contract on a *timeline*.

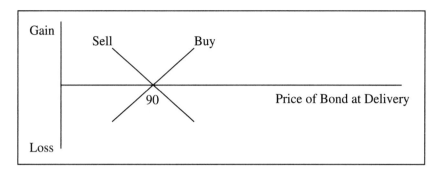

**Figure 24.1** Graphic representation of reverse payoffs.

| Today | December | March |
|---|---|---|
| Contract is signed | Delivery date | Maturity of underlying bond |
| | (Buy or sell T-bill) | (One-quarter Treasury bill) |

At the delivery date next December, Alpha Bank buys the bond from Gamma Bank. If the price has gone above $90, Alpha Bank is making a profit. However, if the price has fallen below $90, it is making a loss. The reverse payoffs apply to Gamma Bank. These payoffs can be represented graphically, as shown in Figure 24.1.

This is an off-balance sheet transaction, as at the origination date, it is just an agreement, with no impact on assets and liabilities. It is also referred to as an *over-the-counter* (OTC) transaction, a transaction between two financial institutions.

However, the financial outcomes of a forward contract could have been achieved with on-balance sheet positions.

## Buy Side

Suppose you borrow money (with a promise to repay $90 in December) and buy a Treasury bill today. Next December, you sell the Treasury bill and repay the debt of $90 (interest included). If the value of the asset exceeds $90, you win, and if it is below $90, you lose, exactly the same financial payoffs as those of a forward buy position.

| Today | December |
|---|---|
| Borrow money | Sell Treasury bill |
| Buy Treasury bill | Repay debt ($90) |

A long forward position to buy is thus equivalent to a 100 percent leveraged (debt-funded) position.

### Sell Side

This is slightly more demanding. In the first step, you borrow the Treasury bill today from a counterparty, with a promise to return it next December. You then sell the bill today and invest the proceeds in a short-term asset that pays you $90 in December. In December, you collect the $90, buy the Treasury bill on the market, and return it to its owner. If the price has gone below $90, you win. If it is above $90, you lose. This financial strategy is referred to as *short selling*.[2]

| Today | December |
|---|---|
| Borrow a Treasury bill maturing next March | Collect $90 |
| Sell Treasury bill | Buy Treasury bill and return it to its owner |
| Invest cash in a risk-free asset maturing in December and yielding $90[3] | |

These two on-balance sheet strategies produce payoffs identical to those of the forward contract. These on-balance sheet strategies are sometimes called *replicating portfolios*, as the payoffs replicate those of off-balance sheet contracts. Replicating portfolios can be used for pricing or for hedging financial derivatives. If two strategies yield the same outcome, they should have the same price. Therefore, the price of a replicating portfolio should be identical to that of an off-balance sheet contract. In hedging, the appropriate replicating portfolio is used to offset, or hedge, the outcome of a position. For instance, short selling could be used to hedge a long position on the forward market.

However, the fact that forward contracts can be replicated with on-balance sheet positions raises the question of why they exist in the first place. If they were redundant instruments that can be replicated, intuition tells you that the forward markets would not be so large.

Aside from cosmetic accounting issues (one appears on the balance sheet, while the other does not) and possible differences in tax treatment (quite often a reason for the emergence of financial innovations), the main difference between the forward and the balance sheet positions is the *counterparty risk*, that is, the losses that would arise if the counterparty defaults and is unable to meet its obligation.

Consider the case of the forward contract to buy the Treasury bill at the price of $90. If Gamma Bank is unable to deliver the bond next December, Alpha Bank can always buy the bond on the market, but at the prevailing price. If the price is higher than $90, Alpha Bank will suffer a loss, as it was expecting to pay $90. Counterparty risk on a forward is thus a form of *replacement risk*, that is, the risk of having to replace the contract with a new one at less favorable terms. The risk refers to an adverse change in the price of the asset ($\Delta$ price).[4]

In the case of the on-balance sheet position, where one party borrows $90, it is the full debt of $90 that is at risk. Therefore, one of the major merits of forward contracts, as opposed to on-balance sheet leveraged positions, is to substantially reduce *counterparty risk* by replacing it with a smaller *replacement risk*.

## FINANCIAL FUTURES

To further reduce the consequences of a counterparty default, financial futures have been introduced successfully around the world. Very much like a forward contract, a financial future is an agreement between two parties to buy or sell a financial instrument (stock, currency, bond, commodity) at a future date (the delivery date) at a price that is fixed today (the exercise or strike price). Financial futures differ from forward contracts in two major ways.

### New Counterparty: A Third Party Is Involved

The first characteristic of a financial future is the introduction of an independent third party in the transaction, the futures exchange. The original contract between Alpha Bank and Gamma Bank is replaced by two new contracts (the legal notion of *novation*) connecting the two banks to the futures exchange. Alpha Bank buys from the exchange. Gamma Bank sells to the exchange. Essentially,

- Gamma Bank sells
- Alpha Bank buys
- The futures exchange buys and sells

The counterparty risk between the two banks has been replaced by a counterparty risk with the exchange. However, the exchange usually has very strong shareholders, in the form of large financial institutions, to guarantee the terms of the transaction. To further reduce counterparty risk, a system of margin accounts, marking of positions to market, and margin calls is put in place. To enter into a futures transaction, each party must deposit a guarantee with the futures exchange. At the end of each day, the position is marked to market, meaning that the exercise price is adjusted to the current price. The party that is winning receives a cash payment, while the party that is losing has to fund its margin account further.

For example, consider the case of the contract between Alpha Bank and Gamma Bank. If the price of the future goes to $91 the next day, the old $90 contract is replaced (marked to market) with a contract to buy and sell at $91. Alpha Bank (on the buy side) is not pleased, as it now has to pay $91 instead of $90, but it receives a cash compensation of +$1 (making the net new marked-to-market position identical to the old $90 contract). In reverse, Gamma Bank (on the sell side) is now selling at $91. Gamma is not happy for long, however, as it will have to make a cash payment (margin call) of −$1. This complex system is put in place to ensure that, as long as a price change does not exceed the amount of the margin account, there is no risk of default by the counterparty. Indeed, if the losing party is not able to replenish its margin, it is replaced by another party. Margin calls can create a liquidity risk,[5] as they affect the bank's cash balance every day.

### Standardized Futures Contracts and Liquidity

A second characteristic of financial futures is *standardization*. Financial futures have standardized sizes (for example, a Treasury bill contract is $1,000,000), standardized underlying instruments (for example, a three-month Treasury bill), and specific delivery dates (usually four per year: March, June, September, and December). The market is open every day, but delivery dates are few. These standardized contracts force all players to concentrate demand and supply on a few instruments, which improves liquidity. Liquidity, or the ability to get into and out of the future contract rapidly without altering prices, is particularly important for speculators, who want to be able to move into and out of contracts rapidly.

The standardized features of futures create a difficulty for banks because the positions that they want to hedge may not be identical to those that are available in the futures market. For instance, a bank may be forced to hedge a four-month T-bill with a three-month T-bill future. As explained later in the chapter, information on the duration of the asset and that of the future can be used to adjust the hedge, but there will always be a risk that the three-month rate and the four-month rate will not move in parallel. Or the bank may want to hedge a November position but finds that only a December futures contract is available.

To help clients, banks offer forward contracts tailored to meet those clients' needs and then hedge them on the futures market. A fee is charged for the risk arising from the imperfect hedge. A new form of financial intermediation is born: risk intermediation. Instead of using deposits to fund loans, the bank sells customized forwards to clients and hedges them with standardized futures.

### Numerical Example of Hedging a Cash Transaction with Financial Futures

In May, you want to price a one-year loan that will be offered next November. To fund the November loan, you anticipate the issue of $10,000,000 in certificates of deposits (one-year-to-maturity CDs) in November. To avoid any interest-rate risk, you would like to lock in (fix) the cost of funds for the CDs. The cash CD rate in May is 7.8 percent (discount basis[6]). The cash one-year T-bill rate is 6.95 percent. The December T-bill futures contract rate is 7.62 percent.

Here is the correspondence between discount yield, prices, and discounts:

| Yield | Money Raised at Issue Time | Discount ($10,000,000 — Money Raised) |
|---|---|---|
| 7.62% | $9,238,000 | $ 762,000 |
| 10.24% | $8,976,000 | $1,024,000 |
| 8.58% | $9,142,000 | $ 858,000 |

1. Work out the hedge in May (that is, do you buy or sell 10 futures contracts?).

2. Given that in November, the cash CD rate is 10.24 percent, the cash T-bill rate is 8.09 percent, and the December T-bill futures rate is 8.58 percent, what is the effective (net) cost of the CDs issued in November? What kind of risk did you retain when you entered the future contract in May?

The summary data are given in Table 24.1. The *cash market* refers to the market in which an asset can be purchased immediately (*on the spot*). The *futures market* refers to an off-balance sheet agreement to buy/sell an asset at some future date.

In May, the risk is that interest rates will have gone up by next November, the time at which the financing of the loan with CDs will take place. To hedge the risk, you would therefore sell 10 financial futures contracts. If interest rates have gone up by next November (which is in fact the case, with the CD rate moving up to 10.24 percent), the increase in the cost of funds will be reduced by the profit on the financial futures.

**TABLE  24.1**

Hedging with Futures: An Example

| Cash Market | Futures Market |
|---|---|
| **May** | **May** |
| Anticipate issuing $10,000,000 of CDs next November | Sell (short) 10 December T-bill futures at 7.62% |
| The cash CD rate is 7.84% (discount basis) | |
| The cash T-bill rate is 6.95% | T-bill price = $9,238,000 |
| The CD/T-bill spread is 89 basis points | (Discount = $762,000) |
| **November** | **November** |
| Issue $10,000,000 of CDs. The cash CD rate is 10.24% | Close December T-bill futures position at 8.58% |
| The cash T-bill rate is 8.09% | T-bill future = $9,142,000 |
| The CD/T-bill spread is 215 basis points | (Discount = $858,000) |
| CD price = $8,976,000 | |

$$\text{Net cost} = \text{November CD cost} - \text{profit on futures}$$
$$= 1,024,000 - (9,238,000 - 9,142,000)$$
$$= 928,000$$

The profit on the futures can also be written as the difference between the two discounts, instead of the difference between the two prices:

$$\text{Net cost} = 1,024,000 - (858,000 - 762,000) = 928,000$$

To understand the source of the residual risk in the hedge, the net cost can be rewritten as follows:

$$\text{Net cost}_{November} = 762,000 - (858,000 - 1,024,000)$$
$$= \text{future discount}_{May} - (\text{future discount}_{November} - \text{cash discount}_{November})$$

The residual risk arising from the hedge must be evaluated using what is known in May. The November cost of funds has two parts. The first one, the price of the futures in May, is known at the time the contract is signed. However, the second part, the difference between the futures discount in November and the cash discount in November, is not known for sure in May, when the hedge is built. The reason is that in November, the cost of funding the CDs is not identical to the discount on a December T-bill future. The instruments are different (CD vs. Treasury bill), and the maturity dates are different (November vs. December). The second term therefore creates some uncertainty in the hedge. This is known as *basis risk*, a random difference between two interest rates at a certain point in time.

It should be noted that most futures contracts are closed before the delivery date. That is, investors are not really interested in buying or selling the underlying asset. They want to benefit from a price increase or decrease for hedging or speculative reasons.

Forwards and futures are off-balance sheet positions. Chapters 18 and 19 introduced repricing gaps and economic value at risk applied to on-balance sheet positions. It would be convenient to have a measure of interest-rate risk that integrates both on- and off-balance sheet items. The next section shows how to integrate futures and forwards into the repricing gap and economic value at risk. The discussion simply uses replicating on-balance sheet portfolios.

## FORWARDS, FUTURES, AND REPRICING GAPS

Consider the forward contract example. Alpha Bank agrees today to buy a three-month Treasury bill from Gamma Bank with delivery next December at a price of $90 fixed today.

| Today | December | March |
|---|---|---|
| Contract is signed | Delivery date (buy) | Maturity of underlying bond |

In December, Alpha Bank makes a profit (loss) if the price of the Treasury bill goes up (down). As this is a three-month-to-maturity instrument, its price (the present value of future March cash flows) will increase if the three-month rate from December to March goes down. To summarize the position: buying a future with delivery next December is to take the view that the three-month rate will fall between December and March. In the repricing gap, the financial future is replaced by a replicating portfolio of on-balance sheet positions. That is, an asset with a specific fixed-rate maturity (from today until March) is created, funded by a fixed-rate funding from today until December

| Today | December | March |
|---|---|---|
| Asset: | | |
| Deposit: | | |

Next December, if the financing of the March asset has to be rolled over until March, there will be a profit if the interest rate goes down in December. From an interest-rate position perspective, the replicating portfolio is identical to the futures contract. A reverse position (a December asset funded by a March debt) would be equivalent to the sell side position. To monitor the total interest-rate risk resulting from on- and off-balance sheet positions, forwards and financial futures are converted into equivalent on-balance sheet positions.

## FORWARDS, FUTURES, AND ECONOMIC VALUE AT RISK

Chapter 19 introduced the concept of economic value at risk, defined as

$$\text{Economic value} = \text{value of assets} - \text{value of debt} = A - D$$

Applying the adjusted duration formula to assets and debt gives $\text{Du}_A$ and $\text{Du}_D$, denoting the adjusted duration of assets and deposits:

$$\frac{\Delta \text{ Economic value}}{\text{Economic value}} = -\frac{A}{EV} \times (\text{Du}_A - \frac{D}{A} \times \text{Du}_D) \times \Delta R$$

Futures can now be introduced. Futures are marked to market, and the profit from the futures is related to the change in the value of the underlying instrument.

Given that FF = position in financial futures, a positive figure indicates a "buy" long position, while a negative figure indicates a "sell" short position.

$\text{Du}_{FF}$ = adjusted duration[7] of financial futures (underlying asset)
Profit on futures = $\Delta$ value of financial futures = $-\text{FF} \times \text{Du}_{FF} \times \Delta R$

Adding the last relation to the first gives

$$\frac{\Delta \text{ Economic value}}{\text{Economic value}} = -\frac{A}{EV} \times (\text{Du}_A - \frac{D}{A} \times \text{Du}_D + \frac{FF}{A} \times \text{Du}_{FF}) \times \Delta R$$

The percentage change in the value of the bank's equity is the product of three terms: leverage, the futures-adjusted duration gap, and the volatility of interest rates.

### Numerical Example

Consider total assets of $1,000,000 funded with $950,000 of debt and $50,000 of equity. The adjusted duration of the assets is 2.87 years, and the adjusted duration of the debt is 1 year. The principal per futures contract is $10,000, with an adjusted duration of 2 years. Compute the number of futures contracts needed to hedge the economic value of the bank for a parallel shift in interest rates of 1 percent.

$$\frac{\Delta \, EV}{EV} = -\frac{1,000,000}{50,000} \times \left[ (2.87 - \frac{950,000}{1,000,000} \times 1) + (N \times \frac{10,000}{1,000,000} \times 2) \right]$$
$$\times \, 0.01 = 0$$

$$N = -96 \text{ (that is, a selling position of 96 futures contracts)}$$

## SWAPS

An interest-rate swap is an exchange of interest payments between two parties on the over-the-counter market. For instance, in a plain vanilla swap, one party, Alpha Bank, promises to make a fixed interest payment each year to the other party, Gamma Bank, and will receive from Gamma a short-term LIBOR interest rate. Interest payments are computed on the basis of a notional principal that is not exchanged. See Figure 24.2

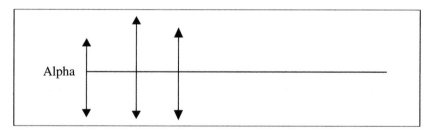

**Figure 24.2** Swaps (pay fixed, receive floating)

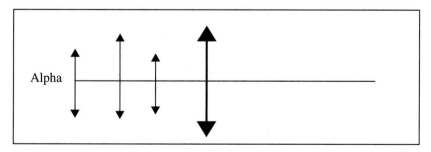

**Figure 24.3** Swaps (pay fixed, receive floating)

The position of Alpha Bank can be visualized graphically on the time line, as shown in Figure 24.3.

From the perspective of Alpha Bank, the fixed arrows represent the fixed cash outflows (interest payments), while the variable arrows represent the variable cash inflows (interest receipts). One way to understand the economics of the swaps is to add to the graph an exchange of principal at maturity (which will not take place, as the positive and negative amounts would cancel out).

It can be seen that one leg of the swap is equivalent to a fixed-rate debt, while the other leg is equivalent to holding a short-term LIBOR asset. As was done with the futures, it is possible to use this replicating on-balance sheet portfolio (a floating-rate asset funded by a fixed-rate debt) to compute a repricing gap or an economic value at risk.

As was the case with forward contracts, the risk related to the default of a counterparty on a swap is a form of replacement risk. Indeed, if the party is unable to meet its obligations some time into the future, it is possible to enter into a new swap at that time, but at the terms prevailing on the market at that time.

## OPTIONS

As the financial futures payoff graph indicates, the downside risk of buying or selling a financial future can be large if you take the wrong position. A major advantage of options is that they keep the profit potential while limiting the downside risk.

A *call* option is a right to buy an asset (stock, bond, currency, or commodity) at a price that is fixed today (the exercise or strike price), with delivery at a date in the future.

A *put* option is a right to sell an asset at a price that is fixed today, with delivery at a date in the future.

The difference between a financial future and an option is represented by one word: the future is an *agreement* to buy or sell, while the option is a *right*. As it is a right, it will be exercised only if it brings a gain to the holder of the option. Options payoffs are often compared to a hockey stick.

### Call Option

A call option is a right to buy a financial asset (stock, bond, or currency) at a price that is fixed today (the exercise or strike price), with delivery at a date in the future (see Figure 24.4).

On the right-hand side of the exercise price of $90, the price goes up and the call option is exercised. The gross profit (before premium

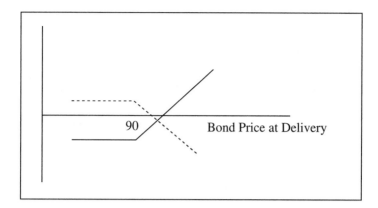

**Figure 24.4** Call option.

expense) is the difference between the market price and the strike price.
On the left side, the price falls below $90 and the option is not exercised.
There is a loss equal to the premium paid to buy the option

Note that for the party selling (writing) the option (dashed line), the
payoffs are completely different—they are the mirror image of those of the
holder of the call. The writer of the call keeps the premium if the option
is not exercised. If the option is exercised, the writer could end up with
heavy losses. The business of writing options is often compared to that of
underwriting insurance. In that business, you collect an insurance premium up front, and you keep it if there is no casualty. However, if there is
a casualty, the insurance liability could be very large.

### Put Option

A put option is a right to sell a financial asset at a price that is fixed today
with delivery in the future (see Figure 24.5).

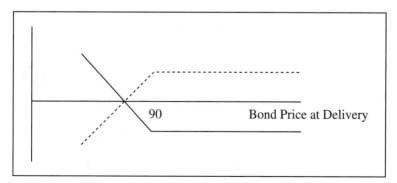

**Figure 24.5** Put option.

On the left side of the exercise price of $90, the price goes down, and the put option is exercised. On the right side on the graph, the price increases to over $90 and the option is not exercised. In that case, the only loss will be the premium paid to buy the option.

Again, for the party selling (writing) the put option, the payoffs are just the opposite. If the price goes above $90, the writer keeps the premium, but if the price goes down, it can be exposed to heavy losses.

### VOLATILITY: A NEW SOURCE OF VALUE AT RISK

The premium (price) paid for an option depends on how likely it is that the price of the bond at the delivery date will exceed the exercise price, and by how much. The well-known option-pricing formula devised by Professors Black and Scholes has been discussed in specialized textbooks.[8] Intuitively, the value of the option will include the exercise price, the current price of the bond, and the bond's volatility (the standard deviation of the probability distribution of the underlying bond). Indeed, if the volatility is large, there is a greater chance of large price movements and large profits.[9]

Banks that hold or write options are facing a new type of risk: the value of their option portfolio can change when

- Prices of bonds change
- The volatility of bond prices changes

To manage option risk, specialists in option portfolios simulate changes in option value for both a change in the price of the underlying bond and a change in the volatility. Simulation is the best way to measure option risk. Including options in a repricing bucket is not recommended because, unlike holding an asset, a future, or a swap, the fact that the option is a *right* creates an asymmetry. For example, the holder of a call option will report a profit when interest rates go down (bond prices go up), but will report nothing when interest rates go up (bond prices go down). Similarly, applying the duration framework is not advised because of the nonlinearity of option values. Selected option portfolio strategies are presented in Table 24.2.

### COUNTERPARTY RISK, CHERRY-PICKING, AND NETTING

As discussed previously, over-the-counter transactions between two financial institutions create counterparty risk. A party that is in financial distress can default on its obligations.[10] A standard measure of counterparty

**TABLE 24.2**

## Option Strategies

| Payoffs | Name | Market Bias | Profit Potential | Loss Potential | Recipe |
|---|---|---|---|---|---|
| | Long call | Bull | Open | Limited | Buy call |
| | Short call | Bear | Limited | Open | Sell call |
| | Long put | Bear | Open | Limited | Buy put |
| | Short strangle | Bull | Limited | Open | Sell put |
| | Bull spread | Bull | Limited | Limited | Buy call at the money Sell call out of the money |
| | Bear spread | Bear | Limited | Limited | Buy put at the money Sell put out of the money |
| | Long butterfly | Mixed (low volatility) | Limited | Limited | Sell call and put at the money Buy call and put out of the money |
| | Short butterfly | Mixed (high volatility) | Limited | Limited | Buy call and put at the money Sell call and put out of the money |
| | Long condor | Mixed (high volatility) | Limited | Limited | Sell call and put slightly out of the money Buy call and put further out of the money |
| | Short condor | Mixed (low volatility) | Limited | Limited | Buy call and put slightly out of the money Sell call and put further out of the money |

*Continued*

| Payoffs | Name | Market Bias | Profit Potential | Loss Potential | Recipe |
|---|---|---|---|---|---|
|  | Long straddle | Mixed (high volatility) | Open | Limited | Buy call and put at the money |
|  | Short straddle | Mixed (low volatility) | Limited | Open | Sell call and put at the money |
|  | Long strangle | Mixed (high volatility) | Open | Limited | Buy call and put out of the money |
|  | Short strangle | Mixed (low volatility) | Limited | Open | Sell call and put out of the money |
|  | Call ratio spread | Mixed (low volatility— bias for rate increase) | Limited | Open on one side | Sell call and put at the money Buy put out of the money |
|  | Put ratio spread | Mixed (low volatility— bias for rate decrease) | Limited | Open on one side | Sell call and put at the money Buy put out of the money |
|  | Call ratio backspread | Mixed (low volatility— bias for rate drop) | Open on one side | Limited | Buy call and put at the money Sell put out of the money |
|  | Put ratio backspread | Mixed (high volatility— bias for rate increase) | Open on one side | Limited | Buy call and put at the money Sell call out of the money |
|  | Box or conversion | Neutral | Absolute (arbitrage) | Absolute (arbitrage) | For example, long a bull spread and long a bear spread |

risk on a financial institution is the spreads on credit default swaps (CDSs)[11] or the LIBOR-OIS spread. An OIS (overnight interbank swap) is a swap in which two parties exchange a fixed LIBOR rate of a specific maturity and the short-term overnight interbank rate. As no principal is

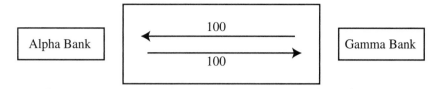

**Figure 24.6** Two transactions between Alpha Bank and Gamma Bank.

exchanged, the fixed-rate leg of the swap essentially reflects the expected forward interbank rates.[12] In contrast, the interbank LIBOR rate with a maturity identical to that of the OIS includes not only the expected future rates, but also a credit spread to incorporate the risk of the borrower's defaulting on the principal. The difference between LIBOR and the long-term leg of the OIS is thus indicative of counterparty risk. During the U.S. subprime crisis in October 2008, this spread increased from 8 basis points observed before the crisis to 286 basis points for a three-month dollar LIBOR.

In the context of bankruptcy proceedings, banks have discovered a new type of risk: *cherry-picking risk*. Consider the example of two transactions between Alpha Bank and Gamma Bank shown in Figure 24.6. They could refer to on- or off-balance sheet transactions.

In the first transaction, Alpha Bank owes $100 to Gamma Bank. On the same date, in a separate transaction, Gamma Bank owes $100 to Alpha Bank. If Gamma goes into bankruptcy, the solicitors in charge of the bankrupt Gamma Bank will default on their obligation of $100, but since Alpha Bank is performing well, it will ask for the full payment of $100. There is an asymmetry: one bank defaults on its obligation, while the other one has to perform. Thus, banks have searched for ways to reduce the counterparty risk. These include netting arrangements, collateral, creation of AAA-rated subsidiaries, and payment-vs.-payment facilities.

## Netting Arrangements

In bilateral netting, the two original contracts are replaced by a single net contract (netting by *novation*). As writing new legal contracts is costly, banks use a *closeout netting* clause. This states that the contracts will be netted only if some conditions are met (such as a downgrade, a fall in capital ratio, or a situation of financial distress). The idea is that netting will take place before bankruptcy. In the previous example, the two transactions are netted to a position of zero. As netting arrangements have sometimes been challenged in bankruptcy courts, various countries have had to adapt their bankruptcy laws to recognize explicitly the validity of closeout netting. Multilateral netting (Ledrut and Upper, 2007) involves the simultaneous netting of transactions across several institutions.

### Collateral

A reduction in counterparty risk has been achieved by mimicking the functioning of futures markets. The positions are marked to market every day, and cash collateral has to be posted by the party having a loss.[13]

### AAA-Rated Subsidiaries

A third way to reduce counterparty risk is to deal exclusively with highly rated counterparties. Some banks have created AAA-rated (well-capitalized) subsidiaries to deal with their derivatives business (DPC = derivative product companies).

### Payment vs. Payment

Another type of risk, settlement risk or Herstatt risk, refers to the fact that the two legs of a transaction (delivery of a security and the receipt of payment) do not always happen simultaneously. There is counterparty risk if a security has been delivered but payment is received later.[14] The German state-owned development bank KfW was called "Germany's dumbest bank" by the leading newspaper *Bild* after it transferred €300 million for currency swaps to Lehman Brothers Holdings on September 15, 2008, the same day that the U.S. securities firm filed for bankruptcy. The largest banks in the world in the foreign currency market have created a *payment-vs.-payment CLS Bank* to ensure that the two legs of a transaction take place at the same time (Lindley, 2008).

## ACCOUNTING FOR DERIVATIVES

Accounting for derivatives is discussed in the appendix to Chapter 18. Here is a summary.

The general principle of the U.S. SFAS 133 and IAS 33 is that derivatives have to be marked to market, with changes in their value being recorded in the income statement. Exceptions to this rule involve "hedge accounting." The issue is as follows: if an on-balance sheet asset or liability is hedged economically (meaning that a change in the value of the asset is offset by an opposite change in the value of the derivative), it would appear reasonable that the net profit in the income statement should not be affected by the change in the value of the derivative. Indeed, successful hedging should minimize the volatility of income. However, since some assets and liabilities are valued at historical cost on the banking book, and since, according to the general rule, derivatives are marked to market, a situation could arise in which a loss of value of a derivative reduces profit, while a capital gain on a fixed-income loan is not reported because of the use of historical accounting for the banking book. In this case, there would be accounting income volatility, although, on a value basis, the bank is fully hedged. To prevent this, specific rules have been designed for hedge accounting:

1. *"Fair value hedge."* The changes in value of both the asset and the derivative go through the income statement. With reference to the previous case, a hedged instrument would create zero volatility in reported profit.
2. *"Cash flow hedge"* (for example, a fixed-rate loan). Divide the results of the hedge into "ineffective" and "effective" parts. The reason for the existence of an ineffective part is that the instrument used for hedging does not match the characteristics of the hedged asset perfectly. The ineffective part goes to the income statement, while the effective part goes to a special account in equity. Profit or loss is recognized on the income statement when the cash flow of the asset affects the income statement.

The European Union has accepted most of IAS 39. A main exception is the hedging of core (demand and savings) deposits. Several countries, such as France, allow banks not to report the change in the value of derivatives in their equity.

## CONCLUSION

The main types of derivatives contracts have been introduced in this chapter: forwards, financial futures, swaps, and options. The chapter has paid attention not only to payoffs, but also to the counterparty risk characteristics of these widely used instruments. Hedging and pricing involve the search for an on-balance sheet replicating portfolio.

## EXERCISE FOR CHAPTER 24

A company is entering into contracts with gas stations to deliver (supply) a fixed amount of oil at a price that is fixed today, with delivery in five years' time. To hedge the risk of an oil price increase, the company is using the oil futures market. More precisely, the company is using what is known as a "stack and roll" hedge, whereby the company is selling short-term futures and, when these mature, renewing (rolling) them into the future.

Identify the various risks that are linked to this hedging strategy.

## Notes

1. For example, Hull (2000) and Rebonato (1996).
2. Many countries have forbidden short selling for years. They did not want to facilitate strategies that involved taking bets on a market's going down. In an exceptional move in September 2008, several countries (including the United States, the United Kingdom, France, and Belgium) prohibited the short selling of stocks of financial institutions because of a fear that falling prices were contributing to the loss of confidence in banks.
3. In an efficient market, the price today of a Treasury bill priced at $90 next December must be the discounted value of $90. This ensures that if I buy and sell the Treasury bill today and invest in a risk-free asset, I can secure a cash flow of $90 next December.
4. Replacement risk was introduced in Chapter 12. Replacement risk is used to measure the Basel I *add-on* for counterparty risk on derivative transactions.
5. Liquidity risk is discussed in Chapter 21.
6. Discount basis quotations are often used for short-maturity assets (such as Treasury bills). A discount of 7.8 percent implies, by definition, that you borrow $92.2 and promise reimbursement of $100 (7.8 = 100 − 92.2).
7. As discussed in Chapter 19, the adjusted duration allows yield curves that are not flat to be taken into account. For a flat yield curve, it is equal to the McAulay duration divided by the interest factor $(1 + R)$.
8. The management of interest-rate options is beyond the scope of this chapter. Useful references include Jarrow (1996) and Rebonato (1996).
9. Unlike the holders of forwards, futures, or swaps, the holder of an option need not worry about large losses, because the fact that an option is a right allows the holder not to exercise it. Note that this reasoning does not apply to the seller of the option, who must honor the request of the holder of the option.
10. During the subprime crisis in 2008 (discussed in Chapter 16), it was the fear of large counterparty losses that led the U.S. government to

      bail out the insurance group AIG and to facilitate the sale of Bear Stearns to JPMorgan Chase.

11. Credit default swaps (CDS) are introduced in Chapter 25.

12. As discussed in the section on forward contracts, pricing will also include a spread for *replacement risk*, as, in case of default, it would be necessary to replace the contract at the going market rates.

13. As an example, many of the swaps sold by the investment bank Lehman Brothers were collateralized. Because of Lehman's default, counterparties were still exposed to the shortfall between the collateral and the cost of replicating the swaps at a time when many banks were bidding up swaps prices.

14. *International Herald Tribune*, September 18, 2008. Note that the KfW story is a case of settlement risk if the second leg of the swaps transaction (the transfer from Lehman Brothers to KfW) had not been completed. This is implicit in the article, but not confirmed explicitly.

# CHAPTER 25

# Credit Derivatives

Credit derivatives are among the most recent and successful financial innovations in the banking industry. By allowing banks to sell or buy the credit risk on a loan or a portfolio of loans, they separate the funding of loans from the holding of credit risk.

Credit derivatives are a form of credit insurance. Consider the case of Alpha Bank, which has funded a loan to corporate client ABC. Alpha Bank is willing to fund the loan and keep it on its balance sheet, but it does not want to face the credit risk, that is, the losses that could result from a default by its corporate client. So, Alpha Bank will search for a counter-party—this could be another bank, an insurance company, or an investment fund—that is willing to assume the credit risk. Credit derivatives facilitate the transfer of credit risk from one party to another party.

Here is the (simplified) balance sheet of Alpha Bank.

### Alpha Bank Balance Sheet

| Loan to corporate client ABC | Deposits |
| --- | --- |
| | Equity |

Three types of credit derivatives instruments will be discussed in this chapter: credit default swaps (CDS), total rate of return swaps (TRORS), and credit-linked notes (CLN). Each type of contract attempts to mitigate some of the weaknesses of other contracts.

## CREDIT DEFAULT SWAPS

Here is the structure of the transaction between Alpha Bank and Gamma Bank. Alpha Bank, which has the initial credit exposure to corporate client ABC, is called the *protection buyer*. Gamma Bank, which is willing to assume the credit risk, is called the *protection seller*. Corporate client ABC, which has borrowed from Alpha, is called the *obligor*.[1] The structure of the CDS is presented in Figure 25.1.

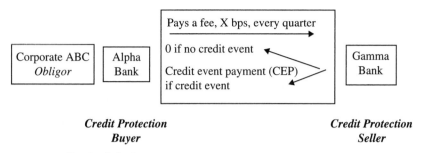

Figure 25.1 Credit default swaps.

In a credit default swap (CDS), the protection buyer, Alpha Bank, agrees to pay a credit insurance fee or spread of $x$ basis points[2] to the protection seller, Gamma Bank, every quarter. If there is no default (no credit event), meaning that the obligor, corporate client ABC, is able to make the interest or principal payment due on the loan, Gamma Bank pays nothing ($0) to Alpha Bank. However, if corporate client ABC defaults (credit event), Gamma Bank agrees to pay a certain amount, the *credit event payment*, to Alpha Bank. It can be seen that a credit default swap is a form of credit insurance. One bank pays an insurance premium to cover the losses arising out of a possible default. As these contracts are traded over the counter (OTC)—that is, directly with a counterparty—the terms can be negotiated freely. The contract terms need to specify

- *The credit event.* The credit event, such as the default of the obligor, a downgrading below a certain grade, or the missing of any contractual payment, such as of interest or principal, is predefined.
- *Credit event payment (CEP).* This is the exchange of the distressed asset for cash or payment of some percentage of the principal value.

However, insurance companies do not always wish to meet their obligations when you call on them. It is therefore important that you define precisely what triggers a credit event and what the credit event payment will be. To ensure some homogeneity of contracts, the derivatives industry professional association, ISDA,[3] has standardized the terms of credit derivative contracts.

In the example just given, the protection buyer was lending money to the obligor, corporate client ABC. But equally, Alpha Bank could have been holding a bond issued by obligor ABC. It could even be that the protection buyer, Alpha Bank, is neither lending to ABC nor holding a bond. It simply wants to trade the insurance premium against a possible credit event payment.

Credit default swaps are the most frequent type of credit derivative contract. They help to insure against the risk of default, or, from the perspective of the protection seller, they enable the taking on of credit risk. In the example just given, Gamma Bank is said to be providing the credit insurance. But, increasingly, insurance companies, pension funds, or investment funds are playing that role.

## Pricing CDS

There are two ways to price CDS. One is to compute the explicit risk-neutral probabilities of default[4] and loss given default to estimate the value of the insurance. The investor receives periodic spread payments (the "fee" leg) and makes contingent payments when default occurs (the "contingent" leg). The value of the CDS is the difference between the expected value of the fee leg and the expected present value of the contingent leg. The second is to price by arbitrage. Indeed, except for counterparty risk arising from a possible default of the protection seller, holding both a risky ABC bond and a CDS is fairly similar to holding a risk-free asset (Duffie, 1999).

Return on risky debt − CDS spread − expected loss due to default of protection seller = return on risk-free asset

During the 2007 subprime credit crisis and the uncertainty surrounding the solvency of financial institutions, LIBOR, the return on bank deposits, was sometimes larger than the risk-free rate + the CDS spread. This difference can be interpreted as either the existence of imperfect arbitrage or the counterparty risk assigned to the protection seller.

In a credit default swap, Alpha Bank is still exposed to two types of risk: market risk and counterparty risk. Market risk refers to the fact that even if there is no default, the value of the loan or bond could change— for instance, because of a downgrade or a change in interest rates. Counterparty risk refers to the fact that the protection seller, Gamma Bank, might not be able to meet its insurance obligations if it is itself in default. The next two types of credit derivative contracts, total rate of return swaps and credit-linked notes, attempt to mitigate those risks.

## TOTAL RATE OF RETURN SWAPS

The structure of a total rate of return swap (TRORS) (Figure 25.2) is very similar to that of a credit default swap. The difference involves the

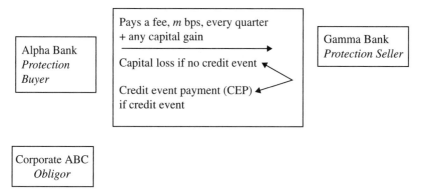

**Figure 25.2** Total rate of return swaps.

exchange of payments between the protection buyer and the protection seller. The protection buyer will pay a fee of $m$ basis points every quarter, plus any positive appreciation in the value of the underlying loans or bonds. Thus, any capital gain is passed to the protection seller. In return, the protection seller not only covers the risk of default, but also compensates the protection buyer for any reduction in the value of the asset (capital loss), even when there is no default. A TRORS therefore provides protection not only against default risk, but also against any change in the value of the underlying loan or bond.

While a TRORS allows Alpha Bank to insure against both default risk and market risk, or the change in value of the underlying assets, the bank is still exposed to counterparty risk, that is, the risk that the protection seller, Gamma Bank, is not able to meet its obligations. The third type of contract, credit-linked notes (CLN), attempts to mitigate that risk.

## CREDIT-LINKED NOTES

In the first two types of contracts, credit default swaps and total rate of return swaps, the protection buyer is exposed to the risk that its counterparty, the protection seller, will be unable to meet its insurance obligations. Is it really possible to mitigate that risk? Through the wonders of financial engineering, it is. Figure 25.3 provides an analysis of credit-linked notes (CLNs).

In the first step, a *protection buyer*, Alpha Bank, borrows from Gamma Bank, issuing a note (a bond). Alpha receives the capital/principal on this issue. In the second step, Alpha Bank pays the interest on the note to Gamma Bank, the *protection seller*. The credit risk insurance is provided through the terms of the repayment of the principal of the note.

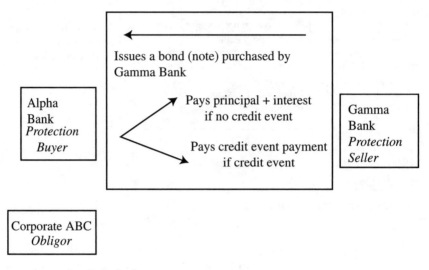

**Figure 25.3** Credit-linked notes.

If corporate client ABC does not default (there is no credit event), Alpha Bank repays the full principal, as it would do in the event of normal borrowing. But if there is a credit event (a default by ABC), the protection buyer, Alpha Bank, repays a smaller amount to the protection seller. This is a clever deal. Indeed, notice that if the protection seller, Gamma Bank, defaults, the credit-linked note is still performing, meaning that Alpha Bank will have to meet the original payment terms of the contract to the solicitors managing the defaulted Gamma Bank. This is magic! The counterparty risk from the protection seller has disappeared. However, as is often the case in financial markets, mitigation of one type of risk creates a new one. Indeed, now the protection *seller*, Gamma Bank, has to worry that the protection *buyer*, Alpha Bank, may default and be unable to repay the credit-linked note! One type of counterparty risk, the risk of default of the protection seller, has been replaced by another type of counterparty risk, the risk of default of the protection buyer.

### SYNTHETIC SECURITIZATION

As discussed in Chapter 16, banks sometimes want to sell loans to reduce their credit risk or to free capital. An alternative to asset sale and securitization is *synthetic securitization* (see Figure 25.4). The bank keeps the loan on its balance sheet, but eliminates (transfers) the credit risk through a credit default swap, for example, with a hedge fund.

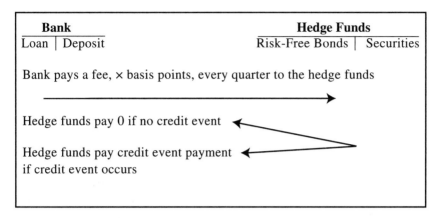

**Figure 25.4** Synthetic securitization.

Investors in hedge funds receive a risk-free rate augmented by the CDS fees if there is no credit event. If there is a credit event, they receive the risk-free rate reduced by the credit event payment.

## SINGLE-NAME CREDIT DEFAULT SWAPS VS. CDS INDEXES VS. BENCHMARK CDS INDEXES VS. CDS INDEX TRANCHES

So far, the discussion has covered the credit risk arising from one single exposure to corporate client ABC. This was a case of a *single-name credit default swap*. However, banks might wish to buy credit risk insurance on a portfolio of corporate clients. This is called a *CDS index* or *basket CDS*, meaning that the credit insurance covers several corporate clients that are included in the index. Moreover, to increase the liquidity of the market, some *benchmark CDS indexes* have been created. Well-known benchmarks include DJ CDX for North America and emerging markets, and DJ iTraxx for Europe and Asia. Standardization applies to both the composition of the reference pool and the structure ("width") of the tranches (Amato and Gyntelberg, 2005). For example, a well-known CDS index in the United States is the five-year Dow Jones North American Investment Grade (CD.NA.IG) index, which includes a reference portfolio of 125 companies. The attachment points to the tranches are 0–3 percent, 3–7 percent, 7–10 percent, 10–15 percent, and 15–30 percent. Similarly, the five-year Dow Jones iTraxx EUR includes a reference portfolio of 125 investment-grade European companies. The attachment points to the tranches are 0–3 percent, 3–6 percent, 6–9 percent, 9–12 percent, and 12–22 percent (Hull and White, 2004). The ABX index represents a basket of credit default swaps on high-risk mortgages.[5]

CDS index tranches allow investors to take a position on specific segments of the CDS index default loss distribution.

## *N*TH-TO-DEFAULT CDS

This is a credit derivative in which the protection seller provides protection on the first, second, third, or *n*th default in a basket of names. The buyer of the protection pays a specified rate (the CDS spread) on a specified notional principal amount either until the *n*th default occurs among a specified set of reference firms or until the end of the contract's life. If the *n*th default occurs before the contract maturity, the buyer of the protection can present the bonds issued by the defaulted entity to the seller of the protection in exchange for the face value of the bonds. Alternatively, the contract may call for a cash payment equal to the difference between the postdefault bond value and the face value (Hull and White, 2004).

Intuitively, the risk borne by the *n*th default tranche is related to the likelihood of there being that many (*n*) loans defaulting at the same time or, to put it in other words, to the correlation across default. Nth-to-default credit derivatives are traded on financial markets to take a view on credit correlation.

## INSIDE THE VALUATION OF CDS TRANCHES AND CDOS: IMPACT OF PROBABILITY OF DEFAULT AND DEFAULT CORRELATION

Whether what is being evaluated is the value of a specific tranche of a CDO (equity, mezzanine, or senior tranche; see Chapter 16 on securitization) or the value of a particular tranche of a CDS index, the net present value of expected cash flows over the maturity of the CDS is computed.[6] As cash flows are related to the eventual default of each of the entities in the basket or index, modeling can be quite demanding. Indeed, it is necessary to model the probability of default at several points in time (default time probability), the recovery in case of default, the market risk or liquidity premium, and the correlation across defaults, which is the risk that many or few assets default at the same time.[7]

### Default Time Probability

The probability of default at a given point in time $t$ ($PD_t$) is defined in relation to the probability of the firm's survival at time $t$, modeled as

$$\text{Probability of survival at time } t = 1 - PD_t = e^{-\lambda t}$$

with $\lambda$ being the default hazard rate or default intensity.

This implies

$$PD_t = 1 - e^{-\lambda t} \quad \text{and} \quad \lambda t = -\ln(1 - PD_t)$$

From the price of a single-name CDS or the spread on corporate bonds, it is possible to estimate the one-year PD, and therefore estimate $\lambda$.

### Recovery Rate

Relying on rating agencies' tables on recoveries on investment-grade debt at the time of financial distress, a fixed recovery rate of 40 percent is often assumed.

### Risk and Liquidity Premium

To avoid the problem of risk premium, a standard methodology is used in option pricing, which is to rely on the use of risk-neutral probabilities of default (RNPD; see Chapter 15). Given observed pricing or spreads, these are the probabilities of default that would prevail in a risk-neutral world. It has been shown that consistent use of risk-neutral probabilities of default allows the pricing of derivative instruments.

## JOINT DEFAULT TIME OR CORRELATION ACROSS DEFAULTS

The standard approach used in the marketplace to model the joint probability of default is the so-called one-factor Gaussian copula (Amato and Gyntelberg, 2005).[8] It assumes identical constant pairwise default time correlations across all firms, normally distributed default times, and a normal joint default probability distribution. These simplifying assumptions make the one-factor Gaussian copula relatively easy to use to calculate variations in values. It is the equivalent of the Black-Scholes option-pricing model. This is also the model used by Vasicek (2002) to model the value of a loan portfolio.

The Vasicek model was discussed in Chapter 22 on credit risk diversification. It is repeated here to facilitate the discussion.

Assume that the assets $A_i, 0$ of a firm are funded with debt with promised reimbursement at the end of the year $Bi$ and with equity. The value of the assets at time $t$, $A_{i,t}$ follows a lognormal distribution:

$$A_{i,T} = A_{i,0} \times e^{\mu_i T - 0.5 \sigma^2 T + \sigma_i \sqrt{T} X_i}$$

The exponent of the exponential function is the instantaneous return on the asset. It incorporates two components: an expected return and the impact of a shock:

$$\text{Instantaneous return} = (\mu_i T - 0.5\,\sigma^2 T) + (\sigma_i\,\sqrt{T}\,X_i)$$

where $\mu_i$ = expected instantaneous annual return on the asset
$\quad\sigma^2$ = variance of annual return
$\quad T$ = number of years from today
$\quad X_i$ = a standardized normal variable

The factor $X_i$ represents the business risk for firm $i$.
Next, assume that

$$X_i = \sqrt{\rho}\,F + \sqrt{(1-\rho)}\,\varepsilon_i.$$

where $F$ is a standardized normal risk factor common to all firms, and $e_i$ is a standardized normal shock specific to Firm $i$. It can then be shown that the variance of $X_i = 1$, and that $\rho$ is the correlation across pairwise asset returns. This model is known as the asymptotic single risk factor (ASRF) model.

As discussed in Chapter 22 on credit risk diversification, it is possible to compute the probability of default conditional on a value of the risk factor $F$:

$$\text{Probability of default} = N\left[\frac{\text{IN}(P_D) - F\sqrt{\rho}}{\sqrt{(1-\rho)}}\right]$$

This is the probability of default conditional on the common risk factor $F$. Relying on the law of large numbers, Vasicek (2002) shows that the unconditional cumulative distribution function of loan losses on a very large loan portfolio is in the limit

$$P(L < \times\,;\rho\,;PD) = N\left[\frac{\sqrt{1-\rho}\,\text{IN}(x) - N(PD)}{\sqrt{\rho}}\right]$$

The probability distribution is highly skewed and leptokurtic, as shown in Figure 25.5.

From the perspective of the investors in the equity tranche, it helps, ceteris paribus, if the cumulative probability of low losses increases (so that holders of the equity tranche make money). In contrast, the holders of the senior tranche suffer if the probability of large losses increases (as they start to share in the losses). It is possible to show that an increase in correlation increases the value of the equity tranche while decreasing the value of the senior tranche (Gibson, 2004). The intuitive explanation is as follows: an increase in correlation implies that if there is a default on one

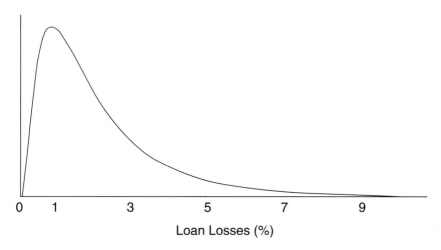

**Figure 25.5** Loan loss distribution (PD = 2%, correlation = 0.1).

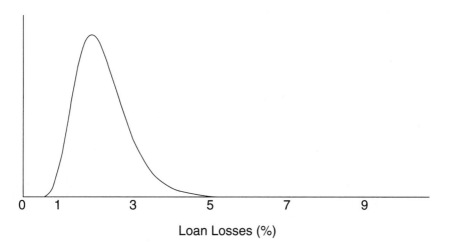

**Figure 25.6** Loan loss distribution (PD = 2%, correlation = 0.02).

loan, there are likely to be many others defaulting, a situation that is referred to as default clustering (bad for the senior tranche). An increase in correlation also means that if one loan does not default, there is a large probability that many others will not default (good for the equity tranche).

Figure 25.6 shows the distribution of loan losses for a lower correlation of 0.02. It is apparent that the probability of large losses is substantially reduced.

The limit distribution can be used to illustrate the impact of a change of correlation.

The loan-loss limit distribution is easily evaluated with a PC spread-sheet. It is used to compute the cumulative probability that applies to an equity tranche (with attachment 0–3 percent), a mezzanine tranche (with 3–6 percent), and a senior tranche (with 6–100 percent).

In Table 25.1, it can be seen that an increase in correlation from 0.3 to 0.5 increases the probability that the senior tranche will suffer from default from 3.06 percent to 4.14 percent.[9]

As a CDS index contains a limited number of names, it is possible to use Monte Carlo simulations (Duffie and Garleanu, 2001, or Fender et al., 2008), numerical approximations, or closed-form solutions (such as those presented in Gibson, 2004, and Hull and White, 2004) to compute the value of a single-tranche CDS index.

The riskiness for a dealer selling a single-tranche CDS—that is, the change in the marked-to-market value of the tranche—is related to the factors affecting the net present value of cash flows. They include changes in the probability of default for all names or for a specific name, changes in risk or liquidity premiums changes in expected recovery rates, changes in correlation, and model risk, as the Gaussian one-factor copula is a simplifi-cation (Belsham et al., 2005; Fender et al., 2008). Delta hedging refers to hedging the value of the single tranche against a small change in the spread of the assets in the reference portfolio. This is hedging a change in the default risk of the underlying asset, as the spread on the asset is related to the probability of default. Convexity or gamma risk refers to the change in value following a large change in the spread on the assets in the reference portfo-lio (Basel Committee, 2005). As the value of a first-to-default credit deriva-tive or the value of senior and equity tranches of CDOs are affected by a change in correlation, they are used by the market to take positions and trade correlations.

**T A B L E   25.1**

Vasicek Limit Cumulative Loan-Loss Distribution for the Area within the Attachment Points (Probability of Default: 1%)

| Correlation | Attachment | | |
| --- | --- | --- | --- |
| | Equity (0–3%) | Mezzanine (3–6%) | Senior (6–100%) |
| 0.3 | 91.53% | 5.41% | 3.06% |
| 0.5 | 92.06% | 3.8% | 4.14% |

## Correlation Smile

From the price of credit derivatives on several tranches, it is possible to back out the implied correlation used by the market, assuming that the single Gaussian risk factor model holds. In this case, the estimate of the implied correlation should be the same for all tranches. In reality, a smile is observed, reminiscent of the volatility smile observed with option pricing. Implied correlations are lower for the mezzanine tranche, and higher for the equity and senior tranches. Correlation and degree of default clustering appear to be higher for these two tranches (Duffie, 2004; Amato and Gyntelberg, 2005).

## CREDIT DERIVATIVES AND RISK MANAGEMENT

Gibson (2007) identifies five sources of risk with credit derivatives:

1. *Credit risk.* Credit derivatives do not eliminate risk, but transfer it to some other parties. The first risk is that a party may not fully understand the credit risk it is holding.
2. *Counterparty risk.* This is the risk that one party in the transaction will default on its obligation.
3. *Model risk.* This refers to a significant difference between the price given by a model and the price of actual transactions in the market.
4. *Rating agency risk.* Given the complexity of the instruments, participants rely on the rating agencies to evaluate the credit risk. However, although credit rating agencies are very transparent about their methodologies, investors may not fully understand the significance of a rating.
5. *Settlement risk.* When an issuer defaults, credit derivatives based on the issuer's debt must be settled. If the volume of derivatives is large relative to the size of the bond issue, a physical settlement can prove difficult.

## CONCLUSION

Financial institutions have devised instruments to transfer credit risk, or credit derivatives. This allows the funding of an asset to be separated from its credit risk. Like the hot potato that children pass from hand to hand, credit risk is transferred across financial institutions. In most of these contracts, the reality of the credit risk transfer depends on the solvency of the seller of credit protection. The U.S. subprime crisis is a reminder of the need to check the solvency of the seller of protection.

## APPENDIX: COPULA FUNCTIONS

Copula, from the Latin word *copula*, refers to connecting or joining together (as in the English word *couple*). A copula is a function that joins together a collection of marginal distributions (the statistical distribution of each random variable taken on its own) to form the multivariate distribution (Sklar, 1959).

Let $X_1, X_2, \ldots, X_n$ be a set of random variables, with joint probability distribution $F(X_1, X_2, \ldots, X_n)$. Define $F_1(X_1), F_2(X_2), \ldots, F_n(X_n)$ as the marginal probability distribution for each variable. Then there exists a copula function $C(.)$ such that

$$F(X_1, X_2, \ldots, X_n) = C[F_1(X_1), F_2(X_2), \ldots, F_n(X_n)]$$

Conversely, for a given joint distribution $F$, there exists a unique copula $C$ satisfying

$$C(u_1, \ldots, u_n) = F[F_1{-}1(u_1), \ldots, F_n{-}1(u_n)]$$

In finance, the normal and student's $t$ copulas are used.

The multivariate normal copula—also referred to as the Gaussian copula—can be defined as $C(u_1, \ldots, u_n, \Sigma) = \Phi_\Sigma[\varphi^{-1}(u_1), \ldots, \varphi^{-1}(u_n)]$, where $\Phi$ is the multivariate normal distribution with variance-covariance matrix $\Sigma$, and $\varphi^{-1}$ is the inverse of the univariate normal distribution (Smithson, 2004).

In the context of credit derivatives, it is the normal Gaussian single risk factor that brings together the marginal risk distributions of risky loans and helps to create a joint distribution of default risk (Hull and White, 2004).

## EXERCISES FOR CHAPTER 25

1. The economy is in a recession. You have private information (known only by you) that it will recover soon. Do you prefer to buy or sell credit protection?

2. Three types of credit derivative instruments have been introduced: credit default swaps, total rate of return swaps, and credit-linked notes. Explain, from a risk dimension perspective, how TRORSs and CLNs differ from CDSs.

3. CDS tranches are written on a large portfolio of loans. Each loan in the portfolio has a PD of 1 percent. The attachment points are as follows: Equity tranche, 0–3 percent; mezzanine tranche, 3–6 percent; and senior tranche, 6–100 percent. The

correlation is 0.1. Using an approximation to the asymptotic single risk factor (ASRF) model, evaluate the probability that cumulative losses will be borne exclusively by the equity tranche, the probability that losses will be borne jointly by the equity and mezzanine tranches, and the probability that the senior tranche will bear some losses. How does the probability of losses for the senior tranche change when the correlation increases to 0.2?

## Notes

1. In this example, Alpha lends money to the obligor ABC. However, a credit derivative can exist in the absence of an original credit exposure.
2. Remember that 1 basis point is equal to 1/100 of 1 percent. For example, 15 basis points is equal to 0.0015.
3. International Swaps and Derivatives Association.
4. The risk-neutral probability of default (RNPD) was discussed in Chapter 15.
5. Fender and Schneider (2008). Markit Group is a provider of credit derivatives indexes (www.markit.com).
6. It is standard to use risk-neutral probabilities of default, as these allow the computation of expected value, bypassing the risk premium adjustment. Risk-neutral probabilities of default were introduced in Chapter 15.
7. Useful references include Gibson (2004), Belsham et al. (2005), Amato and Gyntelberg (2005), and Hull and White (2004).
8. Copula functions are discussed in the appendix to this chapter.
9. It should be noted that the example is used to develop intuition on the impact of correlation. The full impact of correlation on the market value of an index tranche takes into account the expected loss, that is, the contingent payment for various levels of loan losses weighted by their probability.

# CHAPTER 26

# Operational Risk

According to the definition from the Basel Committee, operational risk is the risk of loss resulting from inadequate or failed internal processes, people, and systems or from external events. It includes legal risk, or potential losses resulting from lawsuits. It does not include strategic risk or reputational risk. This chapter first presents the various sources of operational risk, and then it presents the statistical techniques that are used to quantify operational risk. It is an introduction to a topic discussed in actuarial sciences and engineering (McNeil et al., 2005).

## SOURCES OF OPERATIONAL RISK

The Basel Committee uses eight standardized business lines and seven loss types as a general means of classifying operational events (see Table 26.1).

**TABLE 26.1**

Operational Risk: Classification by Business Lines and Types

| Standardized Business Lines | Types of Operational Risk |
|---|---|
| Corporate finance | Internal fraud |
| Trading and sales | External fraud |
| Retail banking | Employment practices and workplace safety |
| Payment and settlement | Clients, products, and business practices |
| Agency services | Damage to physical assets |
| Commercial banking | Business disruption and system failure |
| Asset management | Execution, delivery, and process management |
| Retail brokerage | |

Source: de Fontnouvelle et al., 2006.

Examples include the loss of £860 million by a 28-year-old derivatives trader, Nick Leeson, at the British merchant bank Barings, and the loss of $691 million in 2002 by a rogue foreign currency derivatives trader, John Rusnak, at Allfirst Financial, a U.S. subsidiary of Allied Irish Bank (AIB). In January 2008, the French bank Société Générale (SocGen) announced a loss of €4.9 billion as a result of unauthorized trading by Jérôme Kerviel, trading that had started in 2005 (Société Générale, 2008). A hall of fame of reported operational losses is given in Table 26.2.

Recently, a major effort to measure operational risk in banking is being undertaken. It relies on statistics used in engineering and insurance. As discussed in Chapter 13, the advanced measurement approach (AMA) of Basel II allows banks to calculate the regulatory capital required to cover operational risk based on quantitative models. A model needs to provide information on two variables: the frequency of operational events over a period of time, usually one year, and the severity of each of these losses. Data and intuition show that banks usually face a large number of incidents involving small losses and, fortunately, very few incidents involving

**TABLE 26.2**

### Operational Losses: Hall of Fame

| | |
|---|---|
| January 2008, SocGen | €4.9 billion ($7.2 billion); Jérôme Kerviel, unauthorized trading in equities |
| September 2007, Calyon (Crédit Agricole) | €250 million ($353 million); unauthorized New York trading on credit instruments |
| September 2006, Amaranth Advisor | $6 billion on gas futures; Brian Hunter |
| December 2004, China Aviation Oil | $550 million on oil futures |
| February 2002, Allied Irish Bank | $691 million on currency derivatives; John Rusnak |
| February 1997, National Westminster Bank | £50 million "mispricing errors" on interest-rate derivatives; Kyriacos Papuis |
| September 1996, Sumitomo | $2.6 billion on copper trading; Yasuo Hamanaka |
| August 1996, Deutsche Bank | £230 million on unauthorized equity investments in Luxembourg; Peter Young |
| February 1995, Barings | £860 million on equity futures; Nick Leeson |
| 1995, Daiwa | $1 billion cover-up of bond losses spread over 11 years; Toshihide Iguschi |
| April 1994, Kidder Peabody | $350 million recording phantom profits; Joseph Jett |

Source: *Financial Times*, September 20, 2007.

**TABLE 26.3**

Operational Losses (Expressed in 2002 U.S. Dollars)

| Business Lines | % of All Loss Observations | Quantiles ($ millions) | | |
|---|---|---|---|---|
| | | 50% | 75% | 95% |
| Corporate finance | 4% | 8 | 23 | — |
| Trading and sales | 9% | 10 | 27 | 265 |
| Retail banking | 39% | 5 | 12 | 60 |
| Commercial banking | 16% | 8 | 28 | 123 |
| Payment and settlement | 1% | 4 | 11 | — |
| Agency services | 3% | 9 | 28 | — |
| Asset management | 6% | 8 | 22 | 165 |
| Retail brokerage | 22% | 4 | 13 | 67 |
| Total | 100% | 6 | 17 | 93 |

Source: de Fontnouvelle et al. (2006).

large losses. Banks can rely on both internal and external data to model operational risk. For instance, Algorithmics (owned by the rating agency Fitch) operates an operational loss database OpVantage (www.algorithmics.com), and the British Bankers Association (www.bba.org.uk) has developed a Global Operational Loss Database (GOLD).

De Fontnouvelle et al. (2006) report information on the severity of operational losses. These data, based on the OpVantage database, are reported in Table 26.3.

While retail banking includes a large percentage of observations (39 percent), the 95 percent quantile[1] is small, $60 million. Trading and sales and asset management have fewer observations but potentially much larger losses. The 95 percent quantile is $265 million for trading and sales and $165 million for asset management.

In preparing for the Basel II capital regulation, a major effort has been undertaken to quantify operational risk.

## MEASURING OPERATIONAL RISK

To quantify operational risk, it is necessary to estimate both the *distribution of severity* (size of operational losses) and the *frequency* (number of loss events per year). This chapter will focus on two approaches to estimate the distribution of severity. The first one focuses on large operational losses above a certain threshold. The attempt here is to use data on large operational losses to estimate the tail of the distribution. The second approach attempts to estimate the complete distribution of operational losses. Either one of the two approaches leads to an estimate of the distribution of loss severity per event, and the frequency of events that are likely to occur during one year can than be modeled.

Formally, the problem can be expressed as follows (Dutta and Perry, 2006). A loss event $L_i$ (loss severity) is an incident from which the bank suffers damage that can be expressed in monetary terms. An aggregate loss over a specified period of time can be expressed as the sum ($S$) of these events:

$$S = \sum_{i=1}^{N} L_i$$

where $N$ is a random variable that represents the frequency of losses that occur over the period. It is assumed that the operational losses $L_i$ are independent and identically distributed, and that each $L_i$ is independent of $N$. The distribution of $L_i$ is called the *severity distribution*, the distribution of $N$ over each period is called the *frequency distribution*, and the distribution $S$ is called the *aggregate loss distribution*. This framework is known as the loss distribution approach (LDA). The risk exposure or economic capital that needs to be allocated for operational risk can be measured as a quantile of $S$.[2]

As stated earlier, the measurement of operational risk starts with an estimate of the distribution of loss severity.

## MODELING OPERATIONAL RISK, APPROACH 1: MODELING LARGE OPERATIONAL LOSSES

As shown in the OpVantage database, a practical question for capital regulation is the likelihood of occurrence of a large operational loss. A method that is frequently used is the "peak over the threshold" (POT) approach. It relies on results from extreme value theory. Extreme value theory (EVT) is a branch of statistics that is concerned with the study of extreme phenomena, rare events that lie in the tails of the distribution (McNeil et al., 2005).

### Estimate of Loss Severity

Extreme value theory suggests that the distribution of losses exceeding a high threshold can be approximated by a generalized Pareto distribution (GPD). Let $x$ be equal to $X - u$, where $u$ denotes a threshold value.

For instance, $u$ is \$1 million in the OpVantage database. EVT shows that the limiting cumulative distribution of $x$ as $u$ tends to infinity is given by the generalized Pareto distribution:

$$\begin{aligned} GPD(x) &= 1 - (1 + \xi x / b)^{-1/\xi} && \text{if } \xi > 0 \\ &= 1 - \exp(-x/b)^{-1/\xi} && \text{if } \xi = 0 \end{aligned}$$

The probability that the loss exceeds $x$, given that $X > u$, is therefore $1 - GPD$.

The distribution has two parameters, $\xi$ and $b$, that need to be estimated by the data. The parameter $\xi$ is the shape parameter that determines the heaviness of the tail of the distribution. The parameter $b$ is a scale parameter. Which of the two cases holds depends on the underlying loss distribution. If it belongs to a heavy-tail class (e.g., Burr, Cauchy, loggamma, or Pareto),[3] then convergence is to the GDP with $\xi > 0$. A heavy-tail distribution is one for which the probability of having a large loss is high. If it belongs to a light-tail class (e.g., gamma, lognormal, normal, or Weibull), then convergence is to the exponential distribution ($\xi = 0$). A light-tail distribution is one for which the probability of having a large loss is low.

Furthermore, it can be shown that the distribution of log losses belongs to the light-tail class exponential distribution.

De Fontnouvelle et al. (2006) model the operational losses exceeding \$1 million as

$$f(x) = \frac{1}{b} e^{\frac{x}{b}}$$

with $f(x)$ = probability that the variable will exceed $x$, conditional on losses exceeding \$1 million, and $x$ = log of observed loss $-$ log of \$1 million. With a $b$ estimate of 0.66, the

$$f(x) = 0.01 = \frac{1}{0.66} e^{\frac{\ln(29) - \ln(1)}{0.66}}$$

The 99th and 99.9th percentiles are \$29 million and \$110 million, respectively.[4] For example, it can be verified that a test of the goodness of fit is to plot the empirical quantiles of the log of observed losses against the fitted distribution quantiles (Q-Q plot). Observations should lie on the 45-degree line.[5]

## Frequency of Losses

Once a distribution of loss severity has been estimated, it is necessary to model the distribution of the number of operational losses over a desired time interval, often one year. A common assumption is that the frequency of large losses follows a Poisson distribution with mean lambda ($\lambda$).[6] For large international banks, it has been observed that the number of operational losses exceeding $1 million ranges between 50 and 80 per year.

If $N$, the number of losses sustained by a bank over a certain period, follows a Poisson distribution, then the probability of having $n$ losses over one year will be

$$P(N = n) = \frac{e^{-\lambda} \times \lambda^n}{n!}$$

where $n!$ (read "$n$ factorial") is the product $1 \times 2 \times 3 \times \ldots \times n$.

Once the severity and frequency distributions have been determined, it is then possible to simulate 1 million years' experience of losses exceeding $1 million. The simulation works as follows. For each simulated year, let the computer draw a frequency $N$ from the Poisson distribution. Draw $N$ loss severities from the estimated parametric severity distribution. Sum these $N$ losses to get the aggregate annual loss. These steps can be repeated a million times. The result is a simulated aggregate distribution of operational losses, and the 99.9 percent quantile can then be calculated. This gives an estimate of the economic capital needed to cover operational risk.

## MODELING OPERATIONAL RISK, APPROACH 2: MODELING THE COMPLETE LOSS DISTRIBUTION

An alternative approach to modeling the severity distribution is to estimate the complete (not just the extreme) aggregate loss distribution (loss distribution approach, or LDA). Again, first the severity distribution and then the frequency of events is modeled.

### Distribution of Severity

It can be shown (Hull, 2007) that the extreme value theory yields the result that the unconditional probability that $x > u$ can be approximated by the Power Law:

$$\text{Prob}(x > u) = K \times u^{-\alpha}$$

This yields $\ln[\text{prob}(x > u)] = \ln(K) - \alpha \times \ln(u)$, a linear relationship.

With a large number of observations, it is possible to plot the relation between $\log[V(u)]$ and $\ln(u)$, where $V(u)$ is the proportion of observations for which $x > u$. The relationship should be linear if the Power Law holds and the parameters $K$ and $\alpha$ can be estimated.

Other parametric probability density functions used for modeling operational loss severity include light-tail distributions (exponential, Weibull, gamma, and lognormal) and heavy-tail distributions (loggamma, Pareto, generalized Pareto, Burr, and loglogistic). These are presented in the appendix to this chapter.

### Distribution of Frequency and Aggregate Operational Loss Distribution

Again, once the parameters of the severity distribution have been estimated with the entire data set of observed operational losses, a Poisson-type distribution for the frequency of events is added. Simulation allows the aggregate operational loss distribution to be drawn. de Fontnouvelle et al. (2004) obtain empirical estimates of operational losses similar to those obtained with the EVT.

Empirical estimates of operational losses lead to a figure close to 5 to 9 percent of total capital. For reference, the Basel Committee's expectation is that operational risk capital should be about 12 percent of regulatory capital.

Great care and judgment have to be used in applying quantitative models to the measurement of operational risk. The underlying severity distribution chosen has a major impact on results (Dutta and Perry, 2006). According to Dahen and Dionne (2007), research in this field is still in its embryonic stage.

### CONCLUSION

The first pillar of Basel II invites banks to measure operational risk. This has led to recent efforts to evaluate the probability distribution of operational losses. This distribution needs to incorporate information on the likely severity of losses and on the number of incidents per year. Statistics developed in the field of insurance are applied to the banking sector. The first difficulty is that the occurrence of large operational losses is very rare, making the probability of large losses difficult to estimate. A second difficulty is that changes in the environment—technology, mergers and acquisitions, and cross-border banking—could make historical data obsolete. In 2004, when interviewed by the author, Jaime Carauna, then chairman of the Basel Committee of Banking Supervision (BCBS), responded that one reason to introduce the advanced measurement approach in Basel II was to give banks incentives to develop tools that would allow them to better control and measure operational risk. His call has been met with a large series of research papers on the subject. Only time will tell how well these models capture operational risk.

## APPENDIX: PROBABILITY DENSITY FUNCTIONS (PDFS) USED TO MODEL OPERATIONAL LOSS[7]

### Light-Tailed Distributions

**Exponential**

$$\text{Density} = f(x) = \frac{1}{\lambda} \times e^{-\frac{x}{\lambda}}$$

**Weibull**

$$f(x) = \frac{\kappa}{\lambda} \left(\frac{x}{\lambda}\right)^{\kappa-1} e^{-\left(\frac{x}{\lambda}\right)^{\kappa}}$$

**Gamma**

$$f(x) = \frac{1}{\lambda^{\alpha} \Gamma(\alpha)} x^{\alpha-1} e^{\frac{-x}{\lambda}}$$

where $\Gamma(\alpha)$ is the gamma function

**Lognormal**

$$f(x) = \frac{1}{x\sigma\sqrt{2\pi}} e^{-\left[\frac{\ln(x)-\mu}{\sigma\sqrt{2}}\right]^2}$$

### Heavy-Tailed Distributions

**Loggamma**

$$f(x) = \frac{1}{b\Gamma(c)} \left[\frac{\ln(x)}{b}\right]^{c-1} x^{-\frac{1}{b-1}}$$

## Pareto (also Referred to as Power Law)

$$\text{Density} = f(x) = \frac{1}{\xi} x^{-\frac{1}{\xi}-1}$$

## Generalized Pareto (GPD)

$$\text{Density} = f(x) = \frac{1}{\beta}\left(1+\frac{\xi x}{\beta}\right)^{-\frac{1}{\xi}-1}$$

## Burr

$$f(x) = \left(\frac{\tau}{\beta}\right) x^{\tau-1}\left(1+\frac{\xi x^{\tau}}{\beta}\right)^{-\frac{1}{\xi}-1}$$

## Loglogistic (Also Referred to as the Fisk Distribution)

$$f(x) = \frac{\eta(x-\alpha)^{\eta-1}}{\left[1+(x-\alpha)^{\eta}\right]^{2}}$$

## EXERCISES FOR CHAPTER 26

1. To model aggregate operational losses, banks estimate the random distribution of two random variables. What are these two random variables?

2. Operational losses exceeding $1 million are modeled as follows:

$$f(x) = \frac{1}{0.66} e^{-\frac{x}{0.66}}$$

with $f(x)$ being the probability that the variable will exceed $x$, conditional on losses exceeding $1 million, and $x = $ log of observed loss (log of $1 million).

With the help of a PC spreadsheet, calculate the 99.95 percent quantile of the operational loss distribution.

3. You have estimated that the probability that a variable $v > s$ is given by the

Power Law: $\text{Prob}(v > s) = 50 \times s^{-3}$

Using a PC spreadsheet, estimate the 99.9 percent quantile of this distribution.

## Notes

1. As discussed in Chapter 18, $\alpha$-quantile is the value for a variable such that $\alpha$ percent of the observations of a frequency or probability distribution lie below the quantile value.
2. Basel II requires a quantile of 99.9 percent for the advanced measurement approach (AMA).
3. The probability density functions (pdfs) of these distributions are given in the appendix to this chapter.
4. In their empirical estimates, de Fontnouvelle et al. (2006) also incorporate the probability that an operational loss is reported in a public data set. It is assumed that the probability of reporting increases with the size of the loss. An implication is that it is not possible to rely only on observed data, as doing so would overstate the actual risk if small realized losses are not reported.
5. The threshold of \$1 million was driven by the database. In practice, the selection of the threshold is critical for the application of EVT (Dutta and Perry, 2006).
6. The Poisson distribution is a one-parameter distribution, with the parameter $\lambda$ being equal to both the mean and the variance of the frequency. The parameter value is often chosen as the average number of operational loss events per year. An alternative to the Poisson distribution (less used by banks) is the negative binomial distribution (Dutta and Perry, 2006; Dahen and Dionne, 2007).
7. de Fontnouvelle et al. (2004), Dutta and Perry (2006), and Dionne and Dahen (2007).

## Special Notes

Additional material is being made available to readers of this book online at http://www.mhprofessional.com/bankvaluation. This material consists of Chapter 27, "Islamic Banking (Interest-Free Banking): An Introduction"; Chapter 28, "Prudential Regulations, Safety Nets, and Corporate Structure of International Banks (Branches vs. Subsidiaries"; and "Solutions to Exercises," providing solutions to the end-of-chapter exercises contained throughout this book.

# REFERENCES

Allen, Franklin, and Anthony M. Santomero (1998): "The Theory of Financial Intermediation," *Journal of Banking & Finance* 21, 1461–1485.

Allen, Franklin, and Anthony M. Santomero (2001): "What Do Financial Intermediaries Do?" *Journal of Banking & Finance* 25, 271–294.

Altman, Edward I. (1989): "Measuring Corporate Bond Mortality and Performance," *Journal of Finance* 44, 909–922.

Altman, Edward I., and Heather J. Suggitt (2000): "Default Rates in the Syndicated Bank Loan Market: A Mortality Analysis," *Journal of Banking & Finance*, 24, 229–253.

Amato, Jeffery D. (2005): "Risk Aversion and Risk Premia in the CDS Market," *BIS Quarterly Review*, December, 55–68.

Amato, Jeffery D., and Jacob Gyntelberg (2005): "CDS Index Tranches and the Pricing of Credit Risk Correlations," *BIS Quarterly Review*, March, 73–87.

Artzner, Philip, Freddy Delbaen, Jean-Marc Eber, and David Heath (1999): "Coherent Measures of Risk," *Mathematical Finance* 9, 203–228.

Ausubel, Lawrence M. (1991): "The Failure of Competition in the Credit Card Market," *American Economic Review* 81(1), 50–81.

Baltensperger, Ernst (1982): "Alternative Approaches to the Theory of the Banking Firm," *Journal of Monetary Economics* 6(1), 1–37.

Baltensperger, Ernst, and Jean Dermine (1987): "Banking Deregulation in Europe," *Economic Policy* 4, 63–109.

Balthazar, Laurent (2004): "PD Estimates for Basel II," *Risk*, April, 84–85.

Bank for International Settlements (2001): Annual Report. Basel.

Basel Committee on Banking Supervision (1988): "International Convergence of Capital Measurement and Capital Standards," July.

Basel Committee on Banking Supervision (1996):"Amendments to the Capital Accord to Incorporate Market Risks." Updated version, November 2005. Basel, pp. 1–54.

Basel Committee on Banking Supervision (1997): "Principles for the Management of Interest Rate Risk." Basel: Bank for International Settlements, pp. 1–33.

Basel Committee on Banking Supervision (2001a): "The New Basel Capital Accord." Consultative document. Basel: Bank for International Settlements.

Basel Committee on Banking Supervision (2001b): "The New Basel Capital Accord." Explanatory note. Basel: Bank for International Settlements.

Basel Committee on Banking Supervision (2001c): "Risk Management Practices and Regulatory Capital: Joint Forum."

Basel Committee on Banking Supervision (2003): "High-Level Principles for the Cross-Border Implementation of the New Accord," pp. 1–7.

Basel Committee on Banking Supervision (2004): "International Convergence of Capital Measurement and Capital Standards." Comprehensive version published in June 2006. Basel: Bank for International Settlements.

Basel Committee on Banking Supervision (2005): "Credit Risk Transfer," March, pp. 1–61.

Basel Committee on Banking Supervision (2006): "Studies on Credit Risk Concentration." Working Paper 15, pp. 1–24.

Basel Committee on Banking Supervision (2008a): "Credit Risk Transfer," March, pp. 1–79.

Basel Committee on Banking Supervision (2008b): "Principles for Sound Liquidity Risk Management and Supervision," pp. 1–36.

Basel Committee on Banking Supervision (2008c): "Guidelines for Computing Capital for Incremental Risk in the Trading Book," pp. 1–13.

Belsham, Thomas, Nicholas Vause, and Simon Wells (2005): "Credit Correlation: Interpretation and Risks," *Bank of England Financial Stability Review*, December, 103–115.

Berger, Allen N., and David B. Humphrey (1997): "Efficiency of Financial Institutions: International Survey and Directions for Future Research," *European Journal of Operation Research* 98(2), 175–212.

Berger, Allen N., and Loretta Mester (1997): "Inside the Black Box: What Explains Differences in the Efficiencies of Financial Institutions?" *Journal of Banking & Finance* 21, 895–947.

Berndt, Antje, Rohan Douglas, Darrell Duffie, Mark Ferguson, and David Schranz (2005): "Measuring Default Risk Premia from Default Swap Rates and EDFs," BIS Working Paper 173, pp. 1–48.

Bessis, Joël (2002): *Risk Management in Banking*, 2nd ed. New York: John Wiley & Sons.

Black, Fisher (1970): "Banking and Interest Rates in a World without Money," *Journal of Bank Research*, Autumn, 9–20.

Black, Fisher, and Myron Scholes (1973): "The Pricing of Options and Corporate Liabilities," *Journal of Political Economy* 81, 637–659.

Bodie, Zvi, Alex Kane, and Alan J. Marcus (1996): *Investments*, 3rd ed. Chicago: Irwin.

Boyd, John, Stanley L. Graham, and Shawn R. Hewitt (1993): "Bank Holding Company Mergers with Nonbank Financial Firms: Effects on the Risk of Failure," *Journal of Banking & Finance*, 17 (1), 43–63.

Boyd, John, and David Runkle (1993): "Size and Performance of Banking Firms," *Journal of Monetary Economics*, 31 (1), 47–67.

Bradley, Christine M., and Kenneth D. Jones (2007): "Loss Sharing Rules for Bank Holding Companies: An Assessment of the Federal Reserve's Source-of-Strength Policy and the FDIC's Cross Guarantee Authority," FDIC, 1–23.

Brealey, Richard A., and Michael Habib (1996): "Using Project Finance to Fund Infrastructure Investments," *Journal of Applied Corporate Finance* 9(3), 25–38.

Brealey, Richard A., Stewart C. Myers, and Franklin Allen (2006): *Corporate Finance*, 8th and international eds. New York: McGraw-Hill.

Calandro, Joseph, and Scott Lane (2002): "The Insurance Performance Measure: Bringing Value to the Insurance Industry," *Journal of Applied Corporate Finance*, Winter, 94–99.

Canhoto, Ana, and Jean Dermine (2003): "A Note on Banking Efficiency in Portugal, New vs. Old Banks," *Journal of Banking & Finance* 27(11), 2087–2098.

Chambers, David M., William T. Carleton, and Ronald W. McEnally (1988): "Immunizing Default-Free Bond Portfolio with a Duration Vector," *Journal of Financial and Quantitative Analysis* 23(1), 89–104.

Chen, Andrew H., Nengjiu Ju, Sumon C. Mazumdar, and Avinash Verma (2006): "Correlated Default Risks and Bank Regulations," *Journal of Money, Credit and Banking* 38(2), 375–398.

Committee on the Global Financial System (2001): "A Survey of Stress Tests and Current Practice at Major Financial Institutions." Basel: Bank for International Settlements.

Competition Commission (2002): "The Supply of Banking Services by Clearing Banks to Small and Medium-Sized Enterprises." London.

Cooper, Ian A., and Sergei A. Davydenko (2007): "Estimating the Cost of Risky Debt," *Journal of Applied Corporate Finance* 19(3), 90–95.

Cousseran, Olivier, and Imène Rahmoundi (2005): "Le Marché des CDO Modalités de Fonctionnement et Implications en Termes de Stabilité Financière," *Revue de Stabilité Financière* 6, Banque de France, Juin, 47–68.

CreditMetrics (1997): "Technical Document." JPMorgan.

Credit Suisse Financial Products (1997): "CreditRisk+, a Credit Management Framework." London.

Crouhy, Michel, Dan Galai, and Robert Mark (2000): "A Comparative Analysis of Current Credit Risk Models," *Journal of Banking & Finance* 24, 59–117.

Crouhy, Michel, Dan Galai, and Robert Mark (2001): *Risk Management*. New York: McGraw-Hill.

Dahen, Hela, and Georges Dionne (2007): "Scaling Models for the Severity and Frequency of External Operational Loss Data." Canada Research Chair in Risk Management, WP 07–01, pp. 1–47.

Das, Sanjiv R., Darrell Duffie, Nikunj Kapadia, and Leandro Saita (2007): "Common Failings: How Corporate Defaults Are Correlated," *Journal of Finance* 62(1), 93–117.

Das, Sanjiv R., Laurence Freed, Gary Geng, and Nikunj Kapadia (2006): "Correlated Default Risk," *Journal of Fixed Income*, Fall, 7–32.

de Fontnouvelle P., J. Jordan, and E. Rosengren (2004): "Implications of Alternative Modeling Techniques." Federal Reserve Bank of Boston.

de Fontnouvelle, Patrick, Virginia DeJeus-Rueff, John Jordan, and Eric Rosengren (2006): "Capital and Risk: New Evidence on the Implications of Large Operational Losses," *Journal of Money, Credit and Banking* 38(7), 1819–1846.

Delianedis, Gordon, and Pedro Santa-Clara (1999): "The Exposure of International Corporate Bond Returns to Exchange Rate Risk," in Jean Dermine and Pierre Hillion (eds.), *European Capital Markets with a Single Currency*. Oxford, U.K.: Oxford University Press.

Demirgüc-Kunt, Asli, Baybars Karacaovali, and Luc Laeven (2005): "Deposit Insurance around the World: A Comprehensive Database." World Bank, WPS 3628, pp. 1–59.

Dermine, Jean (1984): *Pricing Policies of Financial Intermediaries*, Studies in Contemporary Economics no. 5. Berlin: Springer-Verlag.

Dermine, Jean (1985a): "The Measurement of Interest Rate Risk by Financial Intermediaries," *Journal of Bank Research* 16(2), 86–90.

Dermine, Jean (1985b): "Taxes, Inflation and Banks' Market Values," *Journal of Business, Finance and Accounting* 12(1), 65–74.

Dermine, Jean (1986): "Deposit Rates, Credit Rates and Bank Capital, the Klein-Monti Model Revisited," *Journal of Banking & Finance* 10, 99–114.

Dermine, Jean (1987): "Measuring the Market Value of a Bank, a Primer," *Finance (Revue de l'Association Française de Finance)* 8(2), 91–108.

Dermine, Jean (1991): "The BIS Proposal for the Measurement of Interest Rate Risk, Some Pitfalls," *Journal of International Securities Markets*, Spring, 3–8.

Dermine, Jean (1993): "The Evaluation of Interest Rate Risk," *Finanzmarkt und Portfolio Management* 7(2), 141–149.

Dermine, Jean (1995): "Loan Arbitrage-Free Pricing," *Financier*, 2(2), 64–67.

Dermine, Jean (1998): "Pitfalls in the Application of RAROC, with Reference to Loan Management," *The Arbitrageur–The Financier* 1(1), 21–27.

Dermine, Jean (2000): "DCF vs. Real Options: How Best to Value Online Financial Companies? (with an Application to Egg)." INSEAD Case Series.

Dermine, Jean (2003): "European Banking, Past, Present, and Future," in V. Gaspar, P. Hartmann, and O. Sleipen (eds.), *The Transformation of the European Financial System*. Second ECB Central Banking Conference. Frankfurt: ECB.

Dermine, Jean (2005a): "How to Measure Recoveries and Provisions on Bank Lending: Methodology and Empirical Evidence," in E. Altman, A. Resti, and A. Sironi (eds.), *Recovery Risk, The Next Challenge in Credit Risk Management*. London: Risk Books (with C. Neto de Carvalho).

Dermine, Jean (2005b): "*Le Taux Modèle — ING Direct, a Success Story*." INSEAD Case Series.

Dermine, Jean (2006a): "European Banking Integration, Don't Put the Cart before the Horse," *Financial Markets, Institutions and Instruments* 15(2), 1–106.

Dermine, Jean (2006b): "Strategic Management in Banking, *in Medio Virtus*," in M. Balling, F. Lierman, and A. Mullineux (eds.), *Competition and Profitability in European Financial Services: Strategic, Systemic, and Policy Issues*. London: Routledge.

Dermine, Jean (2007): "ALM in Banking," in S. A. Zenios and W. T. Ziemba (eds.), *Handbook of Asset and Liability Management*, Volume 2. North Holland Handbooks in Finance Series. Amsterdam:Elsevier Science B.V.

Dermine, Jean, and Youssef F. Bissada (2007): *Asset & Liability Management, the Banker's Guide to Value Creation and Risk Control*, 2nd ed. London: Financial Times/ Prentice Hall. Available in Spanish (FT-Prentice Hall, Madrid, 2003), Portuguese (Atlas, São Paulo, 2005), Chinese (China Financial Publishing House, Beijing, 2003), and Russian (Eksmo Publishers, Moscow, 2008).

Dermine, Jean, and Pierre Hillion (1992): "Deposit Rate Ceilings and the Market Value of Banks, the Case of France 1971–1981," *Journal of Money, Credit and Banking* 24(2), 184–194.

Dermine, Jean, and Fatma Lajéri (2001): "Credit Risk and the Deposit Insurance Premium, a Note," *Journal of Economics and Business* 53, 497–508.

Dermine, Jean, and Cristina Neto de Carvalho (2005): "How to Measure Recoveries and Provisions on Bank Lending: Methodology and Empirical Evidence," in E. Altman, A. Resti, and A. Sironi (eds.), *Recovery Risk, The Next Challenge in Credit Risk Management*. London: Risk Books.

Dermine, Jean, and Cristina Neto de Carvalho (2006): "Bank Loan Losses Given Default, a Case Study," *Journal of Banking & Finance* 30(4), 1219–1243.

Dermine, Jean, and Cristina Neto de Carvalho (2008): "Bank Loan Loss Provisioning, Central Bank Rules vs. Estimation: The Case of Portugal," *Journal of Financial Stability* 4(1), 1–22.

Dermine, Jean, Damien Neven, and Jacques Thisse (1991): "Towards an Equilibrium Theory of the Mutual Fund Industry," *Journal of Banking & Finance* 15, 485–499.

de Servigny, Arnaud, and Olivier Renault (2002): "Default Correlation: Empirical Evidence." London: Standard & Poor's Risk Solutions, pp. 1–27.

Diamond, Douglas W. (1984): "Financial Intermediation and Delegated Monitoring," *Review of Financial Studies* 51, 393–414.

Diamond, Douglas, and Phil Dybvig (1983): "Bank Runs, Deposit Insurance and Liquidity," *Journal of Political Economy* 91, 401–419.

Dimson, Elroy, Paul Marsh, and Mike Staunton (2006): "The Worldwide Equity Premium: A Smaller Puzzle." London Business School, pp. 1–40.

Dionne, Georges, and Hela Dahen (2007): "What about Underevaluating Operational Value at Risk in the Banking Sector?" HEC Montreal, pp. 1–32.

Dowd, Kevin (2005): *Measuring Market Risk*, Hoboken, N.J.: John Wiley & Sons.

Driessen, Joost: "Is Default Event Risk Priced in Corporate Bonds?" *Review of Financial Studies* 18, 165–195.

Drossos, Evangeline S., and Spence Hilton (2000): "The Federal Reserve's Contingency Financing Plan for the Century Date Change," *FRBNY Current Issues in Economics and Finance* 6(15), 1–6.

Duffie, Darrell (1999): "Credit Swap Valuation," *Financial Analysts Journal*, January-February, 73–87.

Duffie, Darrell (2004): "Comment," *Risk*, April, p. 77f.

Duffie, Darrell, and Nicolae Garleanu (2001): "Risk and Valuation of Collateralized Debt Obligations," *Financial Analysts Journal*, January-February, 41–59.

Duffie, Darrell, and Juan Pan (1997): "An Overview of Value at Risk," *Journal of Derivatives*, 3, 7–49.

Duffie, Darrell, Leandro Saita, and Ke Wang (2007): "Multi-period Corporate Default Prediction with Stochastic Covariates," *Journal of Financial Economics* 83(3), 635–665. .

Duffie, Darrel, and Ken J. Singleton (1999): "Modeling Term Structure of Defaultable Bonds," *Review of Financial Studies* 12, 687–720.

Duffie, Darrel, and Ken J. Singleton (2003): *Credit Risk*. Princeton Series in Finance. Princeton, N.J.: Princeton University Press.

Düllmann, Klaus, and Nancy Masschelein (2007): "A Tractable Model to Measure Sector Concentration Risk in Credit Portfolios," *Journal of Financial Services Research* 32, 55–79.

Dutta, Kabir, and Jason Perry (2006): "A Tale of Tails: An Empirical Analysis of Loss Distribution Models for Estimating Operational Risk Capital." Federal Reserve Bank of Boston, Working Paper 06–13, pp. 1–85.

Edwards, Franklin R. (1999): "Hedge Funds and the Collapse of Long-Term Capital Management," *Journal of Economic Perspectives* 13(2), 189–210.

Eisenbeis, Robert A., and George G. Kaufman (2006): "Cross-Border Banking: Challenges for Deposit Insurance and Financial Stability in the European Union." Federal Reserve Bank of Atlanta, Working Paper 15, 1–74.

Estrella, Arturo, and Mary R. Trubin (2006): "The Yield Curve as a Leading Indicator: Some Practical Issues," *Current Issues in Economics and Finance* 12(5), 1–7.

Esty, Benjamin C. (1999): "Petrozuata: A Case Study of the Effective Use of Project Finance," *Journal of Applied Corporate Finance* 12(3), 26–42.

European Commission (2006): "Communication from the European Commission to the European Parliament and the Council Concerning the Review of Directive 94/19/EC on Deposit Guarantee Schemes." Brussels.

Fabozzi, Frank J. (ed.) (1995): *The Handbook of Mortgage-Backed Securities*, 4th ed. Chicago: Probus.

Fabozzi, Frank J. (ed.) (1997): *Fixed Income Mathematics*, 3rd ed. Chicago: Irwin.

Fabozzi, Frank J., and Atsuo Konishi (eds.) (1991): *Asset/Liability Management*. Chicago: Probus.

Fama, Eugene (1980): "Banking in the Theory of Finance," *Journal of Monetary Economics* 6(1), 39–57.

Fama, Eugene (1985): "What's Different about Banks?" *Journal of Monetary Economics* 15, 29–36.

Farin, Thomas A. (1989): *Asset/Liability Management for Savings Institutions*.Chicago: Institute of Financial Education.

Fender, Ingo, and Peter Hördahl (2007): "Overview: Credit Retrenchment Triggers Liquidity Squeeze," *BIS Quarterly Review*, September, 1–16.

Fender, Ingo, and Peter Hördahl (2008): "Overview: A Cautious Return of Risk Tolerance," *BIS Quarterly Review*, June, 1–16.

Fender, Ingo, and Martin Schneider (2008): "The ABX: How Do Markets Price Subprime Mortgage Risk?" *BIS Quarterly Review*, September, 67–81.

Fender, Ingo, Nikola Tarashev, and Haibin Zhu (2008): "Credit Fundamentals, Ratings and Value-at-Risk: CDOs versus Corporate Exposures," *BIS Quarterly Review*, March, 87–101.

Figlewski, Stephen (1997): "Forecasting Volatility," *Financial Markets, Institutions and Instruments* 6(1), 1–88.

Financial Services Authority (2007): "Review of the Liquidity Requirements for Banks and Building Societies." Discussion paper 07/7, December, pp. 1–46.

Financial Stability Review (2000): "Banking System Liquidity, Developments and Issues." Bank of England, December.

Finger, Christopher C. (2002): "Credit Grades Technical Documents." RiskMetrics Group Inc.

Flannery, Mark J., and Kasturi P. Rangan (2002): "Market Forces at Work in the Banking Industry: Evidence from the Capital Buildup of the 1990s," University of Florida, mimeo, pp. 1–48.

Freixas, Xavier (2003): "Crisis Management in Europe," in Jeroen Kremers, Dirk Schoenmaker, and Peter Wierts (eds.), *Financial Supervision in Europe*. Cheltenham, U.K.: Edward Elgar, pp. 102–119.

Freixas, Xavier, and Jean-Charles Rochet (1997): *Microeconomics of Banking*. Boston: MIT Press.

Friedfrank (2004): "The Societas Europaea, Thirty Years Later," pp. 1–15.

Friedman, Milton (1970): "The Social Responsibility of Business Is to Increase Its Profits," *New York Times Magazine*, September 13.

Froot, Kenneth A., and Jeremy C. Stein (1998): "Risk Management, Capital Budgeting, and Capital Structure Policy for Financial Institutions, an Integrated Approach," *Journal of Financial Economics* 47, January, 55–82.

Frye, Jon, and Eduard Pelz (2008): "BankCaR (Bank Capital-at-Risk): A Credit Risk Model for US Commercial Bank Charge-Offs." Federal Reserve Bank of Chicago, Working Paper 3, pp. 1–23.

Gatev, Evan, Til Schuermann, and Philip Strahan (2005): "Managing Bank Liquidity Risk: How Deposit-Loan Synergies Vary with Market Conditions." FDIC Center for Financial Research, Working Paper 2006–3, pp. 1–22.

Gatev, Evan, and Philip E. Strahan (2006): " Banks Advantage in Hedging Liquidity Risk: Theory and Evidence from the Commercial Paper Market," *Journal of Finance* 61, 867–892.

Gibson, Michael S. (2004): "Understanding the Risk of Synthetic CDOs." Federal Reserve Board Research Papers 34, July, pp. 1–27.

Gibson, Michael S. (2007): "Credit Derivatives and Risk Management." Federal Reserve Board Research Papers 47, May, pp. 1–20.

Goodhart, Charles A. E. (2003): "The Political Economy of Financial Harmonization in Europe," in J. Kremers, D. Schoenmaker, and P. Wierts (eds.), *Financial Supervision in Europe*. Cheltenham, U.K.: Edward Elgar, pp. 129–138.

Goodman, Laurie S. (2002): "Synthetic CDOs: An Introduction," *Journal of Derivatives*, Spring, 6–72.

Gordy, Michael B. (2000): "A Comparative Anatomy of Credit Risk Models," *Journal of Banking & Finance* 24(1–2), 119–149.

Gordy, Michael B. (2003): "A Risk-Factor Model Foundation for Ratings-Based Bank Capital Rules," *Journal of Financial Intermediation* 12, 199–232.

Gordy, Michael B., and Eva Lütkebohmert (2007): "Granularity Adjustment for Basel II." Deutsche Bundesbank Discussion Paper #1, pp. 1–24.

Gropp, Reint, Christoffer K. Sorensen, and Jung-Duk Lichtenberer (2007): "The Dynamics of Bank Spreads and Financial Structure." Working Paper Series #714, European Central Bank, pp. 1–50.

Hall, Maximilian J. B. (1989): *Handbook of Banking Regulation and Supervision*. Cambridge, U.K.: Woodhead-Faulkner Ltd.

Hannan, Timothy H., and Allen N. Berger (1991): "The Rigidity of Prices: Evidence from the Banking Industry," *American Economic Review* 81, 938–945.

Hawawini, Gabriel, and Claude Viallet (2007): *Finance for Executives*, 3rd ed., Mason, Ohio:Thomson/South-Western.

Hellmann, Thomas F., Kevin C. Murdock, and Joseph E. Stiglitz (2000): "Liberalization, Moral Hazard in Banking, and Prudential Regulation: Are Capital Requirements Enough?" *American Economic Review* 90(1), 147–165.

Herring, Richard, and Anthony M. Santomero (1990): "The Corporate Structure of Financial Conglomerates," *Journal of Financial Services Research* 4, 471–497.

Herring, Richard, and Til Schuermann (2005): "Capital Regulation for Position Risk in Banks, Securities Firms, and Insurance Companies," in H. Scott (ed.), *Capital Adequacy: Law, Regulation, and Implementation*. New York: Oxford University Press.

Houpt, James V., and James Embersit (1991): "A Method for Evaluating Interest Rate Risk in Commercial Banking," *Federal Reserve Bulletin*, August, 625–637.

Houpt, James V., and James Embersit (1996): "An Analysis of Commercial Bank Exposure to Interest Rate Risk," *Federal Reserve Bulletin*, February, 115–128.

Hu, Jian (2007): "Assessing the Credit Risk of CDO's Backed by Structured Finance Securities: Rating Analysts' Challenges and Solutions." Moodys, pp. 1–26.

Hull, John (2000): *Options, Futures and Other Derivatives*, 4th ed. Englewood Cliffs, NJ: Prentice Hall-International.

Hull, John (2006): "VAR vs. Expected Shortfall," *Risk*, December, pp. 48–49.

Hull, John (2007): "The Power Law," *Risk*, March, pp. 72–74.

Hull, John, and Alan White (2004): "Valuation of a CDO and n-th to Default CDS without Monte Carlo Simulation," *Journal of Derivatives*, 12 (2), 8–23.

Hutchison, David E., and George G. Pennacchi (1996): "Measuring Rents and Interest Rate Risk in Imperfect Financial Markets: The Case of Retail Bank Deposits," *Journal of Financial and Quantitative Analysis* 31(3), 399–417.

International Bureau of Fiscal Documentation (2003): "Survey on the Societas Europaea," pp. 1–78.

Jackson, Patricia, and William Perraudin (2000): "Credit Risk Modelling and Regulatory Issues," Special Issue, *Journal of Banking & Finance*, 24 (1–2), 1–14.

Jarrow, Robert A. (1996): *Modelling Fixed Income Securities and Interest Rate Options*. New York: McGraw-Hill.

Jarrow, Robert A., and Donald R. van Deventer (1998): "The Arbitrage-Free Valuation and Hedging of Demand Deposits and Credit Card Loans," *Journal of Banking & Finance* 22, 249–272.

Jarrow, Robert A., and Donald van Deventer (1998): "Integrating Interest Rate Risk and Credit Risk in ALM," in Kamakura Corporation (ed.), *Asset & Liability Management, A Synthesis of New Methodologies*. London: Risk Books.

Jensen, Michael C. (2001): "Value Maximization, Stakeholder Theory, and the Corporate Objective Function," *Journal of Applied Corporate Finance*, Fall, 8–21.

Jorion, Philippe (2000): "Risk Management Lessons from Long-Term Capital Management," *European Financial Management* 6(3), 277–300.

Jorion, Philippe (2007): *Value at Risk*, 3rd ed. New York: McGraw-Hill.

Kamakura Corporation (1998): *Asset & Liability Management, A Synthesis of New Methodologies*. London: Risk Books.

Kaplan, S., and J. Stein (1990): "How Risky Is the Debt in Highly Leveraged Transactions?" *Journal of Financial Economics* 27, 215–245.

Kashyap, Anil K., Raghuram R. Rajan, and Jeremy C. Stein (2002): "Banks as Liquidity Providers: An Explanation for the Co-Existence of Lending and Deposit-Taking," *Journal of Finance* 57(1), 33–74.

Kay, John, and John Vickers (1988): "Regulatory Reform in Britain," *Economic Policy* 7, 286–351.

Kealhofer, Stephen (2003): "Quantifying Credit Risk I: Default Prediction," *Financial Analysts Journal*, January-February, 30–44.

Klein, Michael A. (1971): "A Theory of the Banking Firm," *Journal of Money, Credit and Banking* 3(2), 205–218.

KMV (2002): "Modeling Default Risk." San Francisco: KMV LLC.

Koller, Tim, Mark Goedhart, and David Wessels (2005): *Valuation, Measuring and Managing the Value of Companies*, 4th ed. New York: McKinsey & Co.

Kozhemiakin, Alexander (2007): "The Risk Premium of Corporate Bonds," *Journal of Portfolio Management*, Winter, 101–109.

Lajéri, Fatma, and Jean Dermine (1999): "Unexpected Inflation and Bank Stock Returns, the Case of France 1977–1991," *Journal of Banking & Finance* 23(6), 939–953.

Lando, David (2004): *Credit Risk Modeling*. Princeton Series in Finance. Princeton, N.J.: Princeton University Press.

Ledrut, Elisabeth, and Christian Upper (2007): "Changing Post-Trading Arrangements for OTC Derivatives," *BIS Quarterly Review*, December, 83–95.

Lindley, Robert (2008): "Reducing Foreign Exchange Settlement Risk," *BIS Quarterly Review*, September, 53–65.

Longin, François M. (2000): "From Value at Risk to Stress Testing: The Extreme Value Approach," *Journal of Banking & Finance* 7, 1097–1130.

Macaulay, Frederic R. (1938): "The Movements of Interest Rates, Bond Yields and Stock Prices in the United States since 1856." Cambridge, Mass.: National Bureau of Economic Research.

Markowitz, Harry M. (1959): *Portfolio Selection: Efficient Diversification of Investment* (Cowles Foundation Monograph 16). New Haven, Conn.: Yale University Press.

McAndrews, James J., and Simon M. Potter (2002): "Liquidity Effects of the Events of September 11, 2001," *FRBNY Economic Policy Review*, November, 59–79.

McNeil, Alexander J., Rüdiger Frey, and Paul Embrechts (2005): *Quantitative Risk Management*. Princeton Series in Finance. Princeton, N.J.: Princeton University Press.

McTaggart, James, Peter Kontes, and Michael Mankings (1994): *The Value Imperative*. New York: The Free Press.

Merton, Robert (1974): "On the Pricing of Corporate Debt: The Risk Structure of Interest Rates," *Journal of Finance* 28, 449–470.

Merton, Robert C. (1977): "An Analytic Derivation of the Cost of Deposit Insurance and Loan Guarantees," *Journal of Banking & Finance* 1, 3–11.

Merton, Robert C., and André Perold (1993): "Theory of Risk Capital in Financial Firms," *Journal of Applied Corporate Finance* 6, Fall, 16–32.

Modigliani, Franco, and Merton H. Miller (1958): "The Cost of Capital, Corporation Finance and the Theory of Investment," *American Economic Review* 48, 261–297.

Monti, Mario (1972): "Deposit, Credit and Interest Rate Determination under Alternative Bank Objective Functions," in K. Shell and G. Szego (eds.), *Mathematical Methods in Investment and Finance*, Amsterdam: North-Holland, pp. 431–454.

Nordea (2004): "Pioneering the Move Towards a European Company." Press release, June 23; www.nordea.com.

O'Brien, James (2000): "Estimating the Value and Interest Rate Risk of Interest-Bearing Transactions Deposits." Finance & Economics Discussion Series #53. Federal Reserve Board, pp. 1–44.

O'Brien, James, Athanasios Orphanides, and David Small (1994): "Estimating the Interest Rate Sensitivity of Liquid Retail Deposit Values," Finance and Economics Discussion Series #15. Federal Reserve Board, pp. 1–26.

Office of Thrift Supervision (2000): "The OTS Net Portfolio Model." http://www.ots.treas.gov.

Oldfield, Georges S., and Anthony M. Santomero (1997): "The Place of Risk Management in Financial Institutions," *Sloan Management Review* 39 (1), 33–46.

Packer, Frank, Ryan Stever, and Christian Upper (2007): "The Covered Bond Market," *BIS Quarterly Review*, September, 43–55.

Peek, Joe, and Eric Rosengren (2000): "Collateral Damage: Effects of the Japanese Banking Crisis on Real Activity in the United States," *American Economic Review* 90, 30–45.

Perold, Andre F. (2001): "Capital Allocation in Financial Firms." Harvard Business School Competition and Strategy Working Paper Series #98–072, pp. 1–38.

Pilloff, Steven J., and Anthony M. Santomero (1998): "The Value Effects of Bank Mergers and Acquisitions," in Yakov Amihud and Geoffrey Miller (eds.), *Bank Mergers & Acquisitions*, Dordrecht:Kluwer Academic Publishers, pp. 59–78.

Pitman, Brian (2003): "Leading for Value," *Harvard Business Review*, April, pp. 41–46.

Platt, Robert B. (1986): *Controlling Interest Rate Risk*. New York: John Wiley & Sons.

Pykhtin, Michael (2004): "Multi-Factor Adjustment," *Risk*, March, 85–90.

Rajan, Raghuram R. (1998): "The Past and Future of Commercial Banking Viewed through an Incomplete Contract Lens," *Journal of Money, Credit and Banking*, 30(3) 524–550.

Rajan, Raghuram R., and Luigi Zingales (2003): *Saving Capitalism from the Capitalists*. New York: Crown Books, Random House.

Rangan, Subramanian (2000): "Seven Myths to Ponder before Going Global," in *Mastering Strategy*. London: Pearson Education, pp. 119–124.

Rebonato, Ricardo (1996): *Interest-Rate Option Models*. New York: John Wiley & Sons.

Repullo, Rafael, and Javier Suarez (2004): "Loan Pricing under Capital Requirement," *Journal of Financial Intermediation* 13(4), 496–521.

Roll, Richard (1986): "The Hubris Hypothesis of Corporate Takeovers," *Journal of Business* 59, 197–216.

Ronn, Ehud I., and Avinash K. Verma (1986): "Pricing Risk-Adjusted Deposit Insurance, and Option-Based Model," *Journal of Finance* 41, 871–895.

Rosen, Dan, and Stavros A. Zenios (2006): "Enterprise-wide Asset and Liability Management: Issues, Institutions and Models," in Stavros A. Zenios and William T. Ziemba (eds.), *Handbook of Asset and Liability Management*, Volume 1. North Holland Handbooks in Finance Series. Amsterdam: Elsevier Science B.V.

Rosengren, Eric (2003): "Comment," in V. Gaspar, P. Hartmann, and O Sleijpen (eds.), *The Transformation of the European Financial System*. Second ECB Central Banking Conference. Frankfurt: ECB, pp. 109–114.

Samuelson, Paul A. (1945): "The Effect of Interest Rate Increases on the Banking System," *American Economic Review* 35, 16–27.

Samuelson, Paul A. (1964): "Tax Deductibility of Economic Depreciation to Insure Invariant Valuation," *Journal of Political Economy* 72, 604–666.

Santomero, Anthony M. (1984): "Modelling the Banking Firm," *Journal of Money, Credit and Banking* 16(4), 576–616.

Santomero, Anthony M. (1995): "Financial Risk Management, The Whys and the Hows," *Financial Markets, Institutions and Instruments* 4, 1–14.

Santomero, Anthony M. (1997): "Commercial Bank Risk Management: An Analysis of the Process," *Journal of Financial Services Research* 12(2–3), 83–115.

Santomero, Anthony M., and E. Chung (1992): "Evidence in Support of Broader Bank Powers," *Financial Markets, Institutions and Instruments*, 1–69.

Saunders, Anthony, and Linda Allen (2002): *Credit Risk Measurement*, 2nd ed. New York: John Wiley & Sons.

Saunders, Anthony, and Ingo Walter (1994): *Universal Banking in the United States: What Do We Gain? What Do We Lose?* Oxford, U.K.: Oxford University Press.

Schoenmaker, Dirk, and Sander Oosterloo (2004): "Cross-Border Issues in European Financial Supervision," in D. Mayes and G. Wood (eds.), *The Structure of Financial Regulation*. London: Routledge.

Shimko, David (ed.) (1999): *Credit Risk, Models and Management*. London: Risk Books.

Sklar, A. (1959): "Fonctions de Répartitions à n Dimensions et leurs Marges," *Publications de l' Institut de Statistique de l' Université de Paris* 8, 229–331.

Smithson, Charles (2004): "Hedging a Portfolio of Structured Credit Assets," *Risk*, October, 66–69.

Société Générale (2008): "Mission Green, Rapport de Synthèse." Paris: Inspection Générale, pp. 1–69.

Solé, Juan (2007): "Introducing Islamic Banks into Conventional Banking Systems." IMF Working Paper 175, pp. 1–26.

Stiglitz, Joseph, and Andrew Weiss (1981): "Credit Rationing with Imperfect Information," *American Economic Review* 71, 393–410.

Stigum, M., and R. O. Branch (1983): *Managing Bank Assets and Liabilities*. Homewood, Illinois: Dow Jones-Irwin.

Stoughton, Neal M., and Josef Zechner (1999): "Optimal Capital Allocation Using RAROC and EVA." Manuscript, University of California–Irvine and University of Vienna, pp. 1–33.

Swiss Re (2003): *The Economics of Insurance*.

Taleb, Nassim N. (2007): *The Black Swan*. New York: Random House.

Tarashev, Nikola, and Haibin Zhu (2007): "Measuring Portfolio Credit Risk: Modeling versus Calibration Errors," *BIS Quarterly Review*, March, 83–96.

Turnbull, Stuart M. (2000): "Capital Allocation and Risk Performance Measurement in a Financial Institution," *Financial Markets, Institutions and Instruments* 9, 325–357.

Vander Vennett, Rudi (2002): "Cost and Profit Efficiency of Financial Conglomerates and Universal Banks in Europe," *Journal of Money, Credit and Banking* 34, 254–282.

van Deventer, Donald R., Kenji Imai, and Mark Mesler (2005): *Advanced Financial Risk Management.* Hoboken, N.J.: John Wiley & Sons.

Vasicek, Oldrich A. (1987): "Probability of Loss on Loan Portfolio." Working Paper, KMV Corporation, pp. 1–4.

Vasicek, Oldrich A. (2002): "Loan Portfolio Value," *Risk*, December, 160–162.

Vassalou, Maria, and Yuhang Xing (2004): "Default Risk in Equity Returns," *Journal of Finance* 59, 831–868.

Wilde, Tom (2001a): "IRB Approach Explained," *Risk*, May, 87–90.

Wilde, Tom (2001b): "Probing Granularity," *Risk*, August, 103–106.

Yamai, Yasuhiro, and Toshinao Yoshiba (2005): "Value-at-Risk vs. Expected Shortfall, a Practical Perspective," *Journal of Banking & Finance* 29, 997–1015.

Zaik, Edward, John Walter, Gabriela Kelling, and Christopher James (1996): "RAROC at Bank of America: From Theory to Practice," *Journal of Applied Corporate Finance* 9(2), Summer, 83–93.

Zingales, Luigi (2008): "Why Paulson Is Wrong." Mimeo, Graduate School of Business, University of Chicago, pp. 1–2.